The Break-Up of Britain

By the same author

The Beginning of the End: France, May 1968, with Angelo
 Quattrocchi (1968)
The Left Against Europe? (1973)
The Enchanted Glass: Britain and Its Monarchy (1988)
Faces of Nationalism: Janus Revisited (1997)
After Britain: New Labour and the Return of Scotland (2000)
Pariah: Misfortunes of the British Kingdom (2002)
Global Matrix: Nationalism, Globalism and State Terrorism,
 with Paul James (2005)
Gordon Brown: Bard of Britishness (2006)
Old Nations, Auld Enemies, New Times: Selected Essays (2014)

The Break-Up of Britain

Crisis and Neo-Nationalism

Third Edition
with an Introduction by
Anthony Barnett

Tom Nairn

VERSO
London • New York

This third edition first published by Verso 2021
First published by New Left Books 1977
Verso edition first published 1981
Common Ground edition first published 2003
© Tom Nairn 1977, 1981, 2003, 2021
Introduction © Anthony Barnett 2021

1 3 5 7 9 10 8 6 4 2

Verso
UK: 6 Meard Street, London W1F 0EG
US: 20 Jay Street, Suite 1010, Brooklyn, NY 11201
versobooks.com

Verso is the imprint of New Left Books

ISBN-13: 978-1-78168-320-0
ISBN-13: 978-1-78960-682-9 (US EBK)
ISBN-13: 978-1-78960-683-6 (UK EBK)

British Library Cataloguing in Publication Data
A catalogue record for this book is available from the British Library

Library of Congress Cataloging-in-Publication Data
A catalog record for this book is available from the Library of Congress

Printed and bound by CPI Group (UK) Ltd, Croydon CR0 4YY

To the memory and cause of
Orlando Letelier,
assassinated September 21st, 1976

The revolutionary spirit's ane wi' spirit itsel'!
Let a'thing else gang to Hell.
Hugh MacDiarmid,
Ode to All Rebels (1934)

Contents

Introduction:
'Tom Nairn Is the One'

Anthony Barnett

'All I'm arguing for is nations, minus the dratted
"ism": democratic-national, independent, diverse,
ordinary, even boring, rather than eighteenth-
century museum pieces, or dictators, or hustlers
like Blair and Berlusconi.'

Tom Nairn, 'Free World's End',
openDemocracy, December 4th, 2004.

Both because of the impact it has already had and because its influence is continuing to grow, the volume you are holding in your
hands is the most influential book on British politics to be published in the last half century, even though it is not a famous best-
seller. Its republication signals the post-Brexit renewal of a call
to arms initially issued in the maelstrom of the 1970s and finally
heading towards success.

All of which means this reprint is no mere antiquarian 'classic'
confined to the interest of specialists. Nor can it be read as a book
in the usual sense of having a beginning, middle and end between
two covers that you can close. Instead, it is the source of an ongoing
argument, one that sprang out of the resistant rockface of Marxism
like a fresh stream and continues to challenge everyone to swim in
its waters.

The first but by no means the only expression of its masterly
analysis lies in the certainty of Scottish independence from Westminster within a generation – that is to say, within the next five
to thirty-five years. For *The Break-Up of Britain* set out the first
arguments that clearly identified and advocated this outcome as a
matter of normalization, showing how it stems from the misfit of
the British state in the modern world, and not from the expression
of romantic tartanry, which the author excoriates.

Certainty is a strong word. At the time of writing what remains of the Westminster political–media caste are doing everything they can to head off demands for a second independence referendum, after the May 2021 elections to the Scottish parliament. Whether or not they succeed, the official emphasis is that the 2014 referendum was a 'once in a lifetime' opportunity. The price, therefore, of repudiating Scotland's power to choose its own future now grants it the right to do so when today's younger generation takes over – a generation that overwhelmingly supports liberation from Downing Street.

Now outside the EU, there is no elixir that can turn the UK into a democratic federation that delivers self-government to its nations. Hence the certainty of the coming break-up of Britain. Labour may seek to defy this with the promise of a referendum that includes the option of entrenched autonomy in a new UK constitution. To be credible this must, in effect, create an English parliament separate from a 'Great British' one. In other words, English nationality must be both aroused and confined for the purpose of keeping Scotland in the Union.[1] Which confirms that whatever happens will intensify not diminish the relevance of the argument initiated by Tom Nairn in *The Break-Up of Britain*. For the book addresses the evolving necessity of nationality – and it will be England's turn to absorb this reality; something that is long overdue. Speaking personally, it is here, south of the border, that I would most like to see new readers enjoy Nairn, not as a dreadful warning of the loss of greatness, or Britishness, but as an inspiration for those who would think as democrats. The time has come for democratic England to find its voice: ecological, networked, liberty-loving, European and republican.

Nairn's Influence

Young readers in England may not be aware of Nairn's standing and the need to reckon with his achievement. Two recent surveys record his impact within Scotland and therefore Britain. John Lloyd's

---

[1] Tory thinking is, as usual, ahead of Labour's. The case for implementing this has been set out in detail on the website of the Constitution Reform Group supported by Lord Salisbury. For a succinct version in a newspaper column, see Nick Timothy, *Telegraph*, January 3rd, 2021.

Should Auld Acquaintance Be Forgot: The Great Mistake of Scottish Independence makes its purpose evident in its subtitle. Interrupted only by a brief and unsuccessful stint as editor of the *New Statesman,* Lloyd has been a life-long star reporter for the *Financial Times.* He is what Nairn calls a Scottish butler. There have been many of them: exceptionally able Scots who come south and make a career out of preserving the Union by saving the English from themselves, while playing their role on a bigger stage than their homeland offers.

Lloyd's book seeks to preserve Great Britain by inquiring into the threat posed by Scottish independence. In a chapter on the growth of a self-conscious Scottish political culture, he says of Tom Nairn, 'This one Scots writer has been more influential in the nationalist cause than any other: one who has achieved what many intellectuals desire; that is, to have a marked influence on a movement or a period.' He then lists twenty-four of us – all men – who had written on the nature and future of the United Kingdom, and reports that only Nairn can be counted on to be a point of reference. His conclusion is unequivocal: 'Tom Nairn is the one … He is the one who has laid down the battle lines of attack, on the Union and on England.'[2]

Nine careful pages then follow on *Break-Up* and its 2002 successor, *After Britain.* But Lloyd cannot find a positive insight in Nairn's arguments that might explain his singular influence, apart from 'the fury and scorn' of his language, which Lloyd regards as quite unjustified.

A more thorough and even-handed view of Nairn's role is set out in a new academic history of nationalist political thought in modern Scotland by Ben Jackson. Four key figures emerge from his detailed account: George Davie, author of *The Democratic Intellect;* Stephen Maxwell, an early press officer for the Scottish National Party (and a big influence on Nairn); Neil MacCormick, professor of public law at Edinburgh; and Tom Nairn. Davie set out a vision of Scotland's distinct educational culture; Maxwell, the socialist case for nationalism; MacCormick, the legal realities and potential of shared sovereignty; while Nairn is given pride of place for having forged the 'intellectual origins of modern Scottish nationalism' in

[2] John Lloyd, *Should Auld Acquaintance Be Forgot: The Great Mistake of Scottish Independence* (2020), pp. 161–2.

London's *New Left Review* in the 1960s. Jackson traces how Nairn's argument developed and altered across fifty years.[3] It reinforces the perspective on Nairn presented by his life-long friend Neal Ascherson in his 2017 pamphlet *Painting Nationalism Red*.[4]

It would be wrong to suggest that all English are unaware of Nairn. A heroic attempt to inject his life-enhancing fluid into the pallid limbs of Labour Party socialism was attempted by Mark Perryman, who lives in Tom Paine's one-time home of Lewes. In 2008–9, as Gordon Brown's premiership seemed to open up the prospect of a creative follow-up to New Labour, Perryman edited two sets of essays that took Nairn's work as a starting point: *Imagined Nation: England after Britain* and *Breaking Up Britain: Four Nations after a Union*. Brown's cautious successor, Ed Miliband, put the brakes on Labour rethinking the national question. His successor, Jeremy Corbyn, revived the English left but harnessed it to the unreformed processes of the Westminster state, with Corbyn going to Scotland to tell its people, 'You can't eat a flag.'[5] The hopeful flowering of English radicalism, triggered by Corbyn's leadership after 2015, was never pollinated by the threefold debate over democracy, the Constitution and national identity now essential for lasting progress.

Eventually, England will have to embrace it. When it does the development of Nairn's arguments, whose strength lies in their openness to elaboration, will play a central role. What is it, then, that makes for the lethal success of the battle lines he first set out in the 1970s? How is it that he is succeeding when, since Tom Paine and Percy Shelley hurled themselves fruitlessly against the monstrosities of British power, generation upon generation of radicals have until now failed to make any lasting impression upon its ruling system, with the sole exception of the suffragettes and despite the success of the anti-colonial movements?

[3] Ben Jackson, *The Case for Scottish Independence: A History of Nationalist Thought in Modern Scotland* (2020), p. 63, an exceptionally helpful contemporary history. See also Ben Wellings and Michael Kenny, 'Nairn's England and the Progressive Dilemma: Reappraising Tom Nairn on English Nationalism', *Nations and Nationalism* vol. 25, no. 3 (2019), pp. 847–65.

[4] Reviewed by Rory Scothorne in the *London Review of Books*, December 6th, 2018.

[5] I write about this in *The Lure of Greatness* (2017), p. 290–1.

Three broad reasons explain the influence of the case originally developed in the pages that follow. First, the ongoing, living character of Nairn's argument. Second, the way he is rooted in Scotland yet speaks to his country from a world perspective and not as a nationalist. Third, his challenge to and moving on from Marxism, for what could be called 'Nairnism' were it not for his systematic repudiation of 'isms' of any kind.

The Living Character of Nairn's Argument

Time and a sense of growing momentum run through *The Break-Up of Britain* itself, for it gathers a set of essays published in *New Left Review* across a seven-year period, from 1970 to 1977. Nor does the book itself stand still. The 1981 reprint had a fascinating afterword, and the 2003 edition a significant introduction. Both are included at the end of this edition and show how Nairn reassesses his argument.

Nor was this process confined to reissues of *Break-Up*. He deepened his analysis in 1988, during the strange dual matriarchy of Margaret Thatcher and Elizabeth II, born within six months of each other. In *The Enchanted Glass*, a pioneering study of the monarchy, Nairn decoded 'the glamour of backwardness' and how the 'Crown ideology' was a 'surrogate nationalism' for Britain.[6] In 1999, *Break-Up* was reworked in *After Britain*, when he felt that change since 1977 had gone 'too far' to warrant republication. To assuage his contempt for Tony Blair's premiership, he published a short philippic in 2002, *Pariah: Misfortunes of the British Kingdom*. His fellow Scot, Gordon Brown, thanked in the 1977 acknowledgements to *Break-Up*, became Prime Minister in 2007. He was a more serious challenge, and John Osmond, at the Institute for Welsh Affairs, published Nairn's *Gordon Brown, Bard of Britishness*. In 2014 Jamie Maxwell and Pete Ramand edited a 400-page collection of Nairn's writings. The first, from 1964, on the British élite, the last on 'Old Nations, New Age' published by *openDemocracy* heralding the replacement of 'Internationalism' by 'inter-nationality'.

Others have battled to find a democratic way out of the airlock generated by the authoritarianism of revolutionary Marxism and

---

[6] *The Enchanted Glass, Britain and Its Monarchy* (1988), p. 277.

xiv

the marketization of social democracy. Their work too can be seen as an argument that arcs across a lifetime rather than being confined to a single book. A striking example is the Welsh writer Raymond Williams, who published *The Long Revolution* in 1961 and reprinted its conclusion over twenty years later in *Towards 2000,* in order to 'reconsider and rework' his starting point.[7]

Like Williams, the impetus behind Nairn's continuous reassessment is not backward-looking. It does not stem from sterile narcissism, such as the desire to prove that one was right or confess where one was wrong, although the former is asserted and the latter admitted when called for. The motivation is to work out how to respond and move forward in a profoundly changing world. This is the beating heart of Nairn's method. He expressed it strongly in 1972 when, in between the essays that make up *Break-Up,* he wrote *The Left Against Europe?* It became a special issue of *New Left Review* and was then published by Penguin as a short book. It is a forensic dissection of the futility of left-wing opposition to EU membership. Nairn writes, 'To be in favour of Europe ... does not imply surrender to, or alliance with, the left's enemies. It means exactly the opposite. It signals recognising and meeting them as enemies for what they are, upon the terrain of reality and the future.'[8]

'Recognise the terrain of reality.' This is Nairn's imperative. When the terrain of reality itself changes then your case for democratic self-government may, and perhaps must, be revised, as the principles behind it are reframed. It meant that when the enormous change of what was called globalization swept all before it after 1989, he was able to reassess the role of nationalism within what

[7] Raymond Williams, *Towards 2000* (1983), p. 20. See also my foreword to the reprint of his *The Long Revolution* (2013). A striking personal parallel is that both Nairn as a Scottish republican and Williams as a Welsh one struggle with taking late Britain seriously. Finding it hard to call the country they felt imprisoned in 'the United Kingdom' with a straight face, Williams satirized it as 'the Yookay' and Nairn as 'Ukania'.

[8] *New Left Review* No. 75 (Sept.–Oct. 1972). By chance I happened to be the issue editor and inherited the decision to dedicate an entire number of the review to a single text. Working on it created my friendship with Tom. As there was no need for the usual list of articles, I ran this quote right across the cover so that it could stand out as a message to the left.

he terms 'globality'.[9] The necessity of independence from Westminster that Nairn argued for in the 1970s remains, but the character of Scotland's independence will no longer be the same because the inter-relationship of countries in the era of globality is altering profoundly. Thus in his 2002 introduction to *Break-Up* he observes the forces carrying Great Britain to its termination were modest when the book came out twenty-five years earlier. Now, they were approaching a thunderous 'waterfall', as Blair mobilized what was left of the country's armed forces to join the US attack on Iraq. At the same time the world had become capitalist in an entirely novel way. The case for the independence of small countries in the 21st century was bound to differ significantly from that made in the 1970s in a world defined by the Cold War.

A further two decades have passed. Nairn's impatience is understandable – I share it. But his frustration, his desire that Scotland 'gets on with it', does not mean his arguments have been proved wrong. Alex Massie has recently deployed what is now a familiar, knee-jerk dismissal: 'Tom Nairn … the most mistaken Scottish intellectual of the past half-century. It is forty-three years since Nairn published *The Break-Up of Britain* … yet here we are not broken up.'[10] But the title of this book expresses the author's definitive judgement on the sustainability of the British state not a news story. A key quotation at the end of the chapter on the English Enigma captures Nairn's perspective: 'The English revolution is the most important element in the general upheaval of British affairs described in this book. It is also the hardest to foresee, and will take longest to achieve. Upon its character – conservative nationalist reaction or socialist advance – will depend on the future political rearrangement of the British Isles as federation, confederation, or modernised multi-national state.' Forty-three years later and Massie is writing in the *Sunday Times* about … 'the English revolution'.[11]

---

[9] For example, in *Global Matrix* (2005) written with Paul James.

[10] In a review of John Lloyd's book in the *Times Literary Supplement*, July 17th, 2020.

[11] 'Britain is splintering beneath the Brexit King', *Sunday Times*, January 2nd, 2021, where Massie writes: 'Brexit, then, was a very English revolution. It has sparked nationalist revivals in Wales, Northern Ireland and Scotland that are, in part, reactions to England's assertion of its prerogatives.'

Nairn's diagnosis that for the British left the empire-state of Westminster and Whitehall is *the main problem* has been amply confirmed. It cannot be the source for the solution of fundamental ills. Any welcome progress made by reforming governments winning a Commons majority thanks to an undemocratic electoral system will be undone by a régime which cannot but default to its reactionary nature. Unless this system of government is replaced by a constitutionally articulated democratization, Nairn foresaw an 'unthinkable' collapse into a hysterical, relic-seeking 'greatness' on the coattails of a failing America.

An assessment from 2002 illustrates the quality of Nairn's judgement. New Labour was at the zenith of its hegemony. Nairn's forecast that Britain would break apart seemed absurd. The political–media caste was uniformly scornful of right-wing anti-Europeans, soon to be dismissed by a Conservative leader as 'swivel-eyed loons'. But Nairn discerned a fatal complacency. He saw the danger of a 'hard-nosed and myopic', primarily English opinion taking shape. If, he argued, it cojoined Neo-liberalism with 'Britain's great-power past', and 'if such a proto-nationalist mythology does indeed become the matrix for popular heartland resentment at decline and loss, and is further aggravated by failure or marginalisation, then, of course, serious problems could be posed'. The term Brexit had yet to be coined. He went on, 'The most important cause ... will not be "Europe" or the misbehaviours and self-assertiveness of minorities, it will be the failure and belatedness of central constitutional reform.'[12] Nairn is far from always right, no one is. *Break-Up* should not be read for answers to exam questions on the nations of the UK. What it teaches us, by its example, is how to place a finger on the deeper pulse of reality.

Scotland, a Homeland on the Globe

Nairn first wrote at length about Scotland in 1968. 'The Three Dreams of Scottish Nationalism', published in *NLR*, is a withering denunciation of the futility of the nationalist movement. Its paragraphs are filled with the bombast of that year. The SNP's Winnie Ewing had just won the Hamilton by-election to become a Westminster MP, a victory that we can now see initiated modern

[12] *After Britain* (2002), pp. 16–17.

Scottish politics. Nairn penned a stern, revolutionary rebuke, directed at those who put their hopes in her surprising success. Her Scottish nationalism, Nairn thundered, 'is the product of a history without truth, a sterility where dream is unrelated to character, and both bear little relationship to what happens … Nationalism, in its current forms, is not the possible attainment of this redemptive dream, but its ultimate betrayal.' There was only one possible answer to Scotland's lumpen and provincial 'bourgeois nationalism', he insisted, with no evidence but all the over-confidence of 1968. This was 'a liberated and revolutionary Nationalism worthy of the name and the times'. The claim went undeveloped. It was simply a stirring final paragraph produced like a 'So there!' as Nairn flounced out of the room of actual politics. His 'Socialist nationalism' was no more than a paper rabbit conjured out of a Phrygian cap.

The SNP's political officer, Stephen Maxwell, wrote that he sent *NLR* 'a reasoned rejoinder', which it didn't publish. Then he and Nairn met. What happened next is best put in Nairn's words, for they describe the origins of *The Break-Up of Britain*.

'It was Stephen who put me right about … the likely character of Scottish nationalism … when I remained over-attached to the fossilised remains of "Internationalism". Like many others I had imagined direct transitions from a personal level of faith on to the overarching sky of totality … and in this imagined passage, nationality was somehow bypassed, or treated as a hereditary accident more likely to impede than assist individual progress towards humanity's capital-letter plane. In that sense, secular internationalists had simply taken over the deeper framework of so many religions … Nationality can't be glossed over or occluded, was the Maxwell message. It has to be incorporated into the contemporary, forward-looking mode of sociality.'[13]

[13] From the foreword to the posthumously published essays of Stephen Maxwell, *The Case for Left Wing Nationalism* (2013), p. 9. It includes Maxwell's review of *The Break-Up of Britain* in which he describes his own response to 'The Three Dreams' and writes, 'The development of Nairn's views on Scottish nationalism has something of an epic quality', p. 63.

Nairn's conversion was to have a formative impact on his home-land. Over time, it helped to clear the way for Scotland's left-leaning civil society and then for the country at large to accept the legitimacy of independence. It did so in part because Nairn's approach was international as well as rooted in Scotland. Of its two aspects, the huge attraction and novelty was its coming from abroad. He was fluent in Italian and French, had studied in Oxford, was on the editorial committee of *New Left Review*, a London outpost of international theory, and had mastered Gramsci (already becoming known in Scotland through the influence of Hamish Henderson). The unquestionable depth and range of Nairn's thinking originated without Scottish traditions. He represented the external world, and it was from its perspective that he was persuaded of the need for national autonomy. This made his conclusions more credible than any call from within, however poetic or articulate. It reassured his country-men and women that they would not be alone if they sought to 'be themselves' and put an end to the self-abasement that he argued was the price of Union. He freed the case for independence from charges of small-minded provincialism or ignorance of the workings of global politics.

At the same time Nairn was not a deracinated theorist who set about lecturing the Scots about how to improve themselves. There is a moral quality to his presence, neither Calvinist, romantic nor patronising, despite his immense learning, but self-contained and modest. In a relatively small country, all those who were interested, whether they agreed with him or not, knew what he was like and how he related to Scotland. Marxist thinkers often don't share with others their relationship to home. When I visited Trier, where Marx grew up, I was astonished by the vast basilica and the huge, gloomy three-storey Roman gate that dominate the skyline as well as the second-century bridge across the Moselle. The theorist of modes of production spent his boyhood in a small town surrounded by enormous structures from when it was a city, the northern military capital of Constantine I. Yet he seems not to have written about this. Like Marx, many who have worked and fought in the framework of historical materialism have been forced into exile or sought out the wider world. Nairn's last paid job was as a professor of globalization in Melbourne, Australia. Yet he always abided with, and wrote with poetic force about, Scotland and his upbringing.

Along with his international perspective, two other crucial attributes of the approach Nairn articulated had a lasting impact on the movement for Scottish independence: his opposition to national*ism* and his advocacy of independence in the European Union. He was not alone. Nairn was part of a significant network of men and women in Scotland. Encouraged by them, he made the case with a unique force and depth that help to explain not just his influence in his own country but also the challenge he still poses for left-wing thought.

Independence Rather than Nationalism

One insight is central to Nairn's embrace of the unavoidable reality of nation-framing in any struggle for the larger principles of democracy and equality. This is the intrinsically dual nature of nationalism, captured in his image of it as a two-faced Janus, the Roman god of doorways, facing both past and future. The concept functions to repudiate the idea that there are intrinsically progressive or 'good' nationalisms, such as the independence struggles against colonialism, and essentially xenophobic or 'bad' nationalisms, such as fascist or populist régimes. Nationalism, Nairn argues, is always *both* good and bad. It must draw on particularistic and exclusivist elements from the past as it seeks a larger meaning for all in the future. Furthermore, this dual character originates with the force that generates nationalism: the impossibility of any escape from the uneven development of capitalism.

Every nationalism denies this. Each presents itself as unique and good. The voice of national*ism* invariably emphasizes its own intrinsic positivity and the vulnerability of its own people to outside threats. This is as true for Norwegianism as for Nazism. But while Nairn embraces the national–democratic character of the need for self-government to ensure meaning and self-belief, he will have none of the bullshit. This is a difficult perspective to sustain in his analysis of the UK's nations for it means different things for England, Scotland, Wales and Northern Ireland. Nairn sought to identify their distinctiveness without validating their ideologies. The essays demonstrate his constant recognition of the dangers of 'believing' in nationalism – of taking it at its own evaluation of itself. At the same time, he insists nationalisms cannot be dismissed as false consciousness. In the UK this is made more complicated by the overlay of Britishness, a nationalism without a nation. The pathbreaking essay on Englishness and race and Enoch Powell, written in 1970, is a revelatory exercise in the demystification this demands.

Nairn's approach appears to be a paradox if, that is, you think nationalism means proclaiming you are special – such as 'world-beating' in the case of Brexit Britain. Hailing one's *uniqueness* is the hallmark of national*ism*. Whereas the case for independence that Nairn sets out advocates becoming *like* other countries. This is the language Scotland's first minister, Nicola Sturgeon, adopted when she said in 2012, 'My conviction that Scotland should be independent stems from the principles, not of identity or nationality, but of democracy and social justice.' In 2017, Sturgeon even said she regretted the inclusion of 'National' in the SNP's name.[14]

Independence in Europe

It is all very well declaring that one is not nationalist but progressive and democratic, as Sturgeon does. But what if independence were actually to happen in the teeth of bitter Anglo-British opposition and the immediate termination of London's budgetary support? Surely the stresses would demand an intolerant mobilization that can't help but be nationalist? Nairn's Janus theory of nationalism shows that this serious risk is inescapable. The answer, he argues, is to look to the external circumstances of independence, for these will determine its inner development. In 1975, in one of his most programmatic statements, made when he was writing *Break-Up*, he told his fellow Scots,

> 'My view is … that self-governing Scotland should try at all costs not only to stay in Europe but to help the Common Market grow into a federal or confederal system of States … a new interdependence where our nationhood will count, rather than towards mere isolation; towards Europe as well as towards self-rule.'

[14] Colin Kidd, 'The Twilight of the Union', *New Statesman*, September 30th, 2020.

This was published in the *Red Paper On Scotland*, edited by the young Gordon Brown, at a formative moment when the Scottish left intelligentsia began to debate the need for Scottish self-government and how socialists and the Labour Party should relate to it.

Nairn had already published *The Left Against Europe?*, so the case he was making had considerable depth. For Scotland, Europe was not just the terrain of reality; there was a darker imperative for membership. Without it, independence could indeed bring forth the demons in Scottish history. Today, the attractions of becoming a European state alongside others of comparable size may be obvious. In 1975 it was much less so. But the idea of membership was transformative. Pure independence would lead to fanaticism. Gaining independence within a European association of sovereignties would not stir the blood, but this was the point – it was practical, collaborative and forward-looking.

In 1978, the rapid rise of SNP influence led to a referendum on a Scottish parliament whose low turnout ensured that it failed. In the wake of the disaster a group was formed in Edinburgh by Stephen Maxwell. The young Alex Salmond participated and Nairn came along, although not as a party member. The SNP's leaders began to shift away from opposition to Europe. In 1983 the party conference backed joining the EU after full Scottish independence. In 1988 its policy became 'Independence in Europe'. Salmond called it 'post-nationalism'. By embracing the case for European membership the independence movement ejected Braveheart bloviating. The road to the SNP becoming the government of a devolved Scotland and eventually an independent state was now open.

Nairn's Challenge to Marxism

In these days of spin and image, talk of policy can be dismissed as mere positioning. This is especially so in England–Britain where, perhaps because Westminster no longer has a genuine interior life that links to public self-belief, almost everything that is political is inauthentic. One of the enjoyable refrains in Nairn's analysis of British government across the decades is his satirizing its constant commitment to 'radical' policies, such as world-beating this or that. The old régime constantly generates the simulacrum of modernization, in a never-ending effort to protect itself from being dispatched to the museum where it belongs. Being brought up in this environment and breathing in its bad faith daily, English readers may instinctively read the two sections above to mean that Nairn offered the independence movement a 'line' on nationalism and another 'line' on the EU, so that its unchanged nationalism could proceed behind the apparent novelty of his arguments.

This is not the case at all. You have to understand that with a huge effort Nairn really has exited the thought-world and mentality of Britishness. The argument Nairn developed really was and is original. It stems from his rethinking how we – especially we on the left – have to view the nature of historical change itself. His essay on 'The Modern Janus' which concludes *Break-Up* is a theory of the development of capitalism. It argues that the mobilization of nationality is essential to it and is not a false consciousness. Socialists who want to grasp the challenge this poses can turn to the final page. Nairn warns against seeking to understand the world today by looking back internally to Marxist or socialist traditions: 'the result is bound to be the perpetuation of sectarian theology in some form, however refined'. Instead, we have to ground our ideas and arguments externally. By recentring historical materialism on the terrain of reality, rather than reinterpretation and reapplication, Nairn releases the tradition of Marxism from the imprisonment of its followers. The chapter says nothing about Britain or its constituent countries. But it plays a crucial part in the influence of *The Break-Up of Britain*. For it initiates the method Nairn arrived at in order to make his analysis: the rethinking that he was obliged to undertake once he had been confronted by Stephen Maxwell, after 1968, with the uncomfortable realization that for all his unequalled grasp of Marx and Gramsci and modern European thought, he could not deny or explain the centrality of the nation in political change.

England Next

English readers who believe they are above or beyond their nation now confront the same painful but emancipating need to engage with it. For Brexit is primarily an English nationalism expressed as British uniqueness. Against it a better Englishness is now essential. This entails repudiating any definition of what it means to be English in the racist terms that Enoch Powell sought, and which

Nairn demolished in his 1970 essay published here as Chapter 6. By making British sovereignty the measure of the country's freedom, the English who backed Brexit have turned the UK into a prison for its smaller nations. The one serious argument now deployed to shake the Scots out of their impertinent desire to remain in the EU is the threat to break them on the economic wheel of English supremacy. How can we English abide this treatment of our neighbours? It is time for the great chorus of lamentation from the progressive columnists (let's not mention my good friend Will Hutton), terrified of being reduced to citizens of their own country, to stop singing counterpoint to the *Spectator–Telegraph* that the Kingdom must remain united. A country that imposes itself on another can never be the home of progress. The poison of mobilizing against Scotland's desire to leave England to join the EU will be fatal for betterment on both sides of the border.

It is, therefore, the duty of progressive England to positively urge Scotland on to independence in Europe. Today, we in England cannot read *The Break-Up of Britain* as something that may be *done to us* by the peripheral nations, which would have been understandable at the time it was written in the 1970s. We are well past that. Because it didn't happen as Nairn hoped. Because the devilish energy of globalization and then the initial skill of New Labour preserved the old régime. Because they swept aside demands for the democratic renewal we failed to insist upon strongly enough. Because of our own history, therefore, we in England have now entered the consequences first discerned in these pages in the 1970s, with all the drama and difficulty of someone sketching the reality of the future should it go wrong. England has caused and now entered the breakdown of the United Kingdom. For Scotland the way out is obvious. For the English the process will be harder but the route is the same. The only exit from the breakdown is a course of action that shatters the spell of the Brexiteers: it is time for the English to insist on the break-up of Britain.

January 2021

1. The Twilight of the British State

'External conflicts between states form the shape of the state. I am assuming this "shape" to mean – by contrast with internal social development – the external configuration, the size of a state, its contiguity (whether strict or loose), and even its ethnic composition . . . We must stress that in the life of peoples external events and conditions exercise a decisive influence upon the internal constitution.'

Otto Hintze, *The Formation of States and Constitutional Development* (1902).

Only a few years ago, the break-up of Britain was almost inconceivable. Southern, catholic Ireland had broken away from the United Kingdom in 1922; but there seemed little reason to believe that the protestants of Northern Ireland or the other minor nationalities of Wales and Scotland would follow their example.

Conditions were different in these other cases. Southern Ireland had been conquered country, displaying most of those features which in this century have come to be called 'under-development'. Upon that basis, and mobilizing the deep-laid cultural differences provided by Catholicism, a largely peasant society had produced the classical nationalist reaction against alien rule which ended in 1922. As the century's history of anti-imperialist struggle unfolded this seemed more and more a typical episode of it. Although unusually close geographically to the metropolitan centre, Southern Ireland had in fact been separated from it by a great socio-political gulf, by that great divide which was to dominate so much of the epoch:

the 'development gap'.

For this very reason, it appeared improbable that other regions of the British Isles would follow Eire's example. There were episodes of conquest in the histories of Northern Ireland, Wales, and Scotland, true enough. But these had been followed or accompanied by episodes of assimilation and voluntary integration – and until the 1960s it looked as if the latter tendencies had triumphed. All three societies had, at least in part, crossed over the main divide of the development process. Unlike Eire, they had become significantly industrialized in the course of the 19th century. All three had turned into important sub-centres of the Victorian capitalist economy, and around their great urban centres – Belfast, Cardiff and Glasgow – had evolved middle and working classes who, consciously and indisputably, gave their primary political allegiance to the imperial state.

Through this allegiance they became subjects of one of the great unitary states of history. Absorption, not federation, had always been the principle of its development. From the period of Norman feudalism onwards, the English state had expanded its hold over these outlying areas and peoples. Until in 1800 – as one constitutional authority puts it – 'there existed the United Kingdom of Great Britain and Ireland, and in the process of its development there was not the smallest element of federation'. None of the constituent countries of this multi-national state 'retained even a modified sovereignty: that of each was melted in the general mass'.[1]

Such is the theory of the British state, and the notion of the British parliament's total sovereignty still praised and defended in current debate. To understand it as more than that would be misleading. The 'general mass' has not, on the whole, been taken to mean civil society. The 'unitary state' in this form was compatible with civil variety in the different countries composing it: it did not necessarily seek to impose a uniform culture, language, or way of life. There have been examples of forced levelling, for instance in Wales or the Scottish Highlands; yet in the main 'Anglicization' was left to the slower, more natural-seeming pressures of one large central nationality upon the smaller peripheric areas.

In spite of the pressure, a lot of latitude was left by the system

[1] C. F. Strong, *Modern Political Constitutions*, 8th revised edition, 1972, ch. 4, section IV.

to the personality of the smaller nations. 19th and early 20th century British imperialism even encouraged such circumscribed patriotisms. A conservative pride in local colour and traditions went well with the grand design. Hence, until the secession of southern Ireland in 1922, a general formula of 'Home Rule' for all three countries was widely discussed and approved of. While the centre remained strong, such an approach did not appear too threatening. On the other hand, for the same reason – the strong, magnetic pull the metropolis had over its fringe lands – pressure for genuine self-government was not very great. Apart from the exception, Catholic Ireland, it remained weak until the 1960s.

Since then, in only a decade, it has swelled into the major political issue of the 1970s. It is worth underlining how quite unexpected and puzzling this change has been. Vague expectations about a possible transformation, or even collapse, of the British system after the defeat of its empire had been commonplace not for years but for several generations. Worried prognostications of this order go back to the 1890s or even earlier. It never took much political imagination to grasp that: (i) Great Britain was quite unusually and structurally dependent upon external relations tied up with its empire; (ii) Britain was due for demotion or outright defeat at the hands of the bigger, more dynamic capitalist states that expanded from the late 19th century onwards. Hence the loss of its critical overseas wealth and connections was bound to promote internal re-adjustments – or perhaps, as left-wing observers imagined with relish, a real social revolution. There was something suitable about this: the most inveterate and successful exploiters ought to suffer the most sensational punishment.

There is no doubt that the old British state is going down. But, so far at least, it has been a slow foundering rather than the *Titanic*-type disaster so often predicted. And in the 1970s it has begun to assume a form which practically no one foresaw.

Prophets of doom always focused, quite understandably, upon social and economic factors. Blatant, deliberately preserved in-equities of class were the striking feature of the English social order. Here was the original proletariat of the world's industrial revolution, still concentrated in huge depressed urban areas, still conscious of being a class – capable of being moved to revolutionary action, surely, when the economic crisis got bad enough. As for the economic slide itself, nothing seemed more certain. A constantly weakening industrial base, a dominant financial sector oriented towards foreign investment rather than the re-structuring of British industries, a non-technocratic state quite unable to bring about the 'revolution from above' needed to redress this balance: everything conspired to cause an inexorable spiral of decline. The slide would end in break-down, sooner rather than later.

Clearly the prophecies were out of focus, in spite of the strong elements of truth in them. The way things have actually gone poses two related questions. Firstly, why has the old British state-system lasted so long, in the face of such continuous decline and adversity? Secondly, why has the break-down begun to occur in the form of territorial disintegration rather than as the long-awaited social revolution – why has the threat of secession apparently eclipsed that of the class-struggle, in the 1970s?

In my view the answer to both of these questions depends mainly upon one central factor, unfortunately neglected in the majority of discussions on the crisis. This central issue is the historical character of the British state itself.

The Logic of Priority

The most important single aspect of the United Kingdom state is its developmental priority. It was the first state-form of an industrialized nation. From this position in the general process of modern development come most of the underlying characteristics of the system. A specific historical location furnished those 'external conditions', in Hintze's sense, that 'exercised a decisive influence upon the internal constitution'.

Critical analysis of the state-form has been retarded by two inter-related factors. The conservative account which has always insisted on the system's uniqueness is in reality a mythology, and has been an important ideological arm of the state itself. But critical rejection of these mystifications, above all by marxists, has normally reverted into complete abstraction. Thus, a pious bourgeois cult of British priority and excellence has been countered by insistence that there is 'in reality' nothing special about the British state: like all others, it represents the dominance of a capitalist class.[2]

[2] 'Marxist political analysis has long suffered from marked deficiencies . . . notably in relation to the nature and role of the state, and has shown little capacity

In developmental terms, it represented the dominance of the first
national capitalist class which emancipated itself from city or city-
state mercantilism and created the foundations of industrialization.
From its example, much of the original meaning of 'development'
was derived. For this reason the English – subsequently 'British' –
political system was, and still remains 'unique' in a non-mystifying
sense. These are peculiarities that owe nothing to the inherent
political virtues of the British, and everything to the conditions and
temporality of capitalist development in the British Isles. The multi-
national state-form that has ruled there from 1688 to the present
time could not be 'typical' of general modern development simply
because it initiated so much of that development.

This initiation goes back to the revolutionary era of English
history, between 1640 and 1688. It is not necessary here to discuss
the various accounts which have been given of the causes or un-

---

to renew itself . . .', notes Ralph Miliband in *The State in Capitalist Society*
(1969, pp. 6–8). Apart from Gramsci, 'Marxists have made little attempt to confront the question of the state in the light of the concrete reality of actual capitalist
societies'. But his own analysis remains focused upon 'the many fundamental
uniformities . . . the remarkable degree of similarity, not only in economic but in
social and even in political terms, between the countries of advanced capitalism'
(p. 9). However, theory-construction equally demands advance on the terrain of
differentiation and specific analysis: the developmental uniqueness of states as
well as their uniformities. A characteristic example of the traditional application
of Marxist theory to Britain is *The British State*, by J. Harvey and K. Hood,
1958 – see particularly ch. 2, 'The Marxist Theory and the British State'.

On the other side there is of course a huge literature devoted to panegyric
of the Constitution, along the lines of Sir David Lindsay Keir's *The Constitutional
History of Modern Britain since 1485*: 'Continuity has been the dominant characteristic in the development of English government. Its institutions, though
unprotected by the fundamental or organic laws which safeguard the "rigid"
constitutions of most other states, have preserved the same general appearance
throughout their history, and have been regulated in their working by principles
which can be regarded as constant.' These institutions 'have all retained, amid
varying environments, many of the inherent attributes as well as much of the
outward circumstance and dignity which were theirs in the mediaeval world of
their origin. In no other European country is the constitution so largely a legacy
from that remote but not unfamiliar age . . .', and so on (8th edition, 1966, ch. 1).
By far the most useful and disrespectful classic of constitutional lore is Walter
Bagehot's *The English Constitution*. Sir Ivor Jennings' *Parliament* (1939) contains two exemplary mainstream summations of myth in its opening sections,
'Authority Transcendent and Absolute' and 'The Importance of Being Ancient'.

folding of the upheaval.[3] But few critics would dispute that it signalled the end of absolutism in the British Isles. By the beginning of the next century only the Celtic areas in the north and west retained a basis for restoring the absolute monarchy; and this attempt failed finally in 1746. Thus, the late-feudal state had effectively disappeared by the end of the 17th century, and the way had been opened – at least – for the development of a bourgeois society.[4]

To the conditions of that society there corresponded a new type of political state, first theorized by Thomas Hobbes and John Locke. 'In the aftermath of the crisis . . . it became clear that despite differences in emphasis there was a strong converging tendency so that by the early 18th century the search for sovereignty was moving almost all the European countries towards the concept of the impersonal state', writes one historian of the idea of the state.[5] This common tendency, in time, produced the modern constitutional state of the 19th century. In 1843 Marx delineated the latter's emergence as follows. The political revolution which had destroyed feudalism 'raised state affairs to become affairs of the people, (and) constituted the political state as a matter of *general* concern, that is, as a real state, necessarily smashed all estates, corporations, guilds and privileges, since these were all manifestations of the separation of the people from the community . . .'. It posited a collection of abstract individuals – 'citizens' – whose collective will was supposedly represented by the abstract authority of the new state. The real life of these individuals, as property-owners, religious believers, workers, family men and women, etc., was consigned to the realm of 'civil society'.[6]

[3] These are summed up in Lawrence Stone's *The Causes of the English Revolution, 1529–1642*, 1972.

[4] In England, Absolutism was 'felled at the centre by a commercialized gentry, a capitalist city, a commoner artisanate and yeomanry: forces pushing beyond it. Before it could reach the age of maturity, English Absolutism was cut off by a bourgeois revolution', writes Perry Anderson in *Lineages of the Absolutist State*, 1974, p. 220. An earlier bourgeois revolution had occurred in the Netherlands, but this model did not lead to a comparable sustained priority of development. There, the 'transitional' state form quickly decayed into a highly conservative patriciate.

[5] J. H. Shennan, *Origins of the Modern European State, 1450–1725*, 1974, p. 113.

[6] Marx, 'On the Jewish Question', in Marx and Engels, *Collected Works*, vol. 3 (1843–4), p. 166.

This relationship between society and state was – as Marx indicates in the same place – first completely formulated by Rousseau, and realized in practice by the French Revolution. This second revolutionary era, from the American revolt of 1776 up to 1815, marked the definitive establishment of modern constitutionalism. Absolutism had been far stronger over most of the European continent than in England. Hence – 'On the Continent, the full development of constitutionalism was delayed until the 19th century, and . . . it took a series of revolutions to achieve it'.[7] It was these revolutions which formed the typical modern idea and practice of the state, imitated and reduplicated on an ever-increasing scale up to the present day. 'With the exception of those of Great Britain and the United States,' points out the same author, 'no existing constitution is older than the 19th century, and most of those which existed in the first half of that century have since either entirely disappeared . . . or been so fundamentally amended and revised as to be in effect new.'[8] But of course the association of the English and American systems is misleading here: the American was the firstborn of the moderns, and only the English represents a genuine survival.

Alone, it represented 'a slow, conventional growth, not, like the others, the product of deliberate invention, resulting from a theory'. Arriving later, those others 'attempted to sum up at a stroke the fruits of the experience of the state which had evolved its constitutionalism through several centuries'.[9] But in doing so (as panegyrists of Westminster have always said) they could not help betraying that experience, which remained (in a sense far less flattering than the panegyrists believe) inimitable. Because it was first, the English – later British – experience remained distinct. Because they came second, into a world where the English Revolution had already succeeded and expanded, later bourgeois societies could not repeat this early development. Their study and imitation engendered something substantially different: the truly modern doctrine of the abstract or 'impersonal' state which, because of its abstract nature, could be imitated in subsequent history.

This may of course be seen as the ordinary logic of develop-

---

[7] C. F. Strong, op. cit., p. 25.
[8] Ibid., p. 36.
[9] Ibid., p. 28.

mental processes. It was an early specimen of what was later dignified with such titles as 'the law of uneven and combined development'. Actual repetition and imitation are scarcely ever possible,
whether politically, economically, socially or technologically,
because the universe is already too much altered by the first cause
one is copying. But this example of the rule had one interesting
consequence it is important to underline in the present context.

Most theory about the modern state and representative democracy has been, inevitably, based upon the second era of bourgeois
political revolution. This is because that era saw what Marx called
'the completion of the idealism of the state', and the definition of
modern constitutionalism. It established and universalized what is
still meant by the 'state', and the relationship of the political state to
society. Hegelian-based idealism and marxism were both founded
upon study of 'The *classic* period of political intellect . . . the
French Revolution' and its derivatives.[10] As such, they naturally –
even legitimately – neglected the preceding evolution of the English state. Far less defined and universalizable, this process embodied, and retained, certain original characteristics that in the
later perspectives seemed 'anomalous', or even inexplicable.[11]

[10] Marx and Engels, op. cit., 'Critical Marginal Notes on the Article "The
King of Prussia and Social Reform, by a Prussian"', p. 199.

[11] The 'marked deficiencies' of analysis noted by Miliband (note 2 above) have
unfortunately an influential origin in the history of Marxist writing: the deficiencies of Marx's and Engels' own views on the British state. The odd situation these
views represent has been insufficiently emphasised by their biographers. From
mid-century onwards the main theorists of the following century's revolutions
lived in the most developed capitalist society, and the central part of their main
achievement, *Capital*, was based to a great extent on study of its economy. Yet
they wrote very little on its state and hegemonic structures. Compilations of their
writings on Britain (e.g. Marx and Engels *On Britain*, Moscow 1953) are among
the thinnest of such volumes. Also, their outstanding writings touching on relevant political questions were all early, and were never improved upon: the striking
examples here are Engels' *Vorwärts!* articles on 'The Condition of England'
(now in the *Collected Works*, vol. 3) and his *The Condition of the Working Class in
England* (*Collected Works*, vol. 4). These date from 1844 and 1845. Marx's own
general political ideas were formed before his exile in England. As Colletti observes in a recent introduction to the 'Early Writings', he 'already possessed a very
mature theory of politics and the state . . . (and) . . . Politically speaking, mature
Marxism would have relatively little to add to this' (*Early Writings*, Pelican
Marx Library, London 1975, p. 45). This 'mature theory' was wholly drawn from
Continental study and experiences. There were to be no farther experiences com-

These traits have remained the preserve of worshippers within, and puzzled comment without. It is for this reason that the present political crisis in Britain raises such far-ranging and theoretical problems. While comparable to other problem-situations in Western Europe in a number of ways – e.g. Italy, as regards its economic dimensions, or Spain and France as regards its neo-nationalism – there is something important and *sui generis* about the British case. It is, in effect, the extremely long-delayed crisis of *the* original bourgeois state-form – of the grandfather of the contemporary political world. The passing of this ancestor calls for more than superficial commentary.

An Imperial State

The non-typical features of the British state order can be described by calling it 'transitional'. More than any other society it established the transition from the conditions of later feudalism to those of modernity. More than its predecessor, the Dutch Republic, it gave impetus and direction to the whole of later social development. Yet for this very reason it could not itself be 'modern'. Neither feudal nor modern, it remained obstinately and successfully intermediate: the midwife of modern constitutionalism, perhaps, as much as a direct ancestor.

Internally, this system presents a number of 'peculiarities' related to its historical location. It replaced late-feudal monarchy by a rule which was – as it remains today – patrician as well as representative. Because in this original case a spontaneously emergent bourgeois 'civil society' created the state, pragmatically, civil society retained an unusual dominance over the state. The only comparable examples were to be in social formations directly hived from Eng-

---

pelling them to a more searching inquiry into the prior universe of the British state: their long exile coincided largely with an era of quiescence and growing stability in Britain, and this seems to have rendered them largely incurious about their immediate political milieu. The absence of curiosity led them to persist in a view (very marked in their occasional articles and letters on Britain) of the state as a façade or mask of capitalist realities. The evident archaism of the state did not, therefore, qualify their vision of these realities as the prefiguration of what other, later-developing societies would have to undergo. But their enormous authority in other directions has always tended to justify this blind spot, and so underwrite the 'marked deficiencies'.

land, like the white colonies or North America. Elsewhere the arma-ture of the state itself was of incomparably greater significance in development: all the progeny of the '*classic* period of political intellect' were to be relatively state-dominated formations, reflect-ing the harder circumstances of historical evolution in the 19th and 20th centuries. In turn, this original English civil hegemony had certain implications for the nature of civil society itself, to which I will return below.

But for the moment it is essential to stress something else. From the outset, all these internal conditions were interwoven with, and in reality dependent on, external conditions. As well as England's place in developmental sequence, one must bear in mind its place in the history of overseas exploitation. As Marx indicated in *Capital,* success on this front was bound up with the primitive accumulation of capital in England itself.[12] The new English state's ascendancy over its competitors in colonization accompanied the crystallization of its internal forms.

Hence, a double priority was in fact involved: the temporality of England's new capitalist social system was in symbiosis with the country's maritime and conquering adventures. The latter re-mained a central feature of world history until the Second World War – that is, until long after English industrial capitalism had lost its pre-eminence, and indeed become a somewhat backward economy by many well-known indices.

It was the extraordinary external successes of the transitional English state that permitted it to survive so long. Otherwise, it would certainly have gone down in the wave of new, state-ordered, nationalist capitalisms which developed in the course of the 19th century. It too would have been compelled to suffer a second, mod-ernizing revolution and the logical reorganization of its constitu-tion and state: precisely that second political upheaval whose ab-sence has been the constant enigma and despair of modern Britain.

But in fact the advantages gained through developmental priority

[12] See *Capital,* Chapter XXXI, 'The Genesis of the Industrial Capitalist': 'The colonial system ripened trade and navigation as in a hot-house . . . The colonies provided a market for the budding manufactures, and a vast increase in accumulation which was guaranteed by the mother country's monopoly of the market. The treasures captured outside Europe by undisguised looting, enslave-ment and murder flowed back to the mother-country and were turned into capital there.' (Pelican Marx Library, London 1976, vol. 1, p. 918).

were for long decisive. As the 'industrial revolution' waned from the mid-19th century onwards the more conscious and systematic exploitation of these advantages compensated for domestic back-wardness. A 'New Imperialism' took over from the old, with the establishment of a financial control of the world market as its core. This mutation accorded supremely well with the character of the patrician state. It safeguarded the latter for another half-century, at the cost of ever-greater external dependency and ever more pro-nounced sacrifice of the domestic economy. As will be suggested in more detail below, this pattern has reproduced itself without fail not only into the last years, but into the last months and days of the present crisis: a slow, cumulative collapse determined not by the failure of 'British capitalism' alone, but by the specific underlying structures of an archaic state and the civil class-system it protects.

'Imperialism', in the sense pertinent to this prolonged trajectory, is somewhat different from the definitions now customarily given to the term.[13] As with constitutionalism, theory has naturally been preoccupied in the main by later and more systematic develop-ments: in this case the formation of modern European empires between 1880 and 1945, and the nature of the informal U.S. system which followed them. However, England's pattern of foreign exploitation and dependency has lasted from the 16th century to the present, uninterruptedly. Like the state-form it made possible, it preceded and conditioned the rise of later rivals and – even while adapting to this new world, as in 'New Imperialism' – remained itself of a somewhat different nature.

This nature is best understood in terms of the social order which it fostered in England. A régime so largely concerned with overseas and naval-based exploitation required, above all, conservative stability at home. It demanded a reliable, respectful hierarchy of

[13] The best review of theories of imperialism is Benjamin Cohen's *The Question of Imperialism: the Political Economy of Dominance and Dependence*, 1973. The general view of imperialism advanced there perceives it as rooted in 'the external organization of states' (p. 234), and to that extent accords with the theory of this book. Unfortunately, Cohen fails to relate this theme of external state-order sufficiently to that of uneven development, and so is forced to fall back on national-ity and nationalism as 'given facts' rather than as developmental functions (see pp. 255–7). In reality uneven development generates these 'given facts' of imperialism and nationalism for the contemporary era (*c.* 1750–2000), not vice-versa.

social estates, a societal pyramid to act as basis for the operations of the patrician élite. This was of course quite a different need from the later forms of imperialism. These emerged into an England-dominated world: 'late developers', often with far greater real resources than the British Isles, impelled by a restless internal dynamic of development. This was to be the case, above all, of Germany.

The later empires were either industrial-based, like Germany; or else strongly militaristic in outlook, by compensation for the lack of economic potential, like the Italian, French and Portuguese systems. Indeed, more or less aggressive militarism was the general accompaniment of later 19th century colonization and expansion. The British empire alone was not in essence either of these things. It had been constituted before the others, on a scale which gave it lasting advantages in the later conflicts. And it had been formed overwhelmingly by naval and commercial strategy in which land militarism was of small account.[14]

The following paradoxes must therefore be taken into account. The pioneer modern liberal-constitutional state never itself became modern: it retained the archaic stamp of its priority. Later the industrialization which it produced, equally pioneering and equally world-wide in impact, never made England into a genuinely industrialized society. Even more evidently, the cramped foundations of the 'industrial revolution' quickly became archaic and *dépassé* when set against the unfolding pattern of general world industrialization from the late 19th century onwards.

The two paradoxes are of course organically connected. No recovery from industrial 'backwardness' has been possible, precisely because no second revolution of the state has taken place in England: only the state could have engendered such a recovery, by revolution from above – but the old patrician structure of England's political system, incapable of such radical action, has also resisted every effort at serious reform up to the present day. This astonishing resistance, in turn, must be explained in terms of external relations.

[14] In his article 'En Route: Thoughts on the Progress of the Proletarian Revolution' (*Izvestia*, 1919, reproduced in *The First Five Years of the Communist International*, vol. 1, New York, 1945), Trotsky commented: 'England's insular position spared her the direct burden of maintaining militarism on land. Her mighty naval militarism, although requiring huge expenditures, rested nevertheless on numerically small cadres of hirelings and did not require a transition to universal military service'.

During the very period when industrial backwardness began to present itself as an inescapable problem, between the 1870s and 1914, and foreign competition began to overwhelm England's economy, the archaic mould of society and state was greatly reinforced there. This was the work of the 'New Imperialism', consolidating and reorienting the vast inheritance of previous colonization and overseas trade. Less and less able to compete with the new workshops of the world, the ruling élite compensated by extended control of the world's money market – by building up a financial centre in the City of London. During the long period when sterling was the world's main trading currency – it lasted until after the Second World War – these unique and formidable financial institutions remained at one level the nucleus of world capitalism. Long after the industrial centre of gravity had moved to North America and Continental Europe, they kept their pre-eminence in the area of capital investment and exchange.[15]

Thus, one part of the capital of England was in effect converted into an 'offshore island' of international capitalism, to a considerable degree independent of the nation's declining domestic capitalism. This type of finance-capital imperialism rested, in other words, on a marked division within British capitalism itself. The latter became the victim of a split between the consistently declining productive sector and the highly successful City sector. Naturally, City institutions monopolized the outstanding talents and energies of the business class; in addition, they exerted virtual hegemony over the state in virtue of the élite social solidarity so strongly rooted in English civil society.

This hegemony provided the material basis of the state's 'backwardness'. It was a 'backwardness' perfectly congruent with the demands of the controlling element in British capitalism – elements which enjoyed the conservative societal hierarchy of 'traditional England' and which, if they did not actually approve of the industrial degeneration, had no urgent reasons for redressing it.[16]

[15] The modern imperialist turning of the U.K. economy is outlined, and its long-term significance suggested, in S. Pollard, *The Development of the British Economy 1914–1950*, 1962; see especially 'Foreign Investment and the Problem of Empire', pp. 19–23.

[16] At a number of places in his celebrated *Imperialism* (1902), J. A. Hobson used southern England as an image of the successful, imperialist side of British capitalism: a countryside of plush 'parasitism' drawing tribute from overseas via the City, supporting 'great tame masses of retainers' in service and secondary

External orientation and control implied external dependency. In this sense, it is true to say that such external dependency provided the essential condition for the original accumulation of capital in England; for both the industrial revolution *and* its 'failure', or at least its incomplete and limited character in England itself; and for the one-sided compensatory development of liberal, City imperialism that has carried the old order into the last quarter of the 20th century.

English Civil Society

In his critique of Hegel's theory of the state, Marx insisted that it was not the idea of the state which constituted civil society; rather, the real new nature of civil society – modern or bourgeois society – was responsible for the state. He posited a typical duality of modern conditions, therefore. The competitive, material anarchy of middle-class society evolved as its necessary complement an abstract political state-order: the new liberal or constitutional state. The key mystery of this relationship was representation. The representative mechanism converted real class inequality into the abstract egalitarianism of citizens, individual egoisms into an impersonal collective will, what would otherwise be chaos into a new state legitimacy.[17]

---

industries, and riddled with ex-imperialist hirelings. 'The South and South-West of England is richly sprinkled with these men', he continued, 'most of them endowed with leisure, men openly contemptuous of democracy, devoted to material luxury, social display, and the shallower arts of intellectual life. The wealthier among them discover political ambitions . . . Not a few enter our local councils, or take posts in our constabulary or our prisons: everywhere they stand for coercion and for resistance to reform' (pp. 150–1, 314, 364–5). Not a few of them were active very recently, in forming para-military and strike-breaking organisations during 1973 and 1974. The only big difference brought by seventy-five years is that the 'niggers' they were aiming to put down were mostly white: the other, 'unsuccessful' side of British capitalism north of them.

[17] 'The most important characteristic which distinguishes the burghers (*burgerliche Gesellschaft*) from the other sections of the national community is their individualism . . . (Civil society) remains basically a multitude of self-seeking individuals, impatient of customs, traditions, and privileges, and apt to conceive freedom as the absence or at least the minimum of political obligations. Such a society threatens not merely the rest of the nation but the supreme public authority itself . . .' This is Z. A. Pelczynski's summary of Hegel's view of the political challenge of bourgeois society (*Hegel's Political Writings*, 'Introductory Essay',

However, as noted previously, Hegel and Marx alike were in part theorizing the later, 'typical' circumstances in which middle classes developed a form of dominance more hastily and competitively, against much greater feudal obstacles, and often by revolutionary effort. Although Marx's view of the priority of civil society applies with particular emphasis to England, the accompanying abstract duality does not. The latter reflected the historical experience of the Continental states.

In the English evolution which had gone before, the middle classes developed more gradually and created a civil society which stood in a substantially different relationship to the state. The conquering social class of the mid-17th century civil wars was an agrarian élite: landlordism in a new form, and with a new economic foundation, but emphatically not the urban bourgeoisie which later became the protagonist of modern European development. Although no longer feudal, and allied increasingly closely to the urban middle class, this class remained a patrician élite and concentrated political power entirely in its own hands. In a way quite distinct from later 'ruling classes' it constituted the actual personnel and machinery of the English state. The latter was not the impersonal, delegated apparatus to be formulated in 19th century constitutionalism. On the contrary, in a way which was not repeatable by any typical bourgeois stratum, one social class *was* the state. Hence, one part of civil society wholly dominated 'the state' and lent it, permanently, a character different from its rivals.

In a standard work on the subject. Samuel Finer points out how: 'The importance of this tradition is that it has preserved not only the mediaeval forms but the mediaeval essence: this was that the

---

1964, p. 61). This political challenge is taken up much more trenchantly in Marx's early critique of Hegel and (as Colletti emphasizes in his presentation of the *Early Writings*, op. cit.) taken to a supremely logical conclusion, 'a critical analysis of parliamentarism and of the modern representative principle itself' (p. 42). The only way forward was the dual dissolution of egoistic 'civil society' and the state power corresponding to it. But this was an enormous short-circuit historically, which failed to question the basic assumption of Hegel's view sufficiently: it was not in fact true that bourgeois society is necessarily 'impatient of customs, traditions', etc., etc., and wholly dependent upon an alienated state-power for its cohesion. It employed customs and traditions (England was the striking example of this), invented others, and generated the cohesive power of nationalism to hold itself together.

king governed – but conditionally, not absolutely. At the heart of the English political system – now embracing the entire United Kingdom – there was always a core of officials, who initiated, formulated and executed policy . . . (and) . . . political opposition has never sought to abolish this key-nucleus of the working constitution, but only to control it . . . The form taken by an Act of Parliament links the present to the past and attests the underlying continuity of the mediaeval conception of government.'[18]

This continuity has not been one of 'mediaevalism' in a literal sense. But what was preserved was the essence of rule from above, in that 'transitional' mode established by 1688: an élite social class took the place of the failed English absolute monarchy – a collective 'Prince' which now employed the symbolism of the crown for its own ends. This class framed representative rules for its own members, in the most limited version of property-owning parliamentarism: less the foundation of 'democracy' (in the Enlightenment meaning) than a new variety of constitutional aristocracy, like a mediaeval republic upon a grand scale. Its landlords became akin to the self-perpetuating and co-optive élite of such a republic – but in a city-state become a nation-state.

In relation to the body of civil society, this ruling class established a tradition of informality (as opposed to the formality of the 'normal' state-form); personal or quasi-personal domination (as opposed to the impersonality inseparable from later states); non-bureaucratic and relatively de-centralized control with a weak military dimension (as distinct from 'rationalized', rigid and militarized control). It established a low-profile state which, with the rapid economic development towards the end of the 18th century, easily became the minimal or laisser-faire state depicted by classical political economy. The patrician state had turned into the 'nightwatchman state' of the Industrial Revolution, and presided over the most dramatic initial phase of world industrialization.[19]

---

[18] S. E. Finer, *Comparative Government*, 1970, ch. 5, 'The Government of Britain', p. 139.

[19] Marxist and other commentators have often been unable to resist the inference that the minimalist Victorian state so devoted to laisser-faire must have registered an internal change of nature: the mythical middle-class take-over (after which Britain's ruling class merely *looked* archaic, and was actually an instrument of industrialism, etc.). Perhaps the most striking expression of this view recently is Harold Perkin's *The Origins of Modern English Society, 1780–*

This minimalist, crypto-bourgeois state form reposed upon two vital conditions. One we have already noticed: the successful commercial and colonial strategy that embraced the interests of both élite and middle class together. The second lay in the constitution of civil society itself. The relative absence of a strong, centralized state armature in the nation dominating world development was possible only because that national society possessed a different kind of cohesion. It is the nature of this cohesion which in many

---

1880, 1969, an analysis justly influential for its account of 18th century hierarchy and the birth of modern class-consciousness. He points out that 'It was . . . the peculiar relationship of the English landed aristocracy to society and hence to the state which created the political climate for the germination of industrialism' (p. 67), and that laisser-faire was not in essence an industrialists' ideology at all: 'The truth is that the English landowners had sold their souls to economic development long before the Industrial Revolution (and) when it came they were more than ready to accept its logic, the freedom of industrial employment from state regulation' (p. 187). Yet he is unable to refrain from depicting a mid-Victorian Triumph of the Entrepreneurial Ideal, and the conventional view that 'the entrepreneurial class ruled, as it were, by remote control, through the power of its ideal over the ostensible ruling class, the landed aristocracy which continued to occupy the main positions of power down to the 1890s and beyond . . . Neither contemporaries nor historian have doubted that the capitalist middle class were the "real" rulers of mid-Victorian England, in the sense that the laws were increasingly those demanded by the business-men and . . . their intellectual mentors' (p. 272). In fact, there was no such Triumph, or change of nature, for the reasons he himself indicates: the ruling elite could adjust relatively easily to the laisser-faire conditions of primitive industrialization – 'seizing on Adam Smith' (in his own words) 'as in an earlier age they had seized on Locke, to justify their instincts by the borrowed light of reason' (p. 187).

If one seriously believes that the 'entrepreneurial class' took over 19th century Britain, then the entire subsequent history of entrepreneurial backsliding and chronic industrial failure becomes incomprehensible. In fact, successful enterprise moved away from industry altogether after the first cycle of industrialization and, far from dislodging the elite or the state, formed a new alliance with them on the foundation of City-centred imperialism. A generation later this ruling complex discovered a new 'borrowed light of reason' in J. M. Keynes. Important studies stressing the continuity of the ruling class include W. L. Guttsman, *The British Political Elite*, 1963, and *The English Ruling Class*, 1969. Ivor Crewe's Introduction, 'Studying Elites in Britain', to *The British Political Sociology Yearbook*, vol. 1, 1974, contains a devastating critique of the failures of social science in Britain to confront its main problem: 'So far no sustained empirical analysis of the British power structure has appeared', he points out, in a society where 'it is natural to conclude that a small, economically and educationally privileged group of high traditional status possesses a pervasive and decisive influence in British affairs' (pp. 13–15).

ways presents the main problem of modern British development, above all in comparative perspective.

It is clearly not the case that English bourgeois society resembled the paradigms imagined by Hegel and Marx: the dissolution of feudal integuments into a 'state of nature', an unadulterated morass of conflicting egoistic drives, the war of each against all first theorized by Hobbes. Certain sectors of the new industrial bourgeoisie may have looked like that; they were certainly pictured as like it in some celebrated literary vignettes of the 19th century. Yet on any broader view the picture is quite unsustainable. The new stratum of 'economic men' were never more than a minority, and a relatively powerless minority (indeed, one way of looking at the subsequent problems of capitalism in England is to say that they have never become nearly strong enough politically and culturally). They existed inside a larger civil order whose striking characteristics were (to a degree still are) practically the contrary of the great anti-bourgeois myths.

In a sense not true of any other contemporary state, Finer notes that the English Constitution is 'a facet, a particular aspect of the wider life of the community. It is an emanation, not an epiphenomenon: it springs out of British social structure and values, it is not something that some group has superimposed upon these.' One symptom of this is what he calls 'the powerful and pervasive role of interest groups... related in turn to the wide proliferation of autonomous private associations' in English life.[20]

This aspect of social structure probably derives from the original, spontaneous development of the state in England. State power was appropriated by a self-regulating élite group which established powerful conventions of autonomy: that is, of forms of self-organization and voluntary action independent of state direction. By their efficacy, these in effect came to function as a civil substitute for the state. They imparted to the body of civil society a consistency that rendered the state-skeleton less significant under English conditions.

Such traditions of autonomous responsibility had a class basis: they represented originally the civil-cum-political authority of the agrarian élite. However, they could be imparted to the bourgeoisie also, given the relatively gradual emergence of the latter class within

[20] S. E. Finer, op. cit., p. 131.

the old patrician mould. There was a sufficient common basis of interest to make this possible.

There were at least three dimensions to this common interest. One lay of course in the successful expansion and defence of overseas empire. A second can be found in the degree of economic homogeneity between the governing landed class and the bourgeoisie: while remaining a genuine social aristocracy, the former had long ago ceased to be a feudal estate economically. During the 18th century it consolidated its position by a successful revolution from above, the 'agrarian revolution' which provided one of the necessary conditions for the better-known industrial development that followed. Using its state hegemony to expropriate the peasantry, the landowning élite built up a capitalist agriculture that prospered in harmony with the industrialization process until the later 19th century, by which time Great Britain had become overwhelmingly dependent on imports of food and the agrarian sector had become relatively unimportant.

The third binding factor – and the one which has aroused most critical attention – consisted in the joint front formed by the landowners and the bourgeoisie against the proletariat which arose in the industrial revolution. There is little doubt that this is the key to understanding the class composition of modern English civil society, for the pattern lasted from the 1840s until after the Second World War. It is also the key – for the reasons already advanced – to an understanding of society-state relations, and so of the state itself.[21]

---

[21] In a critique of my and Perry Anderson's earlier views about this crucial point, Richard Johnson writes that 'their main explanatory notion, aristocratic hegemony, *turns out to be nothing more than the principal theme of English Liberal ideology* . . . (where) . . . the root of evils has been seen *precisely* as "feudal", "aristocratic" or "military" residues in an industrial-democratic world. The New Left Review analysis conforms to this very English tradition of radical liberalism: it does not surpass it, still less unmask it'. ('Barrington Moore, Perry Anderson and English Social Development', in *Cultural Studies*, No. 9, Birmingham, Spring 1976, p. 21). In reality, the author continues, both the elitist phenomena which we stressed and the more blatantly *bourgeois* aspect of British existence were *'pressed into the service of capital as a whole'* (p. 25). However, this critique answers itself. What *is* 'capital as a whole' in the specific circumstances of British social development? Not an undifferentiated and abstract category, but an imperialist formation with a meaningful and sustaining relationship to the retrograde forms our analysis underlined: it was the capture of Liberalism by Imperialism which

The most common pattern in the formation of modern states was that the middle classes, whether in a social revolution or in a nationalist movement, turned for help to the people in their effort to throw off the burden of 'traditional society' (absolutism, feudalism, or the imported oppression of colonial régimes). During the '*classic* period' the French Revolution had given the sharpest and most influential definition to this conflict. However, developmental priority was to impose and retain quite a different pattern on England. The Civil War of the 1640s was the English conflict that most nearly corresponded to the later model (the 'first bourgeois revolution'). Yet, while ending absolutism and opening the way to capitalism, it had given in many respects the weakest and least influential definition to the general movement which followed in Europe. In spite of its importance, its *political* imprint on subsequent developments was almost nil.

The patrician class and state provided the necessary conditions for industrialization. Thus, these material conditions encouraged the middle class to bury its revolutionary inheritance, at the same time as the spread of Enlightenment ideology made the concepts of the previous century (the 'Puritan Revolution') outmoded and useless for farther political progress. Towards the end of the century, external forces were again decisive in cementing the alliance. The prolonged overseas struggle with France ended in a successful war against the French Revolution – that is, against most of the political meaning of the 'classic period'. This crucial victory in the great-power struggle consolidated the paradox: already an archaism in certain obvious respects, the English (now 'British') patrician state none the less remained able to lead and dominate world development for another half century. No rival comparable to the French *ancien régime* would appear until the unification of Germany. During these noon-day generations Great Britain accumulated reserves of capital – and not only economic capital – which would sustain its antique forms for far longer than the radicals and early

nullified the former's radical aspect, and gave the working class the task of recovering and accentuating that radicalism as a necessary part of its own political advance. This 'second bourgeois revolution' remains in that limited sense on the historical agenda, but it is surely not the case that recognizing this entails a general ideological retreat to old-fashioned radicalism. It is true that we did not 'unmask' radicalism; but then, no Marxist analysis ever 'unmasks' any phenomenon in this Phantom-of-the-Opera sense.

socialists of the 19th century dreamed.

In effect, these conditions prevented the 'second bourgeois revolution' in the British Isles – that 'modernizing' socio-political upheaval that ought to have refashioned both society and state in logical conformity with the demands of the new age. This was not because radical intellectuals and movements did not call for such a change. On the contrary, both before and after 1789, a good deal of the blueprints for modernity were drawn up in Britain (and to a remarkable extent they were conceived in the most curious 'state-less society' of the 18th century, Scotland). In the 1830s and 40s what seemed at the time the strongest radical movement in Europe, Chartism, struggled to realize these ideas.

In the *Manifesto* Marx and Engels supplied the most celebrated formula for bourgeois revolution: 'At a certain stage in the development of those means of production and exchange, the conditions under which feudal society produced and exchanged, the feudal organization of agriculture and manufacturing industry, in one word, the feudal relations of property became no longer compatible with the already developed productive forces; they became so many fetters. They had to be burst asunder; they were burst asunder.'[22] The radical formula was not enactable in Britain partly because the 'conditions of feudal society' had already been burst asunder and replaced by pre-modern, transitional ones; partly because of the external triumphs of these transitional forms; and partly because of the threat which the dispossessed and the new proletarian masses presented to them.

This 'threat' would of course have been the opportunity of a bourgeois class desperate to get rid of real feudal 'fetters'. But classes embrace political revolution only when they see no other route forward. In spite of the enormous social tensions of the industrial revolution, this was never the case for the English middle class. It was possible, though not easy, for them to arrive at a workable compromise with the political ruling class. This possibility always determined their long-term course, fortifying them against the social threat from underneath and removing most of the substance from their radicalism. Bourgeois radicalism did not vanish from the British political scene: it reappeared in many guises later in the 19th century, between the 1870s and 1914, represented by leaders

[22] Marx and Engels, *Collected Works*, vol. 6, p. 489.

like Joseph Chamberlain and David Lloyd George, and it is still represented today by certain aspects of both the Liberal and Labour Parties. However, its relegation to a secondary (and often regional) status proved permanent. Patrician liberalism had defeated radical liberalism, and its victory has marked the whole evolution of the political system since then.

This was a 'compromise' quite distinct in nature from the ones arrived at in late-developing nations like Germany and Japan. There also the new bourgeois classes were driven into alliances with landowning élites against the threat of revolt or social turbulence – alliances which also sacrificed the Enlightenment inheritance of egalitarian progress and democratic politics, and encrusted capitalism with all sorts of pre-modern features. But in these other cases a new, forced industrialism was entering partnership with more genuinely archaic landlord classes – with social orders which had never gone through an equivalent of 1640, let alone a 1789. This linkage with military late-feudalism was different in its whole developmental character from the English alliance with a post-feudal, civilian, parliamentary élite. It subordinated capitalism to militarized 'strong states' whose inevitable external aim was to contest Great Britain's already established territorial and economic domination.

Both the cost and the gains from the English class-compromise were less dramatic, more long-term (and of course not so much of a threat to world peace). The cost was the containment of capitalism within a patrician hegemony which never, either then or since, actively favoured the aggressive development of industrialism or the general conversion of society to the latter's values and interests. Permanent social limits were thus imposed upon the 'industrial revolution' and the British entrepreneurial stratum. As we shall see later, in a curious – and again unique – fashion, the emergence of working-class politics would merely confirm these limitations, and in its own way render the 'second political revolution' even more distant.

The gains were represented by the effective social subordination of the lower classes – a structural domination achieved by the re-formation of civil society and the enactment of a long-term social strategy, rather than by state or military means. What the re-formation created was a clearly demarcated order of classes, in the stable form most appropriate to overseas-oriented exploitation.

High social mobility, individualism, egalitarian openness, *la carrière ouverte aux talents,* restless impatience with tradition – the traits of dynamic capitalism were systematically relegated or discounted, in favour of those which fitted Britain's particular kind of empire. From the later half of the 19th century onward a similar neglect and relegation of technical and applied-science education was noticeable – the type of formation most important in all later stages of industrialization, after England's pioneering lead. This imbalance was never to be corrected, in spite of (at the time of writing) almost a century of complaints on the subject.

The Intelligentsia

What did this social strategy of containment consist of? It was pointed out earlier that the civil conventions of self-organization and regulation were imparted to the middle class, on the foundations of growing common interests. This, rather than state bureaucracy or armed repression, would furnish the cohesion of English progress.

However, such a strategy needed an instrument – the civil equivalent of state-directed authority, as it were, a pervasive power capable of acting upon civil society at large. This instrument was the English intellectual class. In a broad sense of the term, stretching from literary and humanist thinkers on one side to the church and 'civil servants' (the English word for functionaries) on the other, the 'intelligentsia' played an unusually central and political role in promoting social integration.

The more habitual use of the term indicates an intellectual stratum distanced from society and state: thinkers and writers distanced from and critical of the status quo. In the English social world, however, almost the reverse is the case. This is undoubtedly another of those anomalies that have made the comparative grasp of British development so difficult. From the inside the phenomenon has been elusive simply because virtually everyone concerned with analysis of the British state has been a member of the class in question: myths of British civilization have rendered self-scrutiny unnecessary. From the outside, judgement has been impeded by the developmental singularity of the thing: an intellectual class of great power and functionality, yet not either created by or in critical opposition to the state – neither a state-fostered technocracy (on the French model) nor an 'alienated' intelligentsia (on the Russian model). In addition, of course, it should be remembered that both sociological and marxist analysis of intellectuals has been very slow in advancing any adequate general theory of intellectual groups.[23]

The nucleus of the English intellectual class was formed by civil society itself, not the state. From the mid-19th century up to the present day, this civil armature has been created by a small number of private, élite educational institutions: the 'Public Schools' and the old universities. Although in recent times the latter have become financially dependent upon the state and enlarged the social basis of their recruitment, this has not altered their essential mode of operation. Originally, patrician liberalism de-

---

[23] The *locus classicus* for critical analysis of this phenomenon has become Noel Annan's essay 'The Intellectual Aristocracy', in *Studies in Social History: a Tribute to G. M. Trevelyan*, edit. J. H. Plumb, 1955. This at least gives some overall sense of the authority of this informal tradition. Unfortunately little advance has been made upon it, not surprisingly in view of Crewe's strictures (Note 19, above). The most useful, though still quite inadequate, way to approach it is via study of the educational system. On the principle that the anatomy of the ape is contained in that of *homo sapiens* the reader could do worse than begin with the Report *Elites and their Education*, by David Boyd (National Foundation for Educational Research, 1973). This demonstrates that since the Second World War there has been very little alteration in elite formation: a slight decrease in 'Public School men' in the ranks of the state bureaucracy has been compensated for by a slight but appropriate increase in the army, the navy, and the banks. Dr Boyd (an American) concludes that the outstanding trait of this immutable Mafia is the near-complete absence of 'inter-generational mobility': the clerisy perpetuates itself to an astonishing extent simply by breeding, and the occasional cooption of a few lower-bourgeois upstarts who normally become the most impassioned defenders of the system. Commenting dolefully on the last of many efforts to 'modernize' the recruitment of higher state cadres, Mr Leslie Moody of the Civil Service Union said: 'The point is, that you can lay down as many provisions as you like, but if the appointment to top jobs is by selection boards, then the preferences of those on the boards will be reflected. You can't legislate prejudice out of people's minds...' (*Guardian*, 30th October, 1973). Mr Moody's hope was that by the 1980s things might be a little better.

On the Marxist side, it is Gramsci's *Gli Intellettuali* which furnishes some elements for the analysis of intellectual strata in traditional societies; but here too little has been added by subsequent work. For a critical account of Gramsci's concept of 'hegemony' see Perry Anderson, *New Left Review* No. 100, 1976-7. Most treatments of the subject have tended to focus on the question of revolutionary intelligentsias (e.g. Alvin Gouldner's recent work) rather than on their role in stable societies like England.

pended upon a supposedly 'natural' governing élite: a land-based stratum with certain social characteristics of caste. The functional intelligentsia formed from the 1830s onwards was in essence a still more artificial perpetuation of this, where civil institutions gradually replaced landowning as the foundation of hegemony.

Discussion of this issue has often been clouded rather than clarified by theories of general élitism. It is often argued that all states depend on some form of élite stratification and specialization, and that democracies engender oligarchies. But the British state is in this respect also distinct: it is a case, and really the only case, where oligarchy engendered democracy through an organic social strategy that preserved its own nature (and, naturally, deeply marked and infirmed the 'democracy' which emerged). In this case, élitism was neither fossil survival nor aberration: it has remained the enduring truth of the state. British Labourism is the story of how working-class politics made its own compact with that truth. The bourgeoisie made an alliance with the English form of landlordism, and this was expressed by the formation of the liberal intelligentsia; in turn, that stratum took charge of the emergent political force of the proletariat in the first quarter of the 20th century. In the archetypal person of J. M. Keynes it conceived the new, most general formula for this second alliance, which has lasted from the Great Depression to the present and seen the Labour Party become the main support of the declining state.

From this forward glance one gains already some idea of the astonishing social strength of the system. Embodied in the intelligentsia, the social strategy responsible for this endurance was neither that of revolution from below, nor that of revolution from above – the two main avenues whose interaction has defined so much of modern history. It averted the former, which remained a possibility until the defeat of Chartism; but without embarking on the latter either. It exorcized the spectre of a second, radical revolution – yet without creating the 'strong state' and the right-wing or nationalist social mobilization which was the alternative way of catching up.

Alone among the major powers of 1815–1945, Great Britain was able to evade the choice. Priority and external success let the country remain socio-economically 'backward' (at least from the 1880s) without driving either the lower class and intellectuals, or the economic ruling class, to despair. And throughout the epoch, such adjustment as proved necessary to maintain the system in being was conceived, publicized, and largely enacted by this exceptionally active, confident and integrated intellectual class. If the external secret of old England's longevity was empire, the internal secret lay here: in the cooptive and cohesive authority of an intelligentsia much more part of the state, much closer to political life and more present in all important civil institutions than in any other bourgeois society.

The world-view of this social group is a conservative liberalism, and in terms of socio-political strategy this entailed the preservation of rule from above by constant adaptation and concession below. The general social conservatism of modern England demanded the retention of fixed distinctions of rank: stability before mobility. Yet in modern conditions such stable cohesion was only possible where the lower classes acquired a minimum of confidence in the system – that is, in English terms, a trust in 'them', the rulers. This belief in the concrete nature of the constitution – our way of doing things, etc., as different from the abstraction of post-1789 constitutionalism – depended in turn on 'their' capacity to offer sufficient concessions. Adequate adaptation thus conserved the patrician essence, and strengthened its accompanying mythology, in a continuing dialectic against the new pressures from below.

A misplaced mysticism has been natural enough, considering the success of the machinery. But in reality such a political order worked through the unique conjunction of two factors: a social stratum able to enact it – the governing intelligentsia – and the material or external conditions enjoyed by the whole society. The long-term strategy in question has certainly never been employed anywhere else (giving rise to the idea of the peculiar 'cleverness' of the British ruling class). It could not be. More centralized and rigid state-systems do not work in that way at all: no administrative bureaucracy – even in the shape of the most dazzling products of the French *grandes écoles* – can function with the powerful, pervasive informality of England's civil élite. Neither the feudal absolute state, nor – in the marxist phraseology – the democratic committee-state of the bourgeoisie could possibly imitate it. But this is merely to say that the *typical* forms of pre-modern and contemporary polity are different.

A strategy of compromise presupposes the restriction of the

political dialogue to what can be demanded or conceded in this fashion. As we saw, the social formula was originally contrived between the post-1688 landlord class and the middle classes, and grew from common interests. The latter furnished sufficient homogeneity among the upper strata for mutual adjustments to be possible, and for the question of power never to be made too acute. This is the point of a flexible compromise-strategy. It keeps the issue of command, or the source of authority, at a distance; instead, the political process is restricted to the apparent exchange of influences – to trading within a social continuum, certain of whose features are seen as unalterable.

However, this plainly poses a problem regarding the integration of the working class. Since the First World War the final form of the English political world, and of its myth, has been the inclusion of the working class. In 1844 Engels wrote that Toryism had begun to alter course (under Peel), because 'it has realized that the English Constitution cannot be defended, and is making concessions simply to maintain that tottering structure as long as possible . . .'.[24] The new, alien element of democracy would destroy it; and in British conditions, democracy would become '*social* democracy', the transition to socialism itself. This was in an essay explaining the Constitution to the readers of *Vorwärts*. It did not occur to Engels, Marx, or other radicals that the tottering structure would absorb the proletariat politically without even becoming 'democratic' in the sense intended. Still less could they conceive how the resultant non-democratic proletarian movement might turn into an essential prop of the archaic state and the essentially inegalitarian society they contemplated with such contempt. The strategy of 'concessions' was enormously stronger than then seemed likely; the 'tottering' aspect of the system was merely its constant motion of adaptation and containment. Provided with both an internal mechanism of development and highly favourable external conditions, it was able to broaden its social basis in successive stages between 1832 and 1918. At the latter date the concession of universal male suffrage coincided with the maximum territorial extension of the British Empire after its victory in the First World War.

[24] 'The Condition of England, II', in *Collected Works*, vol. 3, p. 491 and pp. 512–3.

The Working Class

The working class did not have interests in the social order in the same sense as the middle classes; there was no basis for the same sort of compromise as the latter arrived at with the landlords. However, another proved possible – and indeed so satisfactory that after 1945 the labour movement was to play in many respects the major part in securing another generation of existence for the old state. Far from diminishing with the latter's slide towards collapse after the 1950s, this alliance has if anything grown stronger. It was to be the Labour Party that made the most determined effort to restore the fortunes of British capitalism in 1964–7; when this attempt failed, it became in turn the main political buttress of the state in a more straightforward conservative sense. It rebuilt consensus after the outbreak of class conflict under the Heath Conservative government. This consensus took the form of negotiated suspension of the economic class struggle – the 'Social Contract' – as the precondition for another, more cautious effort at capitalist restoration. Like its predecessors this policy was associated with complete (if not rather exaggerated) fidelity to the Constitution and all its traditions. The House of Lords has become the target of some attacks as an 'anachronism'; this is the limit of Labour's iconoclasm. The very fact of the existence of the 'Social Contract' at this late hour, and with these implications, shows the depth of the real social-class alliance behind it.

The most common version of national class-alliance – as I remarked above – lies between the popular masses and a middle class which undertakes the establishment of a modern state. That is, of a constitutional democracy with standard forms. It is also true that numerous 'deviant' versions exist: the popular support for the middle-class counter-revolutions of 1918–39, and mass acquiesence in many Third World military and one-party régimes. Yet it should be acknowledged that all have something in common, as would-be modernizing states (even if in some cases, as with the fascist dictatorships, this revolutionary side was mainly appearance).

The British variety has been very different. It is a social alliance based not upon a modernizing bourgeois revolution, but upon the conservative containment and taming of such a revolution. Whereas in the former process the masses are normally led by middle-class cadres into the overthrow of an *ancien régime*, in the latter they are deprived of such leadership. Under British conditions the intellectuals were not radicalized: they moved more and more into that peculiar service of the old order mentioned previously, as an extensive, civil-based, autonomous corps of *chiens de garde*. Without the leadership of a militant radicalism, the masses were unable to break the system.[25]

The waves of social revolt generated by early industrialization, from the period of Luddism to the 1840s, fell away in mid-century and revived only in very different forms towards the end of the century. Had there existed a true confrontation between the bourgeoisie and a feudal caste closer to its origins, the political reforms of 1832 would have figured as simple palliatives – a doomed effort to arrest the tide. In fact they signalled a turning-point in the other sense. After 1832 the bourgeoisie became steadily more positively reconciled to the state. And in the wake of this reconciliation, through the defeat of Chartism, the working class became negatively reconciled to the same Old Corruption, to élite hegemony, class distinctions, and deference to tradition.

Having failed to break through, the working class was forced to retreat upon itself. Political defeat and the accumulation of powerful social pressures from above compelled the formation of a deeply defensive, somewhat corporative attitude. This was to be defined most clearly – as the basis of the 20th century workers' movements – by the trade-unionism that arose in the later decades of Queen Victoria's reign. Devoted to the piecemeal improvement of workers' conditions within the existing conservative social framework – a status quo now strengthened by two farther generations of imperial success – this movement moved only very slowly and reluctantly back towards any political challenge to the state. Though increas-

[25] Connoisseurs of these debates on the U.K. Left will know that no statement like this can be made without provoking accusations of crazed idealism, subjectivism, historicism, mere radicalism, neglect of mass struggle, or worse. To anticipate: the specific (imperialist) character of U.K. capitalism and its place in general development led to a particular state-form marked by 'continuity' (traditionalism, etc.) and a high degree of integrative capacity – both of the 'new' entrepreneurial classes and of the working class; but this historical success had as its other face equally distinctive failures (in 'modernization', adaptability, etc.) which, since the 1950s, have become steadily more dominant, presaging a general mutation of the state; the passage towards this crisis is so far led by renascent 'bourgeois radicalism' (in the shape of Scottish and Welsh nationalism) rather than by the class struggle in the metropolis, although this may soon change.

ingly strong in itself, trade-unionism remained mainly deferential to the state and Constitution. Rather than perceiving political revolution as the road to socio-economic betterment (like so many Continental movements), the British workers preferred to see a pragmatic politics evolve bit by bit out of their economic struggle.

This lower-class corporativism has remained easily satirizable as a kind of quasi-feudal life-style: insisting on one's limited rights, while continuing to know one's humble position in the wider scheme of society.[26] Conservative apologists have naturally made much of British working-class political Toryism, undeniably a principal source of straight political conservatism ever since the extension of the suffrage.[27] However, it is difficult to see what alternative pattern of development was available, in a country where all the upper orders had so successfully exploited their unique position of developmental priority, and evolved such a strong civil hegemony at the core of the most successful of imperial systems.

The upper-class compromise carried a certain cost with it, in spite of its irresistable seduction: social sclerosis, an over-traditionalism leading to incurable backwardness. So did the lower-class alliance – though here the cost has been harder to identify, and slower to make its burden apparent. This dilemma is best under-

[26] Two recent articles giving a vivid impression of the current condition of working-class attitudes are Michael Mann, 'The New Working Class', *New Society*, November and December 1976.

[27] For example, R. McKenzie and A. Silver, *Angels in Marble: Working Class Conservatives in Urban England*, 1968. Discussing the 'deference' ideology of lower-class conservatism, the authors point out: 'One of the pervasive conditions promoting the survival of deference is the modest role accorded "the people" in British political culture. Although it is a commonplace of research on stable democracies that general electorates are typically uninvolved in politics . . . it is only in Britain that this is so largely consistent with the prevailing climate of political values. Though modern constitutions typically locate the source of sovereignty in "the people", in Britain it is the Crown in Parliament that is sovereign. Nor is that a merely technical point. The political culture of democratic Britain assigns to ordinary people the role, not of citizens, but of subjects . . .' (p. 251). So far from being a 'technical' point, the concept referred to has dominated the debates on devolution (see below): the crucial constitutional issue (and impossibility) is the conservation of the absolute sovereignty of the Crown in Westminster. At a far deeper level, such distinctions are not bourgeois-constitutional trivia (as so many Marxists have held): they manifest the nature of the state, and the whole material history which produced that state.

stood in terms of the peculiar traits of English nationalism.

The more characteristic processes of state-formation involved the masses in a positive rôle. As it is argued below in one of the essays in this volume ('The Modern Janus: nationalism and un-even development', see below pp. 329–363), the arrival of national-ism in a distinctively modern sense was tied to the political baptism of the lower classes. Their entry into history furnished one essential precondition of the transformation of nationality into a central and formative factor. And this is why, although sometimes hostile to democracy, nationalist movements have been invariably populist in outlook and sought to induct lower classes into political life. In its most typical version, this assumed the shape of a restless middle-class and intellectual leadership trying to stir up and channel popular class energies into support for the new states.

When successful – and of course, though many other factors are involved and nationalist ideology has always exaggerated its part, it has succeeded more often than not – this positive rôle has been prominent in the later political histories of all societies. It has often established the key myth of subsequent political development. At its most characteristic this is perhaps the myth of popular revolution or national-liberation struggle – a model of popular action and involvement which haunts the state, and is returned to repeatedly by later generations (often very blindly and conservatively).

Obviously, this has the implication that where mass initiative was little used in national histories such 'myths' may be correspondingly negative, or easily travestied by states that owe nothing to them: modern Germany and Japan are possibly the most usual examples here. But Britain is also a case in point. The older 17th century revolutionary tradition of the major nationality, England, had been effectively buried. There was no second political revolution, so that the more radical tendencies of the bourgeoisie were diverted and absorbed into the dense machinery of civil hegemony. As this happened the new working class was also diverted and repressed: the defeat of early 19th century radicalism forced it into a curious kind of social and political *apartheid*. This condition was almost the opposite of the active intervention from below which figured in so many modern revolutions; so, therefore, was the mythology, or underlying political consciousness, which it generated.

Nationalism is always the joint product of external pressures and an internal balance of class forces. Most typically it has arisen in societies confronting a dilemma of uneven development – 'back-wardness' or colonization – where conscious, middle-class élites have sought massive popular mobilization to right the balance. But obviously the position of Britain – and in the present argument this means mainland England, on the whole – was unusual in this regard. Here was a society which suffered far less from those external pressures and threats than any other, during a very long period. Now we can see how unusual was the internal class dynamic which corresponded to such external good fortune. The working class was not 'mobilized' in the ordinary sense, except for purposes of warfare: it was neither drawn into a revolution from below nor subjected to a 'revolution from above'. Instead it was contained and stratified into a relatively immobile social order – the one world society which faced practically *no* developmental problem until well into the 20th century.

Thus, the popular 'great power' nationalism formed on this basis could not help being especially conservative. It was innocent of the key, populist notion informing most real nationalism: the idea of the virtuous power of popular protest and action. In its peculiar, dignified concept the People are the reliable backbone of the Nation; not the effective source of its authority, not the real makers of the state. As argued below (see Chapter Seven) this makes for a subtle yet profound difference in the stuff of modern English politics. In its long struggle against economic decline, the political world has been in fact struggling – although largely unwittingly – against the particular absences and defects deriving from this class structure.

Bourgeois radicalism and popular mobilization were eschewed for the sake of conservative stability. This led to a politically-inert nationalism, one too little associated with internal divisions and struggle, too socially complacent and deferential. Given the position of the British Empire until the 1950s, this nationalism was periodically and successfully mobilized for external war – each episode of which farther strengthened its inward conservatism, its conviction of an inherited internal unity. But this very conviction and complacency made it extraordinarily difficult to achieve any kind of internal break – any nationalist renaissance *against* the now hopelessly stultifying inheritance of the state. There was simply no tradition of this kind. Stability had become paralytic over-stability; the adaptive conservatism of the successful 19th century system had turned into the feeble, dwindling, incompetent conservatism of the last generation.

All efforts to break out from this declining and narrowing spiral have failed, whether to the right or to the left. The reason is in part that neither the political right nor the left has any tradition of effective internal popular mobilization at its command: there is neither a revolution nor a counter-revolution embodied in the substratum of popular awareness. Hence, governments have invariably appealed to the nation as a whole, much too successfully. Spurious conservative unity is the bane of modern British politics – not, as so often maintained by superficial critics, insuperable class divisions or party oppositions.

Seen from the side of the working class too, therefore, imperialist society in Britain presents a developmental paradox. This is the country where a deep-laid strategy of class-alliance achieved the highest degree of popular integration into the affairs of the state. But this was never 'integration' in the more typical sense of individualistic break-down of the proletariat, through upward mobility and an aggressive capitalist ideology. Instead, it assumed a more corporate and passive form, in accordance with the traits of post-Industrial Revolution development under imperial conditions. The result was a particularly powerful inter-class nationalism – a sense of underlying insular identity and common fate, which both recognized and yet easily transcended marked class and regional divisions. However, far from being a model of politically effective nationalist ideology, this complex was to become useless outside imperial conditions. The reason is that its pervasive strength is inseparable from an accompanying conservatism – which in turn serves as an inhibitor of radical change or reform.

The bulk of the intelligentsia continues to subscribe to this peculiar variety of nationalism (not surprisingly, since it played such a big role in building it up). But so does the working class, under the aegis of British Labourism. Hence the two main sources of change have remained tied into the old structure. They maintain their historic allegiance to a form of nationalism which is in fact reverence for the overall nature of the modern (post-1688) British tribe. This is a faith in the mystique of that system, not in the people who made it (*they*, the revolutionaries of the 1640s, have been suppressed and travestied throughout the era in which this modern tribalism arose). Such faith is in 'the Constitution', and beyond this fetishization in the capacity of 'we all' to surmount difficulties, win battles, etc. But 'we all', as 'we' are actually organized, means those who effectively control the social order; hence the sentiment is very close to belief that 'they' will continue to see we are cared for (though of course they may need to be reminded of their duties sometimes).

There have been numerous analyses of the economic contradictions of post-empire Britain, depicting a society hoist by the petard of its own past success in industry and finance. But the economic vicious circle is mirrored – and rendered inexorable – by this corresponding contradiction on the plane of politics and ideology. Here also imperialism cast society into a shape inadaptable to later, harder conditions of existence. It forged a state which, although very 'flexible' in certain respects – those most noticed and revered by apologists – is incapable of change at a deeper level. On *that* plane, where the modern political principle of nationality really functions, it is bound by a suffocating, paralytic pride in its own power and past glories.

Nationalism, whether of the right or of the left, is of course never really independent of the class structure. Yet its particular efficacy as a mobilizing ideology depends upon the *idea* of carelessness – upon the notion that, at least in certain circumstances and for a period of time, what a society enjoys in common is more important than its stratification. In England, the specially strong stratification created by the failure of the 'second bourgeois revolution' made the normal egalitarian or radical version of this notion impossible. The ordinary texture of English social life denies it. Hence the only effective version has been one which ignores these class divisions against an 'outside' enemy – at the same time implicitly reconsecrating them, as the tolerable features of a 'way of life' basically worth defending against the world. Time and time again this defence has in turn fortified in-built resistance to radicalism. That is, to all tendencies (democratic or reactionary) which might aim to really demolish the creaking English snail-shell of archaic pieties, deferential observance and numbing self-inhibition.

Origins of the Crisis

'Moderate', 'orderly', 'decent', 'peaceful and tolerant', 'constitutional'; 'backward-looking', 'complacent', 'insular', 'class-ridden', 'inefficient', 'imperialist' – a realistic analysis of the British state must admit these two familiar series of truisms are in fact differing visages of the same social reality. That arcadian England which appeals so strongly to foreign intellectuals is also the England which has, since the early 1950s, fallen into ever more evident and irredeemable decline – the United Kingdom of permanent economic crisis, falling standards, bankrupt governments, slavish dependence on the United States, and myopic expedients. The appealing, romantic social peace is inseparable from the twilight. Though imaginatively distinguishable, resistance to modernity is in reality not separable from the senility of the old imperialist state. They are bound to perish together.

The preceding analysis suggests that the origins of this long crisis, still unresolved, go back a long way.[28] They may also suggest the basic reason why resolution is so difficult, and has been so long delayed. The fact is that emergence from the crisis demands a political break: a disruption at the level of the state, allowing the emergence of sharper antagonisms and a will to reform the old order root and branch. But in this system, possibly more than in any other, such a break has become extremely difficult. The state-level is so deeply entrenched in the social order itself, state and civil society are so intertwined in the peculiar exercise of the British Constitution, that a merely 'political' break entails a considerable social revolution.

The governing élite and the liberal intelligentsia, and the dominant sector of the economic ruling class, all have an obvious vested interest in the state. The industrial bourgeoisie and the working class do not.[29] Yet the latter have never succeeded in undoing and

---

[28] The original analysis to which this one (and all others like it) owe a great debt is Perry Anderson, 'Origins of the Present Crisis', *New Left Review* No. 23, Jan.–Feb. 1964.

[29] In this and comparable analyses the split between finance and industrial capital always receives a great deal of attention, as a basic feature of the underpinning of the state-structure. But in an acute comment in his article 'Imperialism in the 70s – Unity or Rivalry?' (*New Left Review* No. 69, Sept.–Oct. 1971), Bob Rowthorn points out how a division of interests within the industrial sector itself has enormously accentuated the political results of that split. 'Paradoxically', he observes, 'the weakness of the British state is to be explained not by the simple decline of British capitalism as such, but by the very *strength* of the cosmopolitan activities of British capital, which has helped to undermine further its strictly domestic economy' (p. 46). Imperialism left a legacy of very large firms with overseas operations, as well as the City: it is their combined interests which have

modernizing the state, in spite of their potential power. As far as the entrepreneurial class is concerned the absence of will is more understandable. The combination of British-Constitutional ideology, their weak political position in relation to the City, and their fear of 'socialism' has turned them into a particularly supine and harmless sub-bourgeoisie. Since the defeat of Joseph Chamberlain's more industrially-oriented 'social imperialism' – a right-wing attempt at a new, more radical class alliance – they have exerted little substantial influence on the state.[30]

As for the working class, the main lines of their own integration into the 20th century state were decided by the same defeat: the defeat of right-wing imperialism was the triumph of 'liberal imperialism', from 1906 onwards – the permanent victory of the City over the British economy, and of patrician liberalism over the class strategy and outlook of the British state. The era of New Imperialism had put the old class alliance under severe strain, from the 1880s onwards. The external threat from a more militarized and competitive world combined with new internal menaces, from a more restless and organized working class and a tiny yet significant trend to disaffection among the intellectuals.

However, that period of crisis was resolved by a reaffirmation of liberalism – in effect, a reaffirmation of the underlying strategy laid

---

remained largely independent of the U.K. state and its 'strictly domestic' economy, and so have helped cripple all vigorous efforts to revive the latter (by import controls, action against overseas investment, etc.). Hence, he concludes: 'Leading sections of the British bourgeoisie have been effectively "de-nationalized", not through their own weakness but through the weakness of the British state and their own home base. The overseas strength of British big *capital* has compounded the debility of British *capitalism* . . .' (p. 47).

[30] Recent emphasis upon 'buried history' excluded from the Establishment versions has focused mainly upon working-class and popular material; but there is an outstanding quantity of bourgeois data that has suffered a similar fate, no less relevant for understanding the overall pattern's significance. Chamberlain's right-wing, tariff-reform imperialism is an outstanding example of this – the buried relics of a forsaken ruling-class strategy which prefigured a very different state-form in the 20th century. As L. S. Amery put it, for tariff-reformers the State 'should be a creative force in economic life, vigorously directing the nation's energies . . . developing the empire', etc. (*The Fundamental Fallacies of Free Trade*, 1906, pp. 5, 17, 92). Chamberlain himself predicted that if his social-imperialist strategy was defeated by the Free Traders, Britain would fall into a long decline comparable to that suffered by Holland and Venice – see *Imperial Union and Tariff Reform*, his 1903 speeches.

down in the earlier 19th century, and described above. This has become the traditional mode of hegemony, most identified with the Constitution, the British road of compromise, and so on. Now, the problem before it was the more effective incorporation of the working class – of a working class which, in the two decades before 1914, had begun to emerge from trade unionism and demand a limited political voice of its own. Previously the enfranchised part of the working class had given its allegiance to the Liberal Party. But at the very period of that Party's triumphant return to power, in 1906–14, a new Labour Party had been formed. Although extremely moderate in ideology, and more an expression of trade-union interests than a socialist party in the Continental sense, this movement none the less clearly represented a class point of view.

Between 1914 and 1924, when the first Labour government took office, this point of view was effectively subordinated to the underlying consensus. It may be that this achievement was only possible so quickly and so decisively because of the First World War. Indeed, maybe the general strategic victory of liberalism should be attributed as much to this factor as to its electoral and reforming successes in 1906 and 1910–11. It is certainly true that neither the Tory right nor the more militant and syndicalist elements of the working class were really reconciled to the solution up to 1914. The clear threat of both revolution and counter-revolution persisted until then, and the old order was by no means so secure as its later apologists have pretended.

But external success settled the dilemma, in accordance with the main law of British history. The victory of the Allies drew both Tory and revolutionary dissidents back into the consensus. The war effort itself signified a huge development in state intervention, upon lines already present in the Liberal Party's reform programme of Edwardian times: public enterprise and control of the economy, and social welfare. As was to happen also in the second world conflict, the ideological reinforcement of all-British patriotism coincided with important structural developments favourable to working-class interests.

These developments took the form of the constant extension of state activity and influence, and ultimately – after World War II – of the pioneer 'welfare state' which for a brief period served as a model for other capitalist countries. In the above analysis, the emphasis has been placed on the strong élite character of the British state, and its bond with a markedly hierarchical yet cohesive civil society. This may appear in some ways at odds with the great expansion of state functions initiated first by Liberalism and then by Labourism.

But the contradiction is only apparent. In fact, the growth of the state – a theme which fuelled polemic and political debate from the 1880s onwards – has never seriously changed its underlying nature. This has been demonstrated by the character of the growth itself: random, ad hoc formation of new agencies and functions, which rarely question the basic principles of government. This amoebic proliferation has merely surrounded and preserved the essential identity of the British Constitution. The endless pragmatic expediency of Westerminster governments has multiplied state activity in response to successive challenges and demands, above all the challenges of war; it has done so (normally quite consciously) in order to conserve the vital mystique of Britishness, not to change or dilute it.

Externally, this line of development was of course made feasible by imperialism. The ruling class retained a position strong enough, and secure enough psychologically, to pursue the strategy of concession in graduated doses to more organized pressures from below. There was – or seemed to be, until the 1960s – surplus enough for the exercise to be valid, while the particular evolution of the class struggle in Britain strongly favoured its continuation, in spite of the difficult passage of Edwardian times. Working-class politics evolved on the back of trade unionism in Britain, emerging quite empirically as a kind of collective, parliamentary voice for a corporate class interest. Hence internally too there was a notable tendency to accede to the concession strategy. It was only rarely that the political leaders of 'British Socialism' perceived a new state and constitution as the precondition of achieving class demands. Normally, the perception was that *the* state could be bent in the direction of these demands. Class political power of the type which became feasible after 1918 (year of the foundation of the contemporary Labour Party) was only the strongest way of doing this.

The class alliance of 20th century Britain is essentially devoted to the exorcism of 'power' in any disruptive sense, and to the maintenance of social consensus at almost any cost. Obviously the decisive test of this strategy was the attainment of elective power by a working-class based movement. It was argued previously that the intelligentsia had played a key, often ill-understood role in the mechanism of hegemony, as the agents of the state-society bond – the 'state-substitute' officers of civil society, peopling the profusion of para-state or semi-official bodies the English state characteristically depends on. But now a definitely lower-class political force had emerged into the state arena under war conditions, in an irreversible way: the 'masses' whom the patricians were supposed to look after were threatening, though still quite mildly, to look after themselves.

This could only be coped with in terms appropriate to the system by the formation of a new intellectual leadership – the creation of a new bond between this awakened sector of civil society and the old state. Fortunately, the very conditions which had presided over the birth of Labourism were highly conducive to this. The corporative aspect of working-class politics meant that it was weak in ideological leadership, and relatively unaware of the problematic of power: the most articulate ideology of naissant Labour politics, Fabianism, was at its feeblest on this issue. 'Gradualism' did much to pave the way for the shift in power relations that actually occurred.

This shift took the form of the transfer of a substantial part of the old liberal intelligentsia into the ranks of the Labour Party itself. The 'ranks' is of course a formal way of speaking; what they actually migrated to were the higher echelons of the movement, rapidly finding themselves promoted and elected into posts of power. From 1918 onwards an ever-growing stream of intellectuals who would previously have adhered to the Liberal Party (or at least been satellites of Liberalism in the wider sense) moved to the Labour Party. They took Liberalism (in the crucial deeper sense) with them. Their liberal variant of the British state creed was readily accepted as the guiding light of the new movement: British Socialism with that unmistakable, resonantly moderate and pragmatical emphasis on the 'British'. From the same moment onwards, the Liberal Party itself declined. No significant part of the intelligentsia shifted back towards it until the 1960s, when it began to look as if Labour might be drifting into a bankruptcy of its own.

One does not require even the most tenuous form of conspiracy-theory to explain the change. The Liberal Party, after laying the foundations of the 'welfare state', had been deeply discredited by the war experience, and still more by the experiment in coalition government with Conservatism after 1916 – a régime presided over by the one-time chief of Liberal radicalism, David Lloyd George.

Reaction against the war and the post-war slump (when working-class militancy was severely defeated) was therefore also against Liberalism in the old form. The progressive arm of the intellectual class turned to the new movement, where it was overwhelmingly welcomed. In the guise of socialist novelty, tradition established a new lease of life and the integration of the proletariat into the British state assumed a new level of expression. By then, it was only in that guise that the system could perpetuate itself. Liberalism developed better without the vestment of the old Liberal Party.

The change took time, naturally. It was not until the end of the Second World War in the 1940s that the process was complete. But by that time, liberal thinkers like Keynes and Beveridge had forged the intellectual and planning framework for the new era of reform, and the political leadership of Labourism had become wholly dominated by traditional, élite cadres. These created the more interventionist state, and the social welfare systems of post-World War II Britain, in continuity with the Liberal Party pioneers of the early 1900s.[31]

Earlier, middle-class radicalism had been defeated, and a continuity established which 'contained' capitalist development within a conservative social nexus. Now, working-class radicalism had been diverted and blunted in an analogous fashion, and with similar

[31] In his *Politicians and the Slump: the Labour Government of 1929–31*, 1967, Robert Skidelsky warns commentators on attributing too much to the formulated Keynesian doctrines themselves: 'The absence of developed Keynesian theory was not a decisive barrier to the adoption of what might loosely be termed Keynesian policies, as is proved by the experience of the United States, Germany, France and Sweden which in the 1930s all attempted . . . to promote economic recovery through deficit budgeting.' (pp. 387–8). But in Britain such 'social engineering' depended upon 'a resolute government . . . exploiting the differences between industry and the City' (as these had been outlined in the major document of the era, the Macmillan Report on *Finance and Industry*, 1931, Cmnd. 3897). Although correct in the abstract, what such analyses ignore is that the nature of the state is incompatible with this sort of strategy: no such 'resolute' régime has ever come into being, even with the modest equipment in 'social engineering' Labour acquired during and after World War II. The reason is that a strategy of 'making capitalism work' *in that sense* remains semi-revolutionary in British conditions (i.e. it implies radical re-formation of the state in a more than simply administrative way). As Skidelsky has indicated elsewhere, the most 'resolute' proponent of that kind of reform, Oswald Mosley, was driven into the ranks of counter-revolution by the sheer impossibility of the task: see 'Great Gritain', in *European Fascism*, edited S. J. Woolf, 1968, and his subsequent biography of Mosley.

results. This second solution of continuity carried the working class into its own version of 'containment': proletarian opposition to free capitalist development united politically with that of the élite traditionalists. The weakening, ever more backward industrial basis was made to carry not only the old snail-shell but a modern 'welfare state' as well. Its triumph, which has only recently become its disaster, lay in evolving a system which both Dukes and dustmen could like, or at least find tolerable. British Socialism, when perceived in its underlying relationship to the state (or equally, in its inner morality and reflexes) should be called 'Tory Socialism'. In the later 1930s and 40s a new generation of liberal thinkers invented 'social-democratic' forms for the Labour Party, based upon largely spurious parallels with Continental socialist reformism: Evan Durbin, Hugh Gaitskell and (in the 1950s) Anthony Crosland. Failing as competely as most Marxists to focus upon the specific character of the English state and constitution, these pretended that the Labour Party was a movement of modernizing egalitarianism – in effect, that it was engaged on (if indeed it had not already achieved) the second, radical social revolution which the middle class had failed to produce. The events of the period 1964–70 were an ironical refutation of these ideas. The cringing Labour conservatism of 1974–6 has been their annihilation. The Labour Party's so-called 'social revolution' of the post-war years led not to national revival but to what Tony Benn now describes as 'de-industrialization': that is, to rapidly accelerating backwardness, economic stagnation, social decay, and cultural despair.

The immediate origin and political condition of this long-delayed crisis was the political harnessing of the working class to the socially conservative British Constitution. In many polemics this process has been crudely mistaken for 'surrender to capitalism', or 'reformism' – for instance, the social reformism of German Social-Democracy since World War II. In fact the Labourist 'surrender' has been to a particularly antique form of bourgeois society and constitution, and the resultant balance of class forces has been to a significant extent directed *against* capitalism, in the sense of industrial modernity and the individualistic, mobile but more egalitarian social relations accompanying it. The form of capitalism which it actively assisted – foreign-oriented investment and finance capital – was itself a constant impediment to more dynamic industrial growth. Labourism allied the proletariat to the inner conservatism and the main outward thrust of imperialism; not to domestic industrialism. As a result, it became a principal agent of 'deindustrialization'.

One may also argue that it turned into *the* main cause of 'the British malady' (etc.), at least from around 1965 onwards. Nobody would rationally have thought that a capitalist class so socially conservative and so tied to monetary imperialism could easily change its historical skin, and quickly give birth to a régime of dynamic modernization. It was the Labour Party which channelled the 'radical' elements and social forces capable of that. It was Labour which returned to office in 1964 with the only plausible-sounding scheme of such radical change – a programme of combined and concerted social and technological modernization, envisaging the ending of social privilege, and 'putting science and industry first'. Within three years this programme was utterly defeated, and the Harold Wilson of 1970 was reduced to posturing as the Premier of a 'natural governing party' – the party now thoroughly at home with the traditions of British state hegemony, wielding an easy Tory authority over the propertied class once afraid of it.[32]

[32] Among many lugubrious chronicles of conceit and decay, perhaps the most compact and useful is *The Decade of Disillusion: British Politics in the Sixties*, edited by D. McKie and C. Cook, 1972, especially the chapter by Peter Sinclair, 'The Economy – a Study in Failure'. The latter's account of the National Plan fiasco conveys the oscillation between megalomania and incompetence that has characterized most key state operations in recent decades: 'The impression brilliantly conveyed to the electorate in 1964 was that some undefined negative attitude implicit in "stop-go" and some unspecified kind of governmental amateurism were all that had deprived Britain of rapid growth in the 50s and early 60s. Purposive and dynamic government would suddenly restore her rightful rate of growth (i.e. by Planning)'. In reality the National Plan was to consist 'of little more than the printed replies to a questionnaire sent to industries about their estimates of inputs and outputs on the assumption of 25% real growth by 1970 . . . (!) . . . The hope was that this stated assumption would justify itself by encouraging business to create the additional capacity required to make its "prediction" come true . . . The truth is that its targets could not conceivably have been achieved' (pp. 103–4). Shortly afterwards the agency set up to perform this feat of levitation, the Department of Economic Affairs, 'withered away unnoticed and unannaled'. Perhaps the most sobering picture of the actual capitalist reality beyond the various new styles, starts and visionary scenarios punctuating governmental life from 1964 to the present is *British Capitalism, Workers and the Profit Squeeze*, 1972, by Andrew Glyn and Bob Sutcliffe.

External Solutions

Since the final failure of Labourism to achieve (or even seriously attempt) Britain's second political revolution, the state has entered into a historical cul-de-sac from which no exit is visible – that is, no exit along the sacrosanct lines of its previous development. British political life has revolved helplessly in diminishing and sinking circles, from which both main political parties try to strike out in vain. They imagine that 'left' or 'right' wing solutions are feasible without a radical break in the crippling state form which corsets them both and forces all new policies back into a dead centre of 'consensus'.

The party-political system itself (which Labour has become the main defender of) makes it next to impossible to obtain any new departure from within the system. The two-party equilibrium, with its antique non-proportional elective method and its great bedrock of tacit agreement on central issues, was formed to promote stability at the expense of adventure. It was never intended that stability should become catalepsy. But all that 'stability' meant was the comfort of external supports which rendered internal growing-pains unnecessary; now that these have vanished, inert conservatism has inevitably turned into increasing non-adaptation to the outside world.

Nothing is more significant during this last era of thickening twilight than the role of what one might label imaginary external solutions: the magic escape-routes indulged in by one government after another as their economic growth-policies collapse around them, broken in pieces by the contradictions of a non-growth state. Since the 1950s boom, the most important of these has been the European Economic Community. British governments refused to join the EEC earlier, during its expanding phase, because they retained too strong a faith in imperialism. Re-baptized as the 'Commonwealth', they still thought the system might go on furnishing Britain with the external support-area it was used to. This illusion dwindled away in the 1960s. Each administration after the Macmillan Conservative government then turned to the Common Market as the only possible realistic alternative. The Labour Party mouthed strident patriotic opposition to Europe when out of office, in 1961–3 and again in 1970–4; but when returned to power, it always moved back into a negotiating stance with the EEC, and finally staged the referendum that confirmed British membership in 1975.

British entry can therefore be described by the two words which apply to almost everything in post-World War II history: 'too late'. It took place when the long developmental phase of the EEC was nearly over, and world depression was looming – so that the British entered a Community itself falling into stalemate and self-doubt. In addition, entry had taken place for a predictable and illusory reason. Although not exactly a surrogate for Empire (like the Commonwealth or EFTA), the Common Market was beyond any doubt seen as the external answer to the British disease. The stimulus of entering a vigorous, competitive capitalist area was intended to do what domestic economic policy had so obviously failed to do: force the fabled 'regeneration' of British industry. Internal levitation had failed, with a dismal succession of thuds; exposure was supposed to accomplish the miracle instead.

Painful as the effects were expected to be, the assumption was that they would be less awful than drastic internal reform. Europe was perceived essentially as bracing bad medicine. But the point of the treatment was revival of the patient, not decent burial. Even fervent Europeanists still regularly transmitted surreal notions on how good it would be for the Continent to have lessons in democracy from the Mother of Parliaments. Neither side in the debate relaxed its grip on the udders of island constitutionalism for a moment.[33]

In fact it is dubious whether entry could have had much beneficial effect on the British economy even ten years sooner, unless a much more radical internal programme had been adopted – unless (e.g.) the Labour 1964 policies had been taken seriously and fought for, instead of being thrown overboard at the first signs of trouble. Without a programme of (in Benn's sense) 're-industrialization' in some sort of conjunction with the new EEC external field of forces, it was always possible (as opponents argued) that these forces would have been overwhelming economically. But 're-industrialization' is not really a question of economic policy in Britain. This is the characteristic empirical-minded error made by successive govern-

[33] I wrote a short account of this passage in our affairs which appeared as No. 75 of *New Left Review* and as *The Left Against Europe?*, 1973, arguing that from any progressive standpoint ranging from the mildly reforming to the revolutionary no fate could be worse than national isolation in the grip of an unreformed U.K. state.

ments since 1945 (and still made by Benn and his supporters on the Labour left wing). It is, in fact, a call for revolution. More exactly, it is a call for the 'revolution from above' which the British state-system has been built upon denying and repressing ever since the Industrial Revolution. It is a call – therefore – which has not the most remote chance of being effectively answered by the existing state, and the deeply rooted civil structures which sustain it.

This impossibility is the immediate context for both the so-called 'economic crisis' and the problem of peripheral nationalism; as such it deserves closer study. The key-note of all appeals for econo-mic renaissance between the 1880s and the present day has been the industrial sector: the wish is to re-establish the primacy of the productive sector over the City and finance-capital – and hence, of the technologist and the industrial entrepreneur over the banker and the broker, of the 'specialized' scientist or business man over the non-specialized (or 'amateur') gentleman-administrator who has governed both the political system and the state bureaucracy. The exercise is presented as the formation of a new, healthier equilibrium: righting the balance left by aristocracy and empire, 'stimulating' industry to a better performance in comparative terms. Once achieved, this more competitive industrial basis will provide export-led growth, leading to a harder currency and so to a renewed foundation for London finance capital also. Sterling will regain its place as a valid international trading currency (even though second to the U.S. dollar), and this all-round revival would signify new life for the state.[34]

Sometimes the operation has been seen as state-contrived or directed (as under the Wilson government of the 1960s); sometimes as a matter of 'liberating capitalism', freeing the entrepreneurial spirit from state obstructions and burdens (e.g. the Heath govern-ment of 1970–2, whose rhetoric has now been taken up by Mrs Thatcher, with the usual empty radicalism of opposition). Yet these

[34] The most interesting general analysis and verdict on economic policy and the state is that provided by *The United Kingdom in 1980: the Hudson Report*, London, 1975. Its main argument was that failure in economic policy was in-separable from the structure, personnel, ideology and recruitment of the state. This abrasive commonplace produced an unprecedented chorus of abusive dis-missal from virtually the whole corps of *chiens de garde*: the intelligentsia choked as one over this bitter foreign pill. I tried to describe the spectacle at the time in *Bananas*, No. 1, London 1975.

prescriptions are not as different as they appear. Since the whole problem lies in the fact that Britain does not possess a dynamic but frustrated capitalist class capable of responding to 'liberation' in the simple-minded Friedmannite sense, state intervention is in fact inevitable (as Heath swiftly found out). The historical 'balance' that has to be righted is in reality so ancient, so buttressed by manifold social customs and ideology, and the domestic capitalist class is so short-sighted and dependent, that nothing except vigorous intervention from above can conceivably make an impact.

However, there exists no state-class of 'technocrats' or administrators capable of doing this. The political and administrative class is irremediably compromised, socially and intellectually, with the old patrician order. Such 'strategies' exist only as recurring fantasies of liberation: perpetual 'new starts', bold dreams of dynamism solemnly enunciated in manifestos and dramatic 'reports' every year or so when the government changes hands (or even when it does not). These furnish a fleeting euphoria to commentators, wholly founded upon the fact that they and their readers have forgotten the previous instalments. The predictable failure of each new bold initiative is simply suppressed, even as it takes place; by oneiric magic, a new dream-corner materializes which the nation has to get round, into the land of the righted balance and 'soundly-based' prosperity. The external observer perceives a constant decline, with occasional plateaus; the English spirit sees constantly-repeated hard luck, and Chancellors of the Exchequer who failed to 'get it quite right' *this* time, but, *next* time . . .

To interrupt this cycle of delusions would require a change of élites. It would entail the radical removal of the entire traditional apparatus of state and civil intelligentsia – that is, of that stratum which, in spite of its liberalism and constitutional gentility, is as much of a stranglehold upon English society as were the Prussian Junker class, the Italian Risorgimento Liberals, the Spanish landowners or the old Dutch burgher class on their respective countries. Elite changes of that kind never occur by modulation and negotiation: they need a break (which may of course assume many different forms). No state ever reforms itself away into something so strikingly different – least of all one with this degree of historical prestige, residual self-confidence and capacity for self-deception.[35]

---

[35] It should not be assumed that the U.K. state's immutability implies absence of *wish* to reform itself; on the contrary, as with other *anciens régimes* the drowning

From the early 1960s to 1975 the European Community provided a constantly recurring external support for illusions of re-
juvenescence: the vital outside succour which would render internal revolution unnecessary. But as faith in this empire-surrogate
evaporated (almost from the instant of entry) another and still
more potent formula took its place. The procession of quasi-divine
strokes of good fortune and helping hands that had helped the
wheel-chair through the 20th century received an incredible
climax.

From around 1970 it became steadily clearer that oil exploration
in the North Sea was going to yield great results, with the obvious
promise of an eventual reversal of the chronic British balance-of-
payments crisis, a restoration of sterling, and a state-aided industrial
investment programme of modernization. After furnishing the
British state with the greatest colonial domain, the Gold Standard,
victorious allies in two world wars, the EEC and the protective
American Empire for its old age, God out-did his own record of
generous favouritism. The final version of imperial exploitation
was discovered in the mud of the North Sea. Practically from the
grave itself there seemed to arise the last great, miraculous escape-
route, the ultimate external cornucopia.

This last phase in the pattern of external dependency has of
course been perceived by most political leaders in the usual way:
salvation at the eleventh hour. Providence will pay off Great Britain's debts, and allow her ancient state to slither into the 21st
century. In an outbreak of euphoria without precedent, one Minis-

---

sensation produces an almost ceaseless quest for insignificant change. 'In the ten
years between 1964 and 1973', notes one authority, 'this Constitution's quality of
flexibility has been predominant. Never before has there been so much talk or so
much actual change, always within a framework which has been kept intact . . .'
P. Bromhead, *Britain's Developing Constitution*, 1974, p. 217. This wave of
frenetic tinkering was devoted to making the old machine more 'efficient' while
keeping it intact: a contradiction in terms pondered over by many Royal Com-
missions and Inquiries (described in, e.g., Frank Stacey, *British Government
1966–1975*, Oxford, 1975, see especially chapter XII). Possibly the finest monument to this 'stage army of the good' (Stacey, op. cit., p. 215) was the Redcliffe-
Maud reform of Local Government, a superbly unradical and unpopular administrative overhaul that conveyed the maximum impression of novelty with
the minimum of real change. The only genuinely radical reform to emerge, from
the Kilbrandon Commission's Report on Devolution, was brought about by a
threat of death to the framework itself: the political eruption of Scottish and
Welsh nationalism in 1974.

ter after another has conjured up the light at the end of the tunnel. If only the British can hang on, in a few years all will be well. The North Sea income will pay off the debts many times over, and leave a huge surplus for industrial investment. What all Chancellors of the Exchequer failed to do, nature will accomplish. At the same time, like any heiress expecting a fortune, the government has hugely expanded its borrowings from abroad. Combined with the soaring inflation of 1974–6 (which afflicted Britain more than her main industrial competitors) this led to a chronic sterling devaluation crisis. Partly 'managed' by government – in order to favour export industries – this collapse none the less threatened to become total in 1976. While waiting on the oil revenues to flow in, shorter term salvation was obtained by a loan from the International Monetary Fund in December.

Foreign governments, and foreign observers generally, naturally have a differing perspective on this conjuncture. There is no reason why they should take this latest version of the British redemption myth seriously. But there are plenty of reasons why they should conclude that both the IMF loan and North Sea oil will merely be another chapter of false hopes.[36] They will be used to avoid painful changes, not to promote them; to put off drastic reforms once more, not to make them palatable. Consensus and inertia will see to that. To furnish one or two extra 'chances' for a state like this one is meaningless. It involves placing more credence in the re-birth ideology of politicians than in the character of the state which they serve. The former deals in round-the-corner optimism; the latter in a tri-secular accumulation of imperial complacency and slow-moving certainties, all firmly cemented into the instinctive reflexes of the huge extended family that really governs England. As long as that family is there, conducting its business in the drawing-room conversational monotone of tradition, farther stays of execution will be used for its real historic aim: to change just as much as is necessary for everything to go on as before.

Class and Nationalism

The conservative essence of the British political drama occupies a

---

[36] They need only read J. P. Mackintosh's astringent account of the behind-the-scenes manoeuverings around the loan, in *The Times*, December 13th, 1977, should a doubt have crossed their mind that contemporary British statesmanship is invariably myopic farce acted out like Greek tragedy.

smaller and smaller stage, and goes on in an ever-dimmer light. In the declining spiral each new repetition of the play, although advertized by the players as the same, has a new note of hollowness or approaching night. Each time the forces capable of extinguishing the performance move a little closer to the actors and the ancient scenery, and loom more noticeably over events.

There are the outside forces, upon which this analysis has placed so much emphasis. The disappearance of empire and the dwindling place of its child, the City, in the fabric of international capitalism; the failing industrial sector and currency, and the gathering intolerance of the capitalist powers for this chronic malingerer who, in spite of every assistance and sympathy, still cannot shake himself into new life. Internally, the class struggle also advances with its own threat of disruption. Since 1974, when the miners' strike led to the overthrow of a Conservative government, the Labour Party has accomplished apparent miracles in restoration of the consensus: this was (as the *Times* stated then) what it was elected to do. The latest round of crisis-and-redemption has only been possible at all on the frozen ice of the class struggle, obtained by means of the 'Social Contract' – perhaps the last desperate form of that deep class-alliance the state has always relied upon.

How thick the ice looks, in the declarations of Labour Ministers and the trade-union leaders who have supported the agreement! How thin and short-lived it may soon become, as inflation and unemployment continue to increase during 1977! It would be broken altogether by the return of the Conservative Party to office, even before it melts under force of circumstance. And under the ice of this traditional nation-first solidarity, real tradition has been put in reverse. The point of the old, secular social strategy was concession to mounting pressures from below: there was always something to concede, and some reason for the lower classes to retain faith in the British firmament. Sacrifices were made for later gains that came from empire and warfare – but which really did come, until well after the last World War. Under the Social Contract, sacrifices and falling standards are being accepted in exchange for rewards that now hinge (when one discounts the escapism of North Sea oil) genuinely on the capacity of the British state to reform its own society – upon the enactment of the long-awaited, incessantly-heralded 'British economic miracle' putting the country back on a level with its old rivals in Europe.

50

If (one should say 'when') this does not take place, a massive reaction is bound to occur and shake even the very strong structure of English hegemony. Even English patience is not endless. Were it to happen in conjunction with a farther phase of the external crisis – accompanied by a currency collapse, for example – then not even the beleaguered optimists of the Establishment would imagine the political system going on as usual. The very least they foresee is the conventional British 20th century formula for crisis, a 'National Government' of emergency.[37]

But in any case, to these two menacing forces has now been added a third – a third force which, though less powerful and significant than the others, is likely none the less to function as the precipitant of the conflict. The underlying dynamic of class alliance has altered; but so have the rules of the political system itself. The one has been forced by Britain's shrinking economic stature and relations; the other by peripheral nationalism – that is, by a different kind of opposition to the same declining world and philosophy.

Different aspects and modes of this opposition are described in some of the essays in this volume. But in the context of British state-

[37] 'National' or coalition governments, in the sense of 'emergency régimes' where the state faces a crisis, account for 21 years of this century's political history in Britain: 1915–22, 1931–45. The corresponding figures for party rule are – Conservatives, 28 years; Labour Party, 18 years; Liberal Party, 9 years (*British Political Facts, 1900–1968*, 1969, by D. Butler and J. Freeman). It is the normal formula of retrenchment, and will undoubtedly be employed again when the situation becomes critical enough. More important than the time-span of emergency régimes is their pivotal role in state history: the genuinely massive adaptations and changes of balance have taken place in war-time – when the impact of external forces became literally irresistable – and under 'non-party' tutelage. The collapse of the Liberal Party, the crystallization of Labourism, the emancipation of women, the Welfare State, liquor licensing hours, widespread sale of contraceptives, trade-union 'partnership' in the state, juvenile delinquency – very many of the big turning-points and most recognizable traits of modern British life were products of war-time. Warfare provided a forced rupture in the normally stifling continuum of the state Establishment – in effect, a partial, controlled social revolution which gave the system a new lease of life on each occasion (but above all after 1945). The thesis is conveyed in Arthur Marwick, *The Deluge: British Society and the First World War*, 1965, and *Britain in the Century of Total War: War, Peace and Social Change 1900–1967*, 1968. On the Second World War, Angus Calder's *The People's War*, 1968, argues cogently for an interpretation of the War as an abortive, ultimately betrayed, social revolution. The congruence of the thesis with the general emphasis on external relations put forward here is obvious.

history what counts most is the common element they display:
however varied in background and aims, these situations of break-
down and gathering nationalism fall outside the characteristic contours of English constitutionalism. They are not the kind of problem it was slowly formed to deal with, and they will resist or destroy
the typical remedies which it inspires. In summary, almost emblematic form, one might say: London government invents habitual
class remedies to nationalist ailments. Its instinct is to concede,
when sufficiently prodded, then consolidate tradition on the new,
slightly different balance of forces that results. Although notoriously
effective on the front of class struggle and negotiation, the strategy
has no real application to national questions. The philosophy and
practice of conservative empiricism presupposes a stable, consensual framework; the new nationalisms challenge that framework itself.
British constitutionalism makes an arcane mystique of power,
removing it from the arena of normal confrontation and enshrining
it as a Grail-like 'sovereignty'; but nationalism *is* about power, in a
quite straightforward sense. It is a demand for the Grail, or at least
a bit of it (this is of course a demand for the impossible, in English
ideological tradition).

This pattern has been followed to the letter in the development of
intra-British conflict so far. When Welsh and Scottish nationalism
began to advance politically in the 1960s, London government from
the outset assumed that these developments would have to be
adapted to, and nullified, in the habitual way. It noticed that the
demands were different in Wales and Scotland, as were the relative
strengths of the nationalist parties. So of course different concessions would be in order in each region. A Royal Commission was
appointed to work out how this should be done, in the customary
hope that the problem would have solved itself by the time this
body's deliberations were finished. When completed, its recommendations were greeted with universal derision and cynicism.[38]

---

[38] The *Royal Commission on the Constitution, 1969–1973*, 1973, Cmnd. 5460,
two vols., chaired (latterly) by Lord Kilbrandon. The general reaction of parliament and metropolitan opinion to its appearance in October 1973 leaves one in no
doubt that the whole thing would have been consigned to the dungeons as a lost
cause, had the Nationalists not made their dramatic electoral break-through only
a few months later. The lost cause then speedily turned into the dominant theme
of parliamentary existence, as it was seen that the future of the political order
itself was at stake. Among the neglected but entertaining sections of the Report are

The derision vanished with the new election results of 1974. The new Labour government hastily produced legislation embodying some of the Commission's ideas, which became the 'Scotland and Wales Bill' of December 1976.[39] Now that the problems were not going to disappear spontaneously, concessionary tactics would have to be employed. With limited degrees of self-government in domestic matters (extremely limited in the case of Wales), it was believed that the regions would soon relapse into their traditional subordination. Are they not full of basically loyal folk who may have a few grievances but know that Britain is best? Once reasonable note is regally taken of their grudges, surely they will fall into line again, acknowledging their limited yet honoured place in the greater scheme of things? A great deal of fulsome rhetoric of 1960s vintage went into the deal: the legislation was titled 'Our Changing Democracy' and sanctified by speeches on bringing government 'closer to the people', combating impersonal centralism, etc. When set in the historical perspectives of English élitism, this was indecorous to say the least of it: few have seen it as anything but an ideological façade. Like the Local Government reforms which had preceded

---

those on the Isle of Man and the Channel Islands, tiny territories that cast a minor yet revealing light on the vaster fabric they (somewhat vaguely) belong to: 'Unique miniature states with wide powers of self-government', as the Commissioners recorded, 'not capable of description by any of the usual categories of political science . . . full of anomalies, peculiarities and anachronisms, which even those who work the system find it hard to define precisely. We do not doubt that more logical and orderly races would have swept all these away long ago . . .' p. 410, p. 441. Not having made enough nuisance of themselves, these authentic feudal relics have been left in peace: 'We have not approached the Islands in any spirit of reforming zeal', confessed the Commission, 'Indeed, if only the constitutional relationships between the United Kingdom and the Islands could remain as they have been in recent years . . . everybody would be happy, and our task would disappear'.

[39] The progress of 'devolution' from universal contempt to a critical issue of state is best epitomized in Hegel's reflections on the Great Reform Bill of 1832. Reluctantly, it was conceded that – 'The right way to pursue improvement is not by the moral route of using ideas, admonitions, associations of isolated individuals, in order to counteract the system of corruption and avoid being indebted to it, but by the alteration of institutions. The common prejudice of inertia, namely to cling always to the old faith in the excellence of an institution, even if the present state of affairs derived from it is altogether corrupt, has thus at last caved in . . .', *Hegel's Political Writings*, 'The English Reform Bill', op. cit., p. 298.

devolution, the changes were at heart ways of preserving the old state – minor alterations to conserve the antique essence of English hegemony.

There was no real belief in a new partnership of peoples. And in fact, such a partnership – in other words, genuine 'transfer of power' from the old state – was never conceivable without the most radical reform of the centre itself. To give effective power away meant examining, and changing, the basis of power itself: the Constitution, the myth-source of sovereignty, and all that it depends upon. The whole British political system had to be altered. There has been no serious question of doing this, for the sake of the Scots, the Welsh and the Ulstermen. The only political party which advocates it is the one permanently removed from power, the Liberal Party.[40]

Unable to contemplate radical reform of the centre (since its whole modern history has been built on avoiding it) London government has blundered empirically into the usual tactic of graduated response. One commentary after another has explored the self-contradictory nature of the proposals, their liability to generate conflict and escalation of nationalist sentiment and demands.[41]

[40] The Kilbrandon Commission formulated the view of federalism which has become standard in the debates on devolution: 'As far as we are aware no advocate of federalism in the United Kingdom has succeeded in producing a federal scheme satisfactorily tailored to fit the circumstances of England. A federation consisting of four units – England, Scotland, Wales and Northern Ireland – would be so unbalanced as to be unworkable. It would be dominated by the overwhelming political importance and wealth of England. The English Parliament would rival the United Kingdom federal Parliament; and in the federal Parliament itself the representation of England could hardly be scaled down in such a way as to enable it to be out-voted by Scotland, Wales and Northern Ireland, together representing less than one-fifth of the population. A United Kingdom federation of the four countries . . . is therefore not a realistic proposition.' *Royal Commission*, op. cit., para. 531, p. 159. The most persuasive version of the Liberal Party's argument for a federal Britain is Jenny Chapman's *Scottish Self-Government* (Scottish Liberal Party, 1976).

[41] But no commentary has done so more devastatingly than the main parliamentary debate on devolution itself, during the four days of the Scotland and Wales Bill's Second Reading, Monday–Thursday, 13th–16th December 1976 (Hansard *Parliamentary Debates*, vol. 922, nos. 14–17). The student is advised to begin at the end, with the speech of the Lord President of the Council and Leader of the House of Commons, Mr Michael Foot. This poem of embattled Constitutionalism begins: 'The central issue was mentioned by my hon. Friend the Member for Walton (and numerous other hon. Friends and Members) . . .

These criticisms have had little effect on the policy. At the time of writing it may still be obstructed or dropped altogether, because of the vicissitudes of economic crisis and U.K. politics; there is small chance of its being amended into a workable form of federalism.

The Slow Landslide

The foregoing analysis has tried, in all too summary fashion, to isolate some of the elements of fatality in Great Britain's current crisis. It has discovered these, above all, in the historical structure of the British state. As far as 'devolution' is concerned, these are the only sort of reforms which such a state *can* enact, while remaining bound by its distinctive historical identity.

That identity was the product of extraordinarily successful earlier adaptation. Although a developmental oddity belonging to the era of transition from absolutism to capitalist modernity, its anomalous character was first crystallized and then protected by priority. As the road-making state into modern times, it inevitably retained much from the mediaeval territory it left behind: a cluster of deep-laid archaisms still central to English society and the British

---

They expressed their genuine belief that there was a danger of the Bill's undermining and destroying the unity of the United Kingdom. That is the central feature of the debate . . . My reply is that there are many other hon. Members on both sides of the House who support the Bill precisely because they believe it is the best way to strengthen and sustain the unity of the United Kingdom . . .'. Pursuing his theme of mystic unity, the Lord President underlined the point with ever greater emphasis: the whole structure of the measure upholds, even enhances the Sovereign Supremacy of Parliament: 'The fundamental explanation for the way we have devised the Bill is that we want to ensure that this House retains its supremacy . . .' so that, in the event of conflict among the nations, 'We sustain the proposition that the House of Commons . . . and the decisions of Parliament must be respected. That is the way in which we say these matters must be settled. Because we set up other Assemblies with specified powers, rights and duties *does not mean that the House of Commons need not retain its full power to deal with these matters in the future* . . .' (my emphasis). Not only is federalism out of the question; the unitary state will remain as mythically One as all past apologists have depicted it. A Scottish National Party M.P., Mr Gordon Wilson, objected to this ghost of Absolutism being conjured up once more: was it not the case that in some countries, Scotland for example, the people were held to be sovereign, rather than Parliament (more precisely, the Crown in Parliament)? This was, again, the far from 'technical' point referred to by McKenzie and Silver (Note 27, above). But of course it was not even noticed in the context of Mr Foot's Westminster fustian.

state. Yet the same developmental position encouraged the secular retention of these traits, and a constant return to them as the special mystique of the British Constitution and way of life. Once the road-system had been built up, for other peoples as well as the English, the latter were never compelled to reform themselves along the lines which the English revolutions had made possible. They had acquired such great advantages from leading the way – above all in the shape of empire – that for over two centuries it was easier to consolidate or re-exploit this primary role than to break with it.

In terms of modern developmental time, this has been a very long era. During it English society has become thoroughly habituated to the conservative re-exploitation of good fortune; and for most of the period the leaner, marginal countries around England were associated with the act. They too received something of the impress of the curious English class system, and were deeply affected by the traditions of patrician liberalism. They also were for long integrated into its peculiar success–story, in a way quite different from most other minor nationalities, and only possible in these singular developmental conditions. At bottom, this freer, less painful, less regimented form of assimilation was simply a function of the unique imperialism England established in the wider world, and of the state-form which corresponded to it internally.[42]

---

[42] This is related to the criticism which must be made of what is in many respects the best, most comprehensive attempt at an overall analysis of British development and its impact on the smaller nations: Michael Hechter's *Internal Colonialism: the Celtic Fringe in British National Development 1536–1966*, 1975. His account is conducted essentially in terms of over-abstract models of development: the orthodox evolutionary and diffusionist model (which foresaw the gradual elimination of peripheral nationalism) is replaced by the 'internal colonialist' one emphasizing the factors of uneven development, discrimination, etc., present even in the oldest West European states. Although enlightening, the application of the theory to Britain is insufficiently historical, and misses too many of the specifics. It omits the key question of the character of the unitary U.K. state, and has too narrow a view of the significance of imperialism for the whole British order. The differentia of this variety of 'internal colonialism' was that – like the state itself – it was a pre-modern (Absolutist or transitional) form of assimilation, which survived and acquired new vitality through successful external depredations – thus enabling real integrative tendencies to outweigh those of 'uneven development' for a prolonged period. None the less, a discussion founded upon Hechter's analysis would probably be more useful than any other in the future (he himself conceded that 'the models employed here are painfully preliminary', p. 6).

The critique of that form is still at an elementary stage. This is partly a result of the mystifications referred to earlier; but also partly because of the general tardiness with which the study of comparative development has arisen. It is suggested below that the whole question of nationalism has remained enigmatic for the same reason (see Chapter Nine, especially pp. 331, 355). Both the general principles of the nation-state and the particular examples of these principles at work, in fact, can only be properly discerned in this relatively new developmental perspective. Although formulated originally to explain backwardness, it has turned out to be the intellectual framework most appropriate for understanding the 'advanced' states as well: in this case, the original school-master of the process, long left behind by his first disciples and overtaken by others every year now, yet congenitally unable to renounce the habits of primacy.

So, many elements have been quite left out of even this bare outline. The nature and ambiguous function of the English Common Law system, for example, as both guarantor of individual liberty and central buttress of social conservatism. In both senses, the mystique of law extends and supports those aspects of the constitution and legal system mentioned previously. Or the particular importance of modern religious developments in England: as in other contemporary democracies, these have certainly contributed powerfully to the actual substance of the political order, especially on its left-wing side. Both Liberalism and Labourism are structurally indebted to the long-drawn-out English Reformation which extended from late Tudor times until Victorian Nonconformity.[43]

[43] Stein Rokkan's study, 'Nation-building, Cleavage Formation and the Structuring of Mass Politics', in *Citizens Elections Parties: approaches to the comparative study of Processes of Development*, Oslo, 1970, gives an interesting comparative view of the persisting significance of religion in the structure of modern party politics; see especially pp. 101–7. This significance is substantially different in all four British nations, and still constitutes one of the deepest agencies of diversity at work: Catholicism and militant Protestant anti-Catholicism in Ireland; Radical Nonconformity in Wales; and Calvinism in Scotland. In England itself debate on this question has always rightly focused on the famous Halévy thesis: among recent discussions, see particularly Bernard Semmel's edition of Halévy's *The Birth of Methodism in England*, 1971, and the same writer's *The Methodist Revolution*, 1974. The latter attempts to relate the theme to the character of Anglo-British nationalism, pointing out how: 'having long abandoned their 17th century revolutionary inheritance, the sects, implicitly

Or the undoubted significance of emigration, continuous yet hard to quantify in its effects, as the perennial safety-valve of society's restless and unstable fraction. In this basic human sense, 'empire' was anything but an abstraction to many generations of British workers and their families.

However, in spite of these and other omissions, I hope a sufficient idea of this strange, declining social world has emerged. It has always been too easy, at least in modern times, to either praise or condemn the Anglo-British state. On the one hand, its historical role and past grandeur impose themselves on most observers. During the Cold War in particular Britain's faltering economy was compensated for by a renewed cult of ancient Constitutional Liberty and wise pragmatism: an especially holy wayside shrine of the Free World. On the other hand, since the end of the last century nobody who has looked at all critically at the economy or the class-structure has been able to avoid sarcasm, often tending towards despair. Incurious worship and flagellation (including self-flagellation): it has always been hard to steer any sort of critical course beyond these poles, and yet keep the whole object in view.

If critique is becoming more possible, it is probably because the object itself has at last decayed to the point of disintegration. The different Britain now being born may be better able to consider its ancestor dispassionately. The new fragmentation may also bring more space and distance into the British world, mental as well as regional and political. If so, it will become easier to weigh up the old contradictions and form a more balanced, overall estimate of the state's decline. The factors of grandeur and of misery are bound together, in the peculiar dialectic and tempo of Great Britain's fall from empire.

---

following the logic and in part the rhetoric of Cromwellian policy, could see a liberal, Protestant Britain as an elect nation with a divine mission. This was a view which . . . Methodism came to share' (pp. 172–8). In terms of the 'second revolution' argument outlined above, Methodism is perhaps more plausibly interpreted as a surrogate, merely 'cultural' revolution, whose intensity and effects were intensified by the failure of revolution at the state level – rather than as a spiritual barrier to revolution as such. Implicitly following the rhetoric of a lost revolutionary inheritance, without its reality, such 'cultural revolutions' end as reinforcements of the existing state-form. In both England and China they have also served as partial mechanisms of adjustment to industrial or urban existence.

That kind of imperial greatness led inexorably to this kind of inert, custom-ridden, self-deluding misery. In its fall as in its origins, this empire differs from the others. It revolved around a remarkably non-regimented society, civilian in its direction and peaceful in its politics, and informed by a high degree of responsible self-activity. But the absence of bureaucracy was always the presence of an extensive, able, co-optive patriciate: rule from above was stronger, for being informal and personally mediated, not weaker. Peace was paid for by democracy – that is, in terms of the loss of any aggressive egalitarian spirit, in terms of 'knowing one's place' and quietism towards the state. The civility was tied to this permanent malady of class, in a unity essentially archaic in nature, whatever its gestures towards modernity. 'Responsibility', that liberal glory of the English state, was never separable from the huge, passive irresponsibility underneath. It depended on and fostered this working-class apathy, the particular social inertia of England. For its part – with the same long-term inevitability – Labourism merely occupied the terrain of this passivity, camping on it like a new set of well-meaning landlords.

A specific form of containment of capitalism, and an accompanying anti-capitalist spirit, were notable merits of the old order. They too made for a kind of peace, and for a muddled, backward-looking social consensus. Perhaps there are some elements of Arcady in all social formations, premonitions of a future ideal mixed up with the usual nostalgia for lost worlds. In modern England this has always been obvious, and operative in the state. Too many people have been unable for too long to free themselves from the ghost of social harmony these conditions created – unable therefore to withdraw belief from the evolutionary myth which sees the authentic harmony of socialism one day emerging from that ghost. Yet in reality the anti-capitalist consensus has been the slow death of the old system: it gave it longevity, with some help from the Labour Party, but only to render senility and ultimate collapse more certain.

In studying this strange slow-motion landslide, one begins to see the answer to the two questions posed earlier: why has the decline lasted so long, without catastrophe? – and, why does its final disintegration seem to be taking the form of nationalist revolt, rather than social revolution?

The very archaism of the Anglo-British state – its failure to modernize and its slow competitive death – was connected to a remarkable social strength. Its 'backwardness', epitomized in industrial retreat and stagnation, and the chronic failure of government economic policy, was inseparable from its particular kind of peaceful stability, from its civil relaxation of customs, its sloth, even its non-malicious music-hall humour. The Siamese twins of anachronism and social cohesion belonged to each other. It was never in reality feasible to infuse the American or West-German virtues into them without the effective destruction of this unique body politic.

In English mythology the uniqueness is ascribed to a mixture of racial magic and 'long experience'. In fact, it should be ascribed to empire. In a sense quite distinct from the habitual icons of imperialism – militarism, uniformed sadism, cults of violence, etc. – this was (as should surely be expected) the most profoundly and unalterably imperialist of societies. Of all the great states, the British was the most inwardly modelled and conditioned by prolonged external depredations, and the most dependent on fortunate external relations. From the time of its Indian conquests to that of its cringing dependence on the United States, its power was the internal translation of these fortunes. An incorrigibly overseas-oriented capitalism removed much of the need for internal reformation and dynamism; but the absence of this pressure was the ideal ground for maintaining and extending the patriciate, and for imposing a conservative straitjacket on the working class. Time and success were the conditions for this slow, anomalous growth; but these were what the British state had, because of its prolonged priority of development. Hierarchy and deference became the inner face of its outward adventure. Alone among the modern imperialisms, it evolved some of the semblance of an ancient empire, with its mandarinate and its placid urban peasantry.

The contrast between Britain and the more brittle imperial systems that were convulsed by losing their colonies does not lie – as often thought – in the former's less great dependence on empire, or in its ruling class's more civilized deportment. Externally, it rested upon the far greater success of British empire, a system so extensive and so deeply enracinated that it could survive the end of formal colonization. Internally, it lay in the superior strength and cohesion of British class society, proof against shocks fatal elsewhere. No other nation was so dependent on imperialism, or had got more out of it; but also, no other nation had made so much of that accumulated riches, socially speaking, in the shape of a contemporary tribal state of such formidable complacency and endurance. This archaically-based security, in turn, made possible the elements of liberalism in the élite's policy – both at home and abroad.

Slow decline has been the joint product of inner social strength and altering external relations. The former has failed bit by bit, in the successive spirals of the inevitable 'economic crisis' and futile governmental tactics to reverse the trend; the latter have changed less abruptly, and on the whole less unfavourably, than is now remembered in a climate of generalized economic gloom. After the 1939–45 war, Britain was still within its long victorious cycle, although nearing the end. It would still enjoy another brief phase of relative advance and prosperity, in the 1950s, before the European and Japanese economies had reasserted themselves. Even then, American hegemony continued to furnish an important surrogate external force-field, both economically and politically. I have already mentioned the EEC and North Sea oil as farther extrapolations of this quest for imperial substitutes.

The actual degeneration has been slower than most ideological pictures of it; it is also of course different in nature from them. In Great Britain itself Doom has been cried every Monday morning for many generations, following an ancient patrician principle that such announcements instil courage in the masses, and help to exorcise the real peril (whatever that may be). Like internal secrecy, this form of magic appears natural to English-style hegemony. Outside commentators naturally find it difficult to avoid an apocalyptic path influenced by these largely ritual warnings and exhortations. But actually, no one can predict the conjunction of external and internal circumstances that may one day cause the collapse of this resistant state. It might survive the present world recession with at least its main social structures intact.

It is of course the character of these dominant structures which leads to the answer to the second question, why peripheral bourgeois nationalism has today become the grave-digger rather than the intelligentsia or proletariat. The smaller nationalities have lost faith in the old state long before its social opposition. More rapidly and decisively than either the mainstream English intellectuals or the English working class, they have acknowledged the only genuinely predictable verity of British state-history: under *this* socio-political system, no conceivable government can reverse the trend, or fight successfully out of the *impasse* left by an empire at the end of its tether. The reinforced archaic solidarity of metropolitan society has numbed awareness of this truth in England. So it has sunk in to the periphery more readily – that is, into societies which, in spite of their modern political subservience, still retain an alternative historical reality and a potentially different vision of things.

This is the wider context that ought to form the foundation for any political judgement on Britain's new nationalisms. It is insufficient to judge them in terms of their own self-consciousness and ideology, or – the commoner case – quite abstractly in terms of an idealized internationalism versus a supposed 'Balkanization' of Britain.

Against Internationalism?

Politically speaking, the key to these neo-nationalist renaissances lies in the slow foundering of the British state, not in the Celtic bloodstream. This is not to deny the significance of ethnic and linguistic factors – the things usually evoked in accusations of 'narrow nationalism' – above all in the Welsh example. However, in the Scottish case these are relatively unimportant: this is overwhelmingly a politically-oriented separatism, rather exaggeratedly concerned with problems of state and power, and frequently indifferent to the themes of race and cultural ancestry. Yet it incontestibly leads the way, and currently dominates the devolutionary attack on the British system. Before long (and depending partly on the fate of the declining Spanish state) it may figure as the most prominent and successful new-nationalist movement in Western Europe.

A more general theoretical argument lies behind this apparent paradox. In the general analysis of nationalism presented below (Chapter Nine) it is suggested that in any case those ethnic-linguistic features so prominent in the ideologies of nationalism have always been secondary to the material factors of uneven development. The undoubted weight of nationalist ideology in modern history is owed, none the less, to a chronically recurrent dilemma of socioeconomic development – a dilemma so far quite inseparable from the actual capitalist nature of the 19th and 20th centuries. This material contradiction of uneven development has itself assumed many forms; so have the compensatory ideologies which it has invariably generated. Yet it remains true that the notoriously subjective or 'irrational' elements in nationalism are always functionally subordinate to an economic reality, *provided one takes a wide enough developmental context*. This usually means looking beyond the particular state or variety of nationalism one is interested in (and often it means taking continental, or even world history into account). It means – therefore – looking far beyond the sort of ideas about nationalism normally entertained by nationalists themselves, and also by the most passionate opponents of nationalism.

In the case of the British Isles, the factors of internal uneven development are clear. They were of course clear in the older example of Southern Irish nationalism; but essentially the same kind of dilemma, 'under-development' and ethnic-linguistic exclusion, has continued in North and West Wales, and furnished the basis for the more politicized and state-oriented nationalism of the present-day *Plaid Cymru* (see Ch. Four below). In Scotland, a similar but much less important form of under-development has persisted in the Highland area: it still contributes something to the character of Scottish nationalism, and will not be without significance to a future Scottish state. But what has decisively changed the Scottish situation is a different variety of uneven development altogether. As I argue below (see Chapter Three, pp. 185–195) the factors operative there are closer to those observable in Catalonia or the Spanish Basque region: a tendential relative 'over-development'. Obviously linked to the discovery and exploitation of North Sea oil, this new awareness has proved particularly effective in the face of the English decline and political immiseration discussed above. It has awakened the Scottish bourgeoisie to new consciousness of its historic separateness, and fostered a frank, restless discontent with the expiring British world.

These differing patterns of uneven development do not suffice in themselves to explain the basis of neo-nationalism, however. The material basis is completed by recognition of the decisive effect exercised *by the uneven development of Great Britain as a whole* upon these, its constituent parts. This is of course the very theme I have been studying, from the angle of the British state. From the angle of the constituent nations – and this has come to be true even of Northern Ireland – it means that their own contemporary development, and the particular problems they confront in it, have become both entrapped and amplified by this larger drama of developmental failure. The latter's reverberations fuse with the more strictly nationalist initiative and energy now functioning in the British periphery. Both together widen the fissures making for a break-up of the British state.

This wider context furnishes a better basis for estimating the place of peripheral British separatism in history. A better foundation, hence, for pronouncement on their political significance. The larger story is that of the fall of one of history's great states, and of the tenacious, conservative resistance of its English heartland to this fate. Within the more general process, the disruptive trends of the periphery emerge as both effect and cause: products of an incipient ship-wreck, they also function – often unwittingly – as contributors to the disaster itself, hastening a now foreseeable end.

Consequently, judgement of their role hinges upon one's view of the dying state itself. If one does not recognize that it is moribund, like most of the English left, then naturally Scottish and Welsh nationalism will appear as destructive forces – as a basically irrational turning back towards forgotten centuries, as involution at the expense of progress. Whether conservative or socialist, belief in a continuing unitary state of the British Isles entails viewing these movements as a threat – whether the menace is to be countered by 'devolution', or eventually by other means. Of course a good deal of the opposition to peripheral self-government is not even as articulate as this, and has no definite idea of the British state at all: it simply takes it for granted, with or without its more feudal ornaments. But the upshot is the same, politically.

On the other hand, if one perceives the United Kingdom as an *ancien régime* with no particular title to survival or endless allegiance, then the breakaway movements may appear in a different light. The phrase 'We must preserve the unity of the United Kingdom' is currently intoned like a litany by most leaders of British public life. Its magic properties are obviously derived from the cults of Constitution and Sovereignty. Merely to refuse this sacrament allows the observer to begin, at least, to acknowledge some positive side in the cause of the smaller nations. While of course the view – put forward in this book – that the all-British régime is an increasingly contradictory and hopeless anachronism entails another shift in judgement. Countries struggling to free themselves from a sinking paddle-wheel state have, on the face of it, much justification for their stance. As the ancient device goes farther down, this justification will increase, in their own eyes and those of the outside world. If at any point the collapsing metropolis attempts to quell their rise by force or constitutional chicanery, it will become absolute.

The logic of the anti-nationalists is most often obfuscated by another idea, which one might describe as the concept of the viable larger unit. New small-nationality movements tend in this somewhat abstract light to be condemned for opting out of an already achieved and workable progress on some larger scale: lapses into pettiness, self-condemned by a broader common sense. The notion surfaces to some degree in the commonplaces of the devolution debate: 'You could never manage on your own'; 'Surely we're better all together, in one big unit?'; 'It's just putting the clock back'; 'It's irrelevant to people's real problems' – and so on. From a metropolitan angle of vision, these bluff platitudes carry a lot of conviction. Any opponent of them seems to define himself as some kind of dark fanatic.

The mistake in this attitude does not lie in its assertion that bigger units of social organization are good, or necessary, or inevitable. A tendency towards larger-scale organization and international integration has indeed accompanied the growth of nationalism and the proliferation of new national states, throughout modern times. This is certain to go on. Scarcely anyone believes that this dialectic will cease, or that the historical clock can be 'put back' in this sense. Certainly very few of Europe's new nationalists think anything of the kind.

The crucial point is the quite characteristic elision in the metropolitan world-view. What it invariably does is to identify the existing larger state-form with this historical necessity. Yet what neo-nationalism challenges is not the general necessity as such, but the spurious identification hung on to it. In their own day, the Napoleonic Empire, the Hapsburg Empire, Tsardom, Hitler's New Europe and the old British Empire were 'justified' by precisely similar arguments; and in certain of these cases the 'internationalist' defence was put forward by manifestly sincere, progressive thinkers – sometimes by socialists, and marxists. It requires little counter-argument, surely, to point out that not all 'larger units' are equivalent, or equally 'viable', or represent progress. Thus – to make the roughest classification – one finds on the one hand workable federations or confederations of states, or communities, associations like the Nordic Union, the Andean Pact, the European Community, or the United Nations Organization; on the other, an assortment of multi-national units imposed by heredity or conquest, most of which mercifully vanished in one or other of the World Wars and the remainder during the anti-colonial movement after 1946.

To which category does the existing Great-British state belong? Clearly, defenders of the British union locate it unthinkingly in the former camp, as a modern, reasonable sort of wider integration. In fact, an in-depth historical analysis shows that, while not directly comparable to the most notorious relics of the 20th century, like the Hapsburg, Tsarist or Prussian-German states, *it retains something in common with them*. This derives from the features we have examined. Although not of course an absolutist state, the Anglo-British system remains a product of the general transition from absolutism to modern constitutionalism: it led the way out of the former, but never genuinely arrived at the latter. Farthermore, the peculiar hybrid nature impressed by this unique experience was confirmed by its later imperialist success. Possibly only the most successful and long-lived of modern empires *could* have preserved such an anomaly, and kept it in working order until the 1970s. Hence, both in its origination and in its surprising longevity, the British state belongs to the first category rather than the second. It is a basically indefensible and unadaptable relic, not a modern state-form. In its prolonged, empirical survival it has of course gathered many of the latter's aspects and appearances; but this must be distinguished from authentic transmutation, via a second political revolution. No less evidently and profoundly, the modern history of the British state is about the absence of such a change: although in one sense a question of comparative structural analysis, this recessive character is also written openly upon the institutions, rituals and self-advertisement of the system, in ideological terms.

If this is the case, then what is the situation of the British state in the (admittedly) necessary world of new, wider international units and cooperation? Far from belonging there as of right, the existing United Kingdom of Great Britain and Northern Ireland *is not even a possible candidate* in the field. It is not important here to speculate upon how long the International Monetary Fund and the other capitalist states will go on providing for the U.K.'s old age. But it is certainly significant that, in this company, the only useful kind of speculation has assumed a geriatric odour: a motorized wheel-chair and a decent funeral seem to have become the actual horizons of the 1980s, without design or conscious consent.

Other new-nationalist movements have other dilemmas to deal with, of a broadly analogous kind. It is interesting – but too much of a digression at this point – to ask what kinds of reproach they address to (e.g.) the Vth. French Republic, the states of Spain and Italy, or the Federal Government of Canada. I have argued in one of the following chapters (see Chapter Three) that over-easy generalization has dogged the theory of neo-nationalism, and erected an over-abstract defence against metropolitan sermons on Progress and Commonsense. There are undoubtedly different kinds of state failure or inadaptation at work, different grudges and demands, and (presumably) quite different solutions in order. It should be the task of independence movements in these various countries to work out an analogous critique of the dominant state. It may be that these critiques have a common element to them, though I believe that it is not yet clear what this is. Perhaps (to quote the most frequent suggestion) the post-World War II development of the capitalist economy, with its U.S.-centred multinationals and internationalization of the forces of production, has to some extent infirmed and de-legitimized all the older sovereign states – diminishing 'independence' everywhere, therefore, but by the same token making it more plausible to demand this status, even for regions and peoples that would never previously have thought of undertaking the whole armament of nation-state existence.

But even if this is so, such very general economic causes will work to discover widely differing problems and dilemmas. And none of these is likely to resemble the British case very significantly: here, neo-capitalist uneven development has finally exposed the most genuinely anachronistic state of the economically-developed world to the light, an archaic palimpsest covering the entire period from Newton's theories to the thermonuclear bomb, and conserved (above all) by empire and successful warfare. Acceptance of *this* entity as the 'viable larger unit' of British-Isles development strains credulity to the uttermost. Like other social fossils before it, it struggles to survive by utilizing the counter-law of combined development, and importing remedies: the 'white hot' technological revolution, French planning and 'technocracy', non-élitist higher education (as in the Polytechnics), even West German workers' representation (as in the proposals of the Bullock Commission). In reality, that law works the other way, and merely generates grotesque failures (as in the British 1960s) or partial successes which underscore the system's futility, and make plainer the need for a radical change.

As we have seen, doom has been cried too often about the U.K., too stridently and (above all) in too foreshortened a fashion. None the less, doom of a sort is genuinely inscribed in this historical pattern. Sufficiently – at any rate – to wholly discredit the easy metropolitan assumption that it, or something like it, should be defended against nationalist wreckers. Viable larger units of social organization ought to be defended against 'narrow nationalism', or an ethnic parochialism indulged in for its own sake. But defence is only possible when they actually *are* 'viable': which really means, when they are the most modern, democratic, and decentralizable form of organization that current development permits – when, therefore, they are capable of progressive accommodation to the tensions of uneven development, and of contributing positively to new international relations and the foundation of socialist society.

The point is of course underlined farther by consideration of the present character of the British independence movements. Preachers of U.K. unity at all costs imagine latent fascisms, and seize on every scrap of patriotic or anti-British utterance as evidence of this. In reality, the Welsh national party is without doubt the least parochial or 'narrow nationalist' mass movement in British politics. Strongly influenced in earlier times by a sentimental, mediaevalist universalism (see Chapter Four) it is if anything rather exaggeratedly attached to European examples and ideas, and has consistently perceived 'nationalism' as a largely cultural escape-route from the peculiar isolation of Wales. The Scottish National Party has a very different historical basis. But its recent successful development has carried it too towards a far more catholic and outward-looking position. It advances the concept of an Association of British States as the successor to the United Kingdom, to preserve what is indeed functional or 'viable' in the union: negotiated agreements among the constituent parts would separate this out from the reactionary and fetishized London slogan of 'essential unity'. For its part the more recently-founded Scottish Labour Party has from the outset linked the cause of self-government to that of membership of the

European Community – seeing in the latter, obviously, a preferable wider unit of organization from a point of view at once nationalist and socialist.

More generally, the question of the Common Market emphasizes still more cruelly the absurdities in any unreflecting defence of the U.K. *ancien régime*. It is only a year or so since the British state at last reconciled itself to membership of that particular larger unit. And the debate surrounding the event demonstrated that 'nationalism' in the familiar disparaging sense is by no means confined to the smaller nations. 'Narrowness' has nothing whatever to do with size. There is a narrow U.S., Soviet and Chinese nationalism, as well as a Welsh or Scottish one. The difference tends to be that the greater nations remain grandly unaware of their narrowness, because their size, their culture, or their imagined centrality makes them identify with Humanity or Progress *tout court*. Great-British chauvinism belongs to this camp. But it does so – of course – with diminishing reason and increasing delusion. The whole bias of the British imperialist state has led the English people to feel themselves as something naturally bigger, more open and more important than just another nation-state. In reality, this museum-piece has dragged them from empire to something less than a modern nation-state, without letting them become one; the missionary expansiveness has turned into the narrowest, most dim-witted of nationalisms. This is what was deployed (especially by the Labour Party and other sectors of the left) in the futile attempt to 'keep Britain independent' between 1971 and 1975. The vulgar hysteria and patriotic kitsch of *that* 'independence movement' easily eclipsed anything tried in Scotland or Wales.

Metropolitans have often accused those who (like myself) both supported entry to the European Community *and* self-government for smaller nations. There is no contradiction in this. None, that is, unless one thinks that the Community and the old British state are equivalently healthy and acceptable 'larger units' – so that it must be illogical to accept the one and reject the other. In fact there is no common measure between them. In one of the essays below the reader will find a rather pessimistic analysis of the EEC's development (see Chapter Eight). But whatever the shortcomings and contradictions of the new Europe, it is still a modern, voluntary, genuinely multi-national organization, capable of great farther progress and of playing a positive role in a new world order. By contrast, the United Kingdom long ago ceased to be a multi-national entity in any ennobling or forward-looking sense: the nerve of its larger unity passed away with empire, and should not be mourned or resuscitated for that reason. The problem of preserving positive elements left by that union – civil and personal closeness, individual liberties, forms of civilized association – is a genuine one, of which nationalists are conscious.

As things stand, the formula most likely to damage these relations permanently is exactly that which the paladins of U.K. unity at all costs have chosen. This is because another field of forces altogether lies behind their cause, concealed from them by the peculiar missionary nostalgia and phoney *grandeur* of Britishism. Most of this book is about the British periphery, or about the theoretical context of nationalism; all too little of it is on England, the heartland. Yet this is certainly where the longer-term political direction of the British Isles will be settled. The paralytic decline of the old state has given a temporary ascendancy to Scotland and other peripheric problems. Beyond this moment, it is bound to be the post-imperial crisis of the English people itself which takes over – the crisis so long delayed by the combination of inner resilience and outward fortune we have discussed.

However, this social crisis is rendered enigmatic by the cryptic nature of English nationalism. A peculiar repression and truncation of Englishness was inseparable from the structure of British imperialism, and I argue below (see Chapter Six, pp. 274–279) that this is one explanation of the salience of racism in recent English politics. The growth of a far right axed on questions of race and immigration is in fact a comment on the absence of a normal nationalist sentiment, rather than an expression of nationalism: this Mr Hyde represents a congruent riposte to the specific character of the Dr Jekyll state outlined above – to the tradition of gentlemanly authority and liberal compromise. It is less surprising than one would think at first sight that such an antithetical phenomenon should have acquired a degree of leverage over the state power (in the 1960s), and a remarkable prominence in terms of public debate and intellectual apprehension.

The longer the *ancien régime* endures, the more defined and worrying this trend is likely to become. On the analysis presented here, it corresponds to an underlying reality – not mere aberration, or a transient mood of intolerance. The fall of the old system must force a kind of national re-definition upon all the British peoples. This process is most important, but also most difficult, for the English metropolis where all the main roots of the British state are located. There, the very strength of those bases means that it is far harder for system-directed resentment and loss of allegiance to find tolerable expression: the growing exacerbation is forced into an exaggerated antithesis to the state as such. Among the younger intelligentsia this has assumed the progressive shape of marxism (albeit sectarian marxism); but among the masses – separated from the intellectuals by the specific abyss of English class – it has too often taken the form of racist populism. As a matter of fact, the particular breadth and vaguery of residual all-British consciousness decays more readily into racialism than into a defined, territorially restricted nationalism. Once divorced from the powerful liberalism-from-above that previously regulated it, it displays obvious affinities with the old fantasies of the white man's blood and genetic aptitude for civilization.

Hence, it is not mere alarmism to suggest that the persistence of the British régime fosters the most regressive possible side of an eventual English nationalism. Those who defend it *à l'outrance* against the supposed petty patriotism of Scotland and Wales do so in honour of its liberalism and past achievements, hoping these can somehow be saved and perpetuated; they ignore the limitations and central defects tied structurally to these traits, defects which are becoming disastrous as the external situation of the state deteriorates. The latter process is irrevocable. So is the emergence of a new English national awareness, as drastic reform (or even political revolution) is forced by the decline. The more it is delayed, the more certain this awareness is to be inflected to the right, and captured by the forces feeding off the wounds and failures of decline.

There exists in modern history no example of a national state afflicted with this kind of decline and traumatic loss of power and prestige which did *not*, sooner or later, undergo a strong reaction against it.[44] In this sense, England has not yet undergone its own

[44] The obvious exceptions in post-World War II terms are Germany and Italy (although previously they were leading exemplifications of the rule). On the other hand, it can be maintained that in these cases the reverses were so absolute, and the externally-imposed constitutions so successful, that (above all in Germany) there was total interruption of the continuity which such national reactions depend upon. In a more than rhetorical sense, 'new nations' intervened in both cases.

version of Gaullism: the prophet of this kind of conservative-nationalist resurgence, Powell, has been so far rendered impotent by the cohesion of the régime, which gave insufficient purchase for such 'outside' opposition to the system as such. Will this go on being true, as Britain lurches still farther downwards on the road of relative under-development? Nothing is pre-determined as regards the political nature of the break, and one may of course argue that it could be radical or left-nationalist in outlook, rather than re-actionary. But it is hard to overlook the fact that the very conditions of degeneration and all-British impotence are themselves 'determining' events in one way rather than the other. Another brief era of ephemeral 'recovery', another plateau of 'stabilization' on the secular path of British decline, and these forces may well become even stronger.

There is a final interesting implication attached to this prospect. The sharpest 'internationalist' opponents of fringe nationalism in the current debate – like Eric Heffer in England, Leo Abse and Neil Kinnock in Wales, or Norman and Janey Buchan in Scotland – perceive a Britain 'Balkanized' into ethnic struggle and mutual hatreds by the agency of movements like the SNP or Plaid Cymru. There is an element of justified alarm in their vision, which should be taken seriously. But their idea of the machinery by which such conditions could come about is revealingly mistaken. As far as England is concerned, all they see is a rather justifiable 'backlash' against peripheral extremism: in reality, that 'backlash' is the frustrated political potency of the English people, and the dominant force in the British Isles – a force which did not wait on the rise of separatism to take on retrograde and alarming forms. One must distinguish between the movements precipitating the break-up at this moment (which are led by the nationalists) and the deeper causes at work, which have little to do with Scotland and Wales, and everything to do with the long-term, irreversible degeneration of the Anglo-British state. It is these, and these alone, which could in the long run provoke the kind of generalized feuding and resentment such critics fear.

It is of course perfectly true that the minor nationalities of Britain might be forced into a wave of regressive 'narrow nationalism'. This possibility is inseparable from any form of nationalism (it is argued below in Chapter Nine that the causes of the connection lie in the very nature of the uneven-development dilemma underlying nationalism). And this is the grain of truth in the internationalists' alarm. Yet their misconception of the state and their unwillingness to focus upon the specifics of the English situation bring a false perspective to that alarm. Regression is never far away, in the ambiguous reality of any nationalist movement. But a definite triggering mechamism is required, none the less, to compel it into that pattern – to make the recessive trends finally outweigh or cancel its liberating, progressive potential. These critics ignore what that mechanism is virtually certain to be, in British conditions. By ignoring it, they encourage its development. In their panicky defence of the old state and Westminster's sovereignty, they help preserve those very things which are the root-cause of their nightmare: the hopelessly decaying institutions of a lost imperialist state.

The Marxist Argument

The new debate about nationalism in the British Isles recalls some old ones. The most important of these is the mainly pre-1914 argument among marxists, which resulted in the most influential single theory of political nationalism and indirectly determined nationality policies over a large part of today's world.[45] To a great extent that dispute still shapes the marxist left's views of nationalism.

Although it was complicated, the significant opposition most relevant to the new case lay between the positions of Rosa Luxemburg and those of Lenin. In this sector of the left, the period of the IInd International was dominated by expectations of imminent social revolution. The general conviction was that upheaval would come fairly soon, and in the most advanced capitalist countries. When it arrived, it would rapidly become international in character: although born in one nation, its example would be irresistible elsewhere, and in this diffusion the international solidarity of the proletariat would become a proven reality. Hence, the basic task of revolutionary movements lay in preparing the way for this process.

But this formula left one major uncertainty. The era that cul-

[45] J. Stalin, 'Marxism and the National Question', in *Works*, vol. 2, 1907–13, Moscow 1953. There is unfortunately no critical edition of this very important text.

minated in 1914 was not only marked by developing class struggle
and the growth of organized socialism; it was equally one of matur-
ing national struggles, both in Europe and outside it. Inside Europe
the remaining multi-national states like Austria-Hungary and
Tsarist Russia experienced growing strains from their dissident
nationalities, and the Ottoman Empire came near its end. In the
other continents, alert observers perceived the beginnings of a
general, predominantly nationalist revolution against the newer
European imperialisms. Nearly all these movements of national
liberation took place in relatively backward areas (though with notable exceptions like Bohemia and Catalonia).

How were these two sorts of revolt related to one another? This
was the key problem. On one hand thinkers like Rosa Luxemburg
took the view that nationalist struggles ought to be allotted a distinctly secondary place. This was the case above all where the two
threatened in any way to come into conflict with one another.
Where this did not happen (straightforward anti-colonialist wars
were the obvious example) there was no dilemma, and it could be
conceded that nationalism had still a positive function. But wherever
(as in her native Poland) it seemed that workers or intellectuals
might have to make a choice between a national struggle and a class
struggle, the former should *never* be given priority. Thus, given the
situation of the Poles, 'integrated' into the Tsarist domain but
occupying a sensitive buffer position vis-à-vis Germany (perceived
at that time by most marxists as a centre of the coming revolution),
it was their duty to renounce 'narrowly nationalist' aspirations. In
similar European situations, the national struggle was a distraction,
if not a positively hostile barrier, to what really mattered: the imminent break-through of the class-struggle. It mattered relatively
little just where the latter happened. Its non-national values and
impetus would quickly render the whole realm of nationalist
preoccupations anachronistic in any case.[46]

---

[46] The best introduction to Luxemburg's views is Appendix 2, 'The National
Question', of Peter Nettl's *Rosa Luxemburg*, vol. 2, 1966. Her main assumption
was that '. . . national and Socialist aspirations were incompatible and that a
commitment to national self-determination by Socialist parties must subordinate those parties to bourgeois nationalism instead of opposing one to the
other. A programme of national self-determination thus became the first of
Rosa Luxemburg's many indices of an opportunism which tied Socialism to the
chariot of the class enemy . . .' (p. 845). Unfortunately the text Nettl refers to as

Luxemburgist anti-nationalism was criticized and qualified by Lenin, in a series of writings on the issue.[47] Even in Europe, even much closer to the scene of metropolitan revolution, he argued that the nationalist revolts had a more positive meaning. The social forces and passions they harnessed were too great to be genuinely 'renounced'; and in any case they worked to unseat the old dynasties, and so foster conditions generally favourable to social revolution. The break-up of these old states was a necessary (though admittedly far from a sufficient) condition of the kind of change marxists were working towards. In this pragmatic spirit the nationalism of liberation struggles ought to be encouraged, at least up to the moment of their seizure of state power. After that, it would of course become the task of the revolutionaries to disassociate themselves from the nationalists: national liberation would then turn into 'bourgeois nationalism', and a force hostile to the broader revolutionary cause.

Both these stances were infirmed by what actually happened after 1914. The decisive non-event was the 'advanced' social revolution, which had been the common assumption of the whole argument. Revolutionary failure rendered Luxemburg's position an abstract one: defiant moral grandeur, in perpetual rebuke of a fallen world. There had been no room for the ambiguous and yet central phenomenon of nationalism in her heroic world-view. Nothing existed between socialism and barbarism; and the latter appeared to have won, as the European working classes drowned in their various 'anachronisms'.

Leninism was less starkly refuted by the evidence of events. However, their development implied that his more pragmatic attitude to the problem became permanent. It was no longer a provisional, tactical formulation holding good only until revolution came. There was nothing but pragmatism for generations: the

---

her principal statement, *Przegląd Socjaldemokratyczny*, August 1908, No. 6, 'The question of nationality and autonomy', has not yet been translated from Polish to English.

[47] Collected together in, e.g. *National Liberation, Socialism and Imperialism: selected writings*, New York, 1968. Most of Lenin's articles and speeches on the question can be found in vols. 20, 21 and 22 of the *Collected Works* (December 1913–July 1916). I am grateful to Yuri Boshyk for letting me see his unpublished paper 'Lenin and the National Question in Russia: 1913 to February 1917', part of his work on the history of Ukrainian nationalism.

provisional became ever-lasting, as capitalism continued to endure and develop, and uneven development and nationalism prospered along with it. The Central and East European national movements attained their goals, but the result was a generation of mainly authoritarian régimes linked to a resurgence of conservatism, or fascism, in Western Europe. The anti-colonial struggles also won, but over a far longer period of time than was imagined. Their political consequences were equally ambiguous: unaccompanied by revolution in the metropolis, such newly independent nations were formed as the 'under-developed' sector of a still capitalist world – exposed, therefore, to forms of exploitation and to developmental dilemmas which long outlived uniformed imperialism. In one of the essays below national liberation and statehood is depicted as a doorway, like the gate over which the Roman god Janus gazed into both past and future. In reality, this threshold of modernity has been a prolonged, dark passage for most of the world, and has occupied most of the 20th century.

Already made problematic by the post-1914 course of history, Lenin's pragmatism was then fossilized by post-1917 history. He himself went on wrestling with the question until his death. With splendid, agonized clarity he had perceived that it was far from any satisfactory resolution even within the territory won by the revolution, and that the latter could easily fall victim to a renascent Great-Russian nationalism.[48] Locked in one under-developed area dominated by one nationality, the revolution could not help itself becoming joined to a 'narrow nationalism'. In the past, other revolutionary nations had harnessed universalizing, missionary ideologies to their national interests: England had done so with Protestantism, and France with the Enlightenment. Now the Russians employed Marxism in the same way, as a legitimizing creed of state. And as part of this process the Leninist view of the national question was hypostatized, and treated as a largely ritual formula for consecrating judgements convenient to Moscow.

Unfortunately, it was a position that lent itself in some ways to this exploitation. Its virtue had lain in its 'realism', in its cautious recognition that nationalism was a double-faced phenomenon central to revolutionary strategy. In the actual dynamics of its era,

[48] For the part played by national questions in Lenin's last days, see especially chapters 4 and 5 of Moshe Lewin's *Lenin's Last Struggle*, 1969.

before the 1914–18 deluge, this was doubly positive: as practical tactics, and as the basis for a theoretical development of marxist ideas on nationalism. But the post-1918 deformations of communism emptied it of all real content, on both counts. All that remained was a double-faced position, the ambiguity of the formulae without their inquiring, restless tension: polemic mummified into priestly cant.

None the less, it is not impossible to separate out the original impulse from the accretions of mechanical dogma. In my view an amended version of Lenin's old conception is the only satisfactory position that marxists can adopt towards the problem of neonationalism, in the British Isles or elsewhere. Neither Austromarxism nor Luxemburgism offer this possibility.[49]

What are the emendations required by this exercise? They are of two kinds, both essential to any intelligible re-employment of these philosophies of sixty years ago. The first concerns the nature of those states and multi-national societies (including the Soviet Union) where revived nationalism is, or is likely to become, a key issue. The second concerns the general theoretical level – that is, marxist concepts of nationalism's place in historical development, the theoretical reformulation towards which Lenin's ideas pointed, but which never took place. Advance on these fronts of course precludes the sort of ghostly archaeology and hushed citation of texts normally associated with Leninism.

The old argument took place in a context of indubitably archaic state forms: the surviving absolutisms of Central and Eastern Europe. Thus, it could be acknowledged without too great difficulty (as Lenin did) that merely nationalist revolt against these entities

[49] The Austro-marxist theory, crucial to the whole pre-1914 debate, conceived of a solution to the question by distinguishing between autonomy in 'cultural' areas (language, education, etc.) and interdependence in the field of economic relations and external affairs. A useful collection of the Austro-Marxist material (largely untranslated) can be found in G. Haupt, M. Löwy, C. Weill, *Les marxistes et la question nationale 1848–1914*, Paris, 1974: see 'Anthologie', sections IV, V, VI, on the Brünn Programme, Renner and Bauer. The basic criticism made of their position was always that it was simply unrealistic to posit such a distinction: 'cultural' matters of the sort dear to nationalists are in fact intertwined with economic issues, and no effective 'autonomy' can be confined to the former area alone (except in the ideal, somewhat god-like state conditions which the traditions of the Hapsburg Empire encouraged social-democrats to believe in).

had a strongly positive side to it. As we saw, this acknowledgement rested upon a second assumption. There was another category of 'modern' capitalist states, against whom only socialist revolution was justifiable, or indeed conceivable. They were the crux of the future revolutionary process, and as such played a part in the justification of pre-socialist revolution elsewhere.

These categories have ceased to apply in contemporary terms. The world of dynastic empires disappeared in war and revolution; while the second category of relatively 'modern' (or at least non-feudal) capitalist and non-capitalist states has expanded, altered, and ramified in a way that makes simplified overall judgement about it impossible. The failure of the social revolution ensured this. It meant that capitalist state-forms would go on proliferating and evolving internally; and also that socialism, confined to relative backwardness and isolation, would develop its own highly ambiguous forms of state-life in a still nationalist universe. Nothing of this was foreseeable in 1913. It follows that any attempt to recuperate the sense of the political judgements made then can only be in a renewed and much more complex perspective – one that admits, above all, the receding horizon of the socialist revolution and the permanent difference which this has made. It is still possible to do this. There is still a distinction to be made on the left between nationalist and socialist revolutions, and an inter-relationship and order of priorities to be recognized – but how much more nuanced and analytically demanding the judgement has now become!

For example, is the French state of the Vth Republic still identifiable with those Jacobin 'colours of France' which have impassioned one generation after another of radicals, ever since the Great Revolution? Did the events of May 1968 demonstrate this continuity – or the very contrary, a situation in which the best traditions of *la Grande Nation* had succumbed to an ineradicably conservative, centralized machine capable only of great-nation posturing and oppression? One's view of the significance of Breton or Occitan nationalism, of the place of the French Basques or the Alsatians, is partly dependent on this judgement. Is the United States of President Nixon and the Vietnamese war still in essence the democratic state of President Lincoln, which Marx defended against the secessionist nationalism of the Confederacy? Can federal Canada still be upheld, ultimately, against the claims of Québecois nationalism? In Yugoslavia a revolutionary socialist state has defended the most original multi-national régime in the world for a quarter of a century – yet there are still unsolved, and apparently growing, difficulties which cannot be merely dismissed as relics or temporary relapses. In the Soviet Union the same problem is posed much more acutely. Is the new national unrest and agitation against a 'socialist state' explicable and justifiable in the same terms as under the Romanovs or the Hapsburgs?

The list is endless. As endless (one is almost tempted to say) as the reality of the world where the metropolitan revolution is so delayed. The point of presenting it here is not to make principled judgements impossible. It is only to suggest that they are more difficult, more relative, and finer than the prevailing marxist or *marxisant* slogans allow. It is the element of caution and relativity in Lenin's old position that ought to have been developed, as revolution receded or went wrong; instead, it was the element of dogmatism which triumphed, a sectarian icon extracted from its historical context.

Understanding of the state – both the particular state and the inter-state order – is one prerequisite. But this factor of autonomous political judgement implies the second emendation I mentioned above. The point here is (as the case of Great Britain demonstrates most graphically) that the analysis of the state's meaning and function itself depends upon an accompanying view of the inter-state order. States are formed by that order, not only (or even primarily) by an inner dynamic of classes, or a 'national economy' perceived as a separate entity. Consequently, one's general conception of modern historical development is called into play: the overall nature of capitalism's uneven development, which alone can provide an explanation of contemporary state-formations and so of the problematic of secession or resurgent nationality. This means that the very essence of the marxist world-view is called into play. But of course, the entire aim of dogmatism is to avoid that: it is to cultivate the pretence that the world where the revolution has not gone according to plan is the same as . . . the original, imagined, heroic world where it *will* go by the plan, because it must.

In short, these 'emendations' are actually demands for the growth of marxist thought. The first in an area where it has proved congenitally weak: the analysis of political structures and the state, above all the bourgeois-democratic state. This weakness underlies, and partly accounts for, marxism's more notorious inability to come to terms with modern nationalism. The second demands revision in an area where marxism is basically strong, the general framework of historical development – but where, nevertheless, orthodoxy largely paralyzed creative revision until the great growth in development studies of recent years.

As to the British case, I suggest that analysis shows the definitively moribund character of this particular state, the reasons for its longevity and the (closely affiliated) causes of the difficulty of social or political revolution within its heartland. This is simply one chapter in the history of the missing metropolitan revolution. It happens to be about an especially anomalous state-history, and may have small bearing on the other chapters due on other countries. But as far as it goes, it seems to demonstrate the case for the separation of the smaller countries. In relation to *this* specific 'metropolis' (or ex-metropolis), and as long as it endures on its old constitutional tracks, they have good reason to want out, and good cause for claiming that their exit is a progressive action – a step forward not only for their own peoples, but for England and the wider state-order as well.

Lenin argued that nationalist upheavals could contribute to socialist revolution where it counted, in the great centres. With appropriate modifications, one can surely make roughly the same case here. The fact is that neo-nationalism *has* become the grave-digger of the old state in Britain, and as such the principal factor making for a political revolution of some sort – in England as well as the small countries. Yet, because this process assumes an un-expected form, many on the metropolitan left solemnly write it down as betrayal of the revolution. Forces capable of unhinging the state finally appear, out of the endless-seeming mists of British-Constitutionalism; not to be greeted as harbingers of a new time, however. Instead, they are told to mind their own business.

I referred previously to those of the socialist left who still believe in the Constitution, and their consternation is natural enough. But the marxist left which totally spurns Westminster and (on paper at least) wants nothing more than its overthrow, also criticizes the separatists. Their reason is that proletarian socialism is supposed to be the grave-digger, and no one else will do. So they tell the nationalists to drop their shovels and put up with the pathetic limits of 'devolution': the revolution will solve their problems along with the others. Meanwhile they should wait until the time is ripe – i.e. the time for socialism – taking a firm grip on their petty-bourgeois, backward-looking impulses. The essential unity of the U.K. must be maintained till the working classes of all Britain are ready.

The fact is that the new nationalisms of the British Isles represent a detour on the way to revolution, and one which is now generally familiar in terms of 20th century history. It is 'unexpected' only in terms of the rigid anticipation of an imminent social revolution about to break through and lead the way. The crux of Lenin's view was that nationalism could constitute a detour in some degree valid – contributing to the political conditions and general climate favourable to the break-through, undermining conservatism and the inertia of old régimes. Why should this not be true in the British case also? If the social revolution is on the agenda of the heartland at all, then it will be enormously advanced by the disintegration of the state. It cannot fail to be, as the old party-system becomes unworkable through the detachment of Scotland and Wales, as the Constitution itself fails and has to be reformed more or less radically, in circumstances of political flux and innovation not known since the earlier 19th century.

If it is not on the metropolitan agenda, then the problem is different. Different, but scarcely unfamiliar: as we saw, the dominant truth in any reconsideration of the older marxist conceptions is the non-arrival of the metropolitan revolution – whether this be due to 'delay' or a deeper impossibility, whether it implies more patience or a drastic critique of the world-view itself. We have looked at some of the causes of slow change and blocked reform in the U.K. state. But at a certain point clearly this analysis leads into the larger scene: notwithstanding all its many 'peculiarities', it is hardly surprising that Britain has not yet done what nobody has done anywhere in the industrialized world, conducted a successful social revolution.

Should *this* still be the case, then neo-nationalism needs no farther justification at all. Escape from the final stages of a shipwreck is its own justification. If a progressive 'second revolution' still does not take place in England, then a conservative counterrevolution will; and in that case the movements towards Scottish, Welsh, and even Ulster independence will acquire added progressive impetus and lustre, as relatively left-wing causes saving themselves from central reaction. One can readily imagine the sudden sectarian rediscovery of Celtic political virtues under those conditions.

At the moment, the prevailing nostrum is inevitable general approval of 'the right of national self-determination' (not even the Scots or Welsh can be exempted from this, although it has been argued the Ulstermen are – see Chapter Five below), combined with Lenin's supposedly sage qualification that 'we do not in all cases advocate the exercise of that right'.[50] Advocacy depends upon the influence which the nationalism in question is imagined to exert upon the general course of revolutionary politics. As far as the above analysis goes, it will be obvious how that influence is estimated. Obvious, too, the nature of the resulting dilemma. Should there be the possibility of a radical, left-directed break-through at the centre, in which the English people finally shakes off the old hierarchical burden of the British state-system, then the nationalist upheavals will assist them – even though the path should be a tormented one, with a higher degree of intra-British political antagonism and misunderstanding. And in that eventuality, the question would then arise of building up a new, fairer, more federal British order: not the dingy, fearful compromise of 'devolution' but a modern, European multi-national state. Should this possibility not exist, then what the small British (and other) nationalities are facing is another prolonged era of capitalist uneven development, stretching into the next century. It is certain that at some point in this period the British régime will finally founder, and very likely that this will be accompanied by a new, indigenous variety of conservative reaction. Who, in that case, can deny them effective self-determination, not as a moral piety but as an urgently necessary, practical step?

---

[50] The most often-quoted passage in this connection occurs in 'The Right of Nations to Self-determination', Feb.–May 1914 (*Coll. Works*, vol. 20): 'To accuse those who support freedom of self-determination, i.e. freedom to secede, of encouraging separatism, is as foolish and hypocritical as accusing those who advocate freedom of divorce of encouraging the destruction of family ties . . .' (p. 422). Whether one advocates divorce or not in any concrete case depends upon one's judgement of the 'family ties' already existing, and especially of the *paterfamilias*. Should the case be hopeless, and the foreseeable prospect of amelioration dim, then it is correct to move on from affirmation of the 'right to self-determination' to encouragement of actual separation. In that movement (in Nettl's words) the 'autonomous role of the proletariat' implies 'alliances with all elements who historically have to move forward (in a revolutionary sense) before they move back' (op. cit., vol. 2, p. 851).

2. Scotland and Europe

This seems an appropriate moment to reconsider the problem of Scottish nationalism. With its November 1973 electoral victory in the Govan Constituency the Scottish National Party recovered from its setbacks in the 1970 general election. At the same time the Kilbrandon Commission supplied a stimulus to regional self-government in the United Kingdom, by recommending the establishment of Scottish and Welsh parliaments. Both the tenor and the reception of these recommendations indicate, significantly, that nothing will come of them unless they are strongly and vociferously supported in Scotland and Wales. The English majority will not enact such reforms unless pushed. But then, why should it do so? In Ireland we are at the same time witnessing a wholesale alteration of the constitutional status of Ulster. But it is not only the United Kingdom's multi-national state which is in motion. In continental Europe too important movements have arisen in a similar direction. In a recent study of the present condition of the nation-state, Nicos Poulantzas wrote that we are seeing 'ruptures in the national unity underlying existing national states, rather than the emergence of a new State over and above them: that is, the very important contemporary phenomenon of regionalism, as expressed particularly in the resurgence of nationalities, showing how the internationalization of capital leads rather to a fragmentation of the state as historically constituted than to a supra-national State . . .'[1] More recently, *Les Temps Modernes* has devoted a special issue to an extensive survey of national minorities in France, perhaps the most strongly unified of the 'historically constituted' European

---

[1] 'L'Internationalisation des rapports capitalistes et l'état-nation', *Les Temps Modernes*, no. 319, February 1973, pp. 1492–3.

nations at the state level.[2] In Italy, where regional self-government has become a question of practical politics, intellectual concern with the topic is also increasing. Perhaps the most valuable overview of repressed and resurgent nationalities in western Europe is provided by Sergio Salvi's *Le nazioni proibite: Guida a dieci colonie interne dell'Europa occidentale*.[3] Hence, it is indispensable to try and view Scottish or Welsh developments in a European perspective. This is the aim of the present essay. I would like to look at certain aspects of Scotland's nationalism and modern history in a wider, more comparative, and more objective way than has usually been done in the past.

The Theory of Nationalism

What do the terms 'objective' and 'comparative' mean here? 'Real understanding of one's own national history begins only where we can place it within the general historical process, where we dare to confront it with European development as a whole,' writes Miroslav Hroch in his own invaluable comparative study of the genesis of nationalism in seven smaller European lands.[4] More generally still, it should be remarked that the history of theorizing about nationalism displays two dramatic faults. One is a tendency to treat the subject in a one-nation or one-state frame of reference: so that each nationalism has to be understood, in effect, mainly with reference to 'its own' ethnic, economic, or other basis – rather than by comparison with the 'general historical process'. The second (and obviously related) tendency is to take nationalist ideology far too literally and seriously. What nationalists say about themselves and their movements must, of course, be given due weight. But it is fatal to treat such self-consciousness other than extremely cautiously. The subjectivity of nationalism must itself be approached with the utmost effort of objectivity. It should be treated as a psychoanalyst does the outpourings of a patient. Where – as is not infrequently the case with nationalism – the patient is a roaring drunk into the bargain, even greater patience is called for.

[2] *Les Temps Modernes*, nos. 324–6, August–September 1973.
[3] Vallecchi, Florence 1973.
[4] Miroslav Hroch, *Die Vorkämpfer der nationalen Bewegung bei den kleinen Völkern Europas*, Prague 1968, a study of the formation and early stage of nationalism in Bohemia, Slovakia, Norway, Finland, Estonia, Lithuania and Flanders.

In short, the theory of nationalism has been inordinately influenced by nationalism itself. This is scarcely surprising. Nationalism is amongst other things a name for the general condition of the
modern body politic, more like the climate of political and social
thought than just another doctrine. It is correspondingly difficult to
avoid being unconsciously influenced by it.[5]

So we must try and avoid the empiricism of the nation-by-nation
approach, and the subjectivism involved in taking nationalist
rhetoric at its face-value. What exactly should we compare to what,
in circumventing such influences? Broadly speaking, what merits
consideration here is, on the one hand, the characteristic general
evolution of European nationalism, between say 1800 and the major
nationalist settlement of 1918–22; and on the other, whatever ideas
and movement in modern Scottish history can be held to correspond
to that general development. I am aware of course that the general
category begs a number of questions. Nationalism did not come to a
stop in Europe in 1922 after the Versailles agreements. Everyone
knows that nationalism is still extremely alive, if not exactly in good
health, everywhere in present-day Europe. But that is not the point.
It remains true nonetheless that by the time of the post-World
War I settlement European nationalism had gone through the
main arc of its historical development, over a century and more.
And the main lines of that settlement have proved, in fact, remarkably tenacious and permanent. Hence it is the outline provided by
that century's development which – without in any way minimizing
Europe's remaining problems of *terre irredente* – should provide our
principal/model and reference point.

Scottish Belatedness

What corresponds to this now classical model of development in
Scotland's case? Here, we encounter something very surprising

[5] There is no room to discuss this further. The reader will find useful surveys of
nationalist theory in Aira Kemiläinen, *Nationalism: Problems Concerning the
Word, the Concept and Classification*, London 1964, and in Anthony D. Smith,
Theories of Nationalism, London, 1971. One attempt to relate older theories of
nationalism to contemporary developments is P. Fougeyrollas, *Pour une France
Fédérale: vers l'unité européenne par la révolution régionale*, Paris 1968, especially
Part I, chapters 1 and 2.

right away. For what can reasonably be held to correspond to the mainstream of European nationalism is astonishingly recent in Scotland. As a matter of fact, it started in the 1920s – more or less at the moment when, after its prolonged gestation and maturation during the 19th century, European nationalism at last congealed into semi-permanent state forms. Thus it belongs to the last fifty years, and is the chronological companion of anti-imperialist revolt and Third World nationalism, rather than of those European movements which it superficially resembles. While the latter were growing, fighting their battles and winning them (sometimes), Scottish nationalism was simply absent.

I am aware that this assertion of Scottish belatedness also begs many questions. There is much to say about the precursors of nationalism in the 19th century, like the romantic movement of the 1850s and the successive Home Rule movements between 1880 and 1914. These are well described in H. J. Hanham's *Scottish Nationalism*. But all that need be said here is that they were quite distinctly precursors, not the thing itself, remarkable in any wider perspective for their feebleness and political ambiguity rather than their prophetic power. While in the 1920s we see by contrast the emergence of a permanent political movement with the formation of the National Party of Scotland (direct ancestor of the SNP) in 1928. And, just as important, the appearance of the epic poem of modern Scottish nationalism (a distinguishing badge of this, as of most other European nationalisms), MacDiarmid's *A Drunk Man Looks at the Thistle*, in 1926.

So, we have to start with a problem – a problem written into the very terms of any comparison one can make between Scotland and Europe, as it were. Why was Scottish nationalism so belated in its arrival on the European scene? Why was it absent for virtually the whole of the 'founding period' of European nationalist struggle?

But we cannot immediately try to answer this. We must turn away from it and return to it later – for the simple reason that, as I hope to show, the belatedness in question is in no sense merely a chronological fact (as nationalists are likely to believe). It is intimately related to the essential historical character of Scottish nationalism. To understand the one is to understand the other. Hence to approach the problem correctly we must first make some progress at a more fundamental level.

The Tidal Wave of Modernization

Let us turn back to the general European model. How may we describe the general outlines of nationalist development, seen as 'general historical process'? Here, by far the most important point is that nationalism is *as a whole* quite incomprehensible outside the context of that process's *uneven* development. The subjective point of nationalist ideology is, of course, always the suggestion that one nationality is as good as another. But the *real* point has always lain in the objective fact that, manifestly, one nationality has never been even remotely as good as, or equal to, the others which figure in its world-view. Indeed, the purpose of the subjectivity (nationalist myths) can never be anything but protest against the brutal fact: it is mobilization *against* the unpalatable, humanly unacceptable, truth of grossly uneven development.

Nationalism in general is (in Ernest Gellner's words) 'a phenomenon connected not so much with industrialization or modernization as such, but with its uneven diffusion.'[6] It first arose as a *general* fact (a determining general condition of the European body politic) after this 'uneven diffusion' had made its first huge and irreversible impact upon the historical process. That is, after the combined shocks engendered by the French Revolution, the Napoleonic conquests, the English industrial revolution, and the war between the two super-states of the day, England and France. This English–French 'dual revolution' impinged upon the rest of Europe like a tidal wave, what Gellner calls the 'tidal wave of modernization'. Through it the advancing capitalism of the more bourgeois societies bore down upon the societies surrounding them – societies which predominantly appear until the 1790s as buried in feudal and absolutist slumber.

Nationalism was one result of this rude awakening. For what did these societies – which now discovered themselves to be intolerably 'backward' – awaken into? A situation where polite universalist visions of progress had turned into means of domination. The Universal Republic of Anacharsis Cloots had turned into a French empire; the spread of free commerce from which so much had been hoped was turning (as Friedrich List pointed out) into the domina-

[6] 'Nationalism' in the volume *Thought and Change*, London 1964, the most important and influential recent study in English.

tion of English manufactures – the tyranny of the English 'City' over the European 'Country'. In short, there was a sort of imperialism built into 'development'. And it had become a prime necessity to resist *this* aspect of development.

Enlightenment thinkers had mostly failed to foresee this fatal antagonism. They had quite naturally assumed 'a link between knowledge and the increase in happiness', so that (as Sidney Pollard writes) 'Society and its rulers are increasingly able, because of greater knowledge, to combine the individual with the general interest, and the laws of nations will increasingly be changed to increase both. Thus the undoubted future progress of the human spirit will be accompanied by continuous social and individual amelioration'.[7] They imagined continuous diffusion from centre to periphery, from the 'leaders' to the regions still plunged in relative darkness. The metropolis would gradually elevate the rustic hinterland up to its level, as it were. It is, incidentally, worth noting that imperialists to this day always cling to some form or other of this pre-1800 ideology, at least partially.

In fact, progress invariably puts powerful, even deadly weapons in the hands of this or that particular 'advanced' area. Since this is a particular place and people, not a disinterested centre of pure and numinous culture, the result is a gulf (far larger than hitherto, and likely to increase) between the leaders and the hinterland. In the latter, progress comes to seem a hammer-blow as well as (sometimes instead of) a prospectus for general uplift and improvement. It appears as double-edged, at least. So areas of the hinterland, even in order to 'catch up' (to advance from 'barbarism' to the condition of 'civil society', as the Enlightenment put it), are *also* compelled to mobilize against progress. That is, they have to demand progress not as it is thrust upon them initially by the metropolitan centre, but 'on their own terms'. These 'terms' are, of course, ones which reject the imperialist trappings: exploitation or control from abroad, discrimination, military or political domination, and so on.

'Nationalism' is in one sense only the label for the general unfolding of this vast struggle, since the end of the 18th century. Obviously no one would deny that nationalities, ethnic disputes and hatreds, or some nation-states, existed long before this. But this is not the point. The point is how such relatively timeless fea-

[7] *The Idea of Progress*, London 1968, p. 46.

tures of the human scene were transformed into the general condition of national*ism* after the bourgeois revolutions exploded fully
into the world. Naturally, the new state of affairs made use of the
'raw materials' provided by Europe's particularly rich variety of
ethnic, cultural and linguistic contrasts. But – precisely – it also
altered their meaning, and gave them a qualitatively distinct function, an altogether new dynamism for both good and evil.

In terms of broad political geography, the contours of the process
are familiar. The 'tidal wave' invaded one zone after another, in
concentric circles. First Germany and Italy, the areas of relatively
advanced and unified culture adjacent to the Anglo-French centre.
It was in them that the main body of typically nationalist politics
and culture was formulated. Almost at the same time, or shortly
after, Central and Eastern Europe, and the more peripheral regions
of Iberia, Ireland, and Scandinavia. Then Japan and, with the full
development of imperialism, much of the rest of the globe. To
locate at least some of the dimensions of the struggle today is simple.
All one had to do was look around one in 1972 or 1973. Where were
the storm-centres? Vietnam, Ireland, Bangladesh, the Middle East,
Chile. Certain of these troubles may, or may not, have involved
socialist revolutions and projected a non-national and Marxist
image; there is no doubt that every one of them involved a *national*
revolution quite comprehensible in the general historical terms of
national*ism* (even without reference to other factors).

Europe's Bourgeoisies

The picture must be amplified and deepened in certain ways, however, to make it into a model applicable to a particular area like
Scotland. We have glanced at the political geography of uneven
development. What about its class basis and social content?
Sociologically, the basis of the vital change we are concerned with
obviously lay in the ascendency of the bourgeoisie in both England
and France: more exactly, in their joint rise and their fratricidal
conflicts up to 1815. Their Janus-headed 'modernity' was that of
bourgeois society, and an emergent industrial capitalism.

And it was upon the same class that this advancing 'civil society'
everywhere had the principal impact. In the hinterland too there
were 'rising middle classes' impatient with absolutism and the
motley assortment of *anciens régimes* which reigned over most of

Europe. Naturally, these were far weaker and poorer than the
world-bourgeoisies of the West. The gross advantages of the latter
had been denied them by history's unequal development. Now they
found themselves in a new dilemma. Previously they had hoped that
the spread of civilized progress would get rid of feudalism and raise
them to the grace of liberal, constitutional society. Now (e.g.) the
German and Italian middle classes realized that only a determined
effort of their own would prevent utopia from being marred by
Manchestertum and French bayonets. Beyond them, in the still
larger Europe east of Bohemia and Slovenia, the even weaker Slav
middle classes realized that 'progress' would in itself only fasten
German and Italian fetters upon their land and people more firmly.
And so on.

This 'dilemma' is indeed the characteristic product of capitalism's
uneven development. One might call it the 'nationalism-producing'
dilemma. Given the premise of uneven growth, and the resultant
impact of the more upon the less advanced, the dilemma is automatically transmitted outwards and onwards in this way. The result,
nationalism, is basically no less necessary. Nationalism, unlike
nationality or ethnic variety, cannot be considered a 'natural'
phenomenon. But of course it remains true that, as Gellner says,
under these specific historical circumstances (those of a whole era
in which we are still living) 'nationalism does become a natural
phenomenon, one flowing fairly inescapably from the general
situation'.

The Role of Intellectuals

Equally naturally, nationalism was from the outset a 'bourgeois'
phenomenon in the sense indicated. But two farther qualifications
are needed here, to understand the mechanism at work. The first
concerns the intelligentsia, and the second concerns the masses
whose emergence into history was – behind and beneath the more
visible 'rise of the bourgeoisie' – the truly decisive factor in the
transformation we are dealing with. 'The intelligentsia do, indeed,
play a definitive part in the rise of nationalist movements – everywhere', remarks Anthony Smith.[8] In his history of the 'dual revolution' and its impact Eric Hobsbawm is more specific: the motor

[8] A. D. Smith, *Theories of Nationalism*, p. 83.

rôle is provided by 'The lesser landowners or gentry and the emergence of a national middle and even lower-middle class in numerous countries, the spokesmen for both being largely professional intellectuals . . . (above all) . . . the *educated* classes . . . the educational progress of large numbers of "new men" into areas hitherto occupied by a small élite. The progress of schools and universities measures that of nationalism, just as schools and especially universities become its most conspicuous champions.'[9] The dilemma of underdevelopment becomes 'nationalism' only when it is (so to speak) refracted into a given society, perceived in a certain way, and then acted upon. And the medium through which this occurs is invariably, in the first place, an intelligentsia – functioning, of course, as the most conscious and awakened part of the middle classes.

Nationalism and the Masses

But if the intellectuals are all-important in one sense (spreading nationalism from the top downwards as it were), it is the masses – the ultimate recipients of the new message – that are all-important in another. As a matter of fact, they determine a lot of what the 'message' is. Why this is can easily be seen, on the basis of the foregoing remarks. These new middle classes, awakening to the grim dilemmas of backwardness, are confronted by a double challenge. They have (usually) to get rid of an anachronistic *ancien régime* as well as to beat 'progress' into a shape that suits their own needs and class ambitions. They can only attempt this by radical political and social mobilization, by arousing and harnessing the latent energies of their own societies. But this means, by mobilizing people. People is all they have got: this is the essence of the under-development dilemma itself.

Consequently, the national or would-be national middle class is always compelled to 'turn to the people'. It is this compulsion that really determines the new political complex ('nationalism') which comes forth. For what are the implications of turning to the people, in this sense? First of all, speaking their language (or, over most of Europe, what had hitherto been viewed as their 'brutish dialects').

[9] E. J. Hobsbawm, *The Age of Revolution: Europe 1789–1848*, London 1962, pp. 133–5.

Secondly, taking a kindlier view of their general 'culture', that *ensemble* of customs and notions, pagan and religious, which the Enlightenment had relegated to the museum (if not to the dust-bin). Thirdly – and most decisively, when one looks at the process generally – coming to terms with the enormous and still irreconcilable *diversity* of popular and peasant life.

It is, of course, this primordial political compulsion which points the way to an understanding of the dominant contradiction of the era. Why did the spread of capitalism, as a rational and universal ordering of society, lead so remorselessly to extreme fragmentation, to the exaggeration of ethnic-cultural differences, and so to the *dementia* of 'chauvinism' and war? Because that diffusion contained within itself (as it still does) the hopeless antagonism of its own unevenness, and a consequent imperialism; the latter forces mobilization against it, even on the part of those most anxious to catch up and imitate; such mobilization can only proceed, in practice, via a popular mass still located culturally upon a far anterior level of development, upon the level of feudal or pre-feudal peasant or 'folk' life. That is, upon a level of (almost literally) 'pre-historic' diversity in language, ethnic characteristics, social habits, and so on. This ancient and (in a more acceptable sense of the term) 'natural' force imposes its own constraints upon the whole process, lending to it from the outset precisely that archaic and yet necessary colour, that primaeval-seeming or instinctive aspect which marks it so unmistakably.

If one now relates these two central features of the bourgeois dilemma to one another, what is the consequence? One perceives at once the true nerve of political nationalism. It is constituted by a distinctive relationship between the intelligentsia (acting for its class) and the people. There is no time here to explore this interesting general theme in detail. For our purposes it is sufficient to note the name, and some of the implications, of the relationship in question. Political nationalism of the classic sort was not necessarily democratic by nature, or revolutionary in a social sense (notoriously it could be inspired by fear of Jacobinism, as well as by Jacobinism). But it *was* necessarily 'populist' by nature. The political and social variables to be observed in its development are anchored in this constant, which steadily expressed the class machinery of the process.

Thus, we can add to the 'external' (or geo-political) co-ordinates of nationalism mentioned above, a set of 'internal' or social-class co-ordinates. The former showed us the 'tidal wave' of modernization (or bourgeois society) transforming one area after another, and soliciting the rise of nationalist awareness and movements. The latter shows us something of the mechanism behind the 'rise': the bourgeois and intellectual populism which, in existing conditions of backwardness where the masses are beginning to enter history and political existence for the first time, is ineluctably driven towards ethnic particularism. Nationalism's forced 'mobilization' is fundamentally conditioned, at least in the first instance, by its own mass basis.

But then, we are in a manner of speaking still living in this 'first instance'. Nationalism arose after the French and Industrial Revolutions, at the very beginning of the 19th century. But the *anciens régimes* which the new nationalist middle classes had to get rid of in Central and Eastern Europe lasted for more than a century after that. Absolutism was far more tenacious then most bourgeois intellectuals admitted. It learned to borrow from the new world elements of technology and populism, to help it survive. Even when killed at last by the First World War and the 1917 revolutions, its ruinous mass of unresolved 'national questions' and fractured states was enough to poison history for another generation. And, of course, while this inheritance has become steadily less important in post-Second World War Europe, the expanding waves of extra-European nationalism are sufficient to hold us all still in this universe of discourse.

Let me now point out some important implications of this model of nationalism, before going on to consider the Scottish case. Its main virtue is a simple one. It enables us to decide upon a materialist, rather than an 'idealist' explanation of the phenomenon. In the question of nationalism, this philosophical point is critical. This is so, because of the very character of the phenomenon. Quite obviously, nationalism is invariably characterized by a high degree of political and ideological voluntarism. Simply because it *is* forced mass-mobilization in a position of relative helplessness (or 'under-development'), certain subjective factors play a prominent part in it. It is, in its immediate nature, idealistic. It always imagines an ideal 'people' (propped up by folklore studies, antiquarianism, or some surrogate for these) and it always searches urgently for vital inner, untapped springs of energy both in the individual and the mass. Such idealism is inseparable both from its creative historical function and its typical delusions. Consequently a generally idealist mode of explanation has always been tempting for it. It lends itself rather to a Hegelian and romantic style of theorizing, than to a rationalist or Marxist one. This is one reason why Marxism has so often made heavy weather of it in the past.[10]

The Nation and Romanticism

I pointed out earlier, indeed, that theories about nationalism have been overwhelmingly influenced by nationalism, as the prevailing universe of discourse. This is really the same point. For they have been overwhelmingly influenced in the sense of idealism – whether their bias is itself pro-nationalist, or anti-nationalist.[11] The ques-

---

[10] I cannot refrain here from citing a criticism of the author made by the Scottish nationalist writer John Herdman, in his contribution to Duncan Glen's *Whither Scotland?*. He castigates my unduly material conception of the purpose of development (in an earlier essay called 'Three Dreams of Scottish Nationalism', *New Left Review* No. 49, May–June 1968, reprinted in Karl Miller's *Memoirs of a Modern Scotland*, 1970) and observes that: 'To my mind both these (material) purposes are secondary and subservient to the mobilizing of populations for *spiritual* development. I dislike the word but cannot think of a better one . . .' (p. 109). And what does such spiritual development counter? The unacceptable face of 'progress', as shown in 'a nation which has become the very embodiment of anti-civilization, of an amorphous mass culture which is ignoble, ugly and debased'. This is England of course. But it might equally well be France, as once seen by German nationalists; Germany, as once seen by Panslavism; America, as now seen by half the world; the U.S.S.R., as seen by the Chinese . . . and so on. By contrast Scotland's spiritual solution is (again very characteristically) 'the difficult assumption of a cultural independence which will give a new dynamic to the country' (Duncan Glen, op. cit., p. 22).

[11] Naturally, the anti-nationalist bias tends to be somewhat more revealing; yet this is to say little. The most interesting strain of bourgeois anti-nationalism is the conservative one deriving from Lord Acton's essay on 'Nationality' (1862, reprinted in *Essays*, ed. G. Himmelfarb, 1949). But really very little has been added to it since, as one may see by consulting, e.g. Professor E. Kedourie's Actonian volume *Nationalism*, London 1960. It is significant in this connection that the first sensible progress in nationalism-theory was made after the First World War by scholars in America who had established a sufficient distance from Europe (the Hayes and Kohn schools). While with few exceptions further serious contributions have been made via the study of Third World 'development' since the Second World War, especially by sociologists. All three stances (social conservatism, the vantage point of an – at that time – less nationalist U.S.A., and Third Worldism) have permitted varying degrees of psychic detachment from the core of the nationalist thought-world.

tion is, then, which can explain which? It is a fact that while idealist explanations of the phenomenon in terms of consciousness or *Zeitgeist* (however acute their observation may be, notably in German writers like Meinecke) never account for the material dynamic incorporated in the situation, a materialist explanation can perfectly well account for all the most 'ideal' and cultural or ideological symptoms of nationalism (even at their most berserk). Start from the premise of capitalism's uneven development and its real class articulation, and one can come to grasp the point even of chauvinist lunacy, the 'irrational' elements which have played a significant role in nationalism's unfolding from the outset to the end. Start from the lunacy itself and one will end there, after a number of gyrations – still believing, for instance, that (in Hegelian fashion) material development exists to serve the Idea of 'spiritual development'.

Perhaps this can be put in another way. The politico-cultural necessities of nationalism, as I outlined them briefly above, entail an intimate link between nationalist politics and *romanticism*. Romanticism was the cultural mode of the nationalist dynamic, the cultural 'language' which alone made possible the formation of the new inter-class communities required by it. In that context, all romanticism's well-known features – the search for inwardness, the trust in feeling or instinct, the attitude to 'nature', the cult of the particular and mistrust of the 'abstract', etc. – make sense. But if one continues to adopt that language, then it becomes impossible to get back to the structural necessities which determined it historically. And of course, we *do* largely speak the language, for the same reason that we are still living in a world of nationalism.

Lastly let me point out an important limitation of the analysis. So far I have been concerned with the earlier or formative stages of nationalism. That is, with the nationalism which was originally (however much it has duplicated itself in later developments) that of Europe between 1800 and 1870. This is – for reasons which I hope will be clear – what primarily concerns us in approaching the Scottish case-history. But it is certainly true that after 1870, with the Franco-Prussian war and the birth of Imperialism (with a large 'I'), there occurred farther sea-changes in nationalist development. These were related, in their external co-ordinates, to a new kind of great-power struggle for backward lands; and as regards their internal co-ordinates, to the quite different class-struggle provoked by the existence of large proletariats within the metropolitan centres themselves. I have no room here to consider this later phase so closely, but it is important to refer to it at least. Not only has it deeply influenced the development of Scotland (like everywhere else in the world). Also, where I have stated that we still live in a climate of nationalism, it would, of course, be more accurate to say we still inhabit the universe of late nationalism: that is, nationalism as modified by the successive, and decisive, mass experiences of imperialism and total war.

Scotland's Absent Nationalism

Let us now turn to Scotland. How exactly are we to set it over against this general model? I pointed out to begin with the very surprising fact which confronts anyone trying to do this: that is, that for virtually the whole century of nationalism's classical development there is no object of comparison at all. Between 1800 and 1870 for example, the dates just referred to, there simply *was* no Scottish nationalist movement of the usual sort.

It still may not be quite understood how disconcerting this absence is. To get it into perspective, one should compare certain aspects of Scotland's situation just prior to the age of nationalism with those of other European minor nationalities. With (e.g.) the Slav nationalities, Greece, Ireland, or Poland. In any such comparison, Scotland appears not as notably defective but, on the contrary, as almost uniquely *well* equipped for the nationalist battles ahead.

Nobody could, for example, claim that Scotland was a *geschichtsloses Volk*.[12] It had only recently ceased being a wholly independent state. The century or so that had elapsed since 1707 is a fairly insignificant time-interval by the criteria which soon became common under nationalism. Many new 'nations' had to think away millenia of oblivion, and invent almost entirely fictitious pasts.[13]

[12] The outstanding study of the problem of 'historyless peoples' from a Marxist point of view is R. Rosdolsky, *Friedrich Engels und das Problem der 'Geschichtslosen Völker'*, Hannover 1964, offprint from *Archiv für Socialgeschichte*, vol. 4, 1964.

[13] Beginning with modern Greece, that first model and inspiration of nationalist revolts throughout Europe. There the gap between present realities and past history was so enormous that the new intellectuals had to create the new myths

Whereas the Scots not only remembered a reality of independence, they had actually preserved most of their own religious, cultural, and legal institutions intact. Their political state had gone, but their civil society was still there – still there and, in the later 18th century, thriving as never before. Most of backward, would-be nationalist Europe had neither the one nor the other.

Within this civil society Scotland also had at least two of the indispensable prerequisites for successful nationalism. It had a dynamic middle class, a 'rising' bourgeoisie if ever there was one. And (above all) it had an intelligentsia. In fact, it had one of the most distinguished intellectual classes in the Europe of that time, a class whose achievements and fame far outshone that of any other minor nationality. Given the key importance of the intelligentsia in early formulations of the romantic populism associated with 'nation-building', this was clearly a formidable advantage – at least in appearance.

As far as folklore and popular traditions went, Scotland was (needless to say) as well furnished for the struggle as anywhere else. Better than most, perhaps, since – as everybody knew then and knows now – one element in those traditions was an ancient, rankling hostility to the English, founded upon centuries of past conflict. These old conflicts gave Scotland a cast of national heroes and martyrs, popular tales and legends of oppression and resistance, as good as anything in *Mitteleuropa*. True, the Scots did not have a really separate majority language. But any comparative survey will show that, however important language becomes as a distinguishing mark in the subsequent advance of nationalism, it is rarely of primary importance in precipitating the movement. It is heavy artillery, but not the cause of the battle.

And in any case, the Scots had far heavier artillery to hand. They had – to consider only one thing – the enormously important factor of a clear religious difference. The Scottish Reformation had been a

---

de toutes pièces. As one (notably pro-Greek) author says: 'Those who spoke the Greek language . . . had no notion of classical Greece or of the Hellenistic civilization of Roman times . . . The classical ruins were quite unintelligible to early modern Greeks . . . From Roman times the Greeks had called themselves "Romans" and continued to do so up to and during the War of Independence'. D. Dakin, *The Greek Struggle for Independence 1821–1833*, London 1973, pp. 11–22.

wholly different affair from the English one, and had given rise to a distinct social and popular ethos rooted in distinct institutions. There is no need to stress the potential of this factor in nationality-struggles today, looking across to Ireland (even in situations where both sides speak the same language). More important, and more generally, there was no doubt at the beginning of the 19th century – just as there is no doubt today – that 'Scotland' was a distinct entity of some kind, felt to be such both by the people living in it and by all travellers who ventured into it from outside. It had (as it still has) a different 'social ethic', in George Elder Davie's phrase. Analysis of the complex elements going into such a product, the recognizable and felt identity of a nationality-unit (whether state or province), may be difficult. But usually the fact is plain enough. And this is what counts most, as the potential fuel of nationalist struggle.

So why, in circumstances like these, was nationalism to be conspicuous only by its absence in Scotland? This question is interesting enough. But it is time to note that behind it there lies another, much more important in any general perspective, and even more fascinating. If, in a European land so strikingly marked out for nationalism, nationalism failed to materialize, then it can only be because the *real* precipitating factors of the nationalist response were not there. And one may therefore hope to discern, through this extraordinary 'negative example', precisely what these factors were. To understand why Scotland did *not* 'go nationalist' at the usual time and in the usual way is, in my opinion, to understand a great deal about European nationalism in general. I hope the claim does not sound too large (or even nationalist). But, as well as understanding Scotland better in relation to the general European model discussed above, one may also understand Europe better by focusing upon Scotland.

Three Kinds of Nation

To assist us in focusing on what is relevant, let me recall a basic point in the crudely materialist schema adopted previously. I suggested there that nationalism is in essence one kind of response to an enforced dilemma of 'under-development'. What we must do now is define the latter term more concretely, in relation to Europe at the critical period in question – that is, during the original formation of nationalism. European countries at the beginning of the 19th century can for this purpose conveniently be assigned to one or other of three categories. Firstly, there are the original, 'historic' nation-states, the lands formed relatively early into relatively homogeneous entities, usually by absolute monarchy: England, France, Spain and Portugal, Sweden, Holland. Naturally, this category includes the 'leaders', the two revolutionary nations whose impact was to be so great, as well as a number of formerly important ones which had now (for many different reasons) dropped out of the race. Then (secondly) there are the lands which have to try and catch up, under the impact of revolution: the German-speaking states, Italy, the Hapsburg domains, the Balkans, the countries of Tsardom, Ireland, Scandinavia apart from Sweden. These account for by far the greater part of Europe geographically, and in terms of population. They were all to attempt to redeem themselves through some form of nationalism, sooner or later: they were all (one might say) forced through the nationalist hoop.

Finally – thirdly – one needs another category. The two main groups of bourgeois-revolutionary lands and 'under-developed' hinterland are easily classified at this point in time. But what about the countries which either had caught up, or were about to catch up? The countries on the move out of barbarism into culture, those on or near the point of (in today's terminology) 'take-off'? Surely, in an age which thought so generally and confidently about progress of this sort, there were some examples of it?

This third group is a very odd one. It had, in fact, only one member. There was to be only one example of a land which – so to speak – 'made it' before the onset of the new age of nationalism. The European Enlightenment had an immense general effect upon culture and society; but it had only one particular success-story, outside the great revolutionary centres. Only one society was in fact able to advance, more or less according to its precepts, from feudal and theological squalor to the stage of bourgeois civil society, polite culture, and so on. Only one land crossed the great divide *before* the whole condition of European politics and culture was decisively and permanently altered by the great awakening of nationalist consciousness.

North Britain

It was Scotland which enjoyed (or suffered) this solitary fate. The intelligentsia at least had few doubts about what had happened. 'The memory of our ancient state is not so much obliterated, but that, by comparing the past with the present, we may clearly see the superior advantages we now enjoy, and readily discern from what source they flow', ran the Preface to No. 1 of the original *Edinburgh Review* (1755). 'The communication of trade has awakened industry; the equal administration of laws produced good manners . . . and a disposition to every species of improvement in the minds of a people naturally active and intelligent. If countries have their ages with respect to improvement, North Britain may be considered as in a state of early youth, guided and supported by the more mature strength of her kindred country'.

A prodigy among the nations, indeed. It had progressed from fortified castles and witch-burning to Edinburgh New Town and Adam Smith, in only a generation or so. We cannot turn aside here to consider the reasons for this extraordinary success. Ordinarily it is no more than a sort of punch-bag in the old contest between nationalists and anti-nationalists: the former hold that Edinburgh's greatness sprang forth (like all true patriot flora) from indigenous sources, while the Unionists attribute it to the beneficent effects of 1707. It may be worth noting, however, that North Britain's intellectuals themselves normally thought of another factor as relevant. As the *Edinburgh Review* article mentioned above put it: 'What the Revolution had begun, the Union rendered more compleat'. It was by no means the fact of union which had counted, but the fact that this unification had enabled the Scots to benefit from the great *revolution* in the neighbour kingdom. As the great Enlightenment historian William Robertson said, the 1707 agreement had 'admitted the Scottish commons to a participation of all the privileges which the English had purchased at the expence of so much blood'.[14] That is, the Scottish bourgeoisie had been able to exploit (by alliance) some of the consequences of the English bourgeois revolution. After the black, the unspeakable 17th century, Robertson notes, it was 1688 which marked the real dawn in Scotland.

But many other factors were involved too, clearly. The character of Scottish absolutism, for example, the feudalism which 'collapsed

[14] William Robertson, *History of Scotland*, 1803, in *Works*, 1817, vol. 3, pp. 188–200.

as a vehicle for unity, and became instead the vehicle of faction', in T. C. Smout's words.[15] The character of the Scottish Reformation and its inheritance. I doubt if even the stoniest of Unionist stalwarts would deny that part of Scotland's 18th-century 'improvement' was due to her own powers, and the retention of a large degree of institutional autonomy. But what matters most in the context of this discussion is that Scotland's situation was almost certainly unique. It was the only land which stood in *this* relationship to the *first* great national-scale bourgeois revolution: that is, to a revolutionary process which, because it was the first, proceeded both slowly and empirically, and therefore permitted in the course of its development things which were quite unthinkable later on. There was, there could not be, any situation like Scotland's within the enormously accelerated drive of 19th-century development. By then, the new inter-national competitiveness and political culture's new mass basis alike prohibited gentlemanly accords like 1707.[16]

We know at any rate that the success-story was never repeated quite like this anywhere else. There were a number of other zones of Europe where it clearly could have been, and would have been if 'development' had gone on in the Enlightenment, rather than the nationalist, sense. Belgium and the Rhineland, for example, or Piedmont. In the earlier phases of the French Revolution these areas were indeed inducted for 'improvement' into the ambit of the French Revolution, the Universal Republic. But as events quickly showed, this pattern could no longer be repeated.

Enlightenment and the Highlands

The most remarkable comment upon Scotland's precocious improvement was provided by Scottish culture itself, during the Golden Age. The country not only 'made it', in the generation before the

[15] T. C. Smout, *A History of the Scottish People 1560–1830*, 1969, p. 33.

[16] Even more to the point perhaps, one need only think of the period just before 1707 – that is, the period of the Scottish bourgeoisie's last attempt at separate and competitive development through the colonization of Darien. This was destroyed largely through English pressures. Can anyone imagine that under 19th-century conditions this *débâcle* would have been forgiven and realistically forgotten? On the contrary, it would have been turned into a compelling popular reason for still more aggressive separate (i.e. nationalist) development. As things were, in the pre-nationalist age this tailor-made nationalist tragedy led straight to the 1707 Union.

great change (i.e. the generation between the failure of the Jacobite rebellion of 1745, and 1789) – it also produced the general formula for 'making it'. That is, it contributed proportionately far more than anywhere else in Europe to the development of social science. And it did so in the distinctive form of what was in essence a study *of* 'development': a study of the 'mechanics of transition', or how society in general can be expected to progress out of barbarism into refinement. Scottish Enlightenment thinkers were capable of this astonishing feat because, obviously, they had actually experienced much of the startling process they were trying to describe. Not only that: the old 'barbaric' world was still there, close about them. The author of Scotland's sociological masterpiece, the *Essay on the History of Civil Society* (1767), had been brought up in the Highlands.[17]

Scotland's progress was all the more striking because there was this one large part of it which did not 'improve' at all. Scotland beyond the Highland line remained 'under-developed'. This fissure through Scottish society had been left by the failure of later feudalism; now it was, if anything, aggravated by the swift rise of Lowland culture in the 18th century. A 'gulf' was formed which resembles in many ways the gulf that opened across Europe as a whole – that is, the very gap I tried to describe previously, the development-gap with all its accompanying dilemmas and ambiguities. Highland Scotland, like most of Ireland, was in effect a part of Central or Eastern Europe in the West. Therefore it was bound to have a distinct development from the 'successful' civil society south of it. It had, as everyone knows, a distinct history of just this sort – one which painfully resembles the history of Ireland or many of the weaker peoples of *Mitteleuropa*, far more closely than it does that of the Scottish industrial belt. The Highlands were to suffer the fate characteristic of many countries and regions which generated nationalist movements in order to resist. But (here unlike Ireland) Highland society did not possess the prerequisites for *nationalist*

[17] As the editor of the recent Edinburgh edition of the *Essay* states: 'Adam Ferguson *was* a Highlander . . . and undoubtedly behind the *Essay* lies a deeply felt experience of the contrast between these two societies, and the question: what happens to man in the progress of society? Ferguson knew intimately, and from the inside, the two civilizations . . . which divided 18th-century Scotland: the *Gemeinschaft* of the clan, the *Gesellschaft* of the "progressive", commercial Lowlands'. Duncan Forbes, Introduction, pp. xxxviii–xxxix, 1966 edition.

resistance. Its position was too marginal, its social structure was too archaic, and too much of its life had been actually destroyed in the terrible reaction to 1745.

If this general analysis is right, then Scotland's precocious and prenationalist development must clearly be reckoned the true 'uniqueness' of its modern history. In European perspective, this emerges as much more striking than anything else. Nationalists always perorate at length upon the unique charms and mission of their object, I know: this is part of the structure of the nationalist thought-world. So is the fact that, seen from a distance, these ineffable missions resemble one another like a box of eggs. One has to be careful, consequently, before presenting a new candidate for the stakes. But I am comforted in doing so by one thought. This is that my emphasis upon the Enlightenment has never in fact (to the best of my knowledge) figured in such nationalist incantations in the past. On the contrary – for reasons that may be clearer below – if Scottish nationalists have ever been really united on one thing, it is their constant execration and denunciation of Enlightenment culture. In short, the real uniqueness of modern Scotland is the one thing which does *not* (and indeed *cannot*) be admitted into nationalist rhetoric.

There is logic behind this, of course. The same logic which drives one to the following thought: it simply cannot be the case that there is *no* connection between Scottish society's fulminating advance before 1800, and that society's subsequent failure to produce a nationalism of its own. There must, surely, be some relation between these two remarkable, peculiarly Scottish achievements. Let me now go on to suggest what it may consist in.

There are two questions which cannot help dominating much of the cultural debate upon nationalism in Scotland. One we have looked at already: it is the problem of how and why the Scots emerged, so suddenly, from backwardness to rise to the peaks of the Edinburgh Golden Age. The other is how and why – and almost as suddenly – this florescence ended in the earlier decades of the 19th century. So that, as far as the national culture is concerned – runs one typical complaint – 'The historian is left calling Victorian culture in Scotland "strangely rootless" ... We have to recognize that there did not emerge along with modern Scotland a mature, "all-round" literature ... In the mid-19th century the Scottish literary tradition paused; from 1825 to 1880 there is next to nothing worth attention'.[18] And, one might add, not much worth attention from 1880 to 1920 either.

It is inconceivable that the profoundest causes of this dramatic fall did not lie in Scottish society's general evolution. Yet where are these causes to be located? For, as Craig says, 'modern Scotland' – industrial Scotland, the economic Scotland of the Glasgow–Edinburgh–Dundee axis – continued *its* startling progress unabated. In his history T. C. Smout situates the beginning of the movement towards take-off in mid-century, after the 'Forty-five: 'The ice began to break. Slow and unspectacular at first, the process of change then began to accelerate in the 1760s, until by the outbreak of the American War in 1775 practically all classes in Scottish society were conscious of a momentum which was carrying them towards a richer society . . .'[19] The momentum continued until by 1830 the country had 'come over a watershed'. 'In 1828 J. B. Neilson's application of the hot-blast process to smelting the blackband ironstone of the Central Belt gave the Scottish economy the cue for its next major advance . . . it led to the birth of Scottish heavy industry with the swelling boom in iron towns and engineering in the 1830s and 1840s and the gigantic construction of shipyards on Clydeside in the last quarter of the century.'[20]

Thus, the economic 'structure' continued its forward march, across the developmental watershed and beyond, breeding new generations of Scottish entrepreneurs and a new and vast Scottish working class. But certain vital parts of the 'superstructure', far from sharing in this momentum, simply collapsed. On *that* level Scotland abruptly reverted to being a province again: a different sort of province, naturally, prosperous and imperial rather than theoretic and backward, but still (unmistakably) a very provincial *sort* of province. How is one to explain this remarkable disparity of development?

Let me relate it, first, to two other notable absences on the Scottish scene. One has already been several times referred to, since it is the main subject I am concerned with: that is, the absence of political nationalism. The other very striking absence is that of

[18] David Craig, *Scottish Literature and the Scottish People, 1680–1830*, Edinburgh 1961, pp. 13–14, p. 273.
[19] T. C. Smout, op. cit., p. 226.
[20] Ibid., pp. 484–5.

what one might call a developed or mature cultural romanticism. It is indeed the lack of this that constitutes the rootlessness, the 'void' which cultural and literary historians so deplore.

I know that this may be thought a paradoxical assertion. We are all aware of the great significance of both Scotland and Sir Walter Scott in the general mythology of European romanticism. And we are also conscious of the importance in Scotland itself of a kind of pervasive, second-rate, sentimental slop associated with tartan, nostalgia, Bonnie Prince Charlie, Dr Finlay, and so on. Yet I would hold that both these phenomena are misleading, in different ways; and that the existence of neither of them is inconsistent with the absence I am referring to.

Sir Walter Scott: Valedictory Realist

First of all Scott. In his essay on Scott in *The Historical Novel* (1962), Lukács points out that 'it is completely wrong to see Scott as a Romantic writer, unless one wishes to extend the concept of Romanticism to embrace all great literature in the first third of the 19th century'. Indeed, what Scott expresses himself – in spite of the great importance of his historical themes for later romantic literature – is rather 'a renunciation of Romanticism, a conquest of Romanticism, a higher development of the realist literary traditions of the Enlightenment'. Thus, to describe Scott as a 'romantic' is akin to describing Marx as a 'Marxist': he undeniably gave rise to a great deal of this European 'ism', but was not himself part of it. He was not, for example, a 'Romantic' in the sense that his compatriot Thomas Carlyle was, in the next generation (even Carlyle's misunderstanding and denigration of Scott are typically romantic).[21]

Scott's imaginative world arose from the same 'deeply felt experience of the contrast between two societies' mentioned above. That is, it belonged to the literary tradition of Scotland, as well as that of the Enlightenment in general. He brought to this an enormously heightened sense of the reality and values of the 'back-

[21] Lukács' essay is also reprinted in *Scott's Mind and Art*, ed. Jeffares, Edinburgh 1969. Thomas Carlyle's influential essay on Scott appeared in the *London and Westminster Review* (1838), and is partly reprinted in *Scott: the Critical Heritage*, ed. J. Hayden, London 1970.

ward' or pre-bourgeois past – a sense which is, of course, characteristic of the whole period of awakening nationalism. But the typical
course of his own imagination is never consonant with what was
to be the general tendency of that period. It ran precisely counter
to that tendency. As Lukács observes, it continued to run upon the
lines of what he calls Enlightenment 'realism'.

For Scott, the purpose of his unmatched evocation of a national
past is never to revive it: that is, never to resuscitate it as part of
political or social mobilization in the present, by a mythical emphasis upon continuity between (heroic) past and present. On the
contrary: his essential point is always that the past really is gone,
beyond recall. The heart may regret this, but never the head.
As Scott's biographer J. G. Lockhart puts it, quite forcibly, his
idea of nationalism was like his idea of witchcraft: 'He delighted in
letting his fancy run wild about ghosts and witches and horoscopes
. . . (but) . . . no man would have been more certain to give juries
sound direction in estimating the pretended evidence of supernatural occurrences of any sort; and I believe, in like manner, that had
any anti-English faction, civil or religious, sprung up in his own
time in Scotland, he would have done more than other living man
could have hoped to do, for putting it down'.[22] For all its splendour,
his panorama of the Scottish past is valedictory in nature. When he
returns to the present – in the *persona* of his typical prosaic hero-
figure – the head is in charge. It speaks the language of Tory
Unionism and 'progress': the real interests of contemporary Scotland diverge from those of the auld sang.

But in nationalist Europe the entire purpose of romantic historicism was different. The whole point of cultural nationalism
there *was* the mythical resuscitation of the past, to serve present and
future ends. There, people learned the auld sangs in order to add
new verses. Naturally, Scott was read and translated in those
countries according to this spirit – and as we know, his contribution
to the new rising tide of national romanticism was a great one. It
was great everywhere but in his own nation. In his own national
context, he pronounced, in effect, a great elegy. But the point of an
elegy is that it *can* only be uttered once. Afterwards it may be echoed,
but not really added to.

[22] J. G. Lockhart, *The Life of Sir Walter Scott* (1837–8), Everyman's abridged
edition, 1906, p. 653.

Consequently, Sir Walter's towering presence during the vital decades of the early 19th century is not only consistent with the absence of a subsequent romantic-national culture: to a large extent, it explains that absence. The very nature of his achievement – whether seen in terms of his own politics, or in terms of his typical plots and characters – cut off such a future from its own natural source of inspiration. It cut off the future from the past, the head from the 'heart' (as romanticism now conceived this entity). As for the second phenomenon I referred to, popular or *Kitsch* Scotland, this is certainly a sort of 'romanticism'. And it is certainly important, and not to be dismissed with a shudder as most nationalist intellectuals tend to do. I shall have more to say about the great tartan monster below. For the moment, however, I think it is enough to point out that he is a sub-cultural creature rather than a performer in the elevated spheres we are concerned with. Whisky labels, the *Sunday Post*, Andy Stewart, the Scott Monument, the inebriate football patriots of International night: no-one will fail to compose his own lengthy list or discern its weighty role in the land. But this is a popular sub-romanticism, and not the vital national culture whose absence is so often lamented after Scott.

What we have therefore is the relatively sudden disintegration of a great national culture; an absence of political and cultural national*ism*; and an absence of any genuine, developing romanticism, of the kind which was to typify 19th-century cultural life. The three negative phenomena are, surely, closely connected. In fact, they are different facets of the same mutation. And if we now set this change over against the general explanatory model sketched out previously, we can begin to see what it consisted in.

If one views it as a disparity of development, as between the ongoing economic structure and a suddenly and inexplicably collapsed 'superstructure', then the answer is contained in the very terms in which the problem is posed. That is, it is overwhelmingly likely that the cultural decline occurred *because* of the material development itself. Because Scotland had already advanced so far, so fast – to the watershed of development and beyond – it simply did not need the kind of cultural development we are concerned with. It had overleapt what was to be (over the greater part of Europe) the next 'natural' phase of development. Its previous astonishing precocity led it, quote logically, to what appears as an equally singular 'retardation' or incompleteness in the period which followed. This can only have happened because, at bottom, certain material levers were inoperative in the Scottish case; and they were inoperative during the usual formative era of romantic nationalism because they had already performed their function and produced their effect earlier, in the quite different culture-world of the 18th century.

The Absent Intelligentsia

We have some clues as to how this actually worked. Normally nationalism arose out of a novel dilemma of under-development; but it did so through a quite specific mechanism, involving first the intelligentsia, then wider strata of the middle classes, then the masses. The process has been admirably described by Hroch in his comparative inquiry. Initially the property of a relatively tiny intellectual élite (usually reacting to the impact of the French Revolution), nationalism passed through 'phase A' into 'phase B' (approximately 1815-48) where it was generally diffused among the growing bourgeoisie. It was in the course of this prolonged process that the new cultural language of romanticism and the new credo of liberal nationalism were worked out. But even so 1848 was still mainly a 'revolution of the intellectuals' (in Namier's phrase), and failed as such. It was only later that it turned into a mass movement proper ('phase C') with some roots in new working-class and peasant parties, and wide popular appeal. Thus, while the new *Weltanschauung* was (as we noticed) inherently populist in outlook, it took a long time to get to the people: that is, to the mystic source whence, in nationalist myth, it is supposed to spring.

Transfer this picture to the Scottish case: there was no real, material dilemma of under-development; hence the intelligentsia did not perceive it, and develop its perception in the normal way – it did *not* have to 'turn to the people' and try to mobilize first the middle strata then the masses for the struggle; hence there was no call to create a new inter-class 'community' of the sort invoked by nationalism, and no objective need for the cultural instrument which permitted this – 'romanticism'; hence the intelligentsia in Scotland (its previous eminence notwithstanding) was deprived of the *normal* function of an intellectual class in the new, nationalist, European world.

But – it may be objected here – even given that this was so, and that the underlying situation decreed a different politico-cultural fate for the Scots, why did it have to take the sad form of this *collapse* into provinciality, this bewildering descent from great heights into the cultural 'desert' of modern Scotland? Why could the Enlightenment not have continued there in some form, in a separate but still 'national' development? This is another of those questions whose very formulation guides one towards an answer. It was, of course, *impossible* for any such development to take place. Impossible because no one intellectual class can ever follow such a separate path in Europe. Once the general intellectual and cultural climate had altered in the decisive way mentioned, in consort with the unfolding of nationalism, it has altered for everybody.

This was by no means just a question of fashion, or the fact that intellectuals heed what goes on abroad. Nationalism was a general, and a structural state of the whole body politic. Although it was born in the 'fringe' lands under the impact of modernity, its subsequent impact transformed everyone – including the 'source' countries of the bourgeois revolution themselves, France and England. The new, enormous, growing weight of masses in motion broke down the old hierarchies everywhere and forced more or less similar cultural adaptations everywhere. In this violent process of action and reaction, no one part of the wider area concerned could 'escape' nationalism and its culture. It had either to evolve its own nationalist-type culture, or succumb to someone else's (becoming thereby 'provincialized').

Against the Fall

Under these new conditions, what in fact happened to the great Scots intelligentsia? As an intellectual class it belonged, with all its virtues, *entirely* to the pre-1789 universe. Both its patrician social character and its rationalist world-view were parts of that older, more stable, hierarchical world where the masses had scarcely begun to exist politically. Claims have been made for its 'democratic' intellect. 'Democratic' in the deeper sense which now became central it emphatically was not. It was pre-Jacobin, pre-populist, pre-romantic; and as a consequence, wholly pre-national-ist. In the drastically different geological epoch which now supervened, it could survive only for a short time, in somewhat fossil-like fashion. The sad tale is all there, in Lord Cockburn's *Memorials*. 'We had wonderfully few proper Jacobins,' he comments wryly upon the Scottish élite's wholesale slide into reaction, 'but if Scotch Jacobinism did not exist, Scotch Toryism did, and with a vengeance. This party engrossed almost the whole wealth, and rank, and public office, of the country, and at least three-fourths of the population.'[23] Sir Walter himself was, of course, in the front rank, battling (literally) to the death against the 1832 Reform Bill.

Elsewhere in Europe this suicide of former élites did not matter. They were displaced by what Eric Hobsbawm called the 'large numbers of "new men"', who *were* educated into nationalism and the other new rules of populist politics. These new men were awakened into radical dissatisfaction with their fate, and had the sense that without great collective efforts things would not improve much for them in a foreseeable future. They tended to come (as Hroch observes) from 'regions of intermediate social change' – from small towns and rural zones whose old life had been undermined, but for whom industry and urbanization were still remote (and dubious) realities.[24] Out of such regions there arose a new and broader intelligentsia to take the place of the old: modern, romantic, populist, more mobile, mainly petit-bourgeois in background.

But – precisely – in Scotland it did not. No new intellectual class at once national in scope and basically disgruntled at its life-prospects arose, because the Scottish petty bourgeoisie had little reason to be discontented. In the overwhelming rush of the Scottish industrial revolution, even the regions of intermediate social change were quickly sucked in. Hence no new 'intelligentsia' in the relevant sense developed, turning to the people to try and fight a way out of its intolerable dilemma. Hence Hroch's phases 'A' and 'B' were alike absent in Scottish development: there was, there could be, no nationalism or its associated romantic culture fully present in that development. There could only be the 'void'.

This kind of analysis will stick in a number of throats for two reasons: it is materialist in content, and rather complicated in form. How simple the old nationalist theory of the Fall appears, in contrast! It can be compressed into one word: treachery! The old Edinburgh élite was guilty of the (Romantic) original sin: cutting

[23] *Memorials of His Time*, by Lord Cockburn (1856), abridged edition, 1946, pp. 64–5.
[24] Hroch, op. cit., pp. 160–1; see also E. J. Hobsbawm, 'Nationalism', in *Imagination and Precision in the Social Sciences*, London 1972, p. 399.

themselves off from the people. Second only to 'community' in this value-vocabulary is the unpleasant term 'roots'. The Enlightenment intelligentsia sold out its birthright – its roots in the Scottish national-popular community – for the sake of its pottage of tedious abstractions. Sir James Steuart may be forgiven, as he happened to be a Jacobite. The rest were cosmopolitan *vendus* to a man: they may have invented social science, but their attitude towards Scoticisms was unpardonable. It was this wilful rootlessness that started the rot. 'The cultural sell-out of Scottish standards . . . the failure of Scotland's political and cultural leaders to be their Scottish selves has created the intellectual and cultural void which is at the centre of Scottish affairs', states Duncan Glen in *Whither Scotland?* (1971). As for David Hume and that band: 'We should give the opposite answers to those of the great philosopher who failed to rise above the attitudes of his time. Since then, however, we have had two hundred years of the Scottish waste of the potential of the Scottish people and we should surely have learned the correct answers by now . . .'

The simple idealism and voluntarism of this diagnosis should need no further stressing. It amounts to saying, *if only* the intellectuals had behaved differently, then our national history might have left its banks, and changed its course. It is not explanation, but retrospective necromancy. But it has as a consequence that the Scottish Enlightenment (as I pointed out above) recedes into a curious limbo of non-recognition, in the nationalist perspective. That is, the country's one moment of genuine historical importance, its sole claim to imperishable fame, literally does not count in the saga of the Scottish national Self. The triumph of Reason produced a wasteland void, as still thriving Romantic clichés would have us believe: not for the first or last time, the nationalist and the romantic 'theories' are really one.

The Reformation as Scapegoat

Lest it be thought that I am treating romanticism too cursorily, and dismissing its view of Scotland too lightly, I shall turn briefly to the most influential study of this kind. Edwin Muir's *Scott and Scotland* appeared in 1926, and has never been reissued. This is a pity, and rather surprising, for it is a book which has reappeared in other people's books and articles ever since. The copies in the Scottish

National Library and the Edinburgh City Library must be particularly well-thumbed. No-one who has spent any time in the archives of literary nationalism can have failed to notice how often Muir is quoted, nearly always with approval.

How did he diagnose what happened to Scotland in the time of Scott? Muir is impressed particularly by what he calls 'a curious emptiness' behind Scott's imaginative richness. The void is already there, as it were, within the work of the Wizard of the North. What caused it? It reflects the fact that Sir Walter lived in 'a country which was neither a nation nor a province and had, instead of a centre, a blank, an Edinburgh, in the middle of it . . . Scott, in other words, lived in a community which was not a community, and set himself to carry on a tradition which was not a tradition . . . (and) . . . his work was an exact reflection of his predicament'. Scott's predicament was, of course, also one 'for the Scottish people as a whole . . . for only a people can create a literature'. England, by contrast, is 'an organic society' with a genuine centre and true *Volksgemeinschaft*. The English author has something to sink his roots into, while his Scottish colleague cannot 'root himself deliberately in Scotland' since there *is* no soil – no 'organic community to round off his conceptions', and not even any real wish for such a society (i.e. no real nationalism).

The mainspring of this, as of all similar arguments, is that it bestows eternal validity, or 'national' status, upon certain categories of 19th-century culture and politics. It is true that all 19th-century nation-states, and societies which aspired to this status through nationalism, had to foster what one may (although somewhat metaphorically) call 'organic community'. That is, for the specific motives mentioned previously their middle classes invented a type of inter-class culture, employing romantic culture and ideology. It is true also that Scotland was structurally unable to adapt to an age in which these categories and motives became the norm. What is not true – though it is the crux of Muir's position – is that this represented some sort of metaphysical disaster which one must despair over.

Muir then goes on to trace (again in very characteristic terms) the dimensions of both disaster and despair. One learns, with some surprise, that the trouble started in the middle ages. The Enlightenment and capitalism are only late symptoms; it was in fact the Reformation which 'truly signalized the beginning of Scotland's decline as a civilized nation'. The last of 'coherent civilization' in Scotland was at the court of James IV (early 16th century). The metaphysical ailment of the Scots, a split between heart and head, began shortly thereafter, that '. . . simple irresponsible feeling side by side with arid intellect . . . for which Gregory Smith found the name of "the Caledonian Antisyzygy"'.[25] So, after the Catholic 'organic community' had ended there was no hope, and Scotland was simply preparing itself for 'the peculiarly brutal form which the Industrial Revolution took in Scotland, where its chief agents are only conceivable as thoughtless or perverted children'.

A markedly oneiric element has crept into the argument somehow, and one wants to rub one's eyes. Can anybody really think this? Not only somebody, but most literary nationalists: it should not be imagined that this position represents a personal vagary of the author. It does have a bizarre dream-logic to it. Muir himself took his pessimism so seriously that not even nationalism seemed a solution to him. But broadly speaking the dream in question is that of romantic nationalism, and the logic is as follows: modern Scottish society does not fit it, and one has to explain why; since the idea-world (roots, organs, and all) is all right, and has unchallengeable status, it has to be Scotland which is wrong; therefore Scottish society and history are monstrously misshapen in some way, blighted by an Original Sin; therefore one should look further back for whatever led to the frightful Enlightenment ('arid intellect', etc.) and the Industrial Revolution; the Reformation is the obvious candidate, so before that things were pretty sound (a safe hypothesis, given the extent of knowledge about the 15th century in modern Scotland).[26]

Start with Idealism and you end up embracing the Scarlet Woman of Rome. I do not wish to dwell longer on this paradox now (though I shall need to refer to it again below). The aura of madness surrounding it is surely plain enough. Farther exploration of the oddities of nationalist ideology in Scotland had better wait until

[25] This curious bacillus can be traced back to G. Gregory Smith, *Scottish Literature: Character and Influence* (1919). It explodes unpronounceably in the archives of literary nationalism quite often after that – e.g. MacDiarmid: 'The Caledonian Antisyzygy . . . may be awaiting the exhaustion of the whole civilization of which English literature is a typical product in order to achieve its effective synthesis in a succeeding and very different civilization' (*Albyn*, 1927, p. 34).

[26] Edwin Muir, op. cit., pp. 22–4, 73–5.

we come to the formation of the nationalist movement itself, in this century. Before I get to this, some more remarks have to be made about the consequences of the Scottish inability to generate a nationalism in the last century.

The Emigré Intelligentsia

I suggested above that Scotland can be seen as a 'negative image' of general European nationalist development, and one which tells us much about that development. There is a sense in which it tells us more than any 'positive' example could: for, of course, in all actual case-histories of nationalism general and highly specific factors are fused together almost inextricably. Whereas in Scotland, where so many particular factors favoured nationalism so powerfully, it is easier to detect (simply by its absence) what the basic causative mechanism must have been. It is in this sense that one may argue that Scotland furnishes a remarkable confirmation of the materialist conception of development and nationalism outlined previously.

But so far the argument has been couched in over-negative terms. We have seen why the development of bourgeois society in Scotland did *not* decree a form of nationalism, and the various 'absences' which followed from this peculiar evolutionary twist. The Scottish bourgeoisie was *not* compelled to frame its own pseudo-organic 'community' of culture, in order to channel popular energies behind its separate interest. Hence there was no serious romanticism as a continuing 'tradition', and the indigenous intellectual class became in a curious sense 'unemployed' or functionless upon its home terrain. The new Scottish working class, in its turn, was deprived of the normal type of 19th-century cultural 'nationalization': that is, such popular-national culture as there was (vulgar Scottishism, or tartanry) was necessarily unrelated to a higher romantic-national and intellectual culture.

One of the most striking single consequences of this overall pattern was massive intellectual emigration. The 19th century also witnessed great working-class and peasant emigration, of course, but these were common to England and Ireland as well. The Scottish cultural outflow was distinctive, although it had much in common with similar trends in Ireland and the Italian south. The reasons for it are clear enough. The country was well provided with educational institutions and its higher culture did not vanish overnight. However, it certainly changed direction, and assumed a markedly different pattern. Its achievements in the century that followed were to be largely in the areas of natural science, technology and medicine – not in the old 18th century ones of social science, philosophy, and general culture. And of course it was what happened to the latter that is most related to the problem of nationalism, and concerns us here. It is in *this* crucial zone that one may speak of 'unemployment', and hence of the forced emigration of the sort of intellectual who elsewhere in Europe was forging a national or nationalist culture.

After the time of Sir Walter Scott, wrote the Victorian critic J. H. Robertson, '. . . we lost the culture-force of a local literary atmosphere; and defect superinduces defect, till it becomes almost a matter of course that our best men, unless tethered by professorships, go south'.[27] In his *Scottish Literature and the Scottish People* the contemporary critic David Craig makes a similar point: 'During the 19th century the country was emptied of the *majority* of its notable literary talents – men who, if they had stayed, might have thought to mediate their wisdom through the rendering of specifically Scottish experience. Of the leading British "sages" of the time an astonishingly high proportion were of Scottish extraction – the Mills, Macaulay, Carlyle, Ruskin, Gladstone'.[28] This last is an especially characteristic judgement, with its suggestion of retrospective voluntarism: *if only* the émigrés had chosen to stay at home, then it might all have been different. The point was that in reality they had no such 'choice': 'specifically Scottish experience' in the sense relevant here would have been a product of culture, not its natural, pre-existent basis – and since Scottish society did not demand the formation of that culture, there *was* no 'experience' and nothing to be said. This phase of the country's history demonstrates, with exceptional vividness, both the social nature and the material basis of 'culture' in the usual intellectuals' sense. It may look as if it could have simply come 'out of people's heads', by free choice; in reality it could not.

There is no time here to say more about the fascinating history of the émigrés and their impact upon the neighbour kingdom. But in a broad sense there is no doubt what happened: unable, for the

[27] J. H. Robertson, *Criticisms*, Vol. II (1885), p. 67.
[28] Craig, op. cit., p. 276.

structural reasons described, to fulfil the 'standard' 19th-century function of elaborating a romantic-national culture for their own people, they applied themselves with vigour to the unfortunate southerners. Our former intelligentsia lost its cohesion and unitary function (its nature *as* an élite) and the individual members poured their formidable energies into the authentically 'organic community' centred on London. There, they played a very large part in formulating the new national and imperial culture-community. We must all be at times painfully aware of how England to this day languishes under the 'tradition' created by the Carlyle-Ruskin school of mystification, as well as the brilliant political inheritance nurtured by Keir Hardie and J. Ramsay MacDonald.

In one way this can be considered a typical form of 'provincialization' which went on in all the greater nation-states. Everywhere hungry and ambitious intellectuals were drawn out of their hinterlands and into the cultural service of their respective capitals. If there was a significant difference here, it lay surely in the higher level and stronger base from which the Scots started. These enabled them, perhaps, to make a contribution at once more important and more distinctive in character. They did not come from a province of an *ancien régime*, but from an advanced quasi-nation with a high (if now anachronistic) culture of its own, and so had a head-start on other backwoodsmen.

3. Old and New Scottish Nationalism

'Scotland is unique among European nations in its failure to develop a nationalist sentiment strong enough to be a vital factor in its affairs . . . The reason probably lies in the fact that no comprehensive-enough agency has emerged; and the commonsense of our people has rejected one-sided expedients incapable of addressing the organic complexity of our national life. For it must be recognized that the absence of nationalism is, paradoxically, a form of Scottish self-determination. If that self-determination, which . . . has reduced Scottish arts and affairs to a lamentable pass is to be induced to take different forms and express itself in a diametrically opposite direction to that which it has taken for the past two hundred and twenty years, the persuading programme must embody considerations of superior power to those which have so long ensured the opposite process. Scottish opinion is anachronism-proof in matters of this kind . . .'

C. M. Grieve (Hugh MacDiarmid), *Albyn, or Scotland and the Future* (1927).

These 'considerations of superior power' were a long time coming to Scotland. However, they have finally arrived. And as they have come – half a century later than MacDiarmid imagined – that hard-headed, 'anachronism-proof' commonsense has indeed begun to shift its ground. The nostalgic literary nationalism he led from the

20s onwards was not a 'comprehensive-enough agency' to do this. Neither were the political movements that accompanied it. The persuading programme which made the difference was the petroleum business: the largest, richest, most aggressive, and most international form of capitalism in the world.

The result is an astonishing situation. Although (as argued below) the new Scottish separatism of the 70s is in some ways comparable to trends in Brittany, Catalonia, Wales, and other regions of Western Europe, in certain respects it remains unique. Nowhere else has the transformation been so abrupt, or so extensive. Nowhere else have the essential forces at work displayed their nature so nakedly. Nowhere else – therefore – is the resultant conflict and political dilemma quite so clearly defined.

It is a substantially new dilemma. On the face of it what is happening may look like an episode of resurrection unequalled since Lazarus. But in fact, this is not only a chapter in the old book of European nationalism. Still less is it something comparable to contemporary national-liberation struggles in the Third World. Romantic interpretations along these lines are not lacking, of course. This is not surprising, because the conceptual language we have available is predominantly 'nationalist' in just this sense: it looks backwards, or out to those parts of the world still engaged in a life-or-death fight against backwardness. New movements cannot help wearing old clothes.

To Scotland's remarkable and novel dilemma there corresponds a new political movement. Like the dilemma itself, it is in a number of ways analogous to historical or mainstream nationalism. But a more careful consideration shows its different place in history, and its different character and potential. As argued below, it deserves to be called 'neo-nationalism' rather than nationalism. For there is a new character which serves to distinguish this separatism from (e.g.) Czech, Polish, South Slav and other nationalisms of the 19th and early 20th centuries, or from such contemporary national struggles as those in Kurdistan, Eritrea, Bangladesh, and the Portuguese colonies.

Let me try to summarize the difference, in a preliminary and quite incomplete fashion. 'Nationalism', in that sense which has dominated historical development since early in the 19th century, was in essence the forced reaction of one area after another to the spread of capitalism. This process has been awarded other titles too:

'westernization', 'modernization', or simply 'development'. What matters here is that this complex, long-term movement arose chiefly in areas of what one may call absolute deprivation. They were overwhelmingly feudal, or pre-feudal, in social character. They were marked, that is, by illiteracy, landlord-rule, feeble urban development, primary poverty, and absence of the socio-economic infrastructures which modernization demands. This is of course why they became (and soon felt themselves to be) 'backward', or 'underdeveloped'. It is why, equally, they were bound to fall victim to some variety of domination or 'imperialism' – to which the only effective response was in most cases locally-based, popular struggle: nationalism.

Neo-nationalism arises at a different, much later point in the same general process. It remains comparable to elemental nationalism in being a forced by-product of the grotesquely uneven nature of capitalist development. As the latter's blind, lurching progress impinges upon this or that region, it still poses a threat (or more exactly, a combined promise *and* threat) of modernization, 'imperialistic' disruption of old ways, and so on. But this now occurs at a far more advanced stage of general development, in areas which long ago emerged from the absolute 'backwardness' just referred to. Located on the fringe of the new metropolitan growth zones, they suffer from a relative deprivation and are increasingly drawn to political action against this. This action is analogous to old-style nationalism, above all in its ideology. But, precisely because it starts from a higher level and belongs to a more advanced stage of capitalist evolution – to the age of multinationals and the effective internationalization of capital – its real historical function will be different. The impact of the oil industry on Scotland and of the U.S. multinationals on the French *Midi* is provoking a new Scottish and Occitanian separatism; but, to a greater extent than is realized, this is a *sui generis* phenomenon which should not be assimilated to classical European or Third World 'nationalism' at all.

It is the devastating rapidity and scale of the impact of these new conditions that has made Scotland into the exemplar of 'neo-nationalism' in this sense. One need only compare the oil industry's arrival to the previous, gradual (and more generally characteristic) infiltration of international corporations into the Scottish industrial belt during the 1950s, and 60s, to grasp this. Yet this is only one aspect of the situation.

For the dramatic developments of the past few years are busy transforming a deeper historical situation which was, itself, quite unique. MacDiarmid was not quite accurate in saying that Scotland was alone in failing 'to develop a nationalist sentiment strong enough to be a vital factor in its affairs', in the 19th century. In fact, Western Europe is a graveyard of historical nationalities which were suppressed or submerged by the rise of what became the 18th and 19th century 'great powers'. Scotland's real peculiarity lies elsewhere. It lies in the lateness with which such absorption occurred: at the beginning of the 18th century, rather than in the later Middle Ages. It lies in the manner of the fusion: there are many stateless nationalities in history, but only one Act of Union – a peculiarly patrician bargain between two ruling classes, which would have been unthinkable earlier, under absolute monarchy, and impossible later, when the age of democratic nationalism had arrived. And it lies in the results of the bargain: a nationality which resigned statehood but preserved an extraordinary amount of the institutional and psychological baggage normally associated with independence – a decapitated national state, as it were, rather than an ordinary 'assimilated' nationality.

For two centuries after the Jacobite Rebellion of 1745–6, this freak by-product of European history posed no particular problem. The reason was simple: on the whole, the Union bargain worked as it had been intended to. Indeed it far surpassed the hopes placed in it. During the prolonged era of Anglo-Scots imperialist expansion, the Scottish ruling order found that it had given up statehood for a hugely profitable junior partnership in the New Rome. The oddity of the Union has always posed grave cultural and psychological problems in Scotland – problems recognizable, as I shall go on to argue, through a characteristic series of sub-national deformations or 'neuroses'. But it posed no real *political* problem for most of this time.

The political problem returned only with the post-World-War-II decline of the United Kingdom. This has been a slow process. The strength and stability of this old multi-national system, founded on its imperialist successes, has proved resistant to the collapse. None the less, as both great U.K. parties failed to do more than tamper with the underlying crisis, the slow foundering has begun to turn into a rout. In the early 1970s paralysis and incapacity have become undeniable, electorally as well as in terms of party strategies.

It is at this point that conditions have precipitated the neo-nationalist movement in Scotland. The oil industry has collided with the country at a moment of extreme and growing debility in the traditional political apparatus – in that conservative Unionism which a majority of Scots have supported, with little dissension, for two centuries. The consequence is perhaps the most startling aspect of the whole situation. The novel conflict in Scotland has cut into the palsied corpus of Unionism like a knife. More than any other factor, more even than the miners' strikes of 1972 and 1974, it has exposed the senility of the old consensus and its two-party system.

Pious, somewhat sleekit debates about 'Home Rule' for Scotland and Wales have appeared and reappeared in imperial politics since the 1880s. It would have dumbfounded these earlier generations of Home Rulers to see the Greater Britain caving in before new nationalist demands. They sought a modest degree of self-government in order to strengthen the Union, and Great-British nationalism. Nobody thought that one day U.K. parties would fall over one another in a competition to cede wider and wider powers, or that The Thunderer would declare defeat in advance, in a mood of world-weary resignation: 'The Scots are all assembly men now. So the practical question is what kind of assembly. No stability could be expected from setting up a Scottish Assembly in a grudging spirit with the minimum powers that a reluctant government in London felt it had to concede. It is better to devolve the widest powers . . . It could be that once the Scottish people have taken one step along that road they will not be satisfied with any stopping place short of full independence. If so, it would be neither possible nor desirable to keep them within the United Kingdom . . .'[1]

Under these conditions, unforeseeable even a few years ago, the somewhat eccentric inheritance of Scottish sub-nationalism has assumed new meaning. Until the later 1960s it was, in wider European terms, an unclassifiable marginal aberration: an ex-nation turned province, neither one thing nor another – a relic from before the Flood of Europe's mainstream nationalism, as it were, more suitable for jokes than serious political analysis. MacFinnegan had slumbered comfortably through the age of national revivals, with no more than a twitch or two. It could not be imagined, then, that a

---

[1] *Times*, editorial of August 19th 1974, 'All Assembly Men Now'.

drop or two of petroleum spirit would bring him staggering to his feet, demanding the restitution of his lost political kingdom. Still less that English governments would have no alternative but to weakly placate him.

Given this turn of events, neo-nationalism has made such rapid, apparently irresistible strides because it has this old basis to stand on. Headless aberration or not, the Scottish sub-culture is far more than most other submerged ethnic groups in Europe have to start from. Cramped, stagnant, backward-looking, parochial – all these and others are the epithets traditionally and rightly ascribed to modern Scottishness. But deformed as they are, these constitute none the less a strong, institutionally guaranteed identity. It is true that political castration was the main ingredient in this rather pathological complex (such was the point of the Union), and that intellectuals have been unable to contemplate it for a long time without inexpressible pain. Still, there it was: the one thing which the Scots can never be said to have lacked is identity. Once the material circumstances for a new sort of political mobilization had formed, the thistle-patch proved very useful. It gave the S.N.P., in a sense, much more to go on than comparable separatist movements in Wales, Brittany, Corsica, or the other regions.

Thus there seem to be three main ingredients in the situation. The most critical, and the newest, is the incursion of the oil business with its apocalyptic bundle of promises and menaces: this is busy creating a new material basis for political life in Scotland. The second is the decline of the all-British political system, which had already half-formed a vacuum into which new and alternative forces could rush: there is no sign of this disintegration being arrested, either in Scotland, in Ulster, or in England itself. The third is the curious quasi-national legacy of North Britain, which is being reanimated by the new kind of separatism that has made such progress in the last few years.

I do not propose to try and deal here with the first two. In any case, searching examinations of the oil companies and desperate broodings on the fate of Westminster are not lacking from the scene. I would like only to consider the third, under three headings. First, its origins, as what MacDiarmid called a 'paradoxical form of self-determination' which arose instead of nationalism. Secondly, its character in a broad political-cultural sense: the cultural sub-nationalism of tartanry. Third, its likely significance within the

122

wider perspectives of European neo-nationalism and the Common
Market.

I

> 'To begin with, while we have a homogeneous British
> State it must be noted that the organizations and institu-
> tions in civil society which comprise its bulwarks and de-
> fences have an azoic complexity the most significant fea-
> ture of which for us is that civil society in Scotland is
> fundamentally different from that in England. What is
> more, much of our shared "British" ideology as it mani-
> fests itself in Scotland, draws its vigour and strength
> from a specifically Scottish heritage of myths, prejudices
> and illusions . . . If the left is even to begin a serious
> critique of our society then these differences must be
> taken account of.'

> Ray Burnett, 'Scotland and Antonio Gramsci',
> *Scottish International* (No. 9, Nov. 1972)

The theoretical problem posed by these remarks of Ray Burnett's
could be put as follows. To understand any society as a whole,
one must always distinguish between its 'State' or political and
administrative structure, and its 'civil society'. The latter comprises,
for example, its most characteristic non-political organizations, its
religious and other beliefs, its 'customs' or way of life, its typical
jokes, and so on. It is not easy to sum up all that is denoted by this
Gramscian category, and there are things which will not fit neatly
under either heading. But this is relatively unimportant. What
matters is that they are distinguishable, and that the singular identity of a modern society depends upon the relationship between
them.

Amidst these abstractions, it is important to be as specific as
possible. What we are considering is the problem of understanding
modern societies; and within that, the question of what it is that
makes any *one* such society structurally distinct, 'peculiar' in relation to others resembling it in so many ways. Needless to say the
question can be answered quite empirically (and it usually is):
thousands of particular events always make any one place different
from others. Yet this is an evasion of the real problem, which derives

from the fact that societies 'hang together' in some way, as some sort of whole. And *modern* (19th and 20th century) societies hang together especially closely, and in a special way.

Gramsci describes the problem as follows. Within the last two centuries – roughly from the French Revolution to the present – there has arisen a relationship between State and society generally characteristic of modern social formations; 'The revolution which the bourgeois class has brought into the conception of law, and hence into the function of the State, consists especially in the will to conform (hence ethnicity of the law and of the State). The previous ruling classes were essentially conservative in the sense that they did not tend to construct an organic passage from the other classes into their own, i.e. to enlarge their class sphere "technically" and ideologically: their conception was that of a closed caste. The bourgeois class poses itself as an organism in continuous movement, capable of absorbing the entire society, assimilating it to its own cultural and economic level. The entire function of the State has been transformed; the State has become an "educator", etc . . .'. The main point about this modern State-society relationship – quite distinct from that of Antiquity or Feudalism – is that through it the whole people becomes part of society, really for the first time.

Previous State-systems and ruling castes had presided over society. By contrast (Gramsci goes on): 'In my opinion, the most reasonable and concrete thing that can be said about the ethical State, the cultural State, is this: every State is ethical in as much as one of its most important functions is to raise the great mass of the population to a particular cultural and moral level, a level (or type) which corresponds to the needs of the productive forces for development, and hence to the interests of the ruling classes. The school as a positive educative function, and the courts . . . are the most important State activities in this sense: but in reality a multitude of other so-called private initiatives and activities tend to the same end – initiatives and activities which form the apparatus of the political and cultural hegemony of the ruling classes'.[2]

One farther remark is indispensable here. This 'revolution which

[2] Antonio Gramsci, *Selections from the Prison Notebooks*, trans. & edited by Q. Hoare and G. Nowell Smith (1971), pp. 258–60. There is some language barrier for the English-language reader due to Gramsci's formation as a Crocean Idealist. But for an argument substantially similar on the subject of nationalism and written in contemporary sociological language, see Ernest Gellner, 'Nationalism', in the volume *Thought and Change* (1964).

the bourgeois class has brought' necessarily affected the different social formations caught up in it at different times, and in quite different ways. Such deep diversity was inseparable from the process. The huge complexity and variety of pre-existing social evolution meant that each society had a different starting-point, and was struck and transformed by the spreading wave of 'modernization' in different ways. Modernization and all its concomitants (industrialization, political democracy, general literacy, etc., etc.) notoriously tend towards uniformity and the standardization of many aspects of existence. But they have done so, historically, only through prolonged struggle against (and forced compromise with) this social diversity.

This is of course why *nationalism* has been a central, inescapable feature of the development of 'modern society'. There could only be modern societies, in the plural, and they could not help being very distinct from one another – even those at a similar general stage of development, as in present-day Western Europe. The State-society knot Gramsci is talking about was, so to speak, tied in remarkably different fashions in these different places. So, the normal historiographical and sociological model for it is naturally that of *one* society-cum-State. It is this modern and contemporary 'nation-State' that 'has become an educator', has 'raised the great mass of the population to a particular cultural level', generated a particular 'apparatus of political and cultural hegemony', and so forth. And we know only too well that once it has done so, in the way corresponding to its particular historical situation, the resultant particular identity is very resistant indeed to change and attack.[3]

If the general problem is posed in this way, then how does the particular problem of modern Scotland appear? As we observed already, it represents a historical oddity – but one which posed no special or anguishing problem to its own ruling class or to its neighbours in Europe, simply because this freak nature was accompanied by prolonged political quiescence. There was, almost until the present day, no urgent practical reason to decipher the enigma. Romantic superstition did well enough. Indeed (as we all know)

[3] I will seek to deal with the more theoretical questions of nationalism's sociological character and place in history, in the general overview of Chapter Nine below, 'The Modern Janus'.

it became in the 19th century one of those 'bulwarks and defences' of our civil society, a kind of surrogate nationalism.

While strong practical motives were absent, all the new models of nationalist history-writing pointed in another direction: towards what had become the standard European (and later world) pattern of one political State and *its* society, or one distinguishable ethnic society and *its* own State. A world where the civil societies and the States mainly fitted each other, as it were, through the normal developmental struggles of last century and this. By comparison, Scotland was a hippogriff: a manifest bastard, in the world of nationalist wedlock. Incomprehensibly, this composite formation had failed to grow like the others. Although clearly an historic nation, and one which had preserved much of its inheritance after 1707 – thus escaping the *Gleichschaltung* to which so many other old ethnic groups were subjected, as they were 'absorbed' into provinces of greater European powers – Scotland had failed to turn nationalist and create its own political State. It had failed to do the normal thing, at the proper time. It had disobeyed the 'logic of history' – which was of course also the logic of the way people had come to think about modern history, and analyse modern societies.

'Most Scots would, quite rightly, have laughed at the idea that the Scottish nation came to an end in 1707 ... it was the end of an auld sang, perhaps, but it was not yet the end of an auld people', T. C. Smout has written.[4] Only in retrospect, from the point of view of the age of nationalism, did the loss of statehood seem to overshadow the country's history so completely, condemning it to eccentricity and oblivion. Scottish society apart from the State, 'civil society', was guaranteed in its independent existence by the Union. The church, the law, the aristocracy, the bourgeoisie of the Royal Burghs: all these institutions and the dominant social classes linked to them were confirmed in what they had demanded of separate identity. So was the distinct social culture they represented.

The Scots pattern so strikingly counterposed to the usual models is therefore that of a distinct civil society not married to 'its' State. It is one of heterogeneity, not that relative homogeneity which became the standard of nationalist development. A foreign, much

[4] T. C. Smout, 'Union of the Parliaments', in *The Scottish Nation: a History of the Scots from Independence to Union*, ed. G. Menzies (1972), pp. 158–9.

stronger State and political system was imposed on Scotland by
the Union. Through it the country was 'managed', as Rosalind
Mitchison has written, 'by a set of monarchs chosen by English
politicians for English political purposes'. Except at moments of
crisis, this State was 'ignorant of and indifferent to the problems
of Scotland . . .' so that on the whole the country's government was
'ramshackle and confused in structure, improvised and halting in
execution'.[5] One should add of course that this fate was chosen by
the indigenous ruling class. Alien and corrupt it may have been.
Still, it was so much better than what Scotland had known that
they could hardly believe their luck. A later contributor to the same
volume quotes a letter from one of the great Scots 'managers',
Duncan Forbes of Culloden, expressing his relief at the dis-
continuance of the Ministerial post of Scottish Secretary. Ultimate
power was best left in English hands completely: '. . . for some time
at least we shall not be troubled by that nuisance . . . a Scots Secretary, either at full length or in miniature; if any one Scotsman has
absolute power, we are in the same slavery as ever, whether that
person be a fair man or a black man, a peer or a commoner, 6 foot
or 5 foot high, and the dependence of the country will be on that
man, and not on those that made him'.[6]

It is above all the class character of this composite polity which
concerns us here. Naturally, it was only the most restricted 'upper
crust' that had embraced Union in this way, and now looked back
with horror upon the old pre-1707 chaos and tyranny. It was indeed
a perfect specimen of the conceptions of one of those 'closed castes'
Gramsci refers to: an 'essentially conservative' class, still largely
aristocratic in nature, which emphatically did not tend to 'enlarge
its class sphere' ideologically and exert a 'political and cultural
hegemony' in the modern sense. The hegemony it represented
was an older one. It was simply that of aristocratic or patrician
'direction' of a hierarchical social order, from above – one might
almost say (emphasizing the contrast with nationalism) from out-

[5] Rosalind Mitchison, 'The Government and the Highlands 1707–1745',
in *Scotland in the Age of Improvement: Essays in Scottish History in the 18th
Century*, ed. N. Phillipson & R. Mitchison (1970), pp. 24–5.

[6] J. M. Simpson, 'Who Steered the Gravy Train, 1707–1766?', in *ibid.*, p. 49.
For the background to the letter see *The Life and Letters of Duncan Forbes of
Culloden*, by G. Menary (1936), ch. IV, 'The Glasgow Malt Riots of 1725'.

side.[7] The Enlightened spirits of the Scottish ruling élite became vigorous and effective 'Improvers' during the century following Union. To this extent they were of course 'modernizing' and progressive. But none of them had the slightest doubt that this *was* what Progress consisted in: diffusion of light *de haut en bas*, from the educated few above to the vast, passive – if not bigoted and refractory – mass below.

There was nothing unusual about this class character, or the world-view associated with it. It prevailed over most of Europe until 1789. Still less was there anything strange about an old society being politically mismanaged by a distant, alien State: this remained standard procedure over large areas of Europe until 1918 (at least). What was originally unusual about Scotland was something different. And with the passage of time this difference became a situation that was to be quite unique.

The distant State that dominated the Scots was not the standard European Absolutism. England was the first really successful post-Absolutist State; after its revolutions of the previous century it was moving towards the even greater socio-economic transformation which, between the later 18th century and the middle of the 19th, would carry it to industrial and political supremacy. This change went far beyond the bounds of the most Enlightened Despotism, the most Improving of Landowning classes. It was, as a matter of fact, the very prototype of the modern development Gramsci indicates: that 'revolution of the bourgeois class' which involved the progressive 'absorbing of the entire society' into the new State-society relationship emblemized in nationalism.

What really counts here is not only that the Scots rulers were lucky enough to have been taken over by a dynamic bourgeois cul-

---

[7] The patriotism found in some circles of the old ruling class had little in common with nationalism (which in the modern sense always has a populist connotation). For example Andrew Fletcher of Saltoun, that doyen of modern nationalists, proposed in the second of his *Two Discourses on the Affairs of Scotland* (1698) that the 'harmless unemployed' should be returned to a form of slavery. 'Back to servitude' was the cry, notes his biographer: 'He risked his reputation as a lover of liberty by proposing what was difficult to distinguish from a system of domestic slavery'. The 'dangerous unemployed' were to be sold to the plantations or deported to Eastern Europe to fight the Turks, at the same time. W. C. Mackenzie, *Andrew Fletcher of Saltoun: His Life and Times* (1935), ch. VIII, 'On Unemployment'.

ture instead of a stagnant late-feudal one. It is that this was the *first* such 'bourgeois revolution' proceeding on a sufficient territorial basis. Just because it was first, it developed gradually, and in a highly 'empirical' and de-centralized fashion. All those societies which developed later, in its wake, could not help doing so far more competitively, through a much more intense political and State organization. After the first huge strides forward England had made, after her Agrarian and Industrial Revolutions and her colonial and commercial triumphs over France, other lands were forced to be in some sense 'late-comers' – forced, therefore, to compensate for their backwardness by a more conscious, a more State-contrived and militant type of development.

Free from these pressures – which were to be the normal tensions of uneven development in modern times – the post-1707 multinational State permitted a more spontaneous and localized evolution of civil society. By comparison with later arrivals, the British Industrial Revolution was remarkably 'provincial' and self-sustaining in character. This was precisely the situation which the Scots inherited, and were able to exploit. The historical situation was by nature unique, unrepeatable – so in turn was the use which the Scottish bourgeoisie made of it. No other province, no other submerged nationality of Europe, was ever to be in the same conjuncture again. Everywhere else, the rising tide of the bourgeois revolution, the forward drive of capitalist development, confronted marginal or 'backward' peoples with a far starker dilemma: uncompromising 'assimilation' or independent (nationalist) development by means of their own State and army.

Given the priority, and the structural character, of their development, the English ruling class was able to tolerate a high degree of North-British autonomy. Hence the lack of what were to become the standard practices of discrimination, ethnic oppression and *Kulturkampf*. These were not due to the milk of English Benevolence, as so many apologists of the Union have proclaimed.

Benevolence did not flow so noticeably in Ireland, or for that matter in Scotland itself beyond the Highland Line: these were 'incompatible' social formations which could not be brought into bourgeois partnership so easily. They were not to escape the normal dilemma of 'development', and its cruel consequences. The Lowland Scots did escape it, just. Through the peculiar circumstances of the Union and their own astonishing self-development in the

later 18th century, they were able to establish a singular, subordinate position inside the still relatively 'open' and expanding
system of English capitalism.

'In sum', writes William Ferguson, 'the economic development of
Scotland in the 18th century is best regarded as constituting the
so-called "take-off" phase, making possible the emergence of an
industrialized society. The actual achievement of industrialization
. . . was the work mainly of the 19th century'.[8] Thus, Scottish
civil society advanced much farther than had been imagined
possible under its foreign monarchy and State. Its dominant class
had sacrificed statehood for participation in the English and
colonial 'common market' of the day, trusting that this would aid
the diffusion of Polite Society in their tenebrous land. In fact,
society 'took off' beneath their feet, towards a revolutionary condition of industrialization. Within the larger economic area they had
entered, they had created an autonomous sub-system – in effect,
an epicentre now borne along upon the grander tide of English
imperial expansion. They had entered its flow at a moment when,
still in formation, it could tolerate the existence of such a sub-
system. Hence they were neither crushed by it, nor compelled into
nationalist reaction against it – the standard fates which, one can be
certain, they would not have escaped if Union had been delayed
until the end of the 18th century.

As a part of this advance, there occurred a significant florescence
of Scottish national culture. In comparison with the theocratic
gloom of the 17th century, this appeared strange even to some of
its protagonists. In a very celebrated letter, David Hume asked:
'Is it not strange that, at a time when we have lost our Princes,
our Parliaments, our independent Government, even the Presence
of our chief Nobility, are unhappy, in our Accent & Pronunciation,
speak a very corrupt Dialect of the Tongue which we make use of;
is it not strange, I say, that, in these Circumstances, we shou'd
really be the People most distinguished for Literature in Europe?'[9]

---

[8] William Ferguson, *Scotland: 1689 to the Present* (vol. IV of the 'Edinburgh
History of Scotland', 1968), p. 197. See also T. C. Smout, *A History of the
Scottish People 1560–1830*, (1969), especially ch. X, 'The Transformation of the
Economy'.

[9] David Hume, letter to Gilbert Elliot, 1757, in *Letters*, ed. Greig (1932),
vol. 1, p. 255. For the background to the letter, see E. C. Mossner's *The Life of
David Hume* (1954), ch. 27, 'Scotland's Augustans'. Mossner maintains that Hume

The question has been posed and re-posed ever since. It has deeply vexed nationalists, in particular, that the most illustrious phase of our cultural history should have been so strikingly non-national*ist* – so detached from the People, so intellectual and universalizing in its assumptions, so Olympian in its attitudes. This vexation is understandable, yet misplaced. The Edinburgh *philosophes* were neither traitors to their country – as that country then was, and as they perceived it – nor cosmopolitan poseurs. They simply belonged to a unique, pre-nationalist stage of socio-economic expansion. Concentrated in such a small area and time, in a land transported so incredibly quickly out of Barbarity into Civility, they were the chief exemplars of the European Englightenment's vision of Progress. That is, of a vision of development which was everywhere discredited and made impossible, after 1800.

At this point, one can see how important the temporal dimension is for any model of Scottish society. For, in the extraordinarily favourable conditions of the Union, the rapid progress of Scotland's new, bourgeois civil society cannot help appearing 'premature'. This is of course mainly a comparative classification. Few, even among perfervid nationalists, would regret that the country escaped so smartly from the age of witch-burning and feudal futility. But in relation to virtually every other region of Europe, Scottish advance was precocious. In a number of decisive respects, the Scots had crossed the great divide of basic 'development' before the real nature of the problem had even presented itself – in most of what are now Italy and Germany, for instance, in most of Ireland and Scandinavia, and in all of Eastern Europe.

This precocity was bound to be far-reaching in its consequences. For it was Europe, Europe as a whole, which cast the general mould of 'development' and the world-view linked to it. We know what that mould inevitably consisted in: nationalism. Nationalism was

---

was 'certainly overstating the case for Scottish Literature', *ibid.*, p. 389, but is there any overstatement in saying that no other region of Europe comparable in population, size, and previous history was more 'distinguish'd for Literature' at this period? A contemporary list of the 'many Men of Genius this Country produces' is given in Smout's *History*: 'Hume, Smith, Burns, Black, Watt, Telford, Robert Adam and Hutton in the first rank, Ferguson, Millar, Reid, Robertson, Allan Ramsay junior, Raeburn, William Adam, Rennie, Boswell and Hogg in the second, and a third rank crowded with talent . . .' (p. 470).

the forced mode of socio-economic, and political, evolution. It was to be through this that the majority of European 'backward' lands tried to achieve that break-through which history had already granted the Scots (in all essentials) by the 1820s. It was to take most of them several generations of struggle to do it. Some did not begin to succeed until after 1918; others, not until after 1945. As they fought in this direction, the original 'advanced' States, the leaders of development, were compelled into a more imperialistic and aggressive nationalism of their own. Nobody could evade the new climate, the ferocious and exacting conditions of this new epoch, in which even culture was pressed – in a way that would have seemed lunatic to David Hume and the other Edinburgh Augustans – into the service of the nationality-state.

The most significant consequence, from our point of view, lies in the quite different stamp left by these two forms of social development. Normal, nationalist development depended upon the deliberate fostering and mobilization of ethnic, linguistic and other *differentiae*. Through it, the typical backward region or ex-province has levered itself forward into modern times with the help of its own past – in effect, by a curious sort of regression. It is of course this 'regression' which marks a good deal of what anyone will recognize as the psychology of nationalism: the mythicization of the past, evocations of the *Volksgeist*, and so on. *Reculer pour mieux sauter*: the dilemma of nationalist movements is that they have to gaze backwards, and summon up what energy they can from the particular 'inheritance' they are stuck with, in order to leap forward. Otherwise (or so it looks to them) they are bound to be trampled on by the greater powers outside. In the course of the process, all these inherited *impedimenta* – the substance of whatever civil society they have – assumes new meaning. It is transfigured, in a way that would have astonished the previous generations who actually lived the 'national experience'.[10]

This complex of events, feelings and ideas makes up national*ism*: a modern, developmental phenomenon quite distinct from straight-forward national and cultural differences, of the kind there have always been and always will be. In Scotland, it has never happened. The innumerable institutional and popular *differentiae* of Scots life had persisted. Some may have dwindled, in the face of those

---

[10] Transfigured, that is, where it is not simply invented.

'assimilationist' pressures which nationalist paranoia makes so much of; but far more have remained, and certain central bastions were in any case (as we saw) guaranteed by the Union. What counts is that the Scottish middle classes were never compelled to turn to this substantial inheritance and harness it *en bloc*, to mobilize it and the social classes beneath them in a developmental struggle. The usual 'raw material' of nationalism remained, in Scotland, latent and unexploited.

The characteristic stamp left on Scotland by its initial development was very different. In an apt passage describing the history of the Kirk in the 18th century, Ian Clark writes: 'The Moderates can perhaps be compared to typical 18th century "Improvers", who canalized the stagnant stream of the Kirk to form an attractive ornamental water, spanned by elegant balustraded bridges and flanked by well-planted policies and the classical country seats of gentlemen who (of course with a Moderate as tutor) had made the Grand Tour in their youth.'[11] So, under these influences, even the Kirk – that incorrigible core of Scottishry, that veritable ribcage of our civil society – was inducted into Civilization. At least in the case of its élite of luminaries, among whom (the same author says): 'The driving force . . . was a mood of cultural liberation and optimism which made the Moderate clergy aspire to play not merely a national but a European role'.

This patrician culture was not adaptable to the new, typically modern conditions created by Scotland's industrial revolution. 'Before the century was out', continues Clark, 'Nature began to reassert herself, and landscaping in the Moderate manner passed out of fashion'. New social earthquakes overthrew the balustrades and Polite terraces, a new landscape of social class rendered the Classical achievements incongruous and anachronistic. It had, after all, been in certain respects a superficial landscape. And its profoundly non-democratic and anti-populist character made it largely useless as an instrument of hegemony in the new conditions. Under the latter – say from the 1780s to the 1830s – Ferguson points out how 'every aspect of Scottish life was being subjected to change – sometimes slow, sometimes rapid, but seemingly inexorable.

[11] I. D. L. Clark, 'From Protest to Reaction: the Moderate Régime in the Church of Scotland, 1752–1805', in *Scotland in the Age of Improvement*, op. cit., p. 223.

Furthermore, it was revolutionary change, not a mere shift of emphasis within the same system. It affected material conditions, these in turn brought social change, and contingent upon this . . . there arose new beliefs and values'. An emphatically modern society was coming into being in Scotland, an urbanized and industrial society with a rapidly-growing proletariat. It was through this formation that 'the full implications of the changes wrought in 18th century Scotland still remained to be worked out'.[12]

The normal implication of such changes was nationalism. It was in forced reaction to (or anticipation of) such revolutionary material conditions and changes that the new, nationalist beliefs and values imposed themselves across Europe. It was in this transformed milieu that it became indispensable to 'raise the great mass of the population to a particular cultural and moral level' (in Gramsci's words), 'a level . . . corresponding to the needs of the productive forces for development, and hence to the interests of the ruling classes'. This could only be done by means of a new, more accessible culture, one located on a far more particularistic and popular basis. It had to be far closer to the people, to their real ethnic and historical character, their language or modes of expression, and so on. It could only be Romantic in form, not Classical. Only in this way could nationality be elevated into 'nationalism' and an effective mobilization of popular class forces be obtained; equally one may say that, wherever the harnessing of such forces had become less important, this was the only way they could be *contained*.

The emergence of modern Scotland was marked by constant social and radical agitation. This proceeded parallel with that in England but, as E. P. Thompson notes in the preface to *The Making of the English Working Class*, it was 'significantly different': 'Calvinism was not the same thing as Methodism, although it is difficult to say which, in the early 19th century, was worse . . . And the popular culture was very different'.[13] It also poses a significantly different question. This is of course why, under these quite different conditions, it did not result in agitation for *separatism*. In his discussion of England's popular radicalism, Thompson shows how its more revolutionary tendencies were betrayed by lack of support

[12] W. Ferguson, *Scotland*, op. cit., p. 233.
[13] E. P. Thompson, *The Making of the English Working Class* (1963), 'Preface', p. 13.

from above: whatever their dissatisfaction with the *ancien régime*, the new bourgeoisie feared the forces beneath them too much to take this path. Not being compelled along it – because they had already achieved adequate economic emancipation as a class – they blocked it, in an ever-closer alliance with the older landed Establishment. One may say something similar about Scotland. But the important difference is that here they were *also* obstructing and diverting the separatist or nationalist trends which were still implicit in the persistence of such a distinct civil society.

It still may not be grasped quite what an anomaly this presents. People look back nowadays with puzzlement at the country's 19th century lack of nationhood, its near-total absence from the great and varied stage of European nationalism. With resentment or relief (depending on their politics) they wonder: what *was* missing? In every *superficial* respect except one – language – Scotland was quite exceptionally well equipped for the usual nationalist struggles. Unless one accepts a naïve language-theory of nationalism, therefore, it is necessary to look a lot deeper. On the surface, around 1820–30, only one other place looked more like a nation-to-be than Scotland: that other recently deceased State, the epitome and inspirer of so much of the romantic nationality struggle of the century, Poland. Nationalism involves the reanimation of one's history. And there was nowhere else more – to coin a phrase, the needed contrary of 'history-less people' – 'history-ful' than the Scotland of Sir Walter Scott.[14]

The cultural 'raw material' for nationalism – old traditions, folk-heroes, anti-Englishry, etc., etc. – was not only abundant. One can observe it being fashioned in the usual way in (to take only the most obvious example) the radical Robert Burns. This was the Burns who 'knelt at the tomb of Sir John the Graham, the gallant friend of the immortal Wallace' and 'said a fervent prayer for old

---

[14] Here I must refer the reader to the famous discussions in the 19th Century which originally gave currency to the idea that there were nations without a history, or a history worthy of the name. The term 'historyless people' was used by Marx and Engels (amongst others) to denote those so backward and ill-equipped for national struggle they had no hope of making it. The implication was usually that they were unjustified in trying, and should have resigned themselves to assimilation by the 'historical nations'. The best discussion of this mistake is in Roman Rosdolsky, *Friedrich Engels und das Problem des geschichslosen Völker* (1964).

Caledonia over the hole in a blue whinstone, where Robert de Bruce fixed his royal standard on the banks of Bannockburn . . .'.[15] But this historical nostalgia was associated with his sympathy for the American and French Revolutions. 'For Burns in 1793' – the year in which he composed *Scots wha hae* – 'Bannockburn is directly associated with the French Revolution', notes Janet Adam Smith, in the sense that 'Scotland's fight for independence could be the channel of expression, the "objective correlative", for feelings of independence that were not confined to Scotland . . . The swords and staves of Bruce's army must become the carronades sent . . . by Burns to the French Convention'. This was exactly the sort of utilization of historical materials which generally marked the formative, ascendant phases of nationalism in Europe. After Burns, hundreds of kindred spirits were to respond to the revolutionary impact with a similar new mythology, a similar vindication of their own special inheritance and its (real or supposed) universal meaning.

In Scotland however, this promising 'raw material', this newly-rediscovered historical character, could not possibly be developed in the usual way. Here, such ethnic and historical *differentiae* could not be mobilized and made part of a new national, romantic culture. Scottish civil society had advanced too far, too quickly. The new bourgeois social classes inherited a socio-economic position in history vastly more favourable than that of any other fringe or backward nationality. They were neither being ground down into industrial modernity, nor excluded from it. Hence they did not perceive it as alien, as a foreign threat or a withheld promise. Consequently they were not forced to turn to nationalism, to redress the situation. They reacted to the inexorable and revolutionary changes of the crucial period even more fiercely than their English partners – with a conservatism amplified, perhaps, by the uneasy sensation of how much more there was to repress and divert in Scotland.

Scots differentness could not be harnessed in the way that the young Burns and other radicals imagined. But it did not disappear, for that reason. It simply became a problem. This problem was a new one, specific to 19th and 20th century conditions; and I shall go on to argue that in certain respects it was *culturally* insoluble (and led therefore to a persistent alienation of the intelligentsia)

[15] Burns, *Letters* (1931), as quoted in Janet Adam Smith, 'Some 18th Century Ideas of Scotland', *Scotland in the Age of Improvement*, op. cit., pp. 118–23.

although it was *practically* solved by the crude external instrument of imperialism. It was culturally insoluble because the vital transitional period, from the 1790s to the 1830s, had ushered in a new age of more organic communities – of the modern societies in which, to employ Gramsci's terms again, ruling classes had to 'construct an organic passage from other classes into their own', by means of a new, more effective 'apparatus of political and cultural hegemony'. Scotland could not become an 'organic' national community in this sense, with its own distinctive union of civil society and State. But it could not remain in the 18th century either. The problem of its bourgeoisie therefore became – put in the starkest terms – one of *neutralizing* or *repressing* the country's more distinctive and proto-national features.

It was only after this that the model of Scottish development indicated above – heterogeneity as between society and State – poses dramatic questions. Earlier on, it is only by a sort of romantic retrospection that the Scottish ruling class and intelligentsia can be depicted as 'betraying' their particular ethnic-national inheritance. If they spurned Scotticisms and 'uncouth manners', it was because, like similar classes from Norrland to Andalusia and from Flanders to Ruthenia, they believed in a Universal and Enlightened civilization of which – sooner or later – everybody educated would be members. There was nothing reprehensible about being a 'province' in an expanding world like this. But the world did not continue to develop in the same way: it broke down into the separate, national, mass societies of the following century – creating quite new general conditions for culture. And under these conditions Scotland was (so to speak) 'stranded'. It was in an odd, limbo-like state, betwixt and between, where it has remained ever since. It was too much of a nation, had too different a civil society, to become a *mere* province of the U.K.; yet it could not develop its own nation-state on this basis either, via nationalism.

Coping with this anomalous situation accounts for a good deal of the Jekyll-and-Hyde physiognomy of modern Scottishness. Before going on to consider the phenomenon, however, one very important additional modification is required. In the schema traced out so far it is the precocious progress of Scottish civil society in the later 18th and early 19th century that plays the main rôle. But of course, the reference here is entirely to Lowland Scotland, the geographical area of the Enlightenment and the Scottish Industrial Revolution alike (as, earlier, it had been that of the Scottish Reformation).

This zone's vigorous bourgeois advance was counterpointed, in the era we have been looking at, by the wholly different fate of the Highlands. Different as English-speaking Scotland was from its southern neighbour, it actually contained a much greater internal differentiation within its own historical frontiers. The 'problem' described above enclosed another, much acuter problem inside itself. Across the Highland Line there lay a social formation distinct in language and customs, and at a completely different stage of social evolution. Gaelic-speaking Scotland had remained predominantly pre-feudal, while the Lowlands had evolved into a bourgeois society. In the 1830s, observes A. J. Youngson, 'there were still obviously two worlds in Scotland, a poor highland world and a comparatively prosperous lowland world'. Far from the former showing any signs of catching up with the latter, to form one homogeneous civil society, 'The idea of building up the highland economy was over, and was not to be revived for more than a hundred years' (until after 1945).[16]

In developmental terms the contrast is elementary: Lowland society's modern 'problem' was constituted by its fulminating, almost over-rapid advance unaccompanied by what were to be the typical (national) superstructures of State and cultural hegemony; Highland society was incapable of 'advancing' at all, in this sense. It started from too far back (having been left relatively untouched by the weak authority of the Scottish monarchy, during the period of Absolutism) and was then exposed too abruptly, and too brutally, to the very dynamic capitalist societies in proximity to it. Ordinarily – as a typical piece of 'backward' Europe, like a part of the Balkans situated in the West – it should have reacted to the dilemma by generating its own nationalism, upon the basis of its own marked socio-cultural *differentiae*. Such a separatism would of course have been directed as much against the Scottish Lowlanders as against the English. This would have taken a long time, and many hard and complicated struggles – in some parts of Eastern Europe, it was to take well over a hundred years. But in fact the process was unable even to get started in Celtic Scotland, for the simple reason that it was stopped in its tracks by the overwhelmingly powerful reaction

---

[16] A. J. Youngson, *After the Forty-Five: the Economic Impact on the Scottish Highlands* (1973), pp. 189–90.

to the 1745 rebellion.

In this one, exceptional case, the juxtaposition of 'backward' land and 'advanced' (bourgeois) culture was so violently unequal, so hugely disproportionate, that the former had literally no chance – not even the common, difficult, fighting chance of so many nationalist movements. In 1745 an army from these backwoods had struck to within 120 miles of London, bearing with it the menace of restored Absolute monarchy. This incredible near-reverse of fortunes decided the outcome. The *Gaeltacht* was to be allowed no farther opportunity of disrupting civilized progress. In the subsequent English and Lowland invasion its old social structure and culture were pulverized too completely for any later nationalist response to be possible. This would not have been so easy (as other examples show) if there had been a Gaelic middle class and some Gaelic towns – if social conditions had developed even to this later-feudal stage. As things were, these elementary springs of collective resistance – of national as distinct from merely individual or small-community revolt – were lacking, and the near-liquidation of a nationality was possible.

'Scotland', in the sense of Lowland civil society, was a partner with England in this process. It represented one of the strongest common interests of the Scottish and English bourgeoisies. However, the catastrophe of Celtic Scotland had a curious effect upon the Lowlanders. It has haunted them in a remarkable way from the early 19th century to the present day.

II

'We had better remain in union with England, even at the risk of becoming a subordinate species of Northumberland, as far as national consequence is concerned, than remedy ourselves by even hinting the possibility of a rupture . . .'

Sir Walter Scott, 'Letter . . . on the
Proposed Change of Currency' (1826).

'So his tendency was always to the whole, to the totality, to the general balance of things. Indeed it was his chiefest difficulty (and an every-increasing one that made him fear at times cancellation to nonentity) to exclude, to con-

demn, to say No. Here, probably, was the secret of the
way in which he used to plunge into the full current of the
most inconsistent movements, seeking, always in vain,
until he was utterly exhausted . . . to find ground upon
which he might stand foursquare . . . He was always
fighting for the absent, eager for forlorn hopes, a champion of the defeated cause, for those portions of truth
which seemed to him neglected . . .'

C. M. Grieve (Hugh MacDiarmid),
Annals of the Five Senses (1923).

To a surprising extent, we are still living in the Scotland of
Sir Walter Scott. He said nothing about 'modern' Scotland, in the
sense of industrial or working-class Scotland. But he did show us
what to do with our past. And in the context of 19th and early
20th century social development in Europe, this was a most important thing to do. One might say: he showed us, both sentimentally
and politically, how *not* to be nationalists during an age of ascendant
political nationalism.

The Scots bourgeois class to which he belonged had had the
developmental good luck to 'take off' in the tow of England. Now,
in the first half of the 19th century, their entrepreneurial capacity
was granted splendid and growing opportunities. The English
capitalist class did not interfere with them, to hinder or suppress
accumulation or investment in Scotland. The English governing
class did not close its ranks to them. In the Empire, there was room
for them both.

But at the same time, the Scots middle class could not help living
in a society still historically distinct from England – and one which
was, as we noticed, positively replete with all the 'raw materials'
of nationalism. As the cultural climate altered, as Enlightenment
gave way to Romanticism, as a new sense of history spread in Europe, they were bound to acquire a keener consciousness of this.
Their civil society had grown more akin to that of England, economically speaking. Yet in this deeper historico-cultural sense – a
sense that was to become more and more politically important –
they had also to cope with a quasi-national inheritance. The latter's
proper place had been safely defined in the Augustan age: the museums and drawing-rooms of Polite Society. ˙ could not be so safely
dealt with in the new age of democracy and nationalism.

The new romantic *consciousness* of the past was, in itself, irresistable. As a matter of fact, from Ossian to Sir Walter himself, Scotland played a large part in generating and diffusing it for the rest of Europe. What mattered in Scotland itself, however, was to render this awareness *politically* null – to make certain that it would not be felt that contemporary Scotland should be the independent continuation of the auld sang. The whole emotional point of national*ism* was to feel just that: our future development must spring out of this, *our* inheritance from past generations, with its special values, etc. Hence, what the new British-Scots middle class had to do was separate the inevitable new popular-national consciousness from action. One might say, very approximately: separate its heart from its head.

One has to employ such terms with trepidation. They are part of a whole language of romanticism closely intertwined with the history of nationalism; in even uttering them one feels a quicksand clutching at the ankles. It threatens to suck the victim down into the land of the 'Caledonian antisyzygy'.[17] That is, into the realm of an anguished examination of conscience and consciousness, a troubled subjective posturing, to which – for reasons I hope will be partly explained here – Scots intellectuals have been especially prone.

Taken only as metaphors, what is implied is that the complex of realities and ideas most associated with 'nationality', in that sense which had become so historically significant, had to be kept separ-

[17] The 'Caledonian Antisyzygy' is one of the interesting minor examples of myth made out of affliction. Although the cultural reality of split personality to which it refers was of course much in evidence in the 19th century (*Dr. Jekyll*, the *Justified Sinner*, etc.), the formulation itself seems to come from G. Gregory Smith's *Scottish Literature: Character & Influence* (1919). Here the disease is diagnosed as racial propensity to alternate between dour matter-of-fact 'realism' (pp. 5–6) and unrestrained fantasy ('confusion of the senses, the fun of things thrown topsy-turvy, the horns of elfland . . .' pp. 19–20); 'It goes better with our knowledge of Scottish character and history to accept the antagonism as real and necessary', Smith concludes. The idea proved only too popular with the *literati*, and reappears in (e.g.) Edwin Muir's *Scott and Scotland* (1936) and in C. M. Grieve, on those many occasions when 'MacDiarmid' got the better of him: 'The Caledonian Antisyzygy . . . may be awaiting the exhaustion of the whole civilization of which English literature is a typical product in order to achieve its effective synthesis in a succeeding and very different civilization.' *Albyn* (1927), p. 34.

ate from 'practical', or effective politics. Those things which were most evocative, most imaginatively suggestive, had to be relegated all the more strenuously in this way. Yet, in the nature of things, such suppression could only be achieved at a certain cost. It was bound to leave characteristic marks, on both sides of the separation.

On the side of nationality – all those aspects of civil society and its past which might be seen as peculiarly Scottish – this meant a curious sort of over-emphasis on history. A new, more deeply felt historical awareness had become universal. But in Scottish conditions it was to become positively obsessional. It is this emotional displacement which lent such furious energy to Scott's great, exemplary panoramas of the country's past. This gives them that intense, elegiac character at once so seductive and so frustrating. He evoked the past (especially a relatively recent past) more powerfully than anyone else; but part of this magic is the implication that it is a past we have, in certain vital ways, irreparably lost. It is gone for good. This is why we have to be so emotional about it, and also why we have to try so hard to 'preserve', husband, patch up, and generally savour all those relics and ruins it has left behind.

On the other side – the side of the State, the manful realities of our present life, and so on – it meant an equally curious over-emphasis. Here, the stress is upon an unsentimental endorsement of the *status quo*. What is implied is sternly 'realistic' acceptance of the Union, the Great-British political hegemony, as a sort of present without history – that is, without *our* history. The private tears must never run upon this public face. It follows of course that such endorsement can never be thorough enough: nothing but the most supine, cringing, and absolute prostration will do. Hence, what accompanies the various Scottish bourgeois cults of the past is an equally constant over-adaptation to the State.

Sir Walter was the great model for this, as for so many other things. Each absurd, antipathetic detail of the *ancien régime*'s Constitution was sacred to him. The same man who sobbed on The Mound at the very thought of reforming Scots Law and fulminated against the loss of the Scots Banknote, could not bear the loss of one Rotten Borough or aristocratic privilege in England. Reform and the ascent of the Whigs killed him, James Hogg maintained: 'Yes, I say and aver, it was that which broke his heart, deranged his whole constitution, and murdered him . . . A dread of revolution had long preyed on his mind; he withstood it to the last; he fled from it, but it affected his brain, and killed him. From the moment he perceived the veto of democracy prevailing, he lost all hope of the prosperity and ascendancy of the British Empire'.[18] The suggestion of any conflict between these two objects of devotion induced a total Tory reflex: the absolute loss of those precious 'peculiarities' of our civil society is preferable to 'even hinting the possibility of a rupture' from the United Kingdom State.

Scott was a Tory in the party sense. But this must not mislead us. For the all-British conservatism referred to here could, and did, attach itself to other British parties with equal force. Just as there was no Old Tory like a Scotch Old Tory, so there would be no Gladstonian Liberal like a Scotch one, no Imperialist like the North British variety, and no Labourite like the Glasgow Faithfuls. The Labour Party, indeed, has become the ultimate repository of this dour devotion. No speeches conjure up the old Unionist *Geist* nowadays more relentlessly than those of William Ross and John Smith.

Most of the time, the conflict does not threaten in practice. It is submerged in a routine way. Scott was still struggling to define this routine, at the beginning of the century, but later on it became settled enough. The complex of Scottish 'patriotism' was subordinated in a habitual and characteristic fashion to the larger political reality of Empire. If we look ahead to that other typical Scottish intellectual, John Buchan, for example, it is to find him too bleating about the country's 'losing its historic individuality', so that '. . . It seems to many that we are in danger very soon of reaching the point when Scotland will have nothing distinctive to show to the world'. It was urgent, *for the sake of Britain and the Empire*, he went on, '. . . to intensify that consciousness of individuality and idiom, which is what is meant by national spirit . . . I believe that every Scotsman should be a Scottish Nationalist'.[19] Even if it meant a dose of Home Rule, he concluded.

It was not unusual for Empires to try and exploit the more picturesque and *Völkisch* sides of their provinces, to pander to petty

[18] James Hogg, *The Domestic Manners and Private Life of Sir Walter Scott* (1882 edit.), pp. 95–6.

[19] Sir Reginald Coupland, *Welsh and Scottish Nationalism: a Study* (1954), pp. 403–4, quoting Buchan's parliamentary speech of 1932 from *Hansard*. This is the debate which led on to what Coupland calls '. . . the appeasement of Scottish nationalism (by) the setting up of St. Andrew's House in Edinburgh.'

local vanities and precious traditions (particularly military ones). The Hapsburgs and Romanovs used the technique for centuries, and Bismarck raised it to a new pitch of perfection in Germany. What is remarkable in the Scottish case is its success and solidity, and the degree to which it was self-administered. Gramsci used a story, 'The Fable of the Beaver', to illustrate the acquiescence of the Italian bourgeoisie in fascism: 'The beaver, pursued by trappers who want his testicles from which medicinal drugs can be extracted, to save his life tears off his own testicles . . . Why was there no defence? Because the parties had little sense of human or political dignity? But such factors are not natural phenomena, deficiencies inherent in a people as permanent characteristics. They are "historical facts", whose explanation is to be found in past history and in the social conditions of the present . . .'[20]

Adapting the fable to our argument one might say: in the 19th century the Scottish bourgeoisie could hardly help becoming conscious of its inherited *cojones* to some extent, its capacity for nationalism; but this consciousness conflicted with its real, economic interests in an unusual fashion, it was forced to – at least – repress or 'sublimate' the impulse itself. The emasculation was not enforced by gendarmes and Regius Professors from London (this kind of treatment was reserved for Gaels). It was a kind of self-imposed, very successful *Kulturkampf*, one which naturally appears as 'neurosis' in relation to standard models of development. Because of its success the elements of 'pathology' inherent in it have become embedded as modern 'national traits'; but these are not really the natural phenomena, dating back to some Caledonian Original Sin, which people feel them to be. As 'historical facts', their *main* explanation is certainly to be located in the modern era itself – that is, in the last century or so, up to the present.

Let us consider some of the historical facts most relevant to the phenomenon. During the age of nationalism it has come to be taken for granted that the distinctively modern consciousness of nationality is 'natural': people are naturally, instinctively, national-*ists* (and not merely aware of being different from other folk). But in reality nationalism was a historical construct, associated with certain social strata, at a certain characteristic period of their development. Amongst these, none was more important than the

[20] Antonio Gramsci, *Prison Notebooks*, op. cit., pp. 223–4.

intelligentsia. The new commercial and industrial middle class was indisputably the dominant force in the process; yet the way this dominance was exerted – the form of their class hegemony – owed its character to new intellectuals. It was the latter who formulated the new ideologies that were needed, and manned the first new societies, parties and other organizations. It was they who, initially, enabled the bourgeoisie to 'enlarge its class sphere technically and ideologically', and so 'pose itself as an organism . . . capable of absorbing the entire society', etc. By accomplishing this task, the intellectuals also won for themselves a new and greater social significance: no longer the servants of a closed aristocratic élite, they became vital elements in the cohesion of society as a whole.

Nationalism was the most important and effective of such new ideologies. Normally it developed through a recognizable number of phases, over several generations, in all those territories where new middle classes felt that tolerable 'development' for their people was impossible without rapid mobilization of their own resources and rejection of 'alien rule'.[21] Normally, too, this process was a revolutionary one – whether or not it ever resulted in a successful *coup d'état* – in the sense that it meant trying to get rid of a non-adaptable landlord *ancien régime*, its 'reactionary' intellectual caste, corrupt and non-populist 'traditions', and so on. One may say that during this long period, over most of Europe, the standard function of an intellectual class was in this task. This is of course not to maintain that all intellectuals were xenophobes or flag-wavers. But the centre of gravity of their rôle *as* a class, their collective definition within modern social conditions, lay in the way they educated one folk or another.

In Scotland, the intelligentsia was deprived of this typical 'nationalist' rôle. Its new intellectual strata were to be, in a sense, unemployed on their home terrain. There was no call for the usual services. Here, the old régime and its intellectuals had crumbled

---

[21] By far the most useful study of the actual social and class structure of typical nationalist development is that by Miroslav Hroch, *Die Vorkämpfer der nationalen Bewegung bei den kleinen Völkern Europas* (Acta Universitatis Carolinae, Monographia XXIV, 1968), which deals with seven different minor nationalist movements. It is remarkable how closely the recent development of the SNP has repeated the older models he describes. See also Eric Hobsbawm, 'Nationalism', in *Imagination and Precision in the Social Sciences: Essays in Honour of Peter Nettl* (1973).

away without firing a shot: they were overwhelmed by the burgeoning growth of the Scottish Industrial Revolution and the new entrepreneurial bourgeoisie linked to it. No prolonged cultural subversion was required to pull down its bastions. William Ferguson
notes 'The decline of the specifically Scottish intellectualism which
throughout the 18th century had without conscious effort sustained
the concept of a Scottish nation'.[22] This decline was not to be
counterpointed by the rise of a new 'specifically Scottish' culture,
less intellectualist and more romantic, advancing the new concept
of nationality appropriate to the age.

Clearly, the country did not cease to produce individual intellectuals from its own separate and quite advanced educational
system. The point is simply that they could not constitute any
longer a coherent, national 'class', in a sense which it is quite hard
to define but easy to recognize. The fact was emphasized, rather than
disproved, by the well-known prominence of so many Victorian
Scots in fields like medicine, engineering, and the natural sciences.
As Ferguson comments again: 'The reputation won by Scotsmen
in science . . . did little to enhance the culture of their country. This
is far from being a singular case, for science stands independent of
national contexts . . . For good or ill, therefore, science cannot nur-
ture the irrational bonds that make nations'. Irrational bonds: this
overstates the case, and concedes too much to German-romantic
theories of nationalism. The bonds are non-rational and non-
intellectual, rather than those of unreason. But the underlying
point is valid: a 'national culture', in that sense which had become
newly important, entailed an intellectual class able to express the
particular realities of a country, in a romantic manner accessible to
growing numbers of the reading public – a class operating actively
in the zone of general and literary culture (rather than the specializ-
ations Scots became celebrated for).

The relationship between civil society and State in Scotland
precluded a fully national culture in this sense. Instead, what
it led to was a strange sort of sub-national culture. An anomalous
historical situation could not engender a 'normal' culture: Scotland
could not simply be adapted to the new, basically nationalist, rules
of cultural evolution. But since the country could not help being

[22] William Ferguson, *Scotland*, op. cit., p. 319.

affected by this evolution, it produced something like a stunted, caricatural version of it. The best title for this is perhaps 'cultural sub-nationalism'.[23] It was cultural, because of course it could not be political; on the other hand this culture could not be straight-forwardly nationalist either – a direct substitute for political action, like (e.g.) so much Polish literature of the 19th century. It could only be 'sub-nationalist', in the sense of venting its national content in various crooked ways – neurotically, so to speak, rather than directly.

Among the numerous strands in the neurosis, two are especially prominent: cultural emigration, and the Kailyard School. As we shall see, the two phenomena are in fact (and contrary to appear-ances) closely connected. And they are connected in a way which permits one to focus much more clearly upon the significant popular-cultural reality underlying both of them: vulgar tartanry.

In the most authoritative study of the Scottish 19th century cul-tural scene, David Craig remarks: 'The historian is left calling Victorian culture in Scotland "strangely rootless" . . . We have to recognize that there did not emerge along with modern Scotland a mature, "all-round" literature . . .'. Later, he ascribes this sur-prising 'void' in culture to intellectual emigration: 'During the 19th century the country was emptied of the *majority* of its notable literary talents – men who, if they had stayed, might have thought to mediate their wisdom through the rendering of specifically Scottish experience. Of the leading British "sages" of the time an astonishingly high proportion were of Scottish extraction – the Mills, Macaulay, Carlyle, Ruskin, Gladstone'.[24] Unemployable in their own country, these and many later émigrés quite naturally found themselves a function in the development of English culture. For England was a milieu *par excellence* of just that 'mature, all-

[23] The term is derived from V. A. Olorunsola, *The Politics of Cultural Sub-Nationalism in Africa* (1972), a study concerned with ethnic problems in new African States. 'The phrase "one State – many nationalisms" . . . is particularly appropriate in describing the new States', says the author, since in many of these 'the country's nationalism can be jeopardized by its cultural sub-nationalisms'. In spite of this, 'some countries have been able to achieve a level of integration which seems surprisingly quite out of proportion to the degree of their cultural homogeneity', while in others (e.g. Eastern Nigeria) cultural sub-nationalism developed into nationalism proper. Introduction, pp. xiv–xv.

[24] David Craig, *Scottish Literature and the Scottish People, 1680–1830* (1961), pp. 13–14, p. 273. See especially ch. IX, 'Emigration'.

round' and literary thought-world Craig refers to. It was an organic
or "rooted' national-romantic culture, in which literature – from
Coleridge and Carlyle up to F. R. Leavis and E. P. Thompson – has
consistently played a major role.

The rootless vacuum, the great 'absence', the 'cultural schizophrenia' William Ferguson mentions in a similar context: these are
metaphors, which in turn invite decipherment. What was the
actual presence they denote, in Scotland – the books they wrote
and read, the thoughts they had, and so on? They did not ponder
mightily and movingly upon the reality of 19th century Scotland –
on the great Glasgow bourgeoisie of mid-century and onwards, the
new class conflicts, the continuing tragedy of the Highlands.
So what was there, instead of those missing Zolas and George
Eliots, those absent Thomas Manns and Vergas? What there was
increasingly from the 1820s onwards, until it became a vast tide
washing into the present day, was the Scots 'Kailyard' tradition.

This was, in effect, the cabbage-patch, the home 'backyard' left
behind by the emigration of so much high-culture talent. Craig
traces its origins to the time of John Galt's *Annals of the Parish*
(1813) and *Blackwood's Magazine*, but its major triumphs were
later. The opposite of mature all-roundness is presumably infantile
partiality, or fragmentariness. This label certainly fits the Kailyard
industry. In his *Literary History of Scotland* J. H. Millar notes that
in the 1880s two books by J. M. Barrie (*Auld Licht Idylls* and *A
Window in Thrums*) '. . . for some mysterious reason caught the
fancy of the English public to which the greater part of the dialogue
must have been wholly unintelligible . . . The vogue of Mr Barrie's
weaver-bodies and elders of the Original Secession was not long in
bringing into the field a host of rivals; and the "Kailyard" School of
Literature as it has been called, presently burst into existence. The
circulating libraries became charged to overflowing with a crowd
of ministers, precentors, and beadles notable for their dry and
"pithy" wit . . . while the land was plangent with the sobs of grown
men, vainly endeavouring to stifle their emotion by an elaborate
affectation of "peching" and "hoasting" . . .'.[25] Barrie remained

---

[25] J. H. Millar, *A Literary History of Scotland* (1903), pp. 656–8. Singling out
S. R. Crockett's *The Lilac Sunbonnet* (1894) for assault – 'a perfect triumph of
succulent vulgarity' – he adds, in words ringing true down to the present, 'though
. . . how nauseous it is, how skilfully it makes its appeal to some of the worst
traits in the national character, no one who is not a Scot can really know'.

the master of the *genre*, but he acquired important rivals like 'Ian Maclaren' (in reality John Watson, 'an established divine of middle age'), whose *Beside the Bonnie Briar Bush* quickly sold a quarter of a million in Britain and half a million in the U.S.A., and S. R. Crockett (*Bloom of the Heather*, etc.).

Kailyardism was the definition of Scotland as consisting wholly of small towns full of small-town 'characters' given to bucolic intrigue and wise sayings. At first the central figures were usually Ministers of the Kirk (as were most of the authors) but later on schoolteachers and doctors got into the act. Their housekeepers always have a shrewd insight into human nature. Offspring who leave for the big city frequently come to grief, and are glad to get home again (peching and hoasting to hide their feelings). In their different ways, village cretins and ne'er-do-wells reinforce the essentially healthy *Weltanschauung* of the place.

There is surely no need to go on. Everyone in Scotland knows only too well what is being referred to. The Penguin *Companion to Literature* defines the school as 'exploiting the sentimental aspects of Lowland life during the period 1880–1914', mainly through minor writers who 'pursued Scottish country quaintness into whimsical middens'. In fact it arose before 1880 and it prospers at the present day. Naturally, it has been transferred to the TV screen. *Dr Finlay's Casebook* is temporarily absent, but at the time of writing *Para Handy* and *Sutherland's Law* carry the standard on alternate evenings (in London). It is not so long since what one might call the supreme *chef d'oeuvre* of sub-cultural Scotchery flitted across the screen, 'holding up our fellow-countrymen (as J. H. Millar put it) to the ridicule and contempt of all sane and judicious human beings': *Scotch on the Rocks*. In Dundee our own cabbage-patch publishing Mafia, the D. C. Thomson gang, still thrives as George Blake observed it doing forty years ago, through 'the careful cultivation of the Kailyard strain'.[26]

What is the significance of this remarkably powerful and persist-

---

[26] George Blake, *Barrie and the Kailyard School* (1951), p. 85. In one of the few attempts to penetrate the shroud of secrecy around the Thomson empire, it was pointed out recently that *The Sunday Post* is 'arguably the most successful newspaper in the world ... the newspaper which achieves the closest to saturation. In 1971 its total estimated readership of 2,947,000 represented more than 79% of the entire population of Scotland aged 15 or over ...' *The Sunday Times*, July 29th, 1973, 'The Private Life of Lord Snooty', by George Rosie.

ent sub-culture? In one sense, it may seem just another example of a widespread European trend, whereby in the 19th century provincial manners and characters were often made into *Kitsch* images for the new, mass reading public of the cities. Yet the very appeal and longevity of the phenomenon, as well as its huge popularity in Scotland itself, suggest more than this. George Blake (himself a skilled practitioner of the school) made national 'infantilism' the key to his diagnosis. What has modern literature to say about modern society in Scotland, he asks?: 'The answer is – nothing . . . This almost suggests a sort of national infantilism'. It is as if there were a 'conspiracy of silence' about the modern nation. All one can find is this sub-romanticism of villages peopled by picturesque morons. One is forced to admit therefore that '. . . what we call, loosely enough, the Kailyard strain, is persistent in Scottish writing, however much the moderns may deplore the fact, and however gallantly they seek to shock their contemporaries out of their chronic addiction to gossip around the parish pump. We always return to the point that the Scots . . . remain inveterately backward in literary culture – bewildered and sentimental children bleating for the old securities of the parochial life'.[27]

There is a notable psychologism about this censorious judgement. It implies that the literary intellectuals ought to have tried harder: if only they *had* decided to write about modern bourgeois life and Social Problems, all would have been well, or at any rate better. David Craig occasionally suggests something similar: the famous émigrés 'might have thought to' write in Scottish terms, if they had stayed at home. If Thomas Carlyle had chosen 'a final achieved integration with a native way of life' instead of sermonizing in London, then he and Scotland might have been better off.[28] William Ferguson comments upon the 'element of cultural schizophrenia' in 19th century Scotland: 'Loss of confidence led to a virtual collapse of Scottish culture: literature degenerated into mawkish "kailyard" parochialism and painting into "ben and glen" romanticism . . .'[29]

These verdicts miss an important point. The overall structure of this modern culture in fact corresponds exactly to the dilemma

[27] George Blake, op. cit., pp. 80–81.
[28] David Craig, *Scottish Literature*, op. cit., p. 276, pp. 285–6.
[29] William Ferguson, *Scotland*, op. cit., p. 317.

of Scotland's social structure since the Industrial Revolution. Emigration and Kailyardery are not merely individual, subjective responses to the situation, and it is therefore unjust to view them as treachery or loss of nerve. The cultural sub-nationalism they conspired to foster was, in its way, as much of a historical 'necessity' as the major national cultures produced in England, Germany, and the rest.

This may become clearer when one reflects on the extent to which the two main factors in the neurosis are connected. 'Thrums', 'Drumtochty' and 'Tannochbrae' were all creations of émigrés. They and their unspeakable progeny were produced, also, very largely for a foreign reading public (i.e. to pander to hankerings not themselves especially Scottish in origin). The main vehicles of the school's diffusion in Great Britain were the London magazines *British Weekly* and *The Woman at Home*. These were both run, incidentally, by another classical émigré figure called William Robertson Nicoll. He is the archetypal lad o' pairts pilloried (along with Barrie and many others) in T. E. H. Crosland's *The Unspeakable Scot* (1902).[30] 'It is a singular thing', wrote Robert Louis Stevenson to J. M. Barrie, 'that I should live here in the South Seas under conditions so new and so striking, and yet my imagination so continually inhabit that cold old huddle of grey hills from which we come'. Stevenson wrote well above the Kailyard plane as a rule, yet often touched the same register in a revealing way: 'And I have come so far; and the sights and thoughts of my youth pursue me; and I see like a vision the youth of my father, and of his father, and the whole stream of lives flowing down there, far in the north, with the sound of laughter and tears, to cast me out in the end, as by a sudden freshet, on these ultimate islands. And I admire and bow my head before the romance of destiny . . .'.[31]

Whether as the pawky simplicities of village life, or as swagger-

---

[30] T. W. H. Crosland, *The Unspeakable Scot* (1902). The author ended his indictment of the Scots in England with a series of rules 'for the general guidance of young Scotchmen who . . . do not desire to add further opprobrium to the Scotch character'. These include: 'I. Remember that outside Scotland you are a good deal of a foreigner . . . X. IF WITHOUT SERIOUS INCONVENIENCE TO YOURSELF YOU CAN MANAGE TO REMAIN AT HOME, PLEASE DO . . .'

[31] From the dedication to *Catriona*, as quoted in David Daiches, *Robert Louis Stevenson and his World* (1973), p. 100.

ing through the heather claymore in hand, 'Scotland' in the sub-
romantic sense was largely defined by émigrés. The Kailyard was –
and still is – very much the reverse of the coin of emigration. Its
lack of 'human and political dignity' does not express some collective fault in the Scots psyche, but the 'historical fact' of the relationship between the intelligentsia and the people. This relationship
was determined by the fact that the Scottish bourgeoisie did not
face the need to form *its own* 'national community', through the
mediation of a more rooted intellectual class and a more complex
and sophisticated national culture (i.e. more 'mature, all-round',
and so on). This is why it is vain to censure the writers and other intellectuals retrospectively for their failure to come up to European
norms. They could not deal with modern experience in Scotland
because in the relevant sense there *was no* 'modern experience':
such experience was the product of culture, not its pre-existing
social basis. And this culture arose in certain characteristic social
and historical conditions which were, inevitably, lacking here.

Rendered jobless in these circumstances – without a middle
class sufficiently exercised over the usual national problems,
without a national capital-city of the kind which had become indispensable – what could the intelligentsia do? Its natural posture
became to seek work outside, but at the same time (aware of its
distinct origins and history) to look constantly backwards and
inwards, in a typical vein of deforming nostalgia – constantly con-
firming a false, 'infantile' image of the country quite divorced from
its 'real problems'. The real problem, of course, did not lie in the
fact of factories, new cities, bourgeois family dramas, class conflicts, etc. – it lay, for the intellectuals (and therefore for the national
culture) in the fact that these phenomena *did not pose* a cultural
problem that had to be solved in specifically Scottish terms. We
noticed the sort of 'split' in Sir Walter Scott's world-view, and how
that corresponded to the Scottish bourgeoisie's peculiar position in
history. Surely the later history of the intelligentsia can be seen as
the continuation, the farther manifestation, of that same split?
That is, of the figurative 'schizophrenia' imposed upon an intellectual stratum which, although strongly national, was in its material
conditions of existence quite unable to be national*ist* – unable to
secrete a complete national-popular culture like its English or
French peers?

Perhaps the most revealing comment of all upon the truth of the situation was provided by those émigrés like 'George Douglas Brown' (*The House with the Green Shutters*, London, 1901) and 'Lewis Grassic Gibbon' (*A Scots Quair*, Welwyn Garden City, 1932–4) who became aware of the trap and tried to escape it by formulating an 'anti-Kailyard' stance of dour realism. By common critical consent, they found it extremely hard to do so, and produced work still marked by the dilemma.[32] It is almost as difficult for a Scots intellectual to get out of the Kailyard as to live without an alias.[33]

The dilemma is not 'merely' an intellectuals' one. Just as the two horns of it are in fact intimately connected, so the whole thing is related to the much larger field of popular culture. For Kailyard is popular in Scotland. It is recognizably intertwined with that prodigious array of *Kitsch* symbols, slogans, ornaments, banners, war-cries, knick-knacks, music-hall heroes, icons, conventional sayings and sentiments (not a few of them 'pithy') which have for so long resolutely defended the name of 'Scotland' to the world. Annie S. Swan and Cronin provided no more than the relatively decent outer garb for this vast tartan monster. In their work the thing trots along doucely enough, on a lead. But it is something else to be with it (e.g.) in a London pub on International night, or in the crowd at the annual Military Tattoo in front of Edinburgh Castle. How intolerably vulgar! What unbearable, crass, mindless philistinism! One knows that *Kitsch* is a large constituent of mass popular culture in every land: but this is ridiculous!

Ridiculous or not, it is obviously extremely strong. In this sense, as the main body of cultural sub-nationalism, it appears to represent a national-popular tradition which has persisted more or less in the way one would expect. Precisely because it has been un-connected with a 'higher' or normal, nationalist-style culture during the formative era of modern society, it has evolved blindly. The popular consciousness of separate identity, uncultivated by 'na-

[32] The best recent example of the strain is Gordon M. Williams's *From Scenes Like These*, although Alan Sharp's *A Green Tree in Gedde* (1965) is also interesting in this regard. In the case of these authors flight from the Kailyard ('The task of self-realization is like a journey', as Sharp puts it) led in the direction of the American cinema. See also P. Gregory, 'Scottish Village Life 1973: a reassessment', *Scottish International*, vol. 7, no. 1 (Feb. 1974).

[33] See Hamish Henderson's 'Alias MacAlias', in *Scottish International* no. 6 (April 1969). 'We are here on the edge of grey debatable land, and must walk warily', the author cautions.

tional' experience or culture in the usual sense, has become curiously fixed or fossilized on the level of the *image d'Épinal* and Auld Lang Syne, of the Scott Monument, Andy Stewart and the *Sunday Post* – to the point of forming a huge, virtually self-contained universe of *Kitsch*.

Pursuing the metaphor of neurosis father, if the émigré-Kailyard dilemma can be taken to represent the plight of the nation's Ego, here surely is the Id with which the intelligentsia has always had to wrestle. On the higher plane, the level of literature and political self-consciousness, the problem appears from the time of Scott onwards as that of 'exorcising' potential nationalism in a historical situation which had become impossible for it – through (e.g.) over-adaptation to the United Kingdom or Empire, emigration, displacement of sentiment to the past, and so on. However, much of the reality in question could not be conjured away: it simply persisted in the 'repressed' state, correspondingly deformed, as an especially 'mindless' popular culture revolving in timeless circles. As we know, one principal trait of this Id-culture is an extraordinarily blatant super-patriotism – in effect, a kind of dream-nationalism which is almost the contrary of that dour, sensible, waist-coated-and-watch-chained Unionism prevalent on the country's Official Occasions. Like drink, this kind of raving ultra-chauvinism was quite harmless: as long, that is, as the 'British' ego-system remained strong enough to confine it.

There is not space here to pursue farther an analysis of what Ray Burnett calls our 'specifically Scottish heritage of myths, prejudices and illusions'. All I have tried to do is indicate in some general ways how that heritage is accessible to discussion in the Gramscian terms which he proposed. How – that is – we can relate it meaningfully to the underlying characters of our civil society, and to the latter's unusual relationship to the State which controls it. Obviously many subjects could be considered in this way, and there is a huge leeway to make up. Robert McLaughlan noted that 'Among what may be termed the Anglophobic nationalisms – Scottish, Irish, French Canadian, Afrikaaner – the first is unique in having no substantial nationalist historiography . . . the general weakness of Scots historical studies, which persisted until very recently, probably prevented the emergence of such a school'.[34] To take only the most

---

[34] R. McLaughlan, 'Aspects of Nationalism', in *The Scottish Debate: Essays in Scottish Nationalism* (1970), edit. N. MacCormick, p. 24.

obvious example: in any serious critique along these lines one is quickly brought to confront the question of the Kirk and its weight within the complex of cultural sub-nationalism. The Disruption of 1843 can still appear to many historians as 'the most momentous single event of the 19th century for Scotland, whose repercussions were felt not only in most departments of Scottish life but overseas as well'.[35] This momentous event is largely incomprehensible today; so is the real function of the national religion in 19th and 20th century development – at different moments in nationalist discussion, one finds that it is either ignored altogether as an anachronism, or else every imaginable sin and shortcoming of the national ethos is attributed to it (including of course these various 'splits' and sub-cultural faults mentioned here). So the Kirk tradition is both irrelevant to SNP Scotland *and* responsible for every one of the country's numberless unacceptable faces!

Although this and kindred discussions cannot be developed here, one or two farther points need to be made since they relate so closely to the present situation.

Over-concentration upon cultural factors (especially literature) can lead easily to an over-subjective or idealist diagnosis of the country's modern situation. This is regularly found in the annals of nationalism. It must not be forgotten that Scotland's anomalous split personality was rendered possible by – and in sense justified by – its place in a larger framework. This is what that 'paradoxical form of Scottish self-determination' Grieve-MacDiarmid referred to was really about. Ever on the scent of betrayal, nationalists have been inclined to argue that the treacheries of the Enlightenment were followed by those of the intelligentsia and the bourgeoisie in Victorian times: the mess of pottage never ceases. Yet as a way of evading historical truth, this is almost as effective as strait-laced Unionist piety. Scotland does appear as a sort of lunatic or deviant, in relation to normal development during the period in question. But one must never overlook the fact that it had found a comfortable – indeed extremely rewarding – asylum to live in, and consequently chosen to stay there. Loss of figurative 'sanity' was a heavy price, admittedly; but it was richly compensated for, at least until 1914, and every social class in Scotland shared quite consciously

[35] William Ferguson, *Scotland*, op. cit., p. 313.

in that return. Imperialism was *not* imposed upon a reluctant Scots *Volk* pining for its own political identity.

Scottish non-nationalist development worked. It was because it worked, and worked for everyone except the Gaels, that a consequent form of politico-cultural nationalism did not arrive until so recently. It did not even dawn until the 1920s, after all-British imperialism had received its first severe shocks and begun to enter upon its long decline. And when it began to arrive, it could not help being plagued by the uneasy sensation that all this *ought never to have happened*: the very existence of such a bastard polity offends any nationalist's sense of human and political dignity. The easiest way out has always been to evade the issues by looking for scapegoats (the trouble being that, as MacDiarmid's many moments of mad logic make clear, nearly everyone who has lived in the country for the past two and a half centuries *can* be found guilty and retrospectively executed!). Given that those most interested in the nation have so often yielded to temptation, it is really not surprising that 'no substantial nationalist historiography' has come into being. For the left – and above all for those nationalists who incline towards the left – the primary necessity is perhaps simply to look things in the face.

I have mentioned the tartan monster. Most intellectuals – and nationalists chief amongst them – have flinched away from him, dismissing the beast over-easily as mere proof of the debased condition of a nation without a State of its own. It is far more important, surely, to study this insanely sturdy sub-culture. Tartanry will not wither away, if only because it possesses the force of its own vulgarity – immunity from doubt and higher culture. Whatever form of self-rule Scotland acquires, this is a substantial part of the real inheritance bequeathed to it. Prayers to the country's 'essentially socialist' or democratic *Geist* will not make it turn a hair.

In considering the rapport between civil society and State, it is vital to bear in mind that these are never watertight compartments. Were one ever inclined to do so, Scottish cultural sub-nationalism would pull one up with a jerk. For among the most manifest of its characters is something which directly reflects the impress of the old British imperialist State, and reminds us sharply that it was no mere victim of history but a co-conspirator – part of the 'apparatus of political and cultural hegemony', in its own way. Popular militarism is part of that culture – a militarism far more strident than anything found in comparable levels of culture in England. This barbarism was not simply imposed from without: it represented also the 'spontaneous' contribution of Scottish society to the State, and one which deeply affected the masses.

Discussing the origins of the phenomenon, Ferguson points out that 'Until the end of the 18th century Scots did not share the ingrained anti-militarism of the English. They continued to take a pride in their martial traditions and one welcome aspect of the Union of 1707 was the way it consolidated the new prospects for Scots soldiers . . .'[36] The prospects got better and better, as imperialism prospered. They helped reconcile Highlands and Lowlands in an important sense, for after the '45 Gaelic divisions joined the British Army. 'By 1800 all the Scottish regiments, Lowland and Highland, were established, and by the end of the Napoleonic Wars each had an established reputation and a jealously guarded tradition. Quite apart from their exploits in the field these military units played a large part in Scottish life . . . They contributed to the maintenance of national sentiment, and the use by the Highland regiments of "the garb of old Gaul" actually gave a new and unexpected impetus to that sentiment. The Gaels, from being viewed as barbarous nuisances, became regarded as in some ways the very embodiment of Scotland. The kilt and the bagpipes acquired popularity where hitherto they had enjoyed none. The new cult was mawkish and often at variance with the facts of Scottish life . . .'. But, in spite of these Kailyardish aspects, militarism struck deep local roots and had 'effects on the populace (which) as a whole are incalculable'. Thus – 'A host of incidents could stir the blood and titillate national pride . . . and exotic names like Ticonderoga or Seringapatam opened up new dimensions to minds hitherto confined to neighbouring parishes and the place-names of the Bible'.

The inhabitants of Ticonderoga and Seringapatam must be pardoned for taking a different view of events. Those numerous 'lands we harriet' (in Hamish Henderson's phrase) could not know they were bringing Gael and Anglophone together or broadening the horizons of Drumtochty and Barbie. However, they would be less than surprised by the deep disfigurement which really resulted from the process.

In one of his many attempts to reinvent Scottish culture single-

---

[36] Ibid., pp. 263–5.

handed, MacDiarmid comments that: 'Where Scott is strong is in the way in which his work reveals that for a subject nation the firm literary bulwark against the encroaching Imperialism is concentration on the national language and reinterpretation of the national history. Scott's work has real value where a stand is being made against Imperialism . . .'[37] The interest of this is not its misinterpretation of Scott, but its assumptions about Empire. By its precocious development, of course, Scotland had in Scott's own time left the category of 'subject nations' for good and joined the ranks of the 'Imperialists'. It did so in an unusual way, since it did not form its own imperialism like other small countries – Belgium and Holland, for instance. However, its rôle in European colonial depradation may not be inferior to theirs and today the Cain-marks left by the adventure are deeper here.

The Scottish masses were not socialized into a unitary national culture. Inevitably they were forced to compose for themselves a bastard product that was part 'indigenous' – expressing the still quite different life and social ethic of the country – and part Great-British, or imperialist. Thus, the ultra-patriotism of tartanry is accompanied by a tradition of sentimentalized savagery which reflects Scotland's participation in two centuries of Great-British exploits, in the subjugation of many genuine 'subject nations'. All who know it from the inside appreciate that this crude *Weltanschauung* is also the attempt to say something unsayable, yet important, and not wholly to be dismissed for its vulgarity. But then, they must also know that obscurely-sanctioned ferocity which inhabits it, and which is never far away from the mawkish Kailyard bonhomie of 'Wha's like us?' Damned few, and all dead. Well, yes, actually we killed most of them off in our North-British uniforms.

The Jekyll-and-Hyde fragmentation of modern Scottish culture is related in an interesting way to the other great split in our history – that is, to the fact that Scotland is in a sense two nations not one, and that from the 18th century onwards the weaker of the two was systematically destroyed. Because the Anglophone reduction of Celtic society was so successful, the latter proved unable to form its own nationalist-type resistance (the reasons are entirely different from those which apply to the Lowlands). Because of this failure, many of its *differentiae* were appropriated by the English-speakers

[37] C. M. Grieve, *Lucky Poet* (1943), pp. 202–3.

in the ensuing period. The latter plundered the Gaelic raw materials of nationality for their own use, so to speak. It had become safe to do so. Tribal barbarities became 'colourful' traditions.

There is in itself nothing unusual in this sort of cultural borrowing. All over Europe new nationalist movements invented or purloined histories and symbols, with small regard for historical logic or decency. However, in Scotland this borrowing – from which the very name, and so many of the icons of 'tartanry' are derived – was one not in the name of 'nationalism' but in order to enrich a sub-nationalist culture. The latter's characteristic thirst for harmless sentiments and sub-romantic imagery found perfect objects in the debris of a ruined, alien society. On a higher plane, from *Waverley* onwards the emphatic, undeniably 'historic' quality of a deceased culture provided writers with a perfect avenue for that kind of retrospective, once-upon-a-time national feeling which had become mandatory. Once the Stuarts were back in Italy for good, the '45 could become everyone's favourite tale: Prince *Tearlach's* ultimate dynastic inheritance was that boundless realm of short-cake tins, plaid socks, kilted statuettes and whisky-labels that stretches from Tannochbrae to Tokyo.

The remarkable assemblage of heterogeneous elements, neurotic double-binds, falsely honoured shades, and brainless vulgarity which make up 'national culture' here have naturally troubled intellectuals. It is hardly too much to say that they have been unable to look at it. David Craig speaks of 'the uncertain foothold for a national literature in Scotland', and of the characteristic 'feeling that the ground in their country is shifting under their feet'.[38] When, from the 1920s forward, intellectuals began to try and look at

---

[38] David Craig, *Scottish Literature*, op. cit., p. 293. Craig's own general recommendation was that the intellectuals should give up the unequal struggle 'to *have* a national vantage-point', since it was self-defeating. So . . . 'one comes to think that a freer spirit, facing up more openly to experience at large whatever its origins, might better enable the Scottish writer to cope with the problems of living in this place at this time'. A similar spirit can be detected in a previous, less than successful, effort of my own to wrestle with the monster, 'The Three Dreams of Scottish Nationalism', *New Left Review* No. 49 (May–June 1968), reprinted in altered form in *Memoirs of a Modern Scotland* (1970), an émigré anthology edited by Karl Miller. It appears in retrospect as a characteristic expression of the 'Red', outward-bound strain in the intelligentsia, as opposed to the 'Black', stay-at-home one closer to nationalism. I am indebted to Christopher Harvie for this distinction.

what had happened in a more nationalist fashion, panic was the natural response. This is something of the spirit of the remarks from *Annals of the Five Senses* quoted above (as it is of *A Drunk Man Looks at the Thistle*, that great national poem on the impossibility of nationalism): there is no 'ground upon which one may stand foursquare', one *is* forced to exclude, to condemn, to say No to practically everything. The only terrain available is the Kailyard, from which of course flight is obligatory – if not into emigration, then into symbolic emigration, the Cosmic Universalism Mac-Diarmid has made into a second home. One is driven towards 'the totality, the general balance of things' because the particular balance of things in one's country is so intolerable, because its schizophrenia threatens 'cancellation to nonentity'. One must fight for the absent because the present is what it is, for forlorn hopes because the real hopes are so small.

There is a truth at once autobiographical and national in this, as in so many of Grieve's earlier sayings. They contrast markedly with the bloodshot lurchings and geyseric splurgings to which he increasingly gave himself, as one 'inconsistent movement' followed another. It is the lucidity of Grieve we need, rather than the dementia of MacDiarmid (not to speak of the minor bards who have lurched in his footsteps). The former reminds us that it was the situation of the intelligentsia that was hopeless, not that of the country. The problems of intellectuals in a nationalism-less nation are one thing; the real problems and 'faults' of development which produced this cultural situation are another. It is the second range of questions which really matter to the Scottish left. For the most part, left-wing intellectuals here either embraced 'nationalism' in the more or less oneiric sense, or fell back more 'realistically' upon Unionism (occasionally disguised as class or other 'international-ism'). In this fashion, they were really reproducing the classical 'split personality' of the intelligentsia in their own terms.

In the new, quite altered situation it is rapidly becoming fatal to cling to these neuroses. To the extent to which a national move-ment really develops, a different national intellectual class must willy-nilly be constituted, one whose basis is not like that which prevailed between the ages of Scott and MacDiarmid. Are socialists to contribute to its formation? How can they, unless they have their own conception of the country's history and character, worked out through a non-romantic marxist debate in their own ranks?

III

'Le Temps tourne sur ses gonds comme une porte:
et lentement, les peuples étonnés passent d'une situation
à l'autre sans innocents ni coupables: ils sont là, ils n'ont
pas changé de place, mais un jour nouveau les éclaire. Et
nous qui dépendons de cette formidable mouvance, ne
pouvons l'aider qu'en poursuivant notre réflexion sur
nous-mêmes, approfondissant loyalement ce que nous
fûmes, ce que nous sommes'.

Morvan Lebesque,
Comment peut-on être Breton? (1971)

Comment peut-on être Écossais? I have suggested that in trying to
answer this question we must take into consideration certain
aspects of Scottish history since the Union. The peculiar position
of Scottish civil society – too developed and too distinct to be
assimilated, yet no longer requiring to make a State-form of its
own – led to an interrelated series of developmental oddities. It is
easiest to think of these as 'malformations' (comparing them to
nationalist norms elsewhere) provided it is recognized that this
kind of faulted development *worked* well enough, in an economic
and external sense, under the wider conditions furnished by All-
British imperialism. There may even be a case to be made out that
for the industrial and commercial bourgeoisie this was a supremely,
if temporarily, successful mode of development: after all, it
allowed them to devote themselves to their narrower or material
class ends almost entirely, with few worries about culture, nationality, or hegemony. Is this not why, among the multiple caricatures
haunting Scots society, we still find that peculiarly gritty and grind-
ing middle-class 'materialism' – a sort of test-tube bourgeois who
does, indeed, think everything but business to be nonsense?

But although successful in these terms, and sufficiently popular
with the masses to function as a substitute for nationalism, the
system has proved temporary. Its external supports have gradually
slackened and broken, until with the current economic crisis they
look like disappearing. Britain has moved from being master of the
world to being 'the sick man of Europe'. In the essay quoted above
Grieve attributed the first stirrings of real nationalism in Scotland

to the effects of the 1st World War: 'The inception of the Scottish Renaissance synchronized with the end of the War, and in retrospect it will be seen to have had a genesis in kin with other post-war phenomena of recrudescent nationalism all over Europe . . . It took the full force of the War to jolt an adequate majority of the Scottish people out of their old mental, moral and material ruts; and the full force of post-war reaction is bringing them to an effective realization of their changed conditions . . .'.[39] This jolt was soon followed by that of the Depression, under which Scotland began to suffer relatively greater deprivation than many other areas of the United Kingdom. The latter's unity was reforged in certain ways by the 2nd World War and the post-war boom. Then the rot began again, this time apparently more chronically and more irreparably.

Throughout this long epoch – from the Enlightenment, by way of being the 'workshop of the world', to the long disintegration of the last half-century – Scotland conserved a remarkable amount of autonomy. In a recent résumé of the country's independent traits, James Kellas writes: 'While possessing neither a government nor a parliament of its own, it has a strong constitutional identity and a large number of political and social institutions. The Act of Union . . . laid down that Scotland would retain for all time certain key institutions such as the Scottish legal system, the Presbyterian Church . . . the Scottish educational system, and the "Royal Burghs" (local authorities). These became the transmitters of Scottish national identity from one generation to the next . . .'[40]

However, this 'identity' has never been entirely institutional in nature. It involves much wider questions of society and culture. George Elder Davie observes in his history of the Scottish Universities during the 19th century that it is necessary – 'To discredit briefly . . . notions of total assimilation in favour of the rival formula of *unification in politics, separation in ethics*', in order to grasp Scottish development. During the 18th century: 'Submergence in the political-economic system of England was combined with a flourishing, distinctive life in what Marxists conveniently, if not perhaps aptly, call the social superstructure, and a Scotland, which

---

[39] C. M. Grieve, *Albyn*, op. cit., pp. 1–12. 'MacDiarmid' then goes on to predict that the main hope for the Renaissance is Irish immigration and Catholicism, leading a re-Catholicized nation back to 'before the Reformation'!
[40] J. G. Kellas, *The Scottish Political System* (1973), p. 2.

was still national, though no longer nationalist, continued to preserve its European influence as a spiritual force, more than a century after its political identity had disappeared. Throughout the
19th century too, in spite of increasing assimilation . . . the Scots
stuck to this policy of apartness in social ethics.'[41] Such apartness
continued to rest upon what he calls 'the distinctive life of the
country . . . in the mutual interaction of religion, law and education'.

But this is still not wide enough. The 'identity' which it is vital
for us to understand goes beyond these institutions, even in their
mutual interaction; it concerns 'civil society' as a whole, and the
diverse ways in which this separate character was articulated
through both intellectual culture and popular or mass culture. This
made us what we are. It is not a matter of the semi-autonomy of
certain institutions, nor of a straightforward contest between a
Scottish 'social ethic' and assimilationist influences pressuring it
from without. It is a question, rather, of the profound, lacerating
contradictions forced upon Scottish society by its anomalous mode
of development.

'Identity' tends of course to be a term of approval. In the psycho-
logistic terms which inform so much discussion of nationalism,
'identity' is what frustrated nationalities want and nation-states
possess. What this myth refers to is presumably the standard type of
developmental social structure associated with national-based
states (which one may conveniently, if not perhaps aptly, call the
normal structure-superstructure relation). In this sense, Scotland
appears as a highly-developed society (as distinct from simply
being a part of a larger developed area, the United Kingdom) which,
nevertheless, does not possess all the standard fitments of development. It is hard to avoid metaphor in describing the situation –
'decapitation', 'neurosis' or even 'schizophrenia', and so on. What
these mean is that a semi-autonomous, Stateless form of development gave rise to a series of characteristic contradictions between
civil society and the (non-national) State, expressed through the
social culture at different levels. Expressed, therefore, in Scottish
'national consciousness', in ways which have been too little analyzed.[42]

[41] George Elder Davie, *The Democratic Intellect: Scotland and her Universities
in the 19th Century* (1961), 'Introductory Essay', p. xv.
[42] Perhaps the most brilliant and useful recent analysis on these lines is that of
N. T. Phillipson, whose 'Nationalism and Ideology' (in *Government and National-*

In a more realistic, less mythical, sense one can of course say that modern Scotland has its own unmistakable 'identity'. Is it right to refuse 'identity' to a hopeless neurotic, because he is different from others, and unhappy about the fact?

'Drums in the Walligate, pipes in the air,
  The wallopin' thistle is ill to bear.'[43]

The modern Scots can complain about what they are, in the sense of not liking it; but it is mildly absurd of them to complain about lacking identity, in the sense of not being different enough from everybody else. However ill to bear, the thistle can hardly be seen as deficient in character.

I suggested earlier that this relatively well-preserved identity was one of the factors which has enabled the SNP to forge ahead so startlingly, once it had managed to break through the initial barrier. Once our 'cultural sub-nationalism' *had* become politicizable, the process of reconversion was to prove less arduous than in many comparable regions of Europe. This raises another problem, upon which it is important to say at least a word or two here. What was the 'barrier' in question, and why did it take so long for the belated modern movements of Scottish nationalism to cross it – i.e. from the 1920s to the 1970s?

The barrier appears here as another way of denoting that national 'split personality' described above. What it meant was that, in an apparent paradox, 'nationalism' was both very strong in Scotland *and* almost unbelievably feeble. This paradox arises from the different real senses being ascribed to the same word. 'Nationalism' in the sense of cultural sub-nationalism – let us say, the repressed complex of Scottishness – remained strong throughout the modern era. As Kellas says, this bears no direct connection at all with the rises and falls of SNP-type politics: 'Such consciousness is greater than the number of votes won by that party at elections. It is not necessarily concerned, as is the SNP, with "national self-determination", or with political devolution. It is rather an assertion of Scottishness on the part of an amorphous group of interests and individuals, whose identity is caught up with that of Scotland . . .'.[44] Among such interests football is more prominent than politics,

ism in Scotland, ed. J. N. Wolfe, 1969) examines the 'ideology of noisy inaction' inspired by Scott, and the exact way in which the latter 'taught Scotsmen to see themselves as men . . . in whose confusion lies their national character'.
[43] C. M. Grieve, *A Drunk Man Looks at the Thistle* (1926), p. 18.
[44] J. G. Kellas, op. cit., p. 129.

while even in more political issues '. . . there is rarely an overt attack on Scottish institutions from England. Instead, there is a "Scottish" and an "English" division of opinion among the Scots themselves'.

On the other hand, 'nationalism' in the fuller historical sense remained very weak – so weak that until the later 1960s it was almost wholly resistant to even the modest organization of the SNP. In the present situation typically nationalist myths about the continuous and inevitable 'rise' of the latter are bound to be invented.[45] For nationalism time is unimportant: in its nature-mythology the soul is always there anyway, slumbering in the people, and it is of no especial importance that McFinnegan opened his eyes one hundred and fifty years after everyone else. He had to get up *some* time, and what matters is the grandeur of the Wake. In reality, this politicized nationalism remained uncertain and vacillating, a matter of much-debated 'waves' of electoral support that looked anything but permanent to most observers. It could still be said in 1972 that '. . . The SNP has not yet established itself as a permanent force of importance in Scottish politics. Nor has it captured the full extent of national consciousness of Scotland to its own advantage'.[46]

This contradiction between a strong basis and weak political manifestation is a real one, but explicable historically. It corresponded, surely, to the main lineaments of that society-State relationship referred to previously. According to these, the specific character of that basis lay precisely in its marked dissociation from political consciousness – so that its obvious 'strength' (informing as it did most of civil society) was accompanied by 'amorphous', fragmented, parochial and other traits. Its maximal political manifestation was perhaps what Kellas calls 'The empty affirmative of most Scots to the standard survey question: "Do you think Scotland should have more control over its own affairs?"'. The dissociation signified that such 'Scottishness' was almost incapable of being mobilized in a national-political direction: its principle was a refusal *of* that direction. And of course, it was complemented by what one may define as 'over-Britishness' upon the plane of

[45] A recent example of this is provided by a series of articles in the *Irish Times* by Owen Dudley Edwards, who depicts the SNP's rise as analogous to 'a great flood steadily coming in' over the years, in an otherwise admirable analysis of contemporary Scottish nationalism.

[46] J. G. Kellas, op. cit., pp. 136–7, and following pages.

actual, day-to-day political awareness and organization. It was this over-adaptation that turned all Scots sections of United Kingdom parties into indescribable caricatures of their English selves.

Looked at in this light, the puzzle is less why the SNP took half a century to break through, than why it broke through at all. There is no room here to say much about the earlier history of revived political nationalism. It is worth observing though that its dominant oddity, when compared to other forms of nationalism, is what one would expect: its whole career from the '20s to the '60s reproduces the 'split-personality' phenomenon *within the nationalist movement itself*. This took the shape, commented upon by every single observer of the SNP, of the chronic division between 'political' and 'cultural' wings of the movement – a division far deeper and more irreconcilable, one should add at once, than the customary quarrels between idealists and 'practical men' which dog all national parties.[47]

The historical 'barrier' to politicized nationalism began to be overcome when, for the first time, something like the classical 'development gap' was thrust upon Scotland. I argued above that in the country's unusual 19th century situation the middle class did not have to confront normal developmental problems: these had been solved for it by the economic revolution which had followed the Union. There was no 'nationalism-producing' dilemma, and hence no serious nationalist movement or culture. British decline alone did not create such a dilemma for the Scots. It led to uncertain stirrings, no more, and never looked likely to end in a sufficiently painful gap between English and Scottish conditions. But the impact of a new capitalism, from a fresh direction, was a different matter altogether.

Perhaps the most essential single ingredient in this dilemma has

[47] The main source remains of course H. J. Hanham's *Scottish Nationalism* (1969), with its often-quoted diagnoses of the 'small man, small town' character of the old SNP, its anti-intellectualism, etc. Among other oddities are the movement's failure to produce a leader-figure; its extremely pacific and constitutional approach; and of course the clearly wayward nature of so much nationalist culture itself (which made it difficult for a political movement to do anything but shun it). In effect this was a split between a political movement that found it difficult to break-away from over-adaptation to 'British' norms; and a culture which was wholly adrift from them, and engaged upon something close to the fantasy re-creation of the whole of modern Scottish history and social reality.

always been the threat from outside. The 'under-developed' region sees development going on under foreign control, and apprehends it as a process which – if not contested and harnessed quite differently – will simply roll over the country and exploit it. It may of course spread a little local 'development' in its wake, and distribute a few crumbs to the native middle class. The imperialists who are in charge invariably speak of 'progress' in this sense. But this sense is nothing (or so the nationalist feels) compared to what his people would get if they control the process themselves, and put it into 'their own terms'. Only in this way therefore, by a populist mobilization of the country, can the promise of development and modernization be made to outweigh its threat.

Understood in this way, the petroleum industry's incursion into Scotland is quite clearly analogous to the 'classical' historical situation associated with nationalism. It is a .east a simulacrum of the dilemma that almost invariably gave rise to nationalist development. Here of course the threat from outside is not from one power, politically speaking: 'imperialism' can be identified most clearly with the United States, in the sense that most of the multinationals involved are U.S.-based, but this indirect relationship has a logic different from the traditional one. None the less, it has given rise to a version of separate or nationalist-type development. There is a vital discontinuity in the situation – a qualitative leap, as it were – which is hidden from view by the innate structure of that nationalist ideology which has profited so largely from the change. This ideology invariably emphásizes continuity and natural 'inevitability', to the exclusion of 'accidents' and influences from outside. In reality, one may suspect that the process of reconversion of sub-nationalism into an effective separatism which is now going on so rapidly – by which, in Kellas's words, the SNP *is* at last 'capturing the full extent of national consciousness . . . to its own advantage' – would never have occurred without the shock of North Sea oil development.

To compare this situation to the historical one of mainstream nationalism is also to become aware of an important difference. The characteristic socio-economic state of 'under-development' which gave rise to the successive waves of nationalist reaction, from the era of Napoleon to that of 'de-colonization' after the Second World War, normally involved conditions considerably more backward than any in modern Scotland (with the partial exception of the Highlands). Nationalism over most of the world was, and still is, the dominant cultural form of industrialization, or 'modernization'. It is under its banner, and through its peculiar machinery, that feudal and pre-feudal societies have struggled towards literacy, economic development and mass political life, the formation of cities, and so on. Nationalism is in this sense the means by which 'modern society' is built up, in terms tolerable to the inhabitants of what would (otherwise) have been repressed and exploited backwaters, 'historyless' regions. For this reason nationalism informs most modern societies, and one may say that industrialization is (in the widest terms) what nationalism is about.

It needs little reflection to see that in Scotland and comparable regions nationalism can no longer absolve these functions. Such societies have become 'modernized' (and in certain cases, like Scotland, Catalonia, etc., become highly industrialized) without benefit of nationalism. One may not like the 'pathological' manifestations of this atypical development mentioned previously; nonetheless, it happened, and it cannot now be undone. In general, the development of capitalism required nationalism; but in particular marginal cases the system could quite well encompass such deviations, 'mongrel' developments combining features from dominant and subordinate nationalities. The complex of *real* problems facing a belated nationalism which returns to a zone of this kind is necessarily distinct from that characterizing older nationalisms. This must be a good deal of the difference between nationalism and 'neo-nationalism' (as hinted above).

This may become plainer, if one reflects more closely upon the wider field of neo-nationalism. It is a phenomenon which now affects a definite area of Western Europe, most notably the Spanish, French and British States, and the Low Countries. The position in Italy and Germany is significantly different, for reasons associated with the more recent (and prototypically nationalist) development of these countries, with their defeat in the Second World War, and with the relatively advanced forms of regional government both have adopted since 1945. The other, older States were all constituted in certain key respects *before the age of nationalism proper*. They are, as a matter of fact, the 'original' nation-states which fostered modern capitalism, and whose impact upon the rest of the world precipitated the process of general 'development' (imperialism and counter-imperialism) with which nationalism became inextricably linked. For this very reason, as many scholars have indicated, they belong in a rather special category. They themselves evolved prior to the general conditions of uneven development which they foisted on the world. They are not really so much 'nation-States' as 'State-nations', in which the factors of nationality had played a rôle quite distinct from that they would assume in nationalism proper. Put at its most simple: they were in fact multi-ethnic assemblages in which, through lengthy processes of conquest and absorption, one or another nationality had established ascendancy (normally in late-feudal times, through the machinery of absolute monarchy). Then, when these entities were exposed to the new circumstances of the nationalist age (19th–early 20th century) they normally reacted by the maximization of this ascendancy, by reinforcement of French (Langue d'Oïl), Spanish (Castilian), British (English), or Belgian (Walloon) patriotism, most often in a new imperialist framework.

This new situation enabled the historically 'composite' nature of such States to be buried politically for a time (though of course the interment was never as total as it seemed from the vantage-points of London, Paris, etc.). Now, however, with the farther prolonged era of capitalist expansion since 1950 and the formation of the European Common Market, the external conditions which did so much to consolidate the old State-nations have largely gone. Their empires have disappeared, with a few insignificant exceptions. They have dwindled in status to mediocre, second-rate powers whose pretentions far outrange their capabilities. Apart from their function as the incubators of capitalism (now long in the past), they have State and military apparatuses whose main rôle was to terrorize each other and the 'backward' lands they had interests in. But nowadays no one is afraid of them, and their attitudes towards one another are marked by Ruritanian envy and parish-pump bile rather than real aggression. In absurdity, the universal aspirations which still mark the speeches of President Giscard d'Estaing and Mr Wilson are on a level with the uniforms of their Palace Guards.

Once, the intellectual circles of their capitals could despise 'provincial' separatisms and parochial ways because their States stood in the van of development. They did represent civilization and a more universal culture – albeit a civilization which was imperialist in character, and transitory. Nowadays such contempt rests on little but size. Madrid, London, Brussels stand for the brute facts of existence, not for what that existence means: they control larger areas and wield larger powers. Yet these areas are not large enough, in relation to the operations of modern multi-national capitalism and the dominant States of our time, and their powers are feeble and antiquated by the same token. Their 'metropolitan' culture draws every day closer to that ageless joke: the village idiot convinced, against all the evidence, that he still has a thing or two to teach the world. As far as the United Kingdom is concerned, the Scots have at least some consciousness of their 'Kailyard' as a problem; the English are still largely unaware of having arrived there. In Edinburgh people are at least ashamed of *The Sunday Post* and STV; in London their folkloric equivalents are still taken seriously.

Thus, the bourgeois modes of domination which held such polities together have wilted. There is a most important corollary to this, which must not be overlooked. The decline of bourgeois hegemony has not been accompanied by the rise of an alternative – that is, by the emergence of an effective socialist power at the level of the old States. Had the class struggle accelerated politically at the same time, it is doubtful if Scottish and other neo-nationalist movements would have made much headway.

I suggested originally that two factors in combination had created the conditions for nationalist resurgence: the multi-national petroleum business, and the degeneration of United Kingdom politics. But the failure of socialism is surely another way of regarding the second of these. It is the failure of the Left to advance far enough, fast enough, on the older State-nation platforms which history had provided, it is the inability of great-nation socialism to tackle advanced contradictions properly, that has made this 'second round' of bourgeois nationalisms inevitable.

To what extent is history destined to repeat itself here? The original socialist movements of the 19th and early 20th century were on the whole outflanked and contained by those contemporaneous national movements which proved stronger. When revolution came to the world of advanced capitalism, it came as fascism, the ultra-nationalist reaction to the threat of socialist and communist advance (a threat that was in fact remote). It may be worth quoting one recent historical verdict upon the conclusion of that first wave of European nationalism after World War I: 'In contrast with (the older nation states) . . . which enlarged the economic area and operated in the direction of expansion and progress, the newly created nation states of the 20th century became a fetter on efficiency and progress, and lent their power to the turning back of the wheels of history. Similarly, while the former . . . seemed to be fulfilling the destiny of a long and uninterrupted historical evolution, the latter entered upon their heritage in a psychological atmosphere of insecurity, rancour, uncertain frontiers and dissatisfied national minorities, and in consequence their search for autarky tended to be unusually aggressive and uncompromising . . . In a dozen different ways the peace treaties and their political consequences thwarted, hampered and obstructed the economy of Europe in a manner which had not been seen since the Industrial and the French Revolutions. At the same time, in the complex symbiosis in which the economic and the political affect each other, the capitalist economy itself appeared to have lost its capacity for expansion and adaptation . . . whether because of its own inner laws or because of the political responses it had stimulated.'[48]

Neo-nationalism need not repeat these disasters of nationalism: the world may have altered in ways that render its negative potential less great. Still, it must remain perfectly legitimate to ask whether the 'second round', the formation of still other nation states, could not lead to at least partially similar effects? It is no use looking to the intentions of the SNP or any other separatist movement for answers to questions like these. However new nationalism may differ from old, it has inherited much of its ideology; and it is a standard law of such ideology that '*our* nationalism will be different' – i.e. not aggressive, not narrow or 'inward-looking' but progressive and 'outward-looking', not turning back the historical wheels but urging them forward (and so on). As far as Scotland is concerned, this moment of innocence is aggravated by the intense Britishness of the nationalist movement so far: it shows small consciousness of the huge potential for non-constitutional and non-pacific conflicts which are inherent in the situation. Westminster, which enjoyed a first moment of (entirely characteristic) metropolitan contempt for the very concept of devolution, when the Kilbrandon Report appeared, is now tumbling over itself to propitiate and contain separatism.

But it would be absurd to confuse these antics with the reality of the English nation. It is in the logic of the whole situation that the formerly dominant nationalities will themselves be compelled by

[48] S. Pollard, *European Economic Integration 1815–1970* (1974), pp. 132–6.

reaction to rediscover their nationalism – for that nationalism too is, in a quite different sense, 'buried' or concealed by the past equivocations of imperialism and the multi-ethnic State. They will have to 'define themselves anew' against the separatism of their former minorities (in Powell's phrase). In England's case, the prospect is sharpened by the likelihood of a phase of reaction against the prolonged economic crises which have accompanied loss of empire – a reaction which is unlikely to assume any but a nationalist form. It has already been unduly delayed, by the strength of the old political system and the fact that it has been exposed to slow wasting rather than dramatic challenges (like those which ended the IVth Republic, and ushered in Gaullism). Would we then be so far from 'a psychological atmosphere of insecurity, rancour, uncertain frontiers and dissatisfied national minorities', aggravated by bitter disputes over North Sea oil?

The contradictions and possibilities of neo-nationalism require far more study. The phenomenon is much too new to allow ready predictions as to its future course. All one can be reasonably sure of is that it will embody contradictions analogous to those of ancestral nationalism: on the one hand, the perspective of liberation to a more genuine democracy or self-rule, accompanied by emergence from debilitating provinciality and cultural estrangement; on the other hand, the tendency of the very same movement (a tendency inherent in it) towards national narrowness, subjective illusion and conceit, political and economic regression, and romantic nonsense. At different times or in different conditions, one side or another may appear more prominent, or in control. But in reality both belong inextricably to the historical structure of national*ism* as a mode of development – and presumably to that of neo-nationalism also. Given that the latter belongs to a new phase of development – to a far more advanced stage of capitalism and bourgeois society – it is still to be seen how the objective circumstances of these times will make its contradictions display themselves.

IV

'The development of world history is not merely a by-product of national developments but has an independent character; created by nations, in its turn it creates them . . . it often interrupts national developments, and after

> nations have become entangled with each other, it affects
> them to a profound degree.'
>
> Otto Hintze,
> 'The Collective Approach to History' (1897).

The prospect of independence poses a new question to Scotland. Where will this re-emergent nation stand, in the collectivity of states? Will it be a separate yet still 'British' state? A new member of the European Community of states? A candidate for membership of an enlarged Nordic Union? A minor dependency of the United States? Will it fortify the old economic order, by siding with world imperialism, or help to build a new order by siding with the under-developed countries?

These are the problems of Scotland's future external affairs. Consideration of them must start from some conception (often left implicit in the argument) of where Scottish society stands in the world order. Yet this is often the weak point in such debates. For, as I will go on to argue, it is not in fact easy to establish what kind of country Scotland is in this sense. The re-emergent nation-state poses problems dramatically different from those of the old imperial province. We are just beginning to see what these are today. They are too important politically to be left in the limbo of 'Afterwards . . .'.

It is best to begin with the existing order. There is a comfortable myth about the world which regulates most debate on contemporary history. This is the idea that historical development has become essentially a struggle between the privileged and the underprivileged nations. The widening gap between them – between industrialized and 'under-developed', between the advanced world and the Third World (or Third and Fourth Worlds) – has turned into the main motor of historical conflict, *the* great problem whose solution conditions everything else.

The element of comfort lies in the myth, of course, not in the grim facts from which it is derived. In its standard application, the myth tends towards a phoney simplicity and completeness. This in turn tends to be what people agree about: both the Western apologists who still think classical 'development' possible, and the revolutionaries who hold that this has broken down, and that increasingly uneven development will compel the deprived peoples along some other path.

I know that the original Manichaean simplicity of the notion has been modified of late. Theorists are more ready to admit that the 'Third World' is a complex, even contradictory concept capable of obscuring important distinctions and changes. More than that may be wrong with it, however.

Its primary fault may be rather that it takes no proper account of what one may call the 'middle class' of the world order. There is a significant intermediate category of countries which usually gets left out altogether. For some reason these do not fit into the grand overall vision of an élite of *bourgeois* nations fighting against the world proletariat. And it may be that an independent Scotland will belong in this company of misfits.

These awkward customers are not the smaller nations of the élite – not medium-sized industrial powers like France, or prosperous suburbs like the Nordic countries and Switzerland. They are countries which, although equipped in certain respects for that status, have failed to make it. They are societies where the development process has gone wrong in a characteristic way and, instead of bearing them upwards into secure membership of the 'rich man's club', has deposited them in a curious limbo of insoluble problems. This very progress has carried them into collision with the main lines of the geopolitical order; it is the latter's inability to either assimilate them or make space for them that turns them into chronic 'problems' of this kind.

Were such countries merely exceptions, anomalies and oddities, they might be unimportant. But the truth is they constitute a recognizable pattern, and this pattern is mainly one of disturbance. To a remarkable extent they are the trouble-makers of the existing international order (or disorder, if preferred). It may still be true that the mainstream problem of world history is forced under-development. But it is also true that the great battle of rich and poor is largely being fought out through intermediaries – through this middling stratum of non-belongers.

There is an obvious analogy to the phenomenon. In traditional discussions of the internal social order we also find an exaggerated polarity: the small ruling class of property-owners and the mass of disinherited (and of course ideas of the global 'class struggle' have actually been drawn from this source). But in social analysis theorists became more cautious a long time ago: the warier among them understood that the great social battle very rarely takes the shape of direct confrontation between the poles. It has almost invariably been fought out through the agency of assorted middle classes – through declining upper strata, rising or discontented *petits bourgeois*, 'labour aristocracies', *déclassé* intellectuals or adventurers, and so on.

Something of the same kind is true in international affairs. The Third World dispossessed will never 'invade' the advanced world, any more than the factory proletariat has generally taken over the bankers' mansions. In the social field it is the lower middle classes which occupy what Arno Mayer has defined as the 'pivotal role' of contemporary history.[49] So in the larger arena too the 'in-between' nationalities function as the focal points of conflict – the areas in which the deeper stresses actually erupt, and are literally fought out.

A nation's place in the world is only superficially determined by the formality of equal status, 'recognition', and a place at the UN. Its real place is constituted by the singular role it occupies in the development process. The industrial revolution began to knit world history into one story; European and North American imperialism imposed that story on the rest of the globe. Carried along in this ever more unified process, each society has found by its own development a characteristic position: its inherited re-sources and traits are given the stamp of world society, mainly by the relations in which it stands to others.

The broad causes of nationalism in modern history are well known. National-*ism* in this systemic sense arose out of a host of earlier phenomena as the protest of under-developed peoples. It became their way of mobilizing, and trying to catch up with already industrialized areas. Over much of the world, too, it was an ideo-logical weapon of liberation from dominance by the latter.

The imperial countries had their own version of nationalism, as a creed of conquest. Both sides in the great contest came to make use of the same ideas, and this created the notorious ambiguity that still haunts them: nationality had become the basis for both 'national liberation' and 'narrow nationalism', both the sacred principle of self-determination and fascism.

[49] A. J. Mayer, 'The Lower Middle Class as Historical Phenomenon', *Journal of Modern History*, v. 47, No. 3 (1975).

But the semantic confusion does not end there. From quite early on in the process there was a third cross-category. This neglected but significant group turned nationalist in order to liberate themselves from alien domination – yet did so, typically, not from a situation of colonial under-development but from one of relative progress. They were nationalities who struggled to free their own strong development from what they had come to perceive as the backwardness around them – from some larger, politically dominant power whose stagnation or archaism had become an obstacle to their farther progress.

Certain other characteristics usually attach to this nationalism of 'relative over-development'. The peoples and territories concerned are small. They tend to be in 'sensitive' zones of a larger political economy, alongside or in between powerful neighbours. They usually develop so rapidly through the discovery and exploitation of sub-soil resources – coal and iron in the 19th century, petroleum today. And sometimes they occupy a particularly favourable 'cross-roads' position in terms of trade patterns.

Capitalizing on these resources, such areas drive forward developmentally. They feel held back and exploited by the backward state power controlling them. Yet they are most often too small and powerless, too isolated or eccentrically located, to shake free and evolve into members of the world élite. Thanks to their bourgeois development, they are too strong to submerge or liquidate; but not strong enough to fight free. Hence they tend to remain stranded, like unassimilable problem-children of the international order.

Belgium was the first important case of this sort, in the post-Industrial Revolution era. The Belgian revolution of 1830–2 and the new state it created represented much more than a Catholic protest against the overlordship of the Calvinist Netherlands. At that period Belgium had developed rapidly into the most advanced centre of the new industrialism on the continent. The exploitation of coal and iron, and the country's strategic position across the great rivers, had bred an active entrepreneurial middle class – a restless, forward-looking bourgeoisie impatient with Dutch bureaucracy and backwardness.

The Holland of the early 19th century – it should be recalled – bore little resemblance to today's industrial state. It was a decaying mercantile empire given to indulgent contemplation of past glories, and very little inclined to put up with the disruptive strains of industrialization. The liberal Belgian middle class wanted to escape from this palsied grip. They asked originally for limited home rule, and when this was resisted by King William I soon escalated their demands to complete independence.

The Belgians were fortunate. Although dire predictions were made at the time about their weakness and precariousness, they survived. Instead of turning into an ulcer of the international system (as conservatives believed) they established a tolerable intermediate position, both 'buffer-state' and cross-roads between the great powers around them. They became, in fact, something like the remarkable pre-industrial state of middle-Europe, that cross-roads country *par excellence*, Switzerland.

Perhaps this good fortune was related to the earliness of Belgian independence. Certainly later small-country middle-class movements had a harder time, in the fiercer and more imperialist climate which prevailed from the later 19th century to the present.

From mid-century onwards, the relatively developed region of Bohemia reacted against the dead hand of Hapsburg absolutism in a similar fashion. The Czech-speaking middle class formulated a nationalism of its own, and fought for a modern bourgeois state capable of liberating them from the incorrigible parasitism of Austria-Hungary. Although superficially like the other Slav nationalisms in the backward lands of the empire – Slovenia, Slovakia, Serbia – Bohemian-based separatism actually stood on different, more developed ground. This is why the Czech state that eventually appeared in the post-1918 settlement was to be the success-story of Central Europe between the wars.

But this success was short-lived, and difficult. The Czechs were not able to sustain the balancing-act and emulate Switzerland or Belgium. Hence their relative over-development remained an intolerable threat to the dominant political powers. They emerged from German occupation in 1945 only to become a new challenge within the Soviet bloc. Again, their very progress gave birth to a renascent nationalism in the 1960s – the pretext, obviously, for a farther wave of imperial suppression and levelling.

In two other cases, achievement was even more fleeting. In the Iberian peninsula the Basque and Catalan regions had been the natural focus of industrial revolution. Both nationalities enjoyed a relatively privileged situation, either in resources or in trade location; and both straddled the existing political frontiers of the French and Spanish states. Again, varieties of nationalism arose to exploit this advantage and build middle-class states capable of effective modernization. This implied of course breaking from the backward, ex-imperial land-mass mainly dominating them, the old Spanish state.

These countries have never obtained independence. They knew only brief periods of limited 'home rule' in the early 1930s, under the liberal republic. Then the ferocious reaction from the centre subjected them to a still-continuing colonial régime of forced integration.

It is clearly the case that for all these awkwardly-located, potentially troublesome peoples, external relations were extremely important, even decisive. The big powers of the new geopolitical order of 19th century Europe had some interest in Swiss neutrality – an interest which survived even the two great wars of this century. They turned out to have far less in Czechoslovakia: Czech independence has been repeatedly 'betrayed'. And they had virtually none at all in the existence of Catalonia or Euzkadi.

Belgium, Bohemia, Catalonia, Croatia, the Basque Country – there is already a recognizable profile. Its general sense becomes plainer if the horizon is extended outside Europe.

In the extra-European world, as economic development has speeded up, there have already been several nationalist revolts founded on relative over-development. The most obvious examples are the attempt at secession by the Ibo Eastern Region of Nigeria in the 1960s, and the later stages of the Kurdish autonomist movement in Iraq. Both of these were connected with recently discovered petroleum resources, and the prospects of rapid separate growth and real independence that had suddenly been opened up. Both were crushed by straightforward military means, at least temporarily. Neither country got the external support it needed for survival in such difficult circumstances.

In Lebanon, the former Christian-dominated state owed its peculiar character and prosperity to a cross-roads position in world trade. This, rather than any natural resource, had furnished the basis for its over-development in a still poor Arab hinterland. For decades Beirut was advertised as the 'Crossroads of the Levant', the junction of East and West, and so forth.

Faced in the 1970s by a more characteristic Third World rebellion of its own under-privileged, the Christian community has been forced back into a small enclave. This particular island of relative economic advance is unlikely to survive for long. The motives that inspired American defence of it in 1958 no longer apply. The Muslim hinterland itself has evolved since then, and the United States enjoys a different relationship to it; in addition, the civil war has probably destroyed the very foundation of Lebanese *entrepôt* prosperity.

The cases we have looked at so far are all of peoples on their own land. But there is a second category of misplaced development which, though its origins are different, is yet so closely akin to them that it deserves consideration here. This is the relative over-development linked to settler implantation. The usual effect of this factor is to intensify hugely the dilemmas aroused by the kind of uneven growth we are interested in.

Settler implantation has to be distinguished from mere settlement. Most of the ex-colonial world which has now been swept away by the anti-imperialist revolt consisted of relatively superficial 'white settler' régimes. Once the old geopolitical context of empire had dissolved, these were doomed by their own fragility and rootlessness.

In a number of cases, however, settlement has developed more intensively, and produced quite a different pattern of events. The difference does not lie in the time-scale of colonial occupation – if it did, Portuguese Africa and British India would presumably still be with us. The distinction lies, rather, in a combination of social and geographical factors: occasionally, colonization formed genuine, self-sustaining, middle-class societies in locations favourable to their survival.

The fate of these societies has not been the standard post-colonial one. Even on alien soil they evolved into more or less complete social formations, capable of independence and self-defence, and with their own variety of nationalism. Like the other small nations mentioned, they have exploited either resources or a favourable trade situation; like them, they have become so many islands of relative over-development in relation to backward areas around them – and in their case too this advance has frequently provoked chronic problems for the wider political order.

Northern Ireland, White South Africa, Singapore, Israel: these also belong to the category of world misfits, and three of them pose what may be the most anguishing and intractable problems of contemporary history. Of course, the immediate politics of all these situations is different. Whereas the indigenous nationalities affected by over-development were forced into attempts at break-away, these settler-based bridgeheads of development defend an existing state against the 'backward hordes' surrounding them. They see themselves as custodians of a civilization which would 'go under' if they were politically assimilated to native society.

However, the underlying dilemma is much the same, and is insoluble by the usual rules for much the same reasons. Only in the totally exceptional circumstances of Hong Kong – where the largest nation on earth permits a settler enclave to survive on its flank for reasons of its own – do such developmental islands pose no problem. Generally, they are successful capitalist societies which can neither graduate normally into the élite, nor be got rid of through war or assimilation.

The overall physiognomy of this recalcitrant 'middle class' is clearer now. It is the relative socio-economic *advance* of certain smaller nationalities and regions that creates the intractable problems. The point is that this development occurs in the wrong place, or among the wrong people, from the point of view of the prevailing geopolitical order. Rich peoples and poor peoples pose no problem for the latter: as long as they know their place, the balance of power remains tidy. Such tidiness encourages belief in the institutionalization of the world class struggle. Why should a 'New Economic Order' of some sort not be attainable in time, by negotiation between the camps?

But actually this neat Victorian *Weltanschauung* is hopelessly crippled by the gang of parvenus and square pegs we have been looking at. As well as the mainstream of the development process, there are those refractory counter-currents and violent eddies. It is through them that the forces of historical development break into actual conflict and trouble. Nor is there the slightest chance of this category of awkward nationalisms diminishing – on the contrary, as world development accelerates it is certain to grow.

There are bound to be new members of the world's *petite bourgeoisie*, and some of them will derive from 'misplaced' development. Such misplacement is of course only relative to existing power structures: it is the latter which transform natural accident into tragedy. Thus, there would have been no problem – or at any rate not *this* problem – if the coal and iron reserves had been in Holland rather than Belgium; if Iberian industrial growth had taken place on the Castilian plateau rather than on its ethnic fringes; if oil had been discovered in Iraq proper rather than Kurdistan – and so on. But – equally obviously – 'accidents' of this kind will go on occurring in world economic development.

The British Isles already have one such centre of turbulence, in Northern Ireland. There, the British Empire fostered the development of a relatively advanced industrial mini-society on the basis of an old settler community, the Ulster Protestants. When imperialism vanished this bridgehead society remained, still locked in irreconcilable opposition to the more backward conditions of Catholic Ireland. The really interesting question of the moment in Britain is – has the farther decline of the old empire state now created another conflict of broadly the same sort? Will Scotland in turn become a centre of disruptive development, outpacing the somnolent failure to the south of it – and compelled, therefore, along a path of political separation?

Few would now deny that relative over-development in the United Kingdom context has something to do with the startling rise of the Scottish National Party. This is not wholly due to the discovery of North Sea oil. Other factors had (for instance) already made the Scottish industrial belt a choice site for investment by U.S. multinationals in the 1950s and 1960s. However, equally few would deny that the dramatic new prospects disclosed by petroleum development made a big difference. They encouraged a revolution of rising expectations and a new self-confidence (affecting the middle classes most tangibly).

At the same time, the London state and the southern economy have lurched several leagues farther on the downward track they have been following for decades. It would be exaggerated, admittedly, to claim that the U.K. state is yet quite like the Hapsburg Empire or the old Castilian state. But the similarities are notable enough: there is a recognizable composite of archaism, incorrigible economic failure, backward-looking complacency, indurate social conservatism and blind will to survive in the same historic form. Culture has become largely the celebration of these values. The main 'opposition' party, British Labour, is as addicted to them as the overt conservatives.

This is why a Scottish middle class, by nature somewhat less attached to the great English pieties, has begun to see the system as more and more of a frustrating burden. The Scots know quite well that the North Sea will be sucked dry mainly to keep this Model-T Leviathan going. The chances of the new resources being employed effectively for the long-awaited modernization of Britain's industrial economy are absolutely zero. Colossal borrowings have already been made against the oil revenues. Every single barrel of North Sea oil will go on being used to get the Crown Jewels back from the pawn-shop. There will be no significant protest from the English masses against this – on the contrary, it is being applauded as a quasi-divine salvation. The Almighty stands with England, right to the end of the road.

The Scots feel mounting opposition to this vision of the imperial future. By the same sort of natural accident as figured in the other cases, they are able to exploit a differential advantage (had the oil-fields been located off the shores of East Anglia, the problem would not have assumed this shape). They will obviously be prevented from doing so fully, by a dominant neighbouring state which itself desperately needs the resources. Even in its dotage, that neighbour is much more important to the international order than a marginal country like Scotland, and will be able to gather correspondingly more support for its own version of sovereign rights. It will not, however, be able to suppress or assimilate the Scottish revolt: although small and remote in world terms, Scotland is also a relatively developed, bourgeois society with many inner strengths and a long history of separate traditions and culture.

On the face of it, this looks like the recipe for another development ulcer. Indeed it would be hard to find elsewhere in this spectrum of problems such a crude and sharply-defined conflict: in an almost terminal condition an ailing empire discovers the treasure to keep it in this world – only to find it snatched from its grasp by greedy and troublesome natives. The SNP won its startling victories in 1974 on the slogan 'It's Scotland's Oil!' If taken seriously, there can be no doubt that this and other nationalist rhetoric portends a real battle.

What we do not yet know is whether it will be taken seriously. A large part of the Scottish people is now looking towards a future of separate development. But so far they have only voted for it; we do not know how many of them would be prepared to fight for it, if the going became harder.

Equally, we do not know at what point the British state will resist such claims with more decision. The whole movement to date remains veiled in a curious kind of negotiated unreality, which it is difficult to find parallels for in the other situations I have referred to. Scotland and Wales (unlike Ireland) have belonged historically in the United Kingdom, in a sense which applies to none of the other nationalities mentioned. Prolonged civil closeness and political partnership have created bonds that seem comparatively resistant to the strains of uneven development.

However, this may merely mean that both countries are drifting into an inevitable conflict in a jointly unrealistic frame of mind. At the moment the official assumption of Anglo-Scottish relations is that the new differences can be regulated by agreement: by the formation of some sort of revived yet limited Scottish self-government which will appease the new nationalism *and* keep the essential unity of Great Britain intact. For its part, the Scottish nationalist movement has seized the opportunity presented by a pragmatic and strongly constitutional state, and confined its action to peaceful and mainly parliamentary means.

The dominant foreign-policy idea of the nationalists is equally revealing. They tend to believe that a peaceably negotiated independence will usher Scotland into instant membership of the rich man's club. Even a share of the oil revenues would be enough to transform this small land into another Norway. Thus the country's future is automatically identified with established and prosperous nation-states, rather than with the other suppressed or struggling nationalities of Europe (still less with the awkward squad examined here). Like the peaceable nature of the SNP, this vision is of course defensible. Nobody would seriously argue that self-government should not be negotiated, if this is possible; nor that quick graduation into an outpost of the Nordic Union would be an attractive future, at least in certain respects.

At the same time, one may reasonably doubt whether either prospect is a real one. Scotland's future place is less likely to be that of a second Norway, and more likely to be in the world's limbo of. anomalies and stress-points.

Speaking of President Giscard d'Estaing's recent visit to Scotland, the Edinburgh *Scotsman* declared that he 'should know that the desire to make a modest appearance on the international stage is growing in Scotland and is unlikely to diminish. The devolutionary movement is part of a historical process which may be checked but will ultimately demand satisfaction' (June 21st, 1976).

The real historical-process in which re-emergent Scotland has become involved may be much wider and more controversial than this editorialist believed. Looking at the question in British terms, or in terms of geography, you get one picture; but in terms of developmental process and its contradictions, there is another view altogether. In the latter, Scotland's situation is far from unique. But any comfort derived from this recognition may be modified by the company we find ourselves in: Catalonia has much more in common with us than Norway. The SNP ideologists tend to perceive us as paid-up members of the élite already; actually, we may end up as noisy outcasts, breaking the club windows in order to get in.

To isolate properly the elements of unrealism in the Nordic dream would take up too much space here. Yet the gist of the matter can be put like this: neither externally nor internally does Scotland have the characteristics which might let her follow such a course in external affairs.

If the Scots had come upon a natural resource which offended no one else – like Norwegian water-power at the beginning of this century – things might be better. As it is, they are laying claim to a resource which is bound to draw them into external conflict with a powerful neighbour. It is not the case that there will be enough to satisfy everyone. In relation to the great expectations aroused in both Edinburgh and London – and which are bound to grow, not diminish – the resources will always be 'scarce'. The pressures of uneven development will soon prove stronger than civil closeness: the magic of British constitutionalism – already distinctly frayed – will be dispersed altogether.

Internally, Scottish society does not possess the homogeneity of the Scandinavian models. On the contrary, it has always been remarkable for dizzying contrasts of wealth and poverty, depopulated deserts and narrow, crowded conurbations. Its recent political advance is related to a prospect of bourgeois affluence; but this coexists with zones of hopeless urban blight, and the familiar records for alcoholism, disease, and basic poverty. Regionally as well as socially, Scotland has been rendered extremely disparate by prolonged de-centred development.

Hence Scottish independence must confront a great accumulation of problems: external and internal difficulties together will force the country into an arena of hard dilemmas and thorny alternatives. Too many imponderables prevent us seeing far. However, one thing is plain. If this bleaker vision is in any degree more realistic, then external relations will be of critical importance to any Edinburgh government. If Scotland is even partly like the series of development-battles reviewed above, then it will resemble them in this: for small, struggling nationalities foreign relationships are always vital, and often decisive. Existence inside a decaying empire has blunted our sensibilities in this respect.

It goes without saying that any sober perspective on the conditions of independence will be used as an argument by defenders of Great Britain. Why abandon a great state for seas as perilous as this? In reality the argument can be turned in the opposite direction just as easily – in which case the prospect of difficulties becomes the strongest argument for a more decided and unrepentant nationalism.

It depends upon one's conception of the United Kingdom. There are those who believe that this rump of the former empire will last for ever, in an essentially unchanging evolution. Their number includes virtually all England, and a still formidable mass of allies in Scotland, Wales, and Northern Ireland. On the other hand stands the growing opposition – within sight of being a majority in Scotland – which accepts the verdict a great part of the outside world passed on Britain long ago: that it is a matter of time before it founders. Its post-empire crisis is long overdue, and not even to be regretted. What else is likely to revive this polity of stultified anachronism and complacent privilege?

This, rather than 'North Sea oil', is the political substance of the nationalist revivals in the British Isles. For the Scots in particular the implication is not only nationalism, but a nationalism especially outward-looking in nature. We shall be under a particular and pressing necessity to look towards other countries and other national movements, for tolerance and understanding, and eventually for help. This of course entails breaking with the introspective tendency which has in the past deeply marked the Scottish national movement (in common with many others).

Such a break will itself be a sign of maturity. It will indicate a readiness to look more openly at the realities of contemporary history, and to measure ourselves against them – an ability, therefore, to recover genuine dialogue and contact with other nations. To be 'outward-looking' is not (as too often believed) a question of facile attitudinizing. It is the difficult programme for the next generation, and its implementation will be forced by practical need.

It is of course not clear what alliances and links will be formed by an emergent Scottish state. Those who incline to the Scandinavian myth will go on fighting for it, even if its difficulties grow more apparent. Others will be more impressed by the possibilities of the European Community – to which Scotland already belongs indirectly – as a nexus of support. Here, the Scots might find themselves as fellow-members alongside a much larger number of small states with comparable needs: the Netherlands, Belgium, Ireland, Denmark, and possibly in time Greece, Catalonia and Euzkadi, Wales and Northern Ireland, and Portugal.

Scotland is an indirect member of the Atlantic Alliance as well as of the Community. The country's new and sensitive position in the international economy of oil makes this more significant. Would NATO tolerate the removal of its Scottish nuclear base, a measure to which the whole national movement is at present committed? The opinions already coming into play here range from a self-consciously exaggerated fidelity to NATO, to outright neutralism.

Through a growing debate on these future dilemmas, the Scots are endeavouring to re-attach themselves to an outside world. As for that world itself: it would be gratifying if, for once, notice was taken of an emerging international problem some time before it becomes impossible to avoid it.

4. Culture and Politics in Wales

> 'People talk of the betrayal by the Tudors, of the decline of the Welsh nobility; of the disappearance of the bardic profession; of the beginnings of the middle class and wealthy merchants who saw nothing in Welsh culture; of the wrong done to the Welsh language; of the Anglicizing of education ... All these are secondary causes. There was a deeper cause: the thing that destroyed the civilization of Wales and ruined Welsh culture, that brought about the dire plight of Wales today, was – *nationalism* ...'.

It is fifty years since Saunders Lewis electrified the audience at Plaid Cymru's first Summer School with these words.[1] He was of course warning it against the perils of a merely political, power-hungry nationalism – against a development in any way like what he imagined the course of modern English history to have been. And the warning was accompanied by his plea for a distinctively Welsh development: for a spiritual and cultural nationalism founded on native tradition and looking back to the Middle Ages.

It is about fifty years, too, since Scottish nationalism first assumed an embryo yet vaguely recognizable shape with John

---

[1] This paper was presented at the fiftieth Summer School of the movement held at Lampeter in July, 1976. I am glad to be able to express my thanks to Dafydd Williams, Phil Williams, and many others, for this invitation to an extremely lively gathering. Also to Ned Thomas, who published an earlier version in his magazine *Planet*.

MacCormick's National Party of Scotland, in 1928. This broad and already moderate political movement was only one ancestor of today's SNP; but it had begun to lead the way out of what one pioneer, Lewis Spence, saw as the giddy confusion of the cultural nationalists in Scotland. On that side, he wrote, the movement in favour of a national rebirth has attracted '. . . many of the greatest cranks in Christendom . . . a maelstrom bubbling with the cross-currents of rival and frequently fantastic theories, schemes and notions, riotous with timultuous personality and convulsive with petulant individual predilection . . .There is no chart, no plan, nothing approaching a serious, practical Scotsman-like policy in either art or politics'. Within a short time the serious and Scotsman-like trend was to emerge triumphant, expelling the culture-heads and *littérateurs* to a Celtic outer darkness.[2]

Although not many would now swallow Lewis's mediaevalism, or denounce the Scottish literary renaissance quite so sharply, the two images are still quite familiar. They reflect, respectively, a nationalism in which cultural issues have been predominant, and one in which culture has occupied a very secondary place. It would be exaggerated to say that Welsh nationalism was culturist in outlook while Scottish nationalism was philistine. But few would fail to recognize some truth in the contrast.

This contrast is linked to many others, and to a great deal of mutual misunderstanding. Few Scots easily understand or sympathize with the anguishing dilemmas of the language-problem; on the other hand, Welshmen are often puzzled by the very existence of a nationalist movement without a language of its own.[3]

[2] H. J. Hanham, *Scottish Nationalism*, 1969, pp. 154–5, and ibid., p. 160: 'The purge of 1933 (sinister date) gave control of the National Party to those whose aim was . . . Home Rule within the British Commonwealth, and who eschewed romantic literary flourishes. There was no place in the National Party either for Erskine of Marr and the Gaelic militants of the Scots National League, or for most of the wild young literary men. They were driven into the wilderness . . .'

[3] The official version: 'In Wales . . . Welsh, a form of British Celtic, is the first language of the majority of the population in most of the western counties and was spoken by 21% of the population aged 3 years and over (some 542,400 people) at the time of the 1971 census . . . The Welsh Language Act of 1967 affirms the equal validity of Welsh with English in the administration of justice and conduct of government business throughout Wales'. *Britain 1976: an Official Handbook* (HMSO). The contrast with Scotland is very marked. In the latter

The Scot perceives a colossal fuss being made about nothing; the Welsh nationalist is intrigued by a country where there seems nothing to make a fuss about. Welsh nationalism has always been strikingly internationalist in outlook, finding a natural affinity in many movements and personalities on continental Europe. Scottish nationalism has tended to be somewhat solitary, with only its Gaelic fringe seeking actively for such contacts. Although sometimes voicing the proper sentiments about repressed nationalities and minorities, the SNP mainstream shows distinctly greater enthusiasm for bourgeois Scandinavia than for the Bretons or the Basques.

And so on. The two movements still do not understand each other very well. After fifty years, they ought to understand one another better. It has become practically and politically important to do so, as well as culturally desirable. The pre-history of Welsh and Scottish nationalism is over, and we are now launched into the irreversible process of the history of these movements – a history in which Wales and Scotland will have many more common interests and struggles than when they were tame provinces of empire.

However, it is not so easy. Although it is high time one advanced beyond the base-line of sonorous sermons about solidarity and common foes, it is actually difficult to work out a line of march. The trouble is that we still lack reliable charts.

A mere point-by-point comparison between two national movements – or between two nations – will not reveal or explain very much. Anyone can see that Wales and Scotland are remarkably different countries: but in itself, such observation will remain superficial and a matter for anecdotes rather than analysis. To get farther we have to have some kind of theory that embraces both of them, a theory which deals with places like Wales and Scotland and situates them in an intelligible historical context. Only then, surely, will we be able to determine more realistically where they stand, and what they can do together or hope to learn from one another.

---

only about 88,000 persons in 1971, mainly in the Highlands and western coastal regions, were able to speak the Scottish form of Gaelic. This is out of a much bigger total population of 5,226,000 (1974 estimate). For an introduction to the political significance of the language question, see Ned Thomas, *The Welsh Extremist*, 1972.

II

'The small-state concept . . . seems not only a matter of
expediency but of divine plan, and on *this* account
makes everything soluble. It constitutes, in fact, nothing
but the political application of the most basic organizing
and balancing device of nature . . . social *blessings* are
concomitants of social size – *small size*.'

Leopold Kohr,
The Breakdown of Nations (1957), pp. 97–8.

We do not yet have a theoretical framework which will let us do
this properly. But this is not all. The trouble is that a dubious
theory has arisen, a framework which to some extent actively mis-
leads us in the quest. Were we merely in the normal condition of
being in the dark, this would be bad enough. As it is, a lurid light
falls across the landscape, and conveys an over-simplified techni-
colour image.

The theory I have in mind may be called for purposes of argument
that of 'cultural colonialism'. Its key notions are those of cultural
identity and cultural oppression. The identity it focuses on is that
of the smaller, peripheral communities and regions of Western
Europe; the oppression lies in the way they have been treated by
the politically dominant nationalities, the 'core areas'. Metropolitan
domination has of course assumed economic form. It has extracted
what it needed from these regions, in labour power and other resources; and such development as it has fostered there has been
typically lop-sided and transitory. However, the theory characteristically emphasizes cultural robbery rather than economic. Large-
scale, over-centralized capitalism has eroded or destroyed old
community identity. It is through a battle for the recovery of their
culture that these regions are reviving today – a struggle primarily
against 'alienation', and the brontosaural bureaucracy epitomized
by the Swansea Vehicle Licensing Centre.

In *The Centralist Enemy* John Osmond has summed up many
elements of the view as follows: 'The road of the Corporate State
leads to a dead end . . . The only rational alternative is a view of life
that gives precedence to the concept of community. This requires a

new philosophy: one that will put community interests first, even at
the expense of economic interests . . . The first requirement of a
community is that it be given a human scale in which people can
reasonably seek a sense of purpose, responsibility and identity.'[4]
Naturally, communities can fight for this philosophy best when they
have a strong ethnic and linguistic basis. So these particular vehicles
of nationality are seen as especially significant.

I am well aware of the powerful Welsh stake in this new European
Weltanschauung. Twenty years ago Leopold Kohr produced an
advance philosophical benediction of it, in the shape of *The Break-
down of Nations*. More recently, as well as John Osmond, Ned
Thomas's *Planet,* Patricia Mayo, and a number of others, have
played a part in formulating it.[5] It fits many aspects of Welsh
experience rather well, obviously. And as an ideology it probably
appeals particularly to the strong cultural dimension of the Welsh
national movement.

The taproot of this new smallness–and–beauty world–view may
lie in Vienna, like so many others. However, the stirrings of the last
decade have produced many new versions of it. Apart from Wales,
it is probably most influential now in regions like Occitania and
Brittany. Outside Europe it has a certain importance in Canada,
in the more anarchist form given it by George Woodcock and his
school. From North America also have come two recent *tours de
force* on the subject, Michael Zwerin's breathless travelogue of
neo–nationalism, *A Case for the Balkanization of Practically
Everyone*, and Michael Hechter's imposing study of *Internal
Colonialism*.[6]

[4] John Osmond, *The Centralist Enemy*, 1974, p. 13.

[5] *Planet*, the leading English-language cultural review linked to the national
movement in Wales, is published by Ned Thomas from Llangeitho, Tregaron,
Ceredigion (Cardiganshire); P. E. Mayo, *The Roots of Identity: Three National
Movements in Contemporary European Politics*, 1974 (on Wales, Euzkadi and
Brittany); see particularly the *Plaid Cymru* pamphlet *Culture and Politics*,
October 1975, with contributions by Raymond Williams, Ned Thomas, John
Osmond and Phil Williams.

[6] *Les Temps Modernes*, special issue on 'Les minorités nationales en France',
Aug.–Sept. 1973; the Canadian debate can be studied in, e.g., *Nationalism or
Local Control: Responses to George Woodcock*, edited by V. Nelles and A. Rotstein;
Michael Zwerin, *A Case for the Balkanization of Practically Everyone . . . the new
nationalism*, London, 1976; Michael Hechter, *Internal Colonialism: the Celtic
Fringe in British National Development, 1536–1966*, 1975; Sergio Salvi, *Le
nazioni proibite*, Florence 1974.

The latter is particularly important. It represents a definitive academic anointment of the thesis, complete with Ph.D.-worthy tables of figures, a weighty variety of references, and sometimes a corresponding style of argument. Underneath the armour, though, the idea is the same. British capitalist development produced a set of 'internal colonies' in its Celtic fringe, for basically the same reasons as it created external colonization all over the globe. It is the contradictory nature of capitalist growth to do so. After external de-colonization the liberation movements of the interior colonies have begun. 'The most recent crystallization of Celtic nationalism may ultimately be understood as a trenchant critique of the principle of bureaucratic centralism', he writes. Alas (he continues in characteristic vein) 'Bureaucratic administration seldom seems to enable less advantaged groups to achieve resources equal to those of dominant groups', and the under-advantaged finally tumble to this and demand something better.

Their demand has to be couched in cultural terms. This is why Hechter takes such a kindly view of Wales, and such a chilly one of Scotland. Unable throughout his argument to cope with the fundamental error of locating Scotland in the 'Celtic fringe' at all, he ends by chastizing the Scots for addiction to GNP and input-output tables. Still recovering from the shock of being told they were really colonized Celts, most SNP-ers would be even more disconcerted to learn that their party's 'lack of a strong appeal to the separate cultural identity of Scotland' means that the SNP 'tacitly admits the cultural indistinguishability of Scotland from England', and is therefore a form of nationalism 'available for co-optation with appropriate ceremony and rewards' by Mother England.[7]

Something is wrong here. It is not merely that the author fails to realize that there might be another sort of 'cultural identity' altogether, one having little to do with literature or emblems, which Scottish nationalists fail to appeal to only because they feel so secure in it. Nor is it the confusion about Celtic and non-Celtic in Scottish history. There is also something more deeply amiss on the plane of theory.

This theory is wrong because it lumps too many different things together. Both in analysing the causes and in considering the effects of new nationalism in Europe, it is too superficial. It may be

[7] Hechter, op. cit., Chapter 9, '20th Century Celtic Nationalism', pp. 307–8.

effective ideology, but it rests on rather poor history. Both the causes and the results and the probable future of these movements are more various than it allows for. In spite of Hechter's massive attempt at legitimation, the theory remains too abstract, and too neat.

The acid test of this and similar generalizations is the comparison between Wales and Scotland. Although parts of the same geographical island and ruled by the same state, they are possibly the most different of the emerging countries, above all in a deeper historical sense. As I said, we need a theoretical framework to put them together; and they in turn should be the main proving ground of such a theory.

III

'In most respects Wales and Scotland are very different countries. Scotland is, to use 19th century terminology, a "historic nation" . . . Wales on the other hand was a typical "non-historic nation". . . .'.

Eric Hobsbawm,
'The Attitude of Popular Classes towards
National Movements for Independence', 1966.[8]

The new political romanticism perceives Wales and Corsica, Scotland and Galicia, Friesland and the Basque Country as so many detachments of the same army, fighting broadly the same battle. No doubt they do have certain things in common. But the only way of being sure what these are is to take full account, at the same time, of the remarkable differences among these territories and situations.

There is one such difference which we ought to concentrate on. More than any other, I think it may help us to grasp the differential location of Scotland and Wales within the larger process. There are at least two contrasting sorts of problem at work. One might define these, in an admittedly crude way, as the problem of relative under-development and the problem of relative over-development.

[8] From the volume *Mouvements nationaux d'indépendance et classes populaires*, edited E. Labrousse, 1965–1966.

'Under-development' in this context is of course relative to the general conditions of the 'metropolitan' area of Western Europe. It does not imply any wider identification with Third World under-development (an analogy that has frequently been taken much too literally). Here, it refers to those predominantly agrarian regions – usually of peasants or small cultivators – which were exploited as sources of manpower and food or raw materials during the first century and a half of the industrial revolution. They were also typically exploited in a political sense, as the basis for political conservatism in the core areas. And nowadays they have usually become zones of summer holiday development or tourism. Corsica, Occitania, Brittany, Galicia, the Highland region of Scotland, Friesland – these are some among many examples of this situation.

In all these cases uneven development has simply thrust back regions and peoples. It has induced depopulation, cultural im-poverishment, a psychology of powerlessness and dependency, and fostered particularly fragmentary or distorted kinds of econo-mic growth. The 'regional policies' of the big states and the Com-mon Market were intended to counteract this pattern, but were probably too little and far too late to do so.

But there are also a number of regions whose key problem has been determined in a wholly different fashion. They occupy a different location altogether in the general history of the economic development process. These are the areas whose problem is that they developed more rapidly and successfully than the territory surrounding them. They have never been 'relatively over-developed' in relation to the European core-areas of industrializa-tion, of course – the Ruhr, the English Midlands, and so on. But they have been so in relation to the larger states dominating them politically. They became dynamic, middle-class enclaves in a more backward country – capitalist societies struggling to be free, as it were.

Naturally, there are fewer stories of this kind than of the other. Yet there are considerably more of them than one would think, and their importance is greater than most writers on nationalism have realized. Western Europe contains four such zones: Catalonia and the Basque Country in Southern Europe, and Protestant Ulster and Scotland in Northern Europe.

Three of these are notorious problems of European history. In Spain the industrial revolution took place mainly in the periphery of the state, and in countries with strongly marked separate identities. As a consequence, strong bourgeois societies developed around great urban centres like Bilbao and Barcelona, and constituted a permanent threat to the backward and parasitic state centred on Madrid (a state whose social supports lay, incidentally, in underdeveloped provinces like those just referred to, such as Andalusia, Estremadura, and others). The Civil War was fought partly to solve this problem – or rather, as far as the Spanish Conservatives were concerned, to liquidate it. But as we know, it is still there, rendered more acute by forty years of reaction.

In Ireland the industrial revolution also occurred mainly in an ethnic periphery, creating the large Protestant 'city-state' of Belfast. Here too uneven development worked to separate the successful middle-class enclave from the more backward land-mass around it. When that southern region managed to constitute its own political state, the relatively over-developed north refused assimilation, and of course it continues to reject it today. It does so, in spite of the archaic religious dimension of the conflict, essentially as a more advanced ('civilized' is the ideology for this) social formation fearful of being dragged down and preyed upon.

The fourth case, Scotland, has only recently entered the category. Although an old industrial society like Catalonia, with its own cities and native capitalist class, it previously developed at approximately the same rate and with the same cadences as the larger society it was linked to, industrial England. Only with the dramatic decline of the latter, and the sudden differential impetus given to the Scottish middle class by North Sea oil production, has a crisis of uneven development arisen. Although recent, this fissure is growing extremely rapidly, and creating a political situation basically similar to the others. Ever more clearly, the outlook of the previously rather quiescent Scottish bourgeoisie is one of restive impatience with English 'backwardness', London muddle, economic incompetence, state parasitism, and so forth.

Obviously, in any categorization of this kind there are bound to be many qualifications and exceptions. But let us ignore these for the moment, and for the sake of the argument. The two types of nationalist dilemma in Western Europe are, respectively: underdeveloped or pillaged regions that have finally begun to react against this treatment; and quite highly-developed epicentres of industrialization, middle-class cultures who are for one reason or another out of phase with the ruling nation-state, and want separate development to get ahead faster.[9]

Not only are there more of the former than of the latter. They are also much more visible intellectually. In the usual theoretical perspectives they have had a high profile. This is mainly for an interesting reason, very relevant to the comparison between Wales and Scotland. In the general history of nationalism material under-development has always had ideological and cultural over-development as its companion. Faced with the culture of deprivation and enforced ruralism, rebels have always had to compensate with forms of militant idealism. They want to redeem lands devoid of the real powers of redemption – lands without the institutions of self-defence and change, countries by definition robbed of a normally constituted civil society, and so of the normal motor of development. So they have to lay correspondingly extreme emphasis on the ideal society the national movement wants to will into existence, often in a very romantic and dream-like fashion.

The intellectual dominance of ideas reflecting this sort of nationalism is not peculiar to present-day Western Europe, of course. Quite the opposite: their salience in the theory of neo-nationalism is due to the world climate already fostered by extra-European national and anti-colonial movements. Those are the mountain-ranges whose influence leads us to look for and find the same shapes in our native hills. If the shapes are not there, we may even be led to invent them (as I think Hechter sometimes does).

So far I have made this typology purely in developmental terms. However, there is another important set of coordinates we should consider, since they are again very pertinent to the Scotland-Wales contrast. This is the notorious scheme of 'historic' versus 'non-historic' countries.

The notoriety derives from the original misuse: Hegel and Friedrich Engels employed the distinction mainly to discredit the smaller and more backward peoples whom they found a nuisance on the map of Europe. The Slavs, in particular, regularly had this poison served up to them. 'The ruins of peoples', snorted Engels, 'still found here and there and which are no longer capable of a

---

[9] There are examples of the latter in Eastern Europe, like historical Bohemia, and Croatia; and outside Europe, like Eastern Nigeria (Biafra), Singapore, and (at least in aspiration) Kurdistan.

national existence, and are absorbed by the larger nations, or maintain themselves as ethnographic monuments without political significance'.[10] With the exception of Southern Ireland, the ethnographic monuments of Western Europe were not at that time noticeable enough to be worth dismissing.

However – as is usually the case with such thinkers – the basic concept is stronger than its polemical misuse. All it means is that among the great scatter of territories and peoples who had not managed to form their own modern state, some had previous experience of existence as a state and others (the great majority) had not. This state history is very important, although certainly not all-important as they imagined. The inheritance it leaves behind, both institutionally and psychologically, is an enormous asset to any later political movement; even if the institutions are destroyed, the recollection of such a past remains prominent in national consciousness. In the 19th century the story of the re-emergence of the two nationalities which had been awarded the 'historic nation' accolade, Poland and Hungary, demonstrates this very well.

Among the reviving nationalities of Western Europe at present, two seem clearly to be 'historic nations' in this sense: Scotland and Catalonia. These were states whose independent existence ended at about the same moment, in the early 18th century, and then suffered different forms of assimilation by a larger unit. Of course the destruction of the old Catalan state was much more total; but on the other hand it was dramatically revived by the experience of the short-lived Catalan Republic in the 1930s – an experience which has now itself become something like the 'historic nation' to which the contemporary independence movement looks back.

The other two industrially developed areas I mentioned, Euzkadi and Ulster, were not historic entities in the Hegelian sense. They are 19th and 20th century creations. Yet as they now are they do have at least certain aspects of this character. They have both been semi-independent states in living memory: the Basques at the same time as the Catalans, under the liberal Republic of the 1930s, and Northern Ireland from 1922 until 1972. And in quite different ways

---

[10] F. Engels, 'Po und Rhein', 1859, in Marx-Engels, *Werke*, vol. XIII, p. 267; a résumé of the theory can be found in Anthony D. Smith, *Theories of Nationalism*, 1971, pp. 72–5. An interesting example of recent resurrection of this dead theory and its application to Wales is the British and Irish Communist Organization's pamphlet *Is Wales a Nation?*, anonymous, 1972.

this recent state existence will remain the crucial factor in the eventual transition to self-rule.

So, of the four relatively developed countries, it would perhaps be fair to say that the Scots have retained an astonishing amount of the structure of their 'historic nationality'; the Catalans recovered it; the Basques acquired it; and the Ulster Protestants had it thrust upon them. Although the political parabolas of these state histories are wildly divergent, what they have in common is some relation to industrialization and bourgeois development: it is the more 'middle-class' societies which kept or got some kind of statehood. To them that had was it given (and will be given again).

The other, more numerous under-developed countries in Western Europe are 'non-historic' ones whose contemporary efforts to stop being ethnographic monuments mainly take the cultural form mentioned above: the idealist nationalism of compensation against their history of forced transformation into 'ruins of peoples'.

IV

'Recently Professor Brinley Thomas has been showing that it was the industrial revolution which kept the Welsh language alive in the second half of the last century. Were it not for the coal-mining valleys and the industrial undertakings of the South the drift of people from rural Wales would have been the death of Welsh . . .'.

Saunders Lewis,
The Fate of the Language (1962).

Returning now to the Wales–Scotland comparison, it is clear where Scotland is located according to the coordinates we have traced out. It is one of the most evolved societies among the buried nationalities, in the sense of industrial and social-class development; and it is easily the most intact of the historic nations. A constellation of national institutions was left in existence by the peculiar contract of 1707, and is mostly still there. The separate legal system and courts, with the substantial middle class which serves them, the educational system, the Church of Scotland, the administrative apparatus slowly built up through a whole series of devolutionary concessions over the last century – these famous bulwarks are little diminished. They are surrounded by an interminable and growing list of associations, societies, museums, institutes, clubs, foundations, all as 'Scottish' as their titles, and all concerned with this or that national interest.

So the survival of Scotland's 'identity' has never been primarily a question of literature or of a cultivated self-consciousness. The culture it rests on is a deeper, more articulated social structure, and one not necessarily visible on superficial acquaintance. It is like a set of rock formations, which may be almost underwater reefs from many points of view. It is certainly not to be met with while strolling down Princes Street (or even at the annual conferences of the SNP). Indeed, any displays one *is* likely to encounter on Princes Street – in the shape of tartan performances in the gardens, pipe bands or 'Highland' restaurants – are guaranteed to be almost wholly unrelated to these realities.

So Scotland might be depicted as high up on the right-hand corner of the graph, with a high developmental and 'historic-nation' quotient. Where does Wales fit in? I believe that its position could be symbolically depicted as dead centre.

Wales does not belong neatly to either of the two first categories I outlined. This is perhaps its peculiarity in the wider European context: perhaps its peculiar importance as well. Historically Wales shares many of the features of forced under-development: depopulation, cultural oppression, fragmentary and distorted development, and so on. These features are strongly evident in the Welsh national movement too, insofar as it has been a battle for the defence and revival of rural-based community and traditional identity – an identity evoked overwhelmingly by literary and musical culture, and having as its mainspring the language question. But of course in another key respect Wales is more akin to the relatively over-developed group: like them, it is a great secondary centre of the European industrial revolution.

This ambiguous, midway location is explained by the nature of Welsh industrialization. It was unlike the sort of economic development normally inflicted on backward provinces in being massive, and in transforming (eventually) the conditions of life of most of the population. Speaking of the Heads of the Valleys, the Plaid Cymru *Economic Plan* states: 'Somewhere on Blackrock, between Gilwern and Brynmawr, there should be a notice; "Welcome to the birthplace of the modern world" – the birthplace of modern industry. Here the early ironmasters established industry on a scale never before seen throughout the world. South Wales became the centre of the iron and steel industry and the techniques developed were copied in every developing country . . . For once, Wales led the world'.[11] Nothing remotely comparable could be said of any of the other European countries whose nationalisms superficially resemble that of Wales.

However, this industrialization *was* like that of such periphery regions in being overwhelmingly guided from outside: it was not the work of a native entrepreneurial bourgeoisie accumulating capital for itself (as in Scotland or the Basque Country) but much more like an invasion from outside. Previously without the main motor of effective separate development, an urban middle class, Wales now acquired an English or at least highly Anglicized bourgeoisie.[12] This combination, an industrialization at once enormous and de-centred, was probably unique to Wales.

If we turn now to the other broad distinction made earlier, that between so-called historic and non-historic nationalities, the position of Wales is again less clear-cut than might appear at first glance. Although not an example of 'historic' nationhood in the sense of Poland, Scotland or Catalonia, it is not a straightforward case of the 'non-historic' either.

The non-historic features of the Welsh past are very well known: 'a territory inhabited by an agrarian population united by . . . a primitive social and economic structure and by the fact of not speaking English', as Eric Hobsbawm has put it, without much urban development until the industrial revolution, and without an indigenous aristocracy or bourgeoisie. None the less, even in the form which it assumed, the South Wales industrial revolution could not help altering the meaning of these conditions. We saw before how ethnic-linguistic nationalism has been usually a compensatory reaction to retardation. But what is striking about the Welsh re-

[11] Plaid Cymru, *Economic Plan*, Cardiff 1969, vol. 2, pp. 119-20.

[12] On this topic, see Sir Reginald Coupland, *Welsh and Scottish Nationalism: a Study*, 1954, pp. 169-75. For the background to Welsh political development – in a much truer sense than Scottish history of that era, the 'pre-history' of today's nationalism – the most useful analysis is K. O. Morgan's excellent *Wales in British Politics, 1868-1922*, Cardiff, 1963. This and his later studies of David Lloyd George are an exemplary reply to what he calls 'metropolitan provincialism' in British studies (op. cit., 'Preface', p. vii). Unfortunately there is all too little to be compared to his work in Scottish studies of the same period.

action in this comparative view is its size and success.

None of those other European regions knew an institutionalized culture movement comparable to the Welsh one of the 19th century – a movement which, on the foundation of 18th century Welsh Nonconformity, extended from the renewed *Eisteddfod* to the University Colleges of Wales, from the Welsh National Library to the great Museums of Cardiff. Although still in the narrower sense 'cultural' – concerned primarily with *Kultur* – here is a movement which from the beginning passed beyond simple poetic protest or the dreams of small intellectual coteries. It created something like the cultural form, the tracery of a nation where no state had existed. It became a substantial force in the new civil society of 19th and 20th century Wales, even without political, legal, and other institutions.

The movement was in reaction against the Anglicizing capitalist invasion of the South – yet also to some extent based upon it. It sought to defend the language and traditional life – yet also to adapt the nation to a more modern existence. As Saunders Lewis recognized in his famous 1962 broadcast, the industrial revolution which so threatened Welsh language and life also gave it a new chance of life – indeed, the only chance of surviving permanently and avoiding the fate of Cornish, Irish and Scottish Gaelic. By becoming the language of the industrial Valleys, Welsh had come part of the way towards the condition of Catalan, in Western Europe, or Czech or Slovene among the smaller ex-Hapsburg countries of Eastern Europe.[13]

To say that the Welsh situation is unusually central, or suspended between the standard alternatives of European neonationalism, is of course to say that it is unusually divided. It is not necessary here to comment on the strong antagonisms and dilemmas built into the national movement by this history: Welsh versus 'Anglo-

---

[13] Thus by migration from the countryside it avoided the more usual fate of being confined to rural existence – the language of noble savages, identified mainly with 'backwardness', or strong, simple feelings, childhood recollection, and so on. By achieving this transition, it probably accomplished a vital part of its own salvation. Once spoken naturally in an industrialized, urban environment, it has at least the possibility of developing farther, and so avoiding the fate of (e.g.) Irish and Scottish Gaelic. For a comparative view, see Glanville Price, 'Minority Languages in Western Europe', in *The Welsh Language Today*, edit. Meic Stephens, 1973, particularly pp. 8–9, on Catalan.

Welsh', ADFER versus bi-lingualism, ethnic traditionalists versus South-Eastern modernizers, and so on.[14] All that should be stressed is that this internal conflict has a wider comparative significance. It reflects, within Wales and Welsh nationalism, certain deeper dilemmas of choice which can be seen operating everywhere else. In the Welsh knot the usual forces of uneven development have been tied together unusually closely and graphically.

V

'*Do you believe that a "sense of Welsh nationhood" is more consistent with one particular attitude to life and affairs than any other?*

If I catch the drift of the question, I would say that I do feel that the Welsh National spirit has had to bank itself up in the Welsh Language for want of being able to express itself politically . . .'.

John Cowper Powys,
Answer to 'Wales' Questionnaire, 1939,
Obstinate Cymric (1947).

What happens to Scotland on the road to self-government has some significance for other countries. But less than might appear

[14] The logical extreme of cultural-linguistic nationalism is to make language almost literally the key to everything else: there can be no culture and nation worth speaking of without the language. Hence those who have lost it are no longer real nationals: there are no genuine Bretons in eastern Brittany, and no real Welshmen in south-eastern Wales. This implies ultimately redrawing the nation's boundaries to coincide with the linguistic area, and dismissing the rest as a lost cause (the sort of logic that makes some Scots profoundly grateful they speak a world language). The ideal of a smaller but purer Wales is held by ADFER ('Restoration'), a militant branch of *Cymdeithas yr Iaith* ('The Welsh Language Society', founded 1962). Cynog Davies underlines the conflict between this trend and the contemporary evolution of Plaid Cymru: 'As *Cymdeithas yr Iaith* was developing into a political movement it was growing away from *Plaid Cymru*. That party's economic plan for Wales (referred to above, see Note 11), a sophisticated and in many ways idealistic document, described how a free Wales might secure for itself a prosperous niche within the international capitalist system, and its growth-centres strategy implicitly assumed the continued decline of rural society . . . The divison stemmed increasingly from a different philosophy and method', *The Welsh Language Today*, op. cit., pp. 260–1.

superficially. It would be principally through a general demonstra-
tion-effect, by which the constitution of any new state in the West
of Europe will encourage the rest. The paradox of Scotland's strong
'historic-nation' status is that it makes the country less relevant
and weaker as an example, above all in relation to the more typical
countries where cultural nationalism prevails.

What happens to Wales is likely to be far more influential in the
long run. This is the point of the Welsh centrality in the nationalist
spectrum which I have tried to analyze. All Western Europe's
deprived and re-awakened peoples want and need stronger economic development, for example. Given the condition they start
from, such development is bound to be in large measure from outside, whether by multinationals or by investment and aid from
other countries. Wales has already gone through this, in the most
violent and chaotic fashion: such de-centred, invasive industrialization created the whole problem of modern nationalism in Wales.
Hence, how the Welsh national movement – or a future Welsh
political state – copes with the question is directly relevant in all
these places.

If Welsh nationalism can arrive at a viable political integration
of its contending elements, then many others can hope to. If the
ideal, 'cultural' nation can be reconciled with the industrial one
here, then the formula may eventually be copiable elsewhere.
Nationalism has always been a struggle to connect romantically-
conceived tradition and culture with the need for modern social
and economic development. In modern Welsh history these two
things are thrust together with special intensity, perhaps imposing a
duty of political leadership on the nationalist movement.

The romantic theory of cultural colonialism described earlier
sees all the resurgent nationalities as essentially the same (and all
are of course also 'unique' in the same way). The less idealist account
I have tried to begin here perceives them as different, even opposed,
and certainly classifiable in a number of interesting ways. A
materialist theory focuses primarily upon their real location in the
modern process of socio-economic development – it sees them as
real places, in this sense, no less real and diverse than the bigger
nation-states they are still attached to. But I am conscious of having
done little more than suggest the starting-point of a theory of this
kind. There are many things we have not looked at at all here.

For example, the question of the causation of the wave of new nationalist movements in Western Europe. It seems very unlikely that these have arisen out of a general protest against impersonal centralism, or against the synthetic culture of bureaucracy and multinational business. Presumably there are deep economic changes behind the new climate. But why are they especially operative in three of the old states – the United Kingdom, Spain and France – and unimportant or non-existent in others? Why should the new forms of inter-dependence promoted by multi-nationals have undermined these ex-imperial nations but – e.g. – left the Netherlands largely unaffected? Why should Italy, a country marked by gross and long-standing uneven development, have been relatively untroubled by separatism in the recent past?

These are all questions that seem to call for much more discriminating and realistic answers than the ones nationalists are at present tending to give. The same might be said of attempts to prospect a nationalist future. The results, as well as the causes, of new nationalist success are not easy to see. There will be a new map of Europe. But it is not likely to resemble the diagrams of a sub-divided, small-nation continent which became fashionable a few years ago.[15]

Returning – in conclusion – to the Scotland–Wales direct comparison, what farther inferences can be drawn from the argument so far? I have chosen to emphasize the differences, and to plead for a more cautious, sceptical approach to inter-nationalist relations. The aim of this is to reinforce such relations – on the assumption that realism ought to balance ideology, and will preserve what is positive in the latter by doing so.

Like other movements, these ones have the strengths of their weaknesses (or vice-versa). The great Welsh cultural movement, with which Welsh nationalism is so closely associated, may have led to a certain over-emphasis upon these factors. There is a great deal both in Welsh history and in current ideology that under-writes this emphasis. Looking back again to that address of fifty years ago, one cannot help being struck by the extreme prudence – even fear – with which political authority is regarded. 'The Welsh civilizing concept is the only worthwhile argument for self-government', said Lewis, '. . . that being so, we must have self-government.

---

[15] Again Leopold Kohr ranks as a forerunner – see the Appendices to *The Breakdown of Nations*, 'The Principle of Federation in Maps'.

Not independence. Not even unconditional freedom. But just as much freedom as may be necessary to establish and safeguard civilization in Wales.'[16] A political state not one hundred-and-one per cent sanctified by cultural needs and values is, frankly, the work of the Devil of Materialism. Cultural nationality and power-hungry nationalism are conceived as real antitheses.

Unless I am greatly mistaken, this underlying attitude is still quite strongly felt in Wales. It must be the only country where one regularly hears nationalists denouncing nationalism. Since Saunders Lewis's antithesis is not a real one, and no state institutions can ever exist purely and solely to cultivate cultural traditions in that sense, I suppose this is a kind of weakness. I suppose therefore that the Welsh national movement ought to give the Devil his due more than it has done in times past, and try to adopt a mildly more Machiavellian attitude to the state and the other non-cultural institutions of power.

As far as the Scots are concerned, I feel on stronger ground. The weakness of the Scottish national movement is the contrary of the Welsh one: it is the consistent, canny philistinism of the movement from its earliest days, and the chronic divorce between what Lewis Spence called the 'practical, Scotsman-like' policy and the distinctly erratic flights of the intelligentsia. The Scottish movement bene-fits from the existence of a powerful middle class; yet one of the traits of that class tends to be a powerful distrust of culture in any spectacular form. Along with the seriousness and practicality, there is of course a dreadful conceit buried in this outlook. One might describe it as the unjustified conceit of a once 'historic na-tion' which deep down still feels itself to be such. Nor should one forget that, while in Wales Calvinism figures as a creed of pro-longed popular opposition to the high and mighty, in Scotland it has been mainly a creed *of* the high and mighty. The Welsh may be too apprehensive about state power; the Scots are not apprehensive enough. Authority appears to them naturally dressed in a Minister's gown and a halo.

With the imminence of self-government, this Scotsman-like weakness has become a more tangible threat. Never having ima-gined an ideal nation with the visionary enthusiasm found in so many other nationalist movements, they are at a loss. There is a

[16] Saunders Lewis, *Principles of Nationalism*, 1926, pp. 15-16.

sudden, rather belated rush to invent actual things to do. The SNP has produced a philosophy, or something like a philosophy, bearing some distinct resemblances to the radical ideology of other European nationalist movements (I refer to the recently published volume, *The Radical Approach: Papers on an Independent Scotland*). In response to the new mood, one or two intellectuals could be seen circulating quite openly at the recent party conference in Motherwell (1976).

Satire apart, Scottish nationalism desperately needs to counter this malformation, by integrating politics and culture more deliberately than in the past. We need new institutions to do this – new means of forging links between practical politics and cultural ideas, between the institutions of power and the imagination of a new nation. Given the evident complementarity of Welsh and Scottish problems, Wales is one of the places to which Scots look with the keenest sense of useful difference in making this effort. Countries so different can never become 'like each other' in a merely imitative sense. This need not matter. What matters is to learn to change, inevitably in one's own way, through the constant stimulus of contact and studied comparison. This is, for us, the new internationalism which ought to arise out of and along with Europe's new wave of national movements.

5. Northern Ireland: Relic or Portent?

The conflict in Northern Ireland has now lasted for seven years. No solution to it is in sight. More precisely, no peaceful solution acceptable to the contending communities and to the governments in London and Dublin is in sight. The 'solution' of a total war for territory is in sight however – held at bay by a thin and uncertain chain of circumstances.

Ireland is far removed from the storm-centres of today's world politics. Unlike the comparable situations in Palestine, Lebanon and Cyprus, Irish problems have almost no relevance to the geo-political interests of the great powers. This remoteness explains why the Irish war has been largely forgotten by world public opinion: a virulent but tiny open sore in a distant country. It also helps explain why the wound has been allowed to fester so long. Had great-power interests been involved, a solution of some sort would have been imposed long ago. As it is, the small-power interests surrounding Ulster have been unable either to agree or impose an answer.

In spite of its remoteness this desolate tragedy has much signifi-cance. It is not occurring in the Third World, where nationalist conflicts are still commonplace for obvious (and much studied) reasons. It is not even on the extremer margins of Europe, like Cyprus. One of the two communities concerned in the war is a traditionally and highly industrialized one: the Ulster Protestants benefited in their day from the full flourishing of the British indus-trial revolution and the imperial economic order. Their traditional, militant political claim is to belong integrally to this 'advanced' capitalist system – and not to backward, under-developed Catholic Ireland.

In any case, the old 'backward' Ireland of the peasant, the priest and the potato is now rapidly ceasing to be so. No one will deny that social and religious archaisms play a big part in determining the character of the Ulster war. But – I shall go on to argue – their role is also habitually exaggerated in the easy dismissals that take the place of explanations (especially in England). However backward Irish conditions may be in this or that respect, Ireland is still a Western European country. It enjoys (or suffers from) the general socio-political level of this region of the world. Both bits of Ireland are in the Common Market community, both are nominally political democracies, and both make outstanding claims to being 'civilized' as well as Christian.

This is the awkward core of the problem, from a left-wing point of view – indeed, from any progressive viewpoint at all. If only Northern Ireland *could* be dismissed as a wholly exceptional regression from European standards! That was certainly how it looked to begin with. But what has actually happened in Western Europe during these same seven years of warfare?

The most cursory glance at today's political horizons, a reading of one day's newspapers, will show the truth. The United Kingdom and Europe have become perceptibly more like Ireland in these years – not vice-versa. Seven years ago, how many serious observers believed that the region's buried ethnic conflicts would ever again pose real problems? When the first violence broke out in Belfast, how many imagined there would be similar deaths in Corsica, that nationalists would be within sight of political control of Scotland, or that explosion and riot would become commonplace over significant areas of France and Spain?

At that time, models of universalism still dominated thought. On one hand the official ideologists of the new European Community foresaw an early economic and monetary union, leading on to a common political state. The great capitalist process of integration, launched in the 1950s, would produce a United States of Europe well before the end of the century. In this unification – so the visionaries insisted – the fearful antagonisms of the previous century would be definitively overcome. A peaceful, post-nationalist Europe was always the strongest part of their argument.

On the other hand, this new bourgeois Europe was challenged by a new generation of revolutionaries. But, invariably, in the name of a vision no less universal. The new anarchist and communist left which reached its high tide of militancy in 1968 and 1969 foresaw a social revolution: the mass rejection of consumerism and capitalism, not a crisis of the nation-state system. The revolution might erupt here, or there – it would be valid for everywhere, and hence spread over Europe (at least) relatively quickly. The millenarist side of the movement was in concord with the capitalist opponent, oddly enough. In terms of slogans, it was all too easy to insert 'Socialist' into the emerging European United States and argue that revolution alone could make a reality of the dream.

History may yet confound us all. It has certainly disappointed the vanguardists of European union. Since the disappearance of De Gaulle the process has not grown easier; it has foundered in increasing difficulties, as the European governing classes have faced the problem of collaborating in more severe economic weather, and against more definite opposition from the United States. Yet these difficulties have done little to foster the revolutionary left. It is varieties of national reformism – some led by social-democrats, some by Communist Parties – that have made a cautious and limited advance since 1970. This movement is hesitant and doubtful enough in its aims and potential; and it has remained largely confined to the old nation-state frameworks.

In other words, it remains tied to 'socialism in one country'. But what country? This has become as important a question as: 'what socialism?' Capitalist and revolutionary seers alike have been confounded by the fact. Everyone looked forward to some kind of transcendence of the nation-state, on a higher level; nobody thought it might break down, on to an apparently lower level. Multi-national corporations or revolutionary socialists were supposed to be ringing its death-knell, not nationalist insurgents.

It is still easy to argue away the tendency as a passing distemper – a temporary fever of uncertainty, perhaps, after Western Europe's renaissance of the post-war years. For many obvious reasons, the ideological grip of the old great powers centred in Paris, London, etc., has slackened a good deal. Historically, these are warfare states which will never again annex a colony or engage in solitary combat. They have dissipated their ideological substance among American armourers, the Cold War anti-communism of NATO, multi-national business and Europeanism. It is scarcely surprising that their more detached or backward regions are betraying some restiveness. But is there not a long road from this to their actual fragmentation?

Another anodyne formula sometimes echoes this one, mainly on the left. Suppose the trend does develop – the argument goes – why be alarmed anyway? Is the movement not a progressive one in any case? In spite of some archaic trappings, is it not recognizably part of a popular and democratic revolt against the State and bigness? In this way, neo-nationalism can be at least partially recuperated by the new-left ideologists of the 1960s: not exactly power to the people as originally blue-printed, but still, a sort of power claimed for 'people' in one sense of the word. Populism and nationalism are ancient partners in ideological history; it is all too simple to yoke them together again.

Both these positions may have some truth in them. However, their function as tranquillizers is dispelled by any serious inspection of Northern Ireland. I suspect it would be destroyed equally easily by a study of Brittany, the Basque nation, or any of the others. Whatever the general truth is, it is probably more ambiguous and more dangerous than this.

I do not intend to suggest the opposite extreme – that the reappearance of nationalist conflicts in Europe is entirely ominous, or merely the recrudescence of a barbaric past. Again, no closer acquaintance with these movements or regions would really suggest this. They are likely to resemble other varieties of nationalism in this at least, that positive and negative potentialities are mixed up together in their progress.

The point is a different one. It is a wider historical and political perspective that underlines the threat. We are – after all – discussing the area of the world that generated both the structure of the modern nation-state and nationalism. After that, its long capitalist development produced the theories of modern revolution, and both the theory and the fact of counter-revolution. It was the conflicts deriving from that development which dragged the whole world into war twice over. Only after the second war, as the exhausted continent was divided and reorganized by outside forces, did these contradictions seem to lose their creative force, and their venom. In the western half, social conservatism and a remarkable political quiescence accompanied the renewed expansion of capitalism. It was in the era of American-sponsored stability that the Common Market and the movements for European union could get going, and propose the definitive solution for this history of national antagonisms.

The womb which bore that history is fertile yet. This may be the lesson of those stirrings I am describing. If so, it takes a great degree of optimism to view them without some anxiety. Western Europe has become slightly more like Ireland in the past seven years; the similarities are more likely to increase than to diminish in the next seven.

This would not be so, naturally, if the grand panaceas proffered by either the bourgeoisie or the marxist left were capable of application. It is possible that if the great movement of international capitalist growth were resumed in Europe, such regionalist protests would dwindle again. The centripetal dynamic would re-establish its force over the area. If reasonable policies of regional devolution were followed (but students of the question know what a large 'if' this is) then under those conditions separatism might be defused. Uneven development appears inseparable from the pattern of capitalist growth. Still, the centrifugal reactions it provokes might be at least neutralized once more, perhaps for a long period.

Equally, if a social revolution were to establish a new, qualitatively different model of development somewhere in Western Europe, the prospects would plainly change radically. Socialism too would have its own centripetal force. In a different way it would offer new, wider horizons of development which might lessen the appeal of nationality. In a Britain dominated by an England in transition to socialism, it goes without saying that (e.g.) Welsh or Scottish separatism would become – at least in their present form – dubious and backward trends. This influence would reach over the old state frontiers also. One centre of socialist development would have the profoundest effect upon the entire area.

It is because neither of these avenues of evolution appears probable that anxiety over the new national questions is justified. A persisting, fairly prolonged economic crisis is now far more likely; so is a continued stalemate over the European Community's political advance. Farthermore, even if capitalist development takes up once more, it may well be in a relatively undynamic and uncertain key. This would actually aggravate the centrifugal trends of nationalism rather than compensate for them. Most of the past history of nationalism shows that once established with some popular support, it is difficult to eradicate such trends even in favourable circumstances.

Hence, whatever movement towards socialism occurs is likely to be intertwined with these renewed dilemmas of nationalism. What results is a far more chaotic picture than any entertained in the 1950s or 1960s. It is one of a Europe paying a grim price for the failure of political unification – a Europe where the forces of uneven development have reasserted themselves in a fragmentation-process inside the old imperialist states. These are of course 'liberation movements' seen from one angle – seen from below, and from within each one. Yet seen together, in a continental perspective, they would also be the re-emergence of an ancestral curse.

It is quite true that the cultural creativity, the inventiveness of Europe was inseparable from its past divisions. Complacent historians sometimes balance these achievements against the curse. However, that balance belonged to a history where Europe was what it has now ceased to be: the heartland of world development. So it is doubtful whether it would hold good in this possible future we are trying to discern.

The post-war restoration of Europe was based upon the continent's division and political subjugation. Economic development alone never provided an escape from this dependency. The only hope of that was some kind of unification, in the sense of the formation of larger political units able to contain these developmental forces and throw off outside great-power hegemony. In their absence, it is the stresses of uneven development which will triumph, sapping and undermining the old state structures from within. Still more divided and preoccupied with these internal problems, the area will be farther exposed to great-power interference and control. The unstable equilibrium between north and south will overpower the weak cohesion of the Common Market. New conflicts and new, weak states or quasi-states will provide a choice terrain for American and Soviet intrigue. The parliamentary democracy associated with the restoration will weaken, become compromised, or disappear altogether. Such socialist régimes as arise within this unstable landscape will be forced to fight for their lives: they will only be able to do this in strongly nationalist terms (that is, if they are not also nationalist movements to begin with). It should not be forgotten that the whole disposition of post-war Europe hinges upon one unresolved national question: Germany. One of its principal aims was to bury that question forever. But in any new climate of revived national feeling and feuding, it is hard to imagine it staying buried.[1]

I am drawing a dark picture of the future, deliberately, in order to underline the contrast between these possibilities and what most people now instinctively expect when Europe is considered in a geopolitical light. The point is that these expectations have been formed by more than two decades of extraordinary stability, even immobility, in European affairs. Such breaks as have occurred (Suez, Hungary, Czechoslovakia, May 1968, the fall of the IVth Republic) were rapidly mended and covered over: before long nothing of significance seemed to have happened. It is unlikely that this will go on being true in the last quarter of the century.

Only one of these volcanic fissures has proved irreparable – Ireland. There, the new forces and ideas of the 1960s led to an unstoppable chain reaction. Every effort to recompose the old map and the old constitution of society has failed. The struggle has not ended yet, so it may be premature to assess its place in the larger context I have been outlining. But if a new drama of social development is beginning in Europe along those lines, then Northern Ireland will have such a place: it will no longer be an outlandish exception to all the rules. And it becomes important to understand it better.

The Myth of Atavism

Even the dead in their world of decay
For you, if they could, would pray.
But redder still your streets shall glow
And in the gutters still, your lifeblood flow;

[1] In approaching these problems I have benefited greatly from discussions with André Gunder Frank, and from the paper he read (as yet unpublished) at the 'Conference on the Survival of Small Nations', in Nicosia, Cyprus, September 1976. In this he linked a sombre picture of new European nationalism to the wider vista of the Third World in depression: the general triumph of totalitarian and repressive-nationalist states, along the lines established in Latin America. While in an earlier period nationalism could have a progressive class-alliance as its basis, founded on the economics of autarky and import-substitution, this is now impossible, Frank argues. The growth of the transnational economy forces the peripheral and semi-peripheral countries into direct competition on the world market; and in a crisis their rulers can only cope by techniques of direct, intensified repression and exploitation at home.

Peace is sleeping.
Few, few shall live to see the time
When you my city cease to pine.
God is weeping.

'Belfast', anonymous poem in
Love Orange, Love Green:
Poems of Living, Loving and Dying in Working-Class Ulster

The *Oxford English Dictionary* says that atavism is 'Recurrence of the disease or constitutional symptoms of an ancestor after the intermission of one or more generations . . . tendency to reproduce the ancestral type in plants and animals'. There is no doubt this is the most popular diagnosis of the war in Ireland.

Indeed, this 'explanation' has itself recurred over several generations. God is always weeping over Ireland. Speaking in a House of Commons debate in 1922, Winston Churchill expressed the angry incredulity Englishmen still feel on the subject: 'Then came the great war. Every institution, almost, in the world was strained. Great empires have been overturned. The whole map of Europe has been changed . . . The modes of thought of men, the whole outlook on affairs, the grouping of parties, all have encountered violent and tremendous changes in the deluge of the world. But as the deluge subsides and the waters fall short we see the dreary steeples of Fermanagh and Tyrone emerging once again. The integrity of their quarrel is one of the few institutions that has been unaltered in the cataclysm which has swept the world . . .'.

Fifty years on, after the rise and fall of European fascism, another world-deluge, the mighty recovery of international capitalism, and another great crisis, there they are still. Where God weeps, men must despair. If Ireland is a Holy Anachronism, there is nothing we modern people can do about it. The Irish war is a marginal aberration in European politics: a freak side-show for *la société du spectacle*, as it were, the mild TV thrills it produces serving principally to confirm the modernity of Düsseldorf and Turin.

This idea of the Irish question comes into the category of half-truths that are worse than lies. While it is of course true that there are markedly anachronistic aspects to the conflict in Ulster, these are in no real sense its cause. Still less are they its political significance for Europe or the world.

The usual disproportionate emphasis on 'Irish atavism' hides several things. As to Ireland itself, it conceals the fact that the war arises from a crisis of capitalist social development – a crisis as typical of our own day as that of 1922 was of an earlier phase of history. Beyond this (and more significantly) it suppresses the real premise of those archaic forms the war has taken: that is, the persisting general political backwardness of Europe.

One may put this in another way. After seven years of war, the question anyone must ask is: why is no more *civilized* solution possible, or even in sight, for such an intolerable and murderous dilemma? Is the answer only in Irish 'backwardness'?

In his poem 'Conversations in Hungary', the Ulster writer John Hewitt depicts the usual attempt to 'explain' Ireland to the foreigner:

> We tried to answer, spoke of Arab, Jew,
> of Turk and Greek in Cyprus, Pakistan
> and India; but no sense flickered through
> that offered reason to a modern man
> why Europeans, Christians, working-class,
> should thresh and struggle in that old morass.

So, inevitably, the attention moves backwards: only a special historical curse, a luckless and predetermined fate, can account for the war:

> Failing there, we turned to history:
> the savage complications of our past;
> our luckless country where old wrongs outlast,
> in raging viruses of bigotry,
> their first infection . . .
> > > > > > > > > (*Out of my Time*, Belfast 1974).

In reality, one doubts whether the past is so much to blame. The British and European present bears a larger share of responsibility. Even granted that Ulster and Cyprus are 'backward' areas forced for peculiar historical reasons to 'catch up' with European norms belatedly, the question remains: why are these norms unchanged? Why – half a century after the destruction of Smyrna and the Irish civil wars of the 1920s – is there no new, alternative way of resolving such 'archaic' nationality-questions? Why (therefore) are people still forced back to struggle in the old morasses of our history, murdering each other with the old 'traditions' of capitalist development?

The Steeples of Fermanagh

The racist futility of the 'atavism' diagnosis is underlined by a remarkable paradox. Ireland has indeed passed through an era of something like atavism. That is, a period when its two communities did retreat into their respective pasts and proceed to cultify everything most reactionary and obscurantist about them. This lasted from the mid-1920s until the mid-1960s. And what the new conflicts signify is above all the effort to escape from such fossilized backwardness – to leave behind forever the years when the dreary steeples dominated the island's landscape. So far from being a preordained return to ancestral type, they are exactly the opposite.

In the Republic, the generation now ended was that of de Valera's theocratic Constitution of 1934, where power was devolved upwards, from the British Emperor to the Holy Ghost himself: 'In the name of the Most Holy Trinity, from whom is all authority . . . and to whom all actions of states must be referred . . . Humbly acknowledging all our obligations to our Divine Lord Jesus Christ, who sustained our fathers through centuries of trial', and so on. It was the epoch of Counter-Reformation bigotry and small-farmer censorship, of that one-eyed Fenianism Joyce satirized in *Ulysses*: 'It's on the march, says the citizen. To hell with the bloody brutal Sassenachs and their patois . . . To hell with them! The curse of a goodfornothing God light sideways on the bloody thicklugged sons of whores' gets! No music and no art and no literature worthy of the name. Any civilization they had they stole from us. Tonguetied sons of bastards' ghosts . . .'. ('Cyclops', pp. 376–449).

Economically, it was the time of *Sinn Féin* protectionism and isolation from the wider world. This futile and inward-looking stagnation was ended only when it had grown insupportable even to de Valera's nationalist ruling clique. When that is (in the words of a recent historian) 'A serious crisis of confidence had developed by the middle 1950s . . . and even more a widespread anxiety that the general performance of the economy was so poor that the country was falling behind Western European standards, not only in productivity but in the social benefits that productivity might be expected to confer . . .'. (F. S. L. Lyons, *Ireland since the Famine*, 2nd edition, p. 628).

In the partitioned North, meanwhile, an equally odious régime answered Catholic nationalism with its own variety of devout spite and discrimination. Its state power rested upon the revived archaism of the Protestant Orange Order. Damned by the Gaelic-League antics of the 'Citizen' in Barney Kiernan's pub, Leopold Bloom – the spirit of decency – is also rejected by the ambiguous Crofter-Crofton-Crawford, an embodiment of Scotch-Irish Protestantism: 'Is he a jew or gentile or a holy roman or a swaddler or what the hell is he? says Ned. Or who is he? No offence, Crofton. – We don't want him, says Crofter the Orangeman or presbyterian.' (p. 438).

Ages of repression had made Catholicism into a profound popular force in Southern Ireland. This was why Southern nationalism could not avoid its initial regressive and obscurantist forms. But to this regression there was inevitably counterposed another: to the Counter-Reformation *redevivus* there was opposed a militant defence of the Reformation itself, in the more economically advanced and Protestant North-East. Here, an entire community had opted out of the Irish nationalist movement. It protected its identity – and eventually organized its own state – in conformity with the notorious 'siege-mentality'. Everything from its own past had to be dredged up to build these fortifications. Thus, the cults of King William, July 12th and the Protestant Ascendancy answered those of the Holy Virgin, Maynooth and the Gaelic League.[2] To avoid becoming a helpless minority in Catholic Ireland, the Protestants built a (supposedly) 'British' statelet of their own, where they had a helpless minority of Catholics to dominate.[3]

---

[2] 'Our case is desperate . . . our land has become a prey to our traditional enemies. The hundreds of new-made graves, the scars of thousands of mutilated bodies all bear eloquent testimony to Ulster's dark agony. Let us also remember that as our case is desperate so is that of our enemies . . . They know they are most certainly doomed if they are defeated. Hence their madness. They are devotees of that godless monster which has drenched Ireland with blood for many generations – the godless monster of a united Ireland . . .' thus the Rev. Ian Paisley, in his tract *A Call to the Protestants of Ulster*, Belfast, January 1975.

[3] Among recent books, more or less up-to-date on the Troubles, by far the most sympathetic picture of Protestant psychology and attitudes is given by

Ireland did not emerge from this era of hopelessness until the 1960s. Only then had modern capitalism penetrated the island sufficiently to force the break-up of these fossil patterns. The Republic abandoned economic nationalism, and moved from the first Programme for Economic Expansion (1958) to free trade with Britain, and eventually to membership of the Common Market. Politically it moved from de Valera to a new generation of Fianna Fáil, and achieved its first genuinely modern bourgeois government in the Fine Gael-Labour coalition now in office.

During the same period Northern Ireland embarked on a comparable programme of reform and economic modernization. It too tried to alter the small-business, small-town foundation of its power. As even a hostile critic admits, Captain O'Neill's governments of the 1960s stood for '. . . a much-vaunted modernism (with) enough basis in reality as far as the rhetoric of technocracy, public relations consciousness and obeisance to industrialism were concerned . . .'.[4]

A National Question Re-born

What happened next was a direct by-product of this advance. The new 'troubles' came less from ancient genes than from modern aspirations. Multinational corporations and state subsidies re-animated the nationality struggle, not the shade of Finn MacCool.

This was not surprising. Ethnic conflicts do not arise naturally from the coexistence of different groups in one society. As long as society stays fixed in time-honoured customs and narrow expectations (like those of Ireland's long developmental sleep from the 20s to the 60s) they merely simmer on the level of village grudges and personal complaints. It is when conditions improve and horizons enlarge that they become intolerable.[5]

Geoffrey Bell, *The Protestants of Ulster*, London 1976. 'The Protestants of Northern Ireland are the most misunderstood and criticized community in Western Europe', he says in the Introduction, 'They do not deserve to be misunderstood; this book explores whether they deserve to be criticized'. By contrast, Michael Farrell's *Northern Ireland: the Orange State*, London, 1976, gives an extensive and well-documented but orthodox view of Ulster, in the Republican tradition.

[4] Owen Dudley Edwards, *The Sins of Our Fathers*, 1970, p. 18.

[5] An excellent source for the understanding of the underlying strains in the old 'trouble-free' days is Rosemary Harris, *Prejudice and Tolerance in Ulster: a study of neighbours and 'strangers' in a border community*, Manchester 1972.

For it is only then that the disadvantaged group feels the full constraints placed on it. Only then – as the prospect of a more decent modern existence is dangled before it – is an oppressed nationality thrust into clearer awareness of its character and fate, and compelled to act. In Ireland, this was true above all of the Catholic minority in the North.

The earlier history of Irish nationalism had made up a classic episode in the annals of self-determination. There was nothing peculiar about it, except in the banal sense that all nationalisms involve the mobilization or invention of numberless peculiarities for display and veneration. Behind *Cathleen ni Houlihan*'s complaints there lay an ordinary dilemma of development, not some ineffable race-fate. And within this dilemma no aspect was more typical than its result: the partition of Ireland.

The history of Irish oppression goes back many centuries. It is certainly this long pre-history which explains one notable aspect of the present conflicts: religious over-determination. Since the Reformation, English overlordship of the island had ceased to be mere aristocratic control and turned into an alien cultural dominance. Ireland was already the main remaining stronghold of Catholicism in the British Isles. And it reacted against the new imposition by an ever deeper and more popular identification with the old faith. Religion became its politics. Catholicism was its substitute for the state, its native world-view. To the Protestant, Anglo-Irish ruling class this of course served as a proof of irredeemable barbarism. Where Protestantism was also a popular force, in the North-East, it naturally assumed its own sort of over-identification in response – the bloody Bible evangelism still represented today by the Paisley church. However, it is not the case that – as mythologies on both sides claim – there is any simple continuity between this tormented history and today's dilemma. The forces which created the latter arose only in the 19th century, and are little different from those generally observed in nationalist history. One should never confuse the older pre-history of nationality questions with that of national*ism* in the true sense.

In this standard tale of under-development, peasant Ireland was first dragged into modern existence by English industrialism and then forced to a nationalist self-mobilization *against* these same forces. Backward countries generally have had no other choice. The process of capitalist industrial development is so blind, so uneven in impact, and so metropolitan-centred that left unresisted it will crush all less-developed regions into some kind of prolonged colonialism. The latter have to fight back, in order to 'develop' in any acceptable sense themselves. So Catholic Ireland did resist, in the same way as and at the same time as the rest of under-developed Central and Eastern Europe, obtaining its independence very shortly after the main settlement of nationality questions in 1919–21.

The new Irish boundary was one in the interminable list making up this settlement. Like most of them, it was based on crude surgery. Agreement on the carve-up of ethnically mixed areas was hardly ever obtainable, and the great powers enforcing the division were uninterested in such details. However, the Ulster-Eire frontier did express what was supposed to be the main *rationale* of the new maps: separation of the new-nationalist under-developed peoples from their alien oppressors. It corresponded, albeit approximately, to the 'development gap' that had generated the whole problem. As a result both of the earlier Scottish Settlement in the North-East and the dramatic industrialization of the 19th century, this gap ran through the island, rather than between geographical Ireland and Britain. Uneven development had long ago potentially divided Ireland in two, along a ragged fissure at once ethnic, religious, and socio-economic.

Stranded on the wrong side of the boundary, the Catholic-nationalist minority joined the huge number of Europe's displaced persons and communities. In the 1930s these probably numbered around thirty million, spoke at least thirty-six different languages, and dotted the landscape from Fermanagh to the Black Sea. For most of them, notes a leading authority on the question, their situation 'is a matter of such vital and intimate concern as to occupy their thoughts, words, and action to the complete exclusion of reasonable spiritual activity upon any other public topic whatever'.[6] No visitor to today's Ulster can fail to appreciate these words.

There is no mystery about why the Catholic minority should have become restless and begun to agitate for its rights in the 1960s (the only 'mystery', if this is the right word, is why it took so long to do

[6] C. A. Macartney, *National States and National Minorities*, London, 1934, pp. 2–3.

it). There is even less about why 'nationalism' should have been mixed up with the demands of what is, after all, a typical national minority. What is not clear is why these stirrings should have led, so quickly and so belatedly, to the concatenation of violence we have witnessed. What caused this escalation into apparent 'atavism', under advanced social and economic conditions, and in the presence of two governments (Dublin and London) whose efforts from the outset were mainly to prevent it happening?

The Ulster Enigma

The key to an answer to the problem does not lie on the side of Northern Ireland's insurgent minority – it does not lie with the I.R.A., or with the souls and sins of Southern-Irish nationalism. It derives from the other side: from the peculiarity of the Ulster majority, not its minority – from the historical nature of the Protestant community (much more of a genuine freak in developmental history) rather than from Cathleen's centuries of trial and the annals of the 'crucified nation'.

There are important reasons why this historical oddity is little acknowledged. One of them is what the anonymous reviewer of Robert Kee's *The Green Flag* calls – '. . . the superior attraction for the cultivated mind of the winding caravan of Irish nationalism with its poets, assassins, scholars, crackpots, parlour revolutionaries, windbags, mythopoeic essayists, traitors, orators from the scaffold, men of action, emerging from so long and so great suffering of the people to impart an almost mystic quality to their often futile and often brutal deeds – the superior attraction of that to the hard, assertive, obsessive, successful self-reliance of the Ulster Protestant which has about it as much poetical imagination as is contained in a bowler hat.' (*Times Literary Supplement*, May 26th, 1972). The caravan has wound on into the 1970s. Nobody who has attended a political meeting on Ireland can have any doubts about the superb articulacy of its camp-followers and mouthpieces.

The Myth of Anti-imperialism

Another reason lies in the ally which this articulacy has found. Its ally is the pseudo-marxist theory of 'anti-imperialist' struggle in Ireland. Since this is virtually the sole competitor of the 'atavism' perspective, and so many phoney conclusions have been drawn from it, it is necessary to say something about it at this point.[7]

The 'anti-imperialist' myth does have one outstanding attraction: simplicity. It runs as follows. The partition of Ireland and the setting-up of the Ulster state was an imperialist conspiracy, intended to block and defeat the 'natural' course of the Irish national-liberation movement. Thus, it did not rest upon the reality of uneven development, or upon the fact of two differing ethnic communities in the island. While of course the London plot depended upon some cooperation by the population of the North-East, this was in essence the collusion of deluded lackeys.

Precisely because the Protestant people is not a 'real' one in the sense sacramentalized by nationalist belief, it can – in all essentials – be dismissed from history. It is a 'white settler' or colonialist minority, not a minority nationality by the standard canons. While it is unfortunate that this group includes the largest proletariat in (geographical) Ireland, this sociological phenomenon cannot be permitted to disturb the categories. Working-class or not, the group's consciousness is basically *false*: it identifies itself with imperialism (remaining part of 'Britain') and refuses to acknowledge its real interests, which lie with the all-Ireland movement of national liberation from British control.

Consequently, what has been taking place since 1968 is really a continuation of the old Irish-nationalist struggle. As Eamonn McCann said in 1969: 'It's Republicanism, and the idea of the revolution is implanted in the minds of the Irish people surrounded by the glory of 1916 and its martyrs . . . What we have to do is to complete the national revolution by making the theoretical and practical link between what we are doing now and what was fought for in 1916'.[8]

But this completion has a new aspect to it – at least in marxist

---

[7] Michael Farrell's conclusion in the study mentioned above (Note 3) is unfortunately typical: 'The choice in Ireland has become devastatingly simple: between, on the one hand, a semi-fascist Orange statelet in the North matched by a pro-imperialist police state in the South, and, on the other hand, an anti-imperialist and socialist revolution' by the united forces of the all-Irish working class, Protestant and Catholic together. Some figures given by Richard Rose in his analysis *Northern Ireland: a Time of Choice*, London 1976, underline the despair behind this devastating simplicity: 'In the 1975 Convention election in Northern Ireland, the two parties emphasizing class politics as well as constitutional politics – the Northern Ireland Labour Party and the Republican Clubs (supporters of the "Red" Official IRA) – *together polled 3.6% of the vote*', p. 141.

[8] *New Left Review*, No. 55, May–June 1969.

visions. It will also evolve into a working-class based battle *for* socialism, as well as against outside control. And it is in the heat of this battle that the blinded Protestant workers will recover their eyes: as class becomes more important than nationality or cults, so will the possibility of a genuine multi-ethnic society emerge. The theories of the most glorious of 1916's martyrs, James Connolly, are being continued, as well as a nationalist fight for one state in one island. He argued that because of its anti-imperialist character, nationalist war *could* be transmuted into war for socialism. Not merely 'national socialism' of course, but international or class socialism of universal significance.

The simplicity of the theory comes from the easy alignment it affords: there is no problem about why the Northern Irish war is occurring at the same time as the wars in Eritrea, Palestine, Kurdistan, and so on – it *is* the same war everywhere. The nadir of facility in this sense was provided by the title of Lotta Continua's Irish anthology: *Un Vietnam in Europa* (1970) (also published in German by Trikont, Munich: *Ein Vietnam in Europa*, 1971). The Manichaean tidiness of this map of the world effaces the actual problem of Ulster without trace. From there on everything is easy. Implacable logic conducts one to 'critical support' of the I.R.A.

In reality, partition was not a mere conspiracy of empire (although a number of conspiracies were involved in making it); the Protestant community is not a 'white settler' social group comparable to the Rhodesian whites or the Algerian *pieds noirs* (although it shares many features with these, above all on the level of ideology); its consciousness of its identity and separate interests is not a mass delusion (however many illusions are mixed up in it); 'imperialism' *in the sense required* by the theory does not operate in any part of the Irish island, while 'imperialism' in the looser meaning of capitalist or metropolitan dominance and farther development has no interest whatever in saving the Protestant state (although it does have a strong interest in preventing the national question from escalating into the pogrom-situation that has been threatened ever since August 1969).

Because there is no 'anti-imperialist' struggle going on in the requisite sense, there is no chance whatever of that struggle being fused from a 'nationalist' into a socialist or class-based one in the way that Connolly hoped.

The Protestant Community

The unacknowledged kernel of the real problem is the character of Protestant Ulster. Hidden under its bowler hat, the physiognomy of this particular band of tonguetied sons of bastards' ghosts has remained curiously unknown. The inarticulacy is not some racial trait: five minutes in the Shankill Road will show anyone that. Like its opposite, the undrainable eloquence of Southern Ireland, it reflects certain aspects of the community's past cultural development.

Faced with the rise of peasant nationalism in 19th century Ireland, the Protestants chose the British connection. Their material interests (including those of the Belfast workers) were in that direction, as well as their religious and ethnic preferences. It is this solid basis which alone explains the success of the sundry 'imperialist intrigues' surrounding partition. Like the Scots, the Southern Welsh, the Basques, the Bavarians and many other secondary nationalities, the 'Scotch-Irish' threw in their lot with the big battalions of the day. The choice created many problems for them (not to speak of those it created for the over-tidy mental charts we still employ in classifying countries). These problems are not dead today. As I suggested above, the slightest glance at the wide range of separatist and neo-nationalist movements currently at work in Western Europe will show this.

But, within this range of historical marginalia, one was destined to be especially intractable. It had a malignancy built into it unlike any other (with the possible exception of Cyprus) which was bound to re-emerge even under much altered circumstances.

For the Irish North-East 'integration' was particularly problematic. Geographically detached from the great power they had joined, the Protestants were *also* a self-conscious, advanced 'frontier' society. In some ways their frontier ethos and social structure can be compared (e.g.) to that of the old German settlements in Central and Eastern Europe. However, their position was far more precarious because of its double isolation. Confronting their equivalent of the Slav hordes, they never had the 'civilized' power which they claimed to represent really at their backs, either physically or (more important) politically and sociologically. The reasons why they were not 'Irish', in the sense that Catholic-based agrarian nationalism had established, are clear enough. But they were not really 'British' either: they were always, and they still remain, profoundly and embarassingly different from the society they imagine they are a frontier *of*.

In itself, this fact taken singly – like most aspects of the Ulster dilemma – is not peculiar to the Six Counties. Militant colonial or settlement societies have often been hopeless caricatures of their fatherlands. Their real conditions of existence are necessarily so different that, given long enough, they are bound to evolve a character of their own (Ulster has had more than three centuries for this). What distinguishes the Protestant North-East in such company is its massive industrial development.

'Ulster was the only part of Ireland where an urban middle class experienced a "natural" historical growth', comments Peter Gibbon.[9] The enormously greater economic development of this northeast zone in the 18th and 19th centuries gave its middle class different interests from the weaker southern bourgeoisie (quite apart from problems of religion and race). 'They enjoyed an integral link with British industry and commerce', Gibbon continues, 'Their working class was in some respects closer to that of Clydeside than of Dublin. It formed part of the great industrial triangle of the valleys of the Mersey, the Clyde and the Lagan'. For the Catholic middle classes leading Irish nationalism, economic protectionism appeared a necessity: the prerequisite of genuine independence from England. For the north-eastern bourgeoisie it meant the break-up of this great industrial triangle: a recipe for economic death.

Within this irreconcilable conflict, the northern workers took up a position alongside their own ruling class. In terms of the wider history of imperialism and under-development this stance cannot be considered exceptional. As Emmanuel has argued in *Unequal Exchange*, it is more like the norm. What is extraordinary in Ulster is the extremely close bonds among the social classes that resulted. The Orange Order cemented a mythical community of landowners, middle class and workers. It provided both an ideology (militant Protestantism), a geopolitical strategy (the British Connection), and an elaborate series of communitarian emblems and rituals (meetings, marches, banners, etc.). This successful integration

---

[9] *New Left Review*, op. cit.

explains why (in Gibbon's words) 'In Ulster . . . the Unionist and Nationalist Parties form two political blocs, cemented by religion, which collude with and complement each other . . . the natural lines of class struggle have been nearly erased by the traditional party system, which represents a monstrous distortion of the true social structure'.

Like Scotland and Wales, Ulster benefited from its 19th century choice of sides. Like them, it renounced separate or nationalist development. Whatever may have been lost by assimilation, there is no doubt what was gained. Ulster too experienced primary industrialization, and the formation of one of the major capitalist and working-class areas of the British Isles. By the 1960s this stage of industrialism had itself become cramped and backward-looking, and so (like so much of the British economy) liable to renewed pains of modernization. But this should not tempt one to forget its historical significance. It serves to separate Northern Ireland permanently from mere colonial implantations, as well as from the history of Catholic, under-developed Southern Ireland.

This settlement had evolved into a complete bourgeois society. Although on a small scale (more like a 'city-state' than a territorial nation) it possessed the whole range of classes and most of the institutions that typify such a society. Yet this evolution had occurred under the most unusual conditions. The economic integration it rested on was accompanied and modelled by that double isolation already referred to – by the politics and the culture of an especially insecure frontier.

Ulster and Empire

Most of the history of the last hundred years has aggravated this extreme contrast. It was dominated from the 1880s to 1922 by the British government's successive attempts to solve its Irish problems through some sort of Home Rule. That is, by its attempts to liquidate the 'frontier' in Ireland altogether and assimilate the island by more rational and modern means. Naturally, Protestant Ulster resisted and fought this policy: it identified the strategy of English Liberalism as one which would lead to its own disappearance *as* a community.

However, this resistance was never conducted as the real or straightforward expression *of* that community. That is, as the assertion of its own distinct identity and rights, its own capacity for national self-determination in a separatist sense. Instead, it was fought as a desperate battle for the frontier: for imperialism, 'British Ireland' in the old sense, Protestant Ascendancy over the 'natives', civilized settler values, and so on. The kind of over-compensation this involved was not peculiar to Ulster. One can (e.g.) perceive many elements of it in the super-imperialism which also characterized Scotland and Wales in the 19th and early 20th centuries. However, in Irish conditions these traits were magnified to maniac proportions – to dimensions reflecting the double menace that now constituted (as it still does) the real geopolitical environment of the Ulster Protestants.

Threatened by the nationalist development of Catholic and peasant Ireland, they were also threatened by 'betrayal' from Britain. Both threats were (and are) real. It was a fact, not a fantasy, that Southern Ireland was a substantially different society at a distinct stage of development, whose separate character and needs would have overwhelmed them had they become part of it. Equally it was fact, not fantasy, that all the strategies the British ruling class has been able to think up in modern times which were *rational* (in a capitalist sense) implied their dissolution. As a base for capitalist exploitation of the whole island, for penetration of the South, four-county industrialization has some use. As a separate entity it has become quite useless. *Modern* 'imperialism' (in the sense of farther, metropolitan-centred, capitalist development) has its interest in removing the mythic 'frontiers' of racist dominance and inter-ethnic feuds, not in erecting them into actual map-boundaries and customs-posts.

Trapped in this extraordinary way between past and future, Ulster Protestantism was unable to formulate the normal political response of threatened societies: nationalism. Instead, what one observes historically is a lunatic, compensatory emphasis of the two ideologies already strongly present in its community: militant Protestantism and imperialism. It is as aberrant substitutes for nationalism that these idea-systems have to be understood – not as evidence of incorrigible archaism, or indelible racism. I said earlier that Ulster's reaction to Southern-Irish nationalism had been a resuscitation of 17th century icons. Like the fetishization of the Union Jack, King Billy and the Apprentice Boys are really crude surrogates for a separate or national consciousness. Their grotesque coloration and rigid changelessness reflect this function, as do the monotonous ritualism and violence they are linked to.

The Two Nationalities

The Southern-nationalist view of the matter has always been simple. Ireland is one nation, coincident with the geographical island. The queer bunch in the North-East are either erring cousins who will admit their true natures once they have been shot or wooed into the union – or else genuine aliens, who can get out. As Conor Cruise O'Brien has many times pointed out, this curious blank is a structural part of Catholic nationalist ideology, from its origins up to and including the Provo present. One finds it even in Connolly: 'The astonishing and ominous absence in his *Labour in Irish History* is 19th century Belfast . . . The story of labour in Ireland's only large industrial city during the high period of the industrial revolution is simply left out. It is hard to resist the conclusion that the Protestant workers of Belfast, *as they actually were and with the feelings and loyalties they actually had*, were not consistently felt by Connolly to be part of Irish History . . .'.[10]

Opponents of this monolithic view have argued that there are two nations in Ireland, not one (a theory especially associated with the British & Irish Communist Organization in recent years).[11] Yet this dualism can be almost as misleading as what it replaces. There are of course two 'nationalities', in the sense of two distinct ethnic-cultural communities, in geographical Ireland. There are two potential national communities and states. But the malignant

[10] Conor Cruise O'Brien, *States of Ireland*, London, 1974, pp. 90–1.

[11] The British and Irish Communist Organization has published a number of incisive, often witty, statements of the 'Two Nations' theory, denouncing traditional Republican Nationalism and the IRA. Although none of this material is in book form, it can be obtained from Athol Books, Athol St., Belfast 12/4GX. Unfortunately their defence and justification of the Protestant case is accompanied by uncritical belief in the British state. Hence, rather than supporting self-government for the North they subscribe to the old form of Protestant 'self-determination': the claim to be 'British' in the sense of identification with the unitary state and its imperialist mythology (discussed above, Chapter 1). Their attack on my own views, *Against Ulster Nationalism*, 1975, contains a resounding paean of praise for Great Britain and Britishness: a unique episode in Marxist literature, presumably connected with their vision of the British Empire as a generally progressive historical phenomenon.

crux of the whole question arises from the fact that there are *not* two 'nations' corresponding to these communities.

More exactly, it arises from the conjunction of two factors. One lies in the peculiar barriers and deformations that have prevented North-Eastern Protestantism from acquiring true national identity; the other lies in *the social and economic force of the same community*. If the problem had been merely a cultural and religious one, history would already have dealt with it – in the same violent way that virtually every question of this kind was settled during the age of nationalism. There is no doubt at all what, in this sense, is presaged by that 'ominous absence' in Irish nationalist ideology O'Brien comments upon. British *marxisant* liberals may not have noticed it. Every minority in the world knows instinctively what it portends for them.

However, the Protestants were far too strong to suffer the normal fates. Economic development had given them the power not only to resist and fight back, but to influence the politics of the Anglo-Scots state they had affiliated themselves to. They pursued a policy of alliance with the English imperialist and nationalist right wing, from Randolph Churchill to Enoch Powell, and this strategy gave them some leverage in the London party system. Even without that, they counted in a more negative and dangerous sense. Liberals and socialists always disliked and disapproved of the Orange statelet and its authoritarian customs (to the extent that they thought of it at all) but never knew what to do about it. Above all, they could always be blackmailed by the threat of 'something worse'.

What the 'something worse' was became clearer than ever in August 1969. The Protestant community is actually strong enough to *impose its own version* of the nationalist 'final solution' at least over the four or six counties of the partition. This was the threat which brought the British army to Ulster. It is a threat far graver than anything represented by Irish reunification under Dublin (in the new economic conditions of the 1970s, that is).

O'Brien has described the peril of such open civil war in these words: even helped by the Republic's army, the Catholics would not win, so that – 'Ireland would be left, once more, with two States, but of even more virulent shades of green and orange than before. The Orange State would be smaller . . . but homogeneously Protestant, without the tiniest Catholic crack or crevice for a new I.R.A. to take root in . . . Both States would be under right-wing governments, scruffily militarist and xenophobe in character. The principal cultural activities would be funerals, triumphal parades, commemorations, national days of mourning, and ceremonies of rededication to the memory of those who died for Ireland/Ulster. The only check on these orgies would be the urgent need for both States to refurbish their connections with England, equally necessary for both of them.'[12] Their respective Presidents, Charles J. Haughey and the Rev. Ian Paisley, would spend the little time left over from religious rituals in pathetic expeditions to London and Brussels, trying to restore trade relations and the confidence of foreign investors (every single multinational concern having withdrawn from the island during the war period).

This is a scenario of total capitalist disaster. It would mean that the modest capitalist 'modernization' of the 1960s had triggered off a helpless retreat into an insular atavism even worse than the one Ireland was emerging from. So it is scarcely surprising that the bourgeois governments of Britain and Ireland have united in a sustained effort to stave it off. However, it is not certain they have succeeded.

It is, equally, a scenario of complete socialist and marxist failure. Every single representative of the Communist Parties, the Trotskyite groups, the International Socialists and the other sets of communist initials who have assumed 'correct revolutionary positions' on Ireland would be in prison, or dead. Consistent to the end, the few survivors in London would blame the catastrophe on imperialist plotters and lackeys. Labour Party politics on both sides of the new frontier would dwindle to even greater insignificance than today. Glumly pleased that its diagnosis had been proved so right ('The Irish are all mad'), the British public would forget about the problem for good. While another generation of stagnation settled over their country, Conor Cruise O'Brien and Garret Fitzgerald would write new histories of the crisis from exile at different American universities.

The Absent Nation

Were there three *nations* involved, two in Ireland and one in Britain, the whole question would be transformed. It would become an

[12] Conor Cruise O'Brien, op. cit., pp. 280–1.

ordinary bargain or transaction among bourgeois states. Such a large national minority would still cause real difficulties. But these would no longer tend towards apocalypse as they do now. It would be clear how they could be resolved, in principle at least, by the tried and mundane techniques of border-manipulation, minority-guarantees, appeals to U.N.O. and other international tribunals, occasional troop-manoeuvres, etc. Above all, it would become reasonable to envisage the progressive reduction of community hatreds and inequities *through farther economic and social development* (rather than by diving back into the past). If it were possible to give a more planned and socialist form to such development, it goes without saying that these chances would be hugely strengthened.

As things are, the whole question hinges upon the *absence* of one vital factor in the equation. Worse than that, what is there instead hopelessly queers all the resultant sums. The peculiar, fractured development of the Ulster-Protestant nationality is like a 'mad' variable which falsifies every reasonable strategy of escape. A nationality with a strong socio-economic basis in development (and hence far from being a *Volkstrümmer*, an ethnic relic ready to be swept aside) which has yet failed to evolve a coherent nationalism correlated with that development; a people which has for long chosen political retardation to accompany its economic advance; a community that has chosen almost to re-live its past, rather than utilize its past to frame an ordinary national consciousness of the present; a society dedicated to the alien – and now collapsing – identity of 'Britishism' rather than to the research and construction of its own distinct character – these are some of the paradoxes round which the new national politics of Ireland revolves.

At every stage in the last seven years, it was the Ulster Protestant community which really held the key to events. Yet because of its quite incoherent and contradictory political nature, it could only 'determine' history in the direction of catastrophe. It was the Protestant resistance to the minority's Civil Rights Movement which forced the latter back into physical revolt and nationalism. It was the Protestant assault on the Catholic areas of Belfast in 1969 which compelled the sending of a British army. It was the Protestant nation which then sheltered behind that army, by what it considered its historical right, while the I.R.A. developed into a significant force. When 'betrayed' by the demolition of the old

Northern Ireland state in 1972, it was they who developed their own secret armies into a much greater force. Above all, it was they who decisively destroyed the only serious effort at a new, more democratic and inter-communal solution to the question in 1974. The Protestant general strike that brought the new constitution and the Sunningdale Agreement to the ground demonstrated, finally, where the centre of political gravity lies in any farther developments.

In other words, the Protestants incontestably dominate a conflict which they are incapable of controlling. They have propelled it along by a series of blind and violent zig-zags reflecting their own inchoate political character. It is only when and to the extent that this character changes, that any intelligible 'solution' is imaginable.

Ulster Nationalism

Moreover, there is only one direction in which this change can now occur – that is, towards the formulation of a more than nominal 'Ulster nationalism'. If the Protestant community can acquire some political identity more secure than the Jekyll-and-Hydeism which imperialism has bequeathed it, there may be hope of progress. Otherwise, the best that can be hoped for is the mutual exhaustion and stalemate of the contending parties. Not all real historical situations have 'solutions' in the sense that radical or progressive thinkers have to hope for.

Nothing is more typical of Ulster's historical plight than the form in which nationalism has haunted the problem since 1968: the idea of a Protestant 'U.D.I.' Independence is seen here as a Biblical last strait – an almost apocalyptic answer to British perfidy, the awesome threat at the end of the line. This is absurd, in one sense. For self-government is also the boringly normal answer to nationality-conflicts: a now standardized product of centuries of world history.

Wild hysteria and violence cling to the idea in this context only because of the deformations of Ulster nationality, and its peculiar incapacity to face self-rule. This incapacity is structural, not the consequence of 'madness'. What it mirrors is the preponderance of those aberrant religious and old-imperialist surrogates mentioned above. Together, Bible fundamentalism and Union-Jackery made impossible the formation of a normal national intelligentsia. It is part of the pathological asymmetry of Ireland's national question that there is in Ulster practically nothing corresponding to the hiccupping caravanserai on the other side. The absence of an intellectual class explains the bowler-hatted 'inarticulacy' of the community in a public or historical sense. The same absence is related to the notoriously elementary (not to say poverty-stricken) traits of the Protestant political ruling class.

Only during the war has there been the belated emergence of something like an ordinary bourgeois ruling group in Ulster. In effect, the new condition allowed this society to overthrow its old quasi-colonial ruling élite of landowners and military gentlemen for the first time. Captain O'Neill and Major Chichester-Clark were undermining the basis of their own power with their reforms, though they hardly saw it in that light. However, perhaps inevitably, the replacements are an especially *lumpen* middle class. They may be most easily comparable to the new-nationalist ruling classes thrown up by rapid de-colonization in some parts of Africa or Asia. There is no developed or coherent tradition for them to inherit and operate with – that is, no functional culture corresponding to the *real* historical development and nature of the society they will have to govern.

Hence it is not surprising there should be a strip-cartoon aspect to the new Ulster politics unsteadily materialized in the recent United Ulster Unionist Council.

Hence also the remarkable part played by the Protestant working class in making up for these deficiencies. It was the working class which made the Ulster nation. Its 1974 general strike defied, and defeated, three bourgeois governments and the British army. Although they will never concede the fact it relegated the claims of the I.R.A. forever to that historical archive from which they should never have re-emerged. It was without doubt the most successful *political* action carried out by any European working class since the World War.[13] Before that turning-point there was an Irish

[13] Robert Fisk's book *The Point of No Return: the Strike which Broke the British in Ulster*, London 1975, gives a detailed history of the events. Speaking of Dublin's reaction to them, he writes: 'Both Cosgrave (the Prime Minister) and Jack Lynch, the Fianna Fail leader, perceived the new strain of Ulster nationalism which had been germinated during the strike. In future the Irish would have to deal with the Loyalists of Belfast as much as with the politicians at Westminster when they wanted to discuss both parts of their divided Ireland'. (p. 227) Chapter 12 contains interesting general reflections about the significance of this working-class action for other countries.

Protestant nationality confined to the level of pogrom violence, to the archaic inter-class tribalism of the Orange Order, Calvinist bigotry and Kiplingesque empire. After it, there is at least the possibility of a middle-class nation.

Any hope of a solution demands that one identify the real, underlying trend of events – what is actually developing as distinct from (and often in spite of) the ideas of the actors themselves. As I noted above, the 'anti-imperialist' theory discerned the trend as social revolution: nationalist fights would turn into socialist triumphs. The 'revolutionary situation' would make possible a short-cut towards a socialism that would automatically reconcile ethnic and religious feuds.

There are historical examples of this. The Chinese Revolution involved a short-cut of this sort – at least partially, and for a time.

In Europe, the struggle of the Yugoslav nationalities against a common external enemy did make possible the construction of a multi-ethnic and socialist republic. But the trouble with such examples is that all they do is underline how wildly different the position in Northern Ireland is. This is connected with the operations of a largely foreign-owned capitalism, which extended its grip during the 1960s. But such development had nothing in common with the Nazi invasion, or the militant counter-revolution in Russia and China (except for the kind of demonology in which 'capitalism', 'fascism' and 'imperialism' are three indistinguishable black cats in the dark).

As a matter of fact, these operations were largely 'progressive' in their effects and implications for the Irish context. Far from being merely a continuation of that older colonizing imperialism which had plagued Ireland, they came directly into conflict with the older inheritance. They spelt the ruin of the Orange Order and Southern clericalism alike. It was their quarrel with hopeless social and political archaism which was the motor of the new troubles. As Jean-Pierre Carasso pointed out, *bon an mal an* any acceptable capitalist government would be forced to *modernize* Northern Ireland and – 'Only once this modernisation is achieved will the *real questions*, for the moment present in a merely embryonic state, begin to be posed . . . '.[14]

---

[14] Jean-Pierre Carasso, *La rumeur irlandaise: guerre de religion ou lutte de classe?*, Paris 1970: a penetrating anlysis from a libertarian point of view, accompanied by a collection of and commentary upon Marx's and Engels' writings about Ireland. Libertarian accounts have been better than Marxist ones on the

This is why exactly the opposite of the anti-imperialists' prediction has taken place. While socialist ideas played a notable rôle in
promoting action from the outset, beginning with the People'
Democracy of 1968 and 1969, they have been invariably absorbed
into the nationalist movements. Nationalism has overwhelmed
socialism in practice, not vice-versa. Marxists have ended up as the
'critical' *aides-de-camp* of national struggles: the Official I.R.A. and
the Trotskyist parties for Southern nationalism, and the British
and Irish Communists for an emerging Ulster nationalism.[15] The
real needs and tendencies of society have proved stronger than ideology. Those 'real questions' Carasso refers to – the socialist questions of the future, the questions of going beyond 'modernization' -
are in turn forced to await some settlement of the national question

The uncertain, hesitant real evolution of the war has been towards Ulster nationalism. For the anti-imperialists, of course, there
have been neither phases nor real turning-points. The Stormon
state régime disappeared: they scarcely noticed. The Catholic
struggle altered from the defence of the ghettos to a renewed, aggressive war for the forcible reunification of all Ireland; they though
the 'progressive' battle against imperialism had simply widened it:
horizons. Sunningdale and the new Constitution appeared: new
even more sinister forms of imperialist control. The 1974 strike
swept them away: but by the Protestant workers unfortunately
affording one more demonstration of their fascistoid bigotry and
backwardness. The one sensational proletarian class action of the
war had come from the wrong side – so it had to be argued out o

---

whole: see e.g. *The Counter-Revolution in Ireland*, Detroit 1974; S. Van de
Straeten and P. Daufoy, 'La contre-révolution irlandaise' (original of the Detroi
pamphlet), *Les Temps Modernes*, June 1972; Bosers Anderup, 'Contradiction
and Struggles in Northern Ireland', in *Socialist Register*, ed. R. Miliband and
J. Saville, London 1972.

[15] In *Against Ulster Nationalism* my anonymous assailants professed stupe-
faction at this monstrous libel (see Note 11, above). In fact, much of their effort
in the early 1970s were devoted, very justifiably, to giving the Protestants who
would listen to them a more rational collective consciousness: it was in thi
capacity, for instance, that one of their number spoke for Ulster's Protestan
community at the Trieste International Conference of Minorities in July, 1974
They seem unable to grasp why this developing consciousness should at a certain
point have escaped their own sectarian influence and moved towards a separat
identity – towards self-government rather than their own fetish of an idealized
eternally progressive Great Britain.

sight, with a battery of equivocations unusual even by the baggy standards Ireland has established.

The customary left-wing attitude towards Northern nationalism focuses on its supposedly 'reactionary' content. Uneasily conscious that the Protestants *are* the real centre of the historical action, socialists are still tempted to dismiss their right of self-determination in a moralizing sense: such monsters can hardly be accorded the usual privileges. In part, this can be seen as the repetition of a mistake constantly made by liberals and socialists throughout the history of modern nationalism. Beginning with Marx and Engels in 1848, they have *always* tended to say that the so-and-so's have no national rights because they are backward, superstitious, tools of reaction, incorrigibly pogrom-minded, and so forth.

Self-determination is not a moral 'right' in this sense. It is a grim necessity of modern social development, but one which can also be presented and argued for as an ethical principle. Moralism inverts the issue. The point about 'nationalism' for the so-and-so's is that, at a certain historical point, it is the only way they have of *ceasing to be* backward, religion-ridden, lunatic reactionaries, and the rest. This point applies very straightforwardly to the Ulster Protestants. Seven years of warfare have only shown that they, and they alone, can solve the problems of their own nation. These problems have been thrust more and more completely into their own hands. With the 1974 strike they drew a lasting limit to outside interference in their affairs.

Outside the Bowler-Hat

'Mr Seamus Costello, chairman of the national executive of the new Irish Republican Socialist Party, told the 500 people who attended its first public meeting in Dublin on Wednesday night, that the development of class politics in Ireland . . . could be brought about only by the ending of British interference in Ireland . . . Another Left-wing organization was necessary because no other understood the correct analysis of the relationship between the national and the class question'. (*The Irish Times,* February 14th, 1975.)

Mr Costello is right. The resolution of the national question is a precondition of Irish socialist politics; and it certainly demands the British leave Northern Ireland. But he and his party (which includes

Bernadette McAliskey, née Devlin) have misunderstood the national question which is actually there to be resolved. It is not theirs, but Protestant Ulster's. Hence, his strategy of armed struggle for an all-Ireland Republic will entail the suppression of Northern rights of self-determination, and will carry his new group on to the side of reaction. Once more, socialism will serve merely as an alibi for nationalism.

Here, it is difficult to improve on Anderup's verdict: 'The strategy of "national liberation" which the left is presently pursuing is based on a faulty analysis and leads absolutely nowhere . . . The affirmation that Northern Irish Protestants constitute a separa-ate national entity with a right to refuse incorporation in the Re-public is usually considered to be divisive of the working class and therefore anti-socialist. On the contrary I think it is the stubborn affirmation of unity and solidarity where none exists and the extravagant claim of Irish Catholics to the whole island which is divisive. The Catholic left . . . tries to sweeten the pill for Protestants by affirming that this will be a socialist, and *ipso facto* a secular Republic. Protestants would be fools if they believed it. Socialism in Ireland is not for tomorrow . . . The Catholic left has demon-strated that even those who claim to constitute the socialist van-guard are trapped in nationalist ideologies'.[16]

To say this is not to deny that nationalism itself poses problems, as a solution. The first forty years of the Republic's independence demonstrated only too clearly what these may be. Although a necessity of modern social development, nationalism has always and everywhere a reactionary potential, a powerful capacity for in-volution and regression. Nobody can possibly guarantee that a nation built by the Crofter-Crofton-Crawfords will be somehow purer than others, a Dr Jekyll among states, able to disown the raving Mr Hydes that crowd the Belfast landscape. This is not the point. What matters is that the necessity comes first, and is really a precondition – in Ulster as everywhere else – of the battle between the Jekylls and Hydes being coherently fought out at all. National-ism is always a 'bad' solution: it just happens to be the only one that modern capitalist social conditions permit.[17]

[16] Anderup, op. cit., p. 158, pp. 188–9.

[17] In the Republic, the most significant single development since this article was written has been the proposal by the Irish Labour Party (who are partners in the present Dublin coalition government) to delete from the Republic's Con-

Left and Right

The problem posed to the left by Northern Ireland was unusual in the British and United States contexts, though fairly common-place outside. It was that of a historical situation where the interests and tendencies of a dominant segment of the ruling class *coincided with those of socialists*. This coincidence was of course 'objective', not 'subjective'. One runs the risk of labouring the obvious in saying so. For profoundly differing motives, and with absolutely different long-term purposes, these two social forces were none the less in alignment over a particular question.

The interests of multinational business and the governments serving them in London and Dublin lay wholeheartedly in 'modernizing' the whole of Ireland. The socio-religious bogs in both North and South had become impediments to the process. From this (admittedly limited) point of view, it no longer mattered desperately whether it was accomplished by a gradual, *de facto* 'unification' of Ireland or by the *de facto* acceptance of United Kingdom control in Ulster. In either case the border would have ceased to matter seriously. New generations would soon appear mercifully indifferent to the Pope and King Billy.

But the same bogs are even more of an obstacle to socialism than to capitalism. During the years of warfare they have swallowed up every libertarian notion. Only when they have been dried up through more modern conditions will it be possible to form a united working-class or socialist movement in the island. Hence, it was the interest of the revolutionary left to prevent the national question being recaptured by the old Republican ideology; to prevent it assuming an insurrectionary or military form when this had revived; and to stop the war which ensued. Liberal or humanitarian concern and political interest were not opposed. In this particular situation they coincided.

Instead, the extra-parliamentary left succumbed very largely to the anti-imperialist mythology described above. With few exceptions, it could not help identifying the Londonderry Bogsiders with the Vietcong and the British army with the U.S. in Vietnam.

---

stitution the claim to sovereignty over the six Northern Counties. If carried, in a referendum, this would make a great difference to the attitudes of the Ulster majority.

The I.R.A. has naturally exploited the situation, above all in the United States.

Anti-imperialism and Ulster

The left in the advanced world has benefited colossally from the anti-imperialist struggles in other continents (nowhere more so than in the U.S.A.). It in no way detracts from this to point out that there is a negative side to these benefits. Romanticism remains a more important ingredient in the make-up of the western intelligentsias than marxism. Since their basic situation is one of frustration at home, they have found it difficult not to make a mythology of anti-imperialism. There is not much point in blaming intellectuals for being unable to make a revolution themselves: history has forced most of them to be content with home-movies of the world revolution. But one may at least criticize the film.

Countries like Protestant Ulster have little place in the usual show. We have seen some of the peculiarities and contradictions of this community already, as manifested in its history, its relations with Catholic Ireland, and with Great Britain. But these should be completed with a consideration of the position which Ulster and comparable societies occupy in the general history of nationalism.

The dominant progressive myth of anti-imperialism is focussed overwhelmingly upon nationalism as a justified struggle of the repressed poor against the wealthy oppressors. And it goes without saying that there is an epochal truth about this, in the sense that it was the spread of western capitalism that provoked the mainstream movement of resistance or counter-attack we label as 'nationalism'. In the nature of things, this mainstream was bound to be predominantly that of 'backward' or 'under-developed' societies anxious to catch up, and to do so on their own terms (not those thrust down their throats by the metropolis).

However, it has never been the case that this main current exhausts the meaning of nationalism. There have also been a number of what could be termed 'counter-currents' – examples of societies which have claimed national self-determination from a different, more advanced point in the development spectrum. These somewhat more developed social formations have struggled for independence against the 'backward' nationalities around them. They have taken up the ideology of nationalism to do so. Impelled by the same underlying historical force, the mainsteam current, they represent none the less eddies in a contrary direction.

Not surprisingly, the category is mainly one of small nationalities and territories in 'sensitive' geopolitical points. The more advanced and industrialized Belgians developed a successful nationalist movement against the (then) backward and agrarian Netherlands monarchy, between 1815 and 1830. In the later 19th and early 20th century the more economically advanced regions of the Basques and the Catalans developed separatist tendencies against backward central and southern Spain. For a quarter of a century 'western' Israel has fought for independence against the less-developed Arab lands on all sides of it. Among the new-nationalist movements in Europe Scotland is (at least potentially) a new addition to this camp: its National Party perceives a future of super-development based on North Sea oil resources, in contrast to the declining industry of England.

The Ulster Protestant territories clearly belong to this group. And one must put the same question about them as about the other members of this rather marginal and select 'rich mens club'. Does it follow that they have no right to self-determination because they are (relatively) economically developed? Within the club – it is worth noting – the Ulster Protestants and the Israelis have more in common than the others. Their situation is complicated by the two striking dilemmas which they share: they can be accused by the more *echt*-looking nationalists around them of being on somebody else's land; and they have a religiously-based national ideology of unusual power, derived from a history of being under siege.

Multi-national Solutions

There is an easy answer to the question. Developed societies have no right to nationalism because they *are* in advance: it is their historical duty to transcend that stage of evolution. In practice, this implies their duty is to merge their national identity with the less fortunate. The Belgians should have found a multi-national *modus vivendi* with their Dutch neighbours; the Basques ought to embrace the less well-off Castilians and Andalusians, not fight them; it is the moral obligation of the Israelis to set up a lay bi-national state with the Palestinians – and so on.

Such sermons hide an awkward fact. This fact is so central to modern history, and so unpalatable to intellectuals, that it is hardly an exaggeration to say it dominates such discussions by its absence. The requests for saint-like behaviour tend to come from London and New York. However, they are certainly not founded on observation of the saintly behaviour of the masses in Western Europe or North America. No doubt it would be for the good of history if the Ulstermen and the Israelis led the way. But they really would be leading the way. One can scarcely pretend that the societies and states of the larger industrialized world have beaten out a path of nationalism-free self-abnegation for them.

Metropolitan homilies instruct the Scots and the Kurds to share their petroleum-wealth with needy neighbours. Yet if these peoples pay any attention to the way the metropolis behaves, as distinct from the way some of its intellectuals write, they will grab their 'national resources' and make the most of them. Crass national egotism, of course. But then, something like that is the normal condition of the U.S.A., Britain and France – the condition of the working classes, not merely of a small exploiting clique.

In other words, 'nationalism' is not confined to lands where under-development or a colonial history lend it a halo of justification; it is not even confined to them and the counter-cases just mentioned; it is a general fact of modern history, rooted in the development of the great powers as well as of the under-privileged. It ought not to be so; but there it is. And because it is, it seems both unrealistic and somewhat invidious of socialists in the West to preach at small, beleaguered nationalities. The truth about ideal, multi-national formulae is probably roughly like that about socialism: it can only emerge from the most advanced, mainstream societies at a higher stage of socio-economic organization than they have yet reached. Also, the two things may be much more closely interconnected than past socialist theorizing has recognized.

It is – incidentally – something of this general logic which echoes through the sermons themselves. At least a little of the heat given off in (e.g.) familiar censures of the Israelis comes from recognition that they – like the Basques, Ulstermen, etc. – are *also*, in effect, fragments of the 'advanced' industrial world. They are, and to a certain extent they behave, like tiny 'great powers'. In some degree their nationalism does have an ugly streak of possessiveness – a proprietorial exclusiveness at odds with the *pieds nus* claims of Third Worldism. It is not infrequently anti-socialist and reactionary (the earlier history of Basque nationalism is a good example here). So it is all too easy to unload the sins and guilty conscience of the real imperialist world on to them, in a familiar kind of compensation effect. The failures of the great families are visited upon their distant minor relatives.

Ulster Failures

The point is emphasized in North-East Ireland by the failure of the recipes which have actually been attempted there. Unlike Palestine, it has seen the imposition of a bi-national state form on the contending parties. But the experiment failed completely.

In 1972 the escalating violence forced the Conservative government in London to break with the long British tradition of reluctant, last-minute intervention in Irish affairs. It abolished the old Protestant regional parliament and administration, and introduced a new constitution. Usually called the 'power-sharing' constitution, this was founded on the concept of proportionally dividing power between the two communities at every level. It was accompanied by plans for a Council of Ireland, in which North and South would have been reconciled in a shadowy form of union with very limited powers. On paper it was a more advanced scheme than any yet tried for problems of this sort (in Europe, at least). It envisaged some progress towards all-Irish unity. It was supported by liberals, capitalists, social-democrats, and soldiers, as well as by the Dublin government. Outside Ulster itself, vocal opposition came mainly from the extreme right and the sectarian left.

None the less, the plan proved completely impracticable. As noted already, it was destroyed simply by the determined opposition of the majority community in Ulster. As an official White Paper commemorating the disaster puts it: 'In plain terms the Ulster Workers' Council . . . brought down the Executive, which, in a spirit of partnership, had undertaken the tasks of government in Northern Ireland since January 1st, 1974. In the political history of these islands, few men had ever undertaken a more arduous yet honourable task . . .' (*The Northern Ireland Constitution*, July 1974). They objected to effective power-sharing with the Catholic minority; and – perhaps even more violently – to the prospect of even a ghostly union with the Republic.

The 1973 Constitution was the last possible solution to the

Ulster war, in the sense of a pacific agreement imposed from without. After it London had a Convention elected, to work out still another power-sharing constitution: the idea was that since a British-imposed scheme had failed, the Ulstermen should work out a comparable model for themselves – the condition is still imposed that it must be founded on the democratic and willing participation of both communities. The Convention failed in its task. Meanwhile the murderous conflict dragged on in the background. Current speculation centred ever more on the imminence of open civil war – accompanied, almost certainly, by the withdrawal of the British army and some kind of territorial re-partition.

The paradoxes mixed up together in this situation are so startling that it is worth while trying to recapitulate them again. The Protestant community maintains its claim to be part of 'Britain', against hell and high water; but since it has refused to *be* 'British' in the fairly elementary sense of obeying the British government's plans for the province, the claim has become in practice a form of nationalism. Popular support for or interest in the Protestant case is minimal in England, and very reduced even in Scotland. The British government wants at all costs to be rid of the problem, in order to concentrate on the deteriorating economic situation and the class-struggle at home. On the other hand, sensing the coming collapse and the departure of the British troops, the I.R.A. still foresees the victory of its own nationalist cause: the final re-unification of Ireland by force. This prospect has come to be disowned by the Dublin government almost as totally as Protestant extremism is by London. Even if attainable (which it is not) it would saddle the Catholic Republic with the insupportable problem of ruling the North-East.[18]

Divorced in this way from the political support of the nations surrounding them, the Ulster communities are still forced to fight it out. The conflict is largely out of control. O'Brien's picture of the future two-state Ireland quoted above is nearer realization now than when he wrote it. It is more likely than not that the E.E.C. and U.N.O. will be graced before the end of the present decade by an improbable newcomer with about two-thirds the size and population of the existing Northern Ireland.

[18] O'Brien, op. cit., p. 139.

Even the acknowledgement of this likelihood has been taboo on the left until recently. The very words 'Ulster independence' led to a familiar litany: the unviability of such a tiny state, entirely deprived of international or great-power backing; the regressiveness of narrow nationalism; the superiority of a social-revolutionary solution, Irish or 'British'; the dreadful human cost of the operation – and so on. It is not necessary here to pursue these arguments farther. The taboo was understandable. But it has become unfortunately irrelevant – indeed something of an obstacle – to political appreciation of Ulster's realities.

The more important question is: why has the only possibility become that of making the miserable best of an extremely bad job, in the shape of independence of Protestant Ulster? The failure underlying this avalanche is not only in Ireland. It was always wrong to imagine that six Irish counties could bring forth a revolutionary answer which has eluded most of the rest of the world – including the 'advanced' societies where most of the criticism comes from. Backwardness has sometimes certain advantages in history, and can lead to short-cuts – but not here.

The larger society of which Northern Ireland is only one part has not provided the means of settling its problems. Neither the antiquated – and now disintegrating – framework of the United Kingdom, nor the elementary new constitution of the European Community gave the necessary support to the power-sharing scheme. Unfortunately, it was ahead of its time for Western Europe, as well as for Ireland.

How far ahead, we shall probably find out in the coming decade. Whatever now befalls Ulster, its agonies will not be detached from this greater history. How can the revolt against the existing big states be prevented from assuming catastrophic forms? How can the new nationalisms and demands for regional self-government be reconciled with a viable larger political framework – one which will express and harmonize them, instead of levelling them like the old imperialist states? How can the real values of smaller, more recognizable communities be obtained without large-scale political chaos and dependency? In what ways can socialist development be related to a new multi-national culture and politics? These are not the dilemmas of Ireland, but of the future of industrialized society in general.

Postscript

Since the original version of this chapter was written, the principal developments in Northern Irish politics have been the world-famous Peace Movement, and a noticeable drift towards the idea of independence as the only possible way out of the dilemma. In his new study *Northern Ireland: a Time of Choice*, Professor Richard Rose observes: 'Many talk about a solution to Ulster's political problem but few are prepared to say what the problem is. The reason is simple. *The problem is that there is no solution* – at least no solution recognizable in those more fortunate parts of the Anglo-American world that are governed with consensus. In such lands disagreements about what government should do are continual, but there is consensus about how the nation is defined and how it should be governed'.[19] The 1976 Peace Movement led by Mairead Corrigan, Mrs Betty Williams and Ciaran McKeown is probably best seen as a final, exasperated popular response to this unique situation where no 'political' solution looked feasible. Only in such conditions would a 'non-political' movement assume such remarkable momentum, and attract this degree of world acclaim and support. This consideration should qualify the most common criticism made of it – its a-political, purely moral and emotional foundation. On the other hand, the limits of such a movement remain undeniable, however much foreign enthusiasm it has generated.

At the same time, remarks Jonathan Power, the trend towards recognition of Northern-Irish self-government has proceeded: 'The call for Ulster's independence . . . is now attracting a wide measure of support. It first publicly surfaced in early November 1976 when nine of Northern Ireland's Protestant paramilitary groups announced that they wanted an Independent Northern Ireland . . . with Catholic participation in the Cabinet, i.e. a kind of power-sharing. The debate broadened when the Catholic Social Democrats at their annual SDLP conference in December passed a resolution to study the question' (see *Encounter*, March 1977, 'Can the Peace People Bring an Irish Peace?'). This amounts to a veiled return to the 'power-sharing' constitution proposed by the British government in 1973–4 – with the vital difference that, instead of being imposed from outside, it would now be created

[19] p. 166.

from inside as the basis of a negotiated form of self-government. This would of course be broadly consonant with the framework of devolution which the United Kingdom government is, for quite different reasons, trying to set up elsewhere.

Is it possible that the popular, community impetus behind the Peace Movement could be turned into support for such a solution? If it is not then, in spite of its achievements, it is all too likely to vanish back into the morass of sectarianism. But if it does, then it might play an important role in rendering the independence formula viable. Is it only the desperate, Christian wish-fulfilment of two peoples who perceive no earthly escape from the terrible dilemma of Northern Ireland? Or does it contain the seeds of a new, non-sectarian society capable of building a new identity beyond the terms of the old dilemma altogether? If it does not, Rose's final bleak predictions (one among so many) may still come true: 'We will only know that the Troubles have once again ended because of the palpable, even brutal, evidence that someone has lost.'[20]

[20] Op. cit., p. 166.

6. English Nationalism: the Case of Enoch Powell

> Every nation, to live healthily and to live happily, needs a patriotism. Britain today, after all the changes of the last decades, needs a new kind of patriotism and is feeling its way towards it . . .
>
> Enoch Powell, Speech at Louth, 1963.

In certain respects, the Right Honourable John Enoch Powell has long seemed the most original of Britain's bourgeois politicians – a figure whose every speech is awaited with eager interest and anxiety, who may be adored or hated but is universally felt to be important. Powell represents something new in British politics. If this something new is also something very old – nevertheless its impact, meaning, and possible results are all novel. Powell rose to this doubtful eminence mainly on the impact of his celebrated Birmingham address of April 20th, 1968. This was the speech in which he met 'a quite ordinary working man' who suddenly told him 'If I had the money to go, I wouldn't stay in this country . . . In this country in 15 or 20 years time the black man will have the whip hand over the white man.' After a scarifying catalogue of further revelations, Powell concluded: 'As I look ahead, I am filled with foreboding. Like the Roman, I seem to see "the River Tiber foaming with much blood"'. The message was that Britain's coloured immigrant population does indeed present a mortal threat to the British (or rather, to the *English* – for he pointed out that 'in practice only England is concerned') and must be got to return home whence they came. As Powell has modestly stated himself, the speech 'provoked a political furore without precedent since the end of the war'.

Naturally, he came to be regarded as the champion and chief spokesman of the various racist and anti-immigrant movements. He has also been widely accused of inconsistency (vis-á-vis his earlier statements on the issue) and of rabid demagoguery.[1] However, both the inconsistencies (which Powell of course presents as the natural evolution of his views) and the blatant demagoguery serve a deeper, and perfectly consistent, purpose. This underlying purpose has been obscured by too narrow a concentration on the question of race and immigration. The narrow focus itself serves Powell's purpose very well, by turning what is really only a right-wing tactic into an obsession for left-wing and liberal opponents – while in fact, there are wider and far more dangerous trends at work. Referring back to England's last bout of immigration-mania, against the Jewish immigrants of the period 1890–1905, Paul Foot remarks that in 1970 'all that has changed is that new scapegoats must be found for the homelessness, the bad hospital conditions, and the overcrowded schools . . .'.[2] But in reality, though England's coloured population has of course become a scapegoat for capitalism's ills, very much more has changed than the scapegoat itself. Powell knows this. Indeed, it is his sense of these profounder historical changes which supplies the real bite to his attack on the immigration question. The 'New Right' he represents is rooted in such changes, as both symptom and aggravation of the historical decline of English conservatism, and so must be regarded in longer historical perspective.

1. The Old English

> From Guilsboro' to Northampton, all the way
>> Under a full red August moon,
> I wandered down . . . Yet the air
>> Seemed thronged and teeming, as if hosts

[1] These charges are described and re-affirmed in Paul Foot's study *The Rise of Enoch Powell: An Examination of Enoch Powell's Attitude to Immigration and Race* (Penguin 1969), which also contains the relevant facts on the immigration issue up to 1969.

[2] In this period, noted Elie Halévy, 'An unmistakable wave of anti-semitism came over public opinion . . . The Act of 1900 against usury was perhaps the first symptom . . . The (Conservative) Cabinet had succeeded in finding a question on which the working classes were naturally protectionist.' The culmination (then as

Of living presences were everywhere;
   And I imagined they were ghosts
Of the old English, who by tower and spire,
   Wherever priest and sexton's spade
In church or graveyard round about the shire
   Their unremembered bones had laid,
Now in the warm still night arising, filled
   The broad air with their company,
And hovering in the fields that once they tilled,
   Brooded on England's destiny.

                    (Enoch Powell,
      Poem XXIV, *Dancer's End*, 1951; written 1940–5).

Powell's basic concern is with England and the – as he sees it –
half-submerged nationalism of the English. His real aspiration is to
redefine this national identity in terms appropriate to the times –
and in particular, appropriate to the end of empire. England's
destiny was once an imperial one; now it has to be something else.
Powell is not really sure what it is. But he feels that he, Enoch
Powell, carries some intimation of it within his own breast, and he
has consistently striven to construe this sense of fate.

   In 1964, speaking to the Royal Society of St. George,[3] he return-

---

now!) was the Aliens Act of 1905 which – Halévy continues – 'was a complete
reversal of the previous legislation, or rather absence of legislation . . . and the
foundation stone of an entire edifice of anti-alien measures, which amounted in
the end not merely to protection, but absolute prohibition'. (*History of the English
People in the 19th Century*, vol. 5, III, II, 5).

[3] This Society, unknown to most Englishmen, was founded in 1894 in the
flood-tide of imperialist delirium. Its aim was aptly conveyed by the first number
of its journal *The English Race*: 'There is some fear that the English stock is
getting deficient in that healthy and legitimate egotism which is necessary to self-
preservation . . . The Englishman must assert his indefeasible birthright.' *The
English Race* was uncomfortably aware that the Scots, Irish and Welsh (to say
nothing of real foreigners) seemed to have more national consciousness than
Englishmen: 'Above all other racial elements in the British system, the English
needs to be distinguished and preserved.' Each issue contained a 235-strong list of
'names to remember on April 23rd', ranging from Alfred the Great to William
of Wykeham, patriotic poems and profiles, articles on such subjects as bell-
ringing and Morris-dancing, and a thundering editorial, e.g.: 'Within the last
century we English have absorbed an appreciable number of Scottish Celts and
Saxons, Irish and Welsh Celts, and Jews . . . So far as the United Kingdom and the
Empire are concerned, the knell of the pure-blooded Celtic race as a distinct

ed to the theme of the 'old English': 'There was this deep, this providential difference between our empire and others, that the nationhood of the mother country remained unaltered through it all, almost unconscious of the strange fantastic structure built around her . . . England underwent no organic change as the mistress of a world empire. So the continuity of her existence was unbroken . . . Thus, our generation is like one which comes home again from years of distant wandering. We discover affinities with earlier generations of English, who feel no country but this to be their own . . . We find ourselves once more akin to the old English . . . From brass and stone, from line and effigy their eyes look out at us, and we gaze into them, as if we would win some answer from their inscrutable silence. "Tell us what it is that binds us together; show us the clue that leads through a thousand years; whisper to us the secret of this charmed life of England, that we may in our time know how to hold it fast." What would they say . . .?'

In 1964, when the post-war Conservative régime ended, Powell still did not know what they would say. Twenty years of brooding on England's destiny had availed him little. By April 1968 the ancestors had, finally, said something: approximately, 'Go home, Wogs, and leave us in peace!' This prodigious clue to a thousand years of history has, however, a meaning beyond its superficial absurdity.

For the *dilemma* to which it appeals is a real one. It is quite true that the English need to rediscover who and what they are, to re-invent an identity of some sort better than the battered cliché-ridden hulk which the retreating tide of imperialism has left them – and true also (for reasons described below) that the politics of the last 20 years have been entirely futile in this respect. Powell's

element has sounded. The Celt will continue to undergo a process of gentle absorption, or share the fate of the aboriginals of America and New Zealand, the "Redskin" and Maori . . . The racial instinct of the English is ever-present, far down and deeply-rooted; too dormant, too unassertive, unaggressive yet uneradicable.' (Vol. II, No. 16, April 1913). In 1939, *The English Race* changed its title to *England*. By 1950 even St. George had gone from the cover, and (a parable of imperial decline) it had dwindled into a genteel newsheet replete with pictures of thatched cottages and royalty, and appeals for funds. Powell's 1964 address is included in *Freedom and Reality* (Selected Speeches, ed. J. Wood, 1969). The reader's attention is drawn specially to the last section of the book, 'Myth and Reality', which Powell himself describes as the most important.

recipe for the growing vacuum is the – at first sight – incredible patchwork of nostrums expounded in his recent speeches: economic laissez-faire, Little England, social discipline, trade before aid, loyalty to Ulster, and racism. But no critique of such incoherence can afford to ignore the need upon which it works: in relationship to reality, it may possess a driving-force which it lacks when considered simply as a set of ideas. After all, very few past Conservative heroes have been noticeably 'coherent' in this sense: compared to those of Churchill, Joseph Chamberlain, or Disraeli, Powell's career so far is an epitome of logical sobriety. Only in the context of the twilit conservatism of the 1960s does his cynical opportunism appear startling, or even unusual. British conservatism has always been profoundly 'illogical' since the time of Edmund Burke, by an instinct rooted in the great historical conditions of its existence. It has been only too happy to rule, and leave logic to the 'opposition'.

The odd ingredients of Powellism are held and fused together by a romantic nationalism with quite distinctive cultural origins. Powell worked his way up from the lower middle-class (both parents were elementary school teachers) via a Birmingham grammar school to Cambridge. Thus early in life this solitary and rigid *bourgeois* industriously acquired the traditional culture of the English ruling élite: Greek and Latin. He became Professor of Greek at the University of Sydney at the age of 26, a remarkable tribute to ungentlemanly energy and self-discipline.[4] At the same time, he wrote verse in an appropriately archaic romantic mode derived mainly from A. E. Housman and the Georgians. The theme is usually death, or else the passing of youth, innocence, and love:

> Oh, sweet it is, where grass is deep
>   And swifts are overhead,
> To lie and watch the cloud, and weep
>   For friends already dead.[5]

[4] 'A distinguished scholar and churchman (remembers) . . . visiting the prodigy on his arrival at Trinity College, Cambridge. He found Powell, on a bitter November morning, in an attic room in New Court. There was no fire in the grate and Powell covered in an overcoat and rugs, was reading Thucydides. His visitor asked him if he would care to come to tea; Powell simply replied "No". In a renewed effort to break the ice, his school friend sauntered across the room and lit a cigarette. "Please don't smoke," said Powell'. (T. E. Utley, *Enoch Powell: the Man and his Thinking*, 1968, p. 48).

[5] Poem XXIX, *First Poems* (1937).

These wholly sentimental reveries and sighing dramas go on in the rustic English limbo first popularized by Housman:

> I dreamt I was in England
>   And heard the cuckoo call,
> And watched an English summer
>   From spring to latest fall,
>   And understood it all . . .
> And I lay there in England
>   Beneath a broad yew-tree,
>   Contented there to be.[6]

This tradition of abstract upper-class kitsch arose in the same epoch which witnessed England's attempt at the Higher Imperialism, the Boer War, the Syndicalist Revolt, the Constitutional Crisis of 1911, and the Aliens Act.[7] It gives sublime expression to the hopelessly *rentier* mentality into which a large part of the English intelligentsia had now lapsed, to the despair of militarists like Lord Roberts, imperial administrators like Curzon and Milner, national-efficiency zealots like Sidney Webb, and such 'committed' intellectuals of the day as Rudyard Kipling and Henry Rider Haggard.

As if knowing instinctively how impossible it would prove to save British imperialism from its own ramshackle self, the poets turned towards a safer past. This movement of involution led them – in a pattern which has also characterized other intellectual trends of the English 20th century – to a conservative dream-world founded on an insular vein of English romanticism. Powell revelled in it. It never occurred to him that this week-end landscape was far more synthetic than the most plastic products of Hollywood. 'Ours is an age when the engines of bad taste possess great force,' he declared in his Inaugural Lecture at Sydney in 1938, 'With rare exceptions, the cinema, the newspaper and the wireless tend powerfully to promote vulgarity, by day and by night in our cities the eye and the ear are continually assaulted by objects of bad taste . . . I once heard Housman, when referring in a lecture to a certain corrupt epithet in Lucretius, remark that "a modern poet, I suppose, might write

---

[6] Poem XV, *Dancer's End* (1951).
[7] The first of the five volumes of *Georgian Poetry* (a collection of verse signalling the new 'Georgian' as distinct from the old 'Edwardian' era) appeared in 1912, with poems by Rupert Brooke, Graves, Masefield, W. H. Davies, Drinkwater, and Walter de la Mare.

252

such a phrase as that and fancy that it was good, but Lucretius could never have done so". The words echo in my mind today; and whenever I have achieved a daring adjective in a poem "and fancy that it is good", my conscience asks me whether Lucretius and Housman would have thought the same or not. That illustrates exactly what I mean by the cultivation of taste . . .'.[8]

It goes without saying that he mastered the techniques of Georgianism, and produced suitably 'tasteful' rhymes. The Prussian assiduity which took him to the Sydney Chair saw to that. Later in life, he even learned to fox-hunt, and penned a Housmanesque jingle on this important political experience. With this background, it was quite natural that the 'old English' should materialize to Powell primarily 'by tower or spire' or in old country churches – rather than, say, in a sooty Wolverhampton cemetery or the ruins of a factory. He still partially inhabits this Disney-like English world where the Saxon ploughs his fields and the sun sets to strains by Vaughan Williams.

This is, in fact, a romantic nationalism which retains nothing of the original energy of either romanticism or nationalism. In England, a country of ancient and settled nationality, romanticism did not serve as the instrument of national liberation, it could not help forge a new national-popular consciousness. It could not even function as substitute for a real national being and consciousness – as, for instance, it did in Scotland. All too easily, it turned into an escapist or conservative dream-world, negating the Victorian bourgeois régime at one level only to confirm it at another. By the time of Housman and the Georgians it had become a sickly parody of itself, expressive only of the historic stalemate into which the English bourgeoisie was falling. Powell's poetic nationalism, in turn, is nothing but a pallid echo of the parody, incongruously surviving into the later 20th century.

However, the very absurdity and archaism of this re-heated romanticism poses a problem. If English nationalism *can* still be identified with such inadequate symbols, it is because of an odd weakness at its heart. The saccharine countryside of the Old English is a reflection of something persistently missing, something absent from English national identity itself. In part, this void is clearly

[8] *Greek in the University*, Inaugural Lecture to the University of Sydney, May 7th, 1938.

associated with the positive and distracting presence of something
else, for so long: English imperialism.

2. The Imperial Crown

> Still the black narrow band of shimmering road,
> A thousand miles the same . . .
> . . . Then on the Eastern hand
> The skyline suddenly fell sheer away
> And showed the smoky Delta; to the right
> Rose sharp and blue against the desert's brown
> The pyramids; and to our astonished sight
> Described, above it all, the Imperial Crown.
> > (Enoch Powell, Poem XXXIII, *Dancer's End*).

Powell was once the most passionate of imperialists. When he left
Sydney for the Indian Army at the outbreak of war, India burst upon
him like a revelation.[9] He admitted recently: 'I fell head over heels
in love with India. If I'd gone there 100 years ago, I'd have left
my bones there.' (*The Times*, February 12th, 1968.) Here, surely,
was the true sense and purpose of England's being. That the grandeur had been fatally undermined half a century previously, that
England's imperialism was more and more of a theatrical charade,
that the Imperial Crown was now held up by the dollar-sign – all
this meant nothing. His enclosed imagination saw 'Edward the
First, Plantagenet' as having held the imperial destiny in one hand
already (in the 13th century):

> The rod thou holdest in thy right
> Is raised thy enemies to smite
> > And shatter their impuissant hate,
> But in thy left already lies
> The image of the earth and skies,
> > Foreboding universal power . . .
> > (Poem L, *Dancer's End*).

[9] English political conservatism has always owed much to empire, and in
particular to India. The most interesting statement of English conservative
thought in the later 19th century, by that distinguished Victorian judge and bully
James Fitzjames Stephen (*Liberty, Equality and Fraternity*, 1873), was also

But in this imperial fervour there lay a basic uncertainty, an ambiguity which marks every facet of English imperialist culture in the era from the 1870s – when England began to become self-consciously imperial – up to the evident decline of the 1920s and 30s. On the one hand, English imperialism could scarcely avoid the most soaring ambition: it possessed so much, and had dominated so much of the world for so long, that its power could not help looking 'universal'. Yet on the other, the English were always uneasily conscious of the great discrepancy between this appearance and the substance behind it.

The old days of informal, economic empire were over, in the teeth of German and French competition; yet England's 'empire' remained a heterogenous assemblage of units belonging to this bygone era, approximately held together by her navy. On one hand there was the boundless delirium of Rhodes and the music-hall: 'His Majesty rules over one continent, a hundred peninsulas, five hundred promontories, a thousand lakes, two thousand rivers and ten thousand islands … The Queen found the revenues of the Empire at £75 million; she left them at £225 million … The Empire to which Victoria acceded in 1837 covered one-sixth of the land of the world; that of King Edward covers nearly one fourth. The Union Jack has unfolded itself, so to speak, over two acres of new territory every time the clock has ticked since 1800…'. But on the other hand, the English universal power was incapable even of governing the British Isles, as the Irish proved every few years. The immensity was also empty. If the English had ever taken their imperial delusion seriously, it would have required the largest army in the world as well as their navy, a new and quite different English State, and a total reform of English society away from the lazy conservatism into which it subsided.

Whatever imperialist zealots like Kipling, Webb or Joseph Chamberlain said, there was never any real chance of such reform taking place. The great weight of English conservatism was against it. And if that were not enough, so was the pressure of the City of London, lender-in-chief to the world and – on the whole – happy

inspired by the author's Indian experiences. India, he wrote, was 'the best corrective in existence to the fundamental fallacies of Liberalism'. Out there "You see real government'. (See Introduction to the 1967 edition, the first since 1874, by R. J. White).

[10] St. James Gazette, on the accession of Edward V11, January 1901, quoted in W.S. Adams, *Edwardian Heritage* (1949).

with the slack old ways: there were as good profits to be had invest-
ing outside the English territorial 'empire' as inside it (in the U.S.A.
or South America, for instance). The first issue of *The English Race*
contained an appropriately vigorous article by the Duke of Glou-
cester on 'The Value of Pageantry'. There was, indeed, little behind
the pompous pageantry of Edwardian imperialism which had not
been there some decades before, when the governing philosophy
had been that colonies were a political nuisance to be got rid of as
soon as the march of Progress would allow. The hollowness sounds
through the English imperialist mind in a thousand forms: in
Rider Haggard's necrophilia, in Kipling's moments of gloomy
doubt, in the self-pitying pessimism of Housman, in the sadness
of Elgar, or in the gloomy cosmic truth of Forster's Marabar caves.

For Powell, however, it was all good as new a generation later.
In this narrow, rigidly-focused sensibility, imperialism had joined
forces with the English pastoral mode. He devoted his disciplined
energy to crazy schemes for the retention of India by military force
and, later, even to plans for its re-conquest when the Conservative
Party came back to power in 1951.[11] This was, in fact, the main
motive which had driven him into political life in the first place.
The world was unthinkable without the British Empire. That is,
Powell's imaginary world was unthinkable without it – the world
where, now, Old English and grateful brown-skinned multitudes
jostled bizarrely together.[12]

The unthinkable happened. Independence was conceded to India
and Pakistan by the Labour government of 1945, and after 1951 it
became clear that even under Churchill it would not be undone.
Powell's fantasia was rudely jarred by the fact: it took him some
years to recover from the blow. England's destiny had received a
mortal wound.

When he did recover, it was by a familiar machinery of over-

[11] See Paul Foot, op. cit., p. 19.
[12] 'The curse outstrips the wind
And on the shores of Ind
Takes form again.
A boat heaves to;
Out stretch ten swarthy hands,
And there the spectre stands . . .
He turns with parted lips,
While graceful on his hips
The dark hands fall . . .
    (Poem XXVIII, *Casting Off*, 1939).

compensation. The most truly remarkable speech of Powell's career has not been on immigration, or the virtues of capitalism, or the social services which he administered for three years as a Minister in the Macmillan government, from 1960 to 1963. It was on the British Empire. It was delivered, not to an audience of ravening Conservative militants, but in the academic detachment of Trinity College, Dublin, and is easily the most interesting comment on imperialism by a Conservative spokesman in this century – at least, since Joseph Chamberlain's famous 'Tariff Reform' address of 1903.[13]

'The life of nations' – he begins – 'no less than that of men is lived largely in the imagination.' Consequently, what really matters in national life is the nation's 'corporate imagination'. Within 'that mysterious composite being, the nation', nothing can be more important than 'the picture of its own nature, its past and future, its place among other nations in the world, which it carries in its imagination. The matter of this imagining is nearly all historical . . .'. The *form* of such imagining, however, is myth. The politician's task – as Plato stated in *The Republic*, that bible of the English élite – is to 'offer his people good myths and to save them from harmful myths'. And (the point is) the current myths of the English corporate imagination are bad ones. The most important of such myths is the delusion that 'Britain was once a great imperial power, which built up a mighty empire over generations and then . . . lost or gave it up'. It is only because of the presence of this pernicious myth that the English believe they are in *decline*: they imagine they once stood upon a great height, hence they cannot help feeling in the shade today. But the conclusion (and by implication the whole of British politics since around 1918) is as mistaken as the premise.

'The myth of the British Empire is one of the most extraordinary paradoxes in political history,' continues Powell. Everyone believes it existed, but it never did: 'Until very nearly the Diamond Jubilee of Queen Victoria (1897) if you mentioned "the Empire" to a man in the street in London, he would think you meant the United Kingdom, with its three capitals, London, Edinburgh and Dublin . . .'.[14] But what of India, Powell's old love, a British political

---

[13] Speech at Dublin, 1946, in *Freedom and Reality*, op. cit., p. 245.

[14] This is of course wildly inaccurate. As Richard Koebner's study of the introduction of terms like 'empire' and 'imperialism' into English usage shows, 'empire' was used in the early 1800's and 'imperialism' was perfectly familiar by the

dependency since the 18th century? Easy: 'India is the exception which proves the rule'. Otherwise, 'imperialism' was largely invented by the Conservative government of 1895–1905, for narrowly political reasons ('because one could make stirring speeches about Empire without needing actually to alter anything') and the particular culprit was his own predecessor from the West Midlands, Joseph Chamberlain (then Colonial Secretary). 'And so it was' – he concludes – 'that just in the very last years when Britain's relationship with her overseas possessions could by any stretch of fiction be represented as imperial, the Conservative Party first, and then the British people, came to believe instinctively, implicitly, that they had an empire – a belief that was to colour their thoughts, emotions and actions for the next 70 years and to set a gulf between them and the rest of the world, the same gulf which exists between a man in the grip of a hallucination and those around him who do not share it.'

How familiar are these particular tones of disenchantment! In the 1950s the whole western world rang to them – the lugubrious ex-votaries of Stalin who, unable to bear what their idol had become, turned to denounce the god that had failed them. Powell reacted in the same way towards the political collapse of imperialism. Given that the failure, the disenchantment, had occurred, what was once the all-embracing, seductive truth *could* only be a tissue of lies. There is in Powell's anti-imperialism exactly that weird mixture of sharpened perception and utter lunacy which one finds in ex-communist tirades on communism.

It is true indeed that England's high imperial moment was largely compounded of myth and pretence, that Chamberlainism was a practical impossibility, and that the Conservative Party had a strong vested interest in the charade. It is also quite true that the experience has left a deep subjective mark upon English national consciousness and culture (as Powell's own previous career had made abundantly clear). But it is grotesque to suggest that there was, literally, 'nothing' behind the theatricality of Edwardian imperialism. The reality behind it was, of course, the varied nexus of econo-

---

1880s, both in more or less the modern sense. 'Imperialism' had made considerable inroads in the 1870's, in fact: Disraeli's first important imperialist speeches were in 1872, while Dilke's *Greater Britain* (which did much to popularize the imperial idea among the upper classes) came out first in 1868. See *Imperialism: the Story and Significance of a Political Word, 1840–1960* (1964).

mic relationships built up by English trade and industry since the
17th century, which had made the English Industrial Revolution
possible in the first place, and then been enormously extended by
England's manufacturing primacy. There was all too little relationship between this mainly economic reality and the new pretentions
aroused by military challenge and the desire to emulate Germany.
It was impossible to systematize the conglomeration into an 'empire' in the Roman, French or German sense, except in fantasy.
Yet this does not signify that such economic power (a different,
more 'informal' empire than any other in history till then) did not
exist.

This is, however, precisely what Powell is driven to maintain.
He can allow no degree of truth or reality whatever to the cause
which disappointed him. After the imperial myth, the second most
notorious legend still gripping England's imagination is that England was once 'the workshop of the world'. In truth, it never was:
this is no more than the 'identical twin' to the empire myth, and
'the characteristics of British industry which are supposed today
to account for loss of ground to other nations were just as evident in
the Victorian hey-day, when Britain enjoyed the preponderant share
of the world trade in manufactured goods.' The very words belie
the intended meaning. If Britain enjoyed 'the preponderant share
of world trade in manufactured goods' at that time, it could not
possibly have been for any other reason than that she enjoyed a
preponderancy in world manufacture, which is all that was meant
by calling her the 'workshop of the world'.

England's decline into 'her own private hell' has been – consequently – a dream process, just as the myth of empire was 'our own
private heaven'. To cure herself, all England need do is wake up:
'If Britain could free herself from the long servitude of her 70-
year-old dreams, how much that now seems impossible might be
within her power. But that is another story, which has not yet begun . . .'. That was in 1964. One can scarcely resist the thought that,
for Powell, the awakening must have begun at last, with his racist
speech of April, 1968.

By May 1967, he already had some intimations. Referring with
admiration to General de Gaulle (one of his heroes), he commented:
'The face which we see in de Gaulle's mirror is our own, and we had
better look at it firmly and steadily . . . What sort of people do we
think we are? We have been hovering over the answer for years . . .

a nation of ditherers who refuse to make up our minds.'[15] After a brisk review of the 'schizophrenia' which has long characterized British policy (the Pound, 'peace-keeping', the growth fetish, and so on) he returned to the question: 'What sort of people do we think we are? The question waits for its answer. In psychiatry a sign of convalescence is what is called "insight" – when the patient begins to regain a self-knowledge hitherto rejected . . . How is Britain to fulfil the Delphic command "Know thyself"? How can you and I and the Tory Party help in resolving the national dilemma, re-uniting the split personality and banishing delusion?'

The reply was still cloudy, though. Powell concluded somewhat feebly, not in the tones of the Delphic Oracle: 'The politician is a voice . . . We do not stand outside the nation's predicament: we are ourselves part of it . . . All we can do is to speak out what we feel, to try and identify and describe the contradictions, and the phobias which we see around us, in the hope that . . . we may wake a chord that will reverberate.' Less than a year later, the Oracle had spoken, and the chords had finally begun reverberating to his satisfaction. The intimations of destiny in the Powell ego had at last found national 'contradictions and phobias' to identify with. The English had begun to know themselves once more. In the obscene form of racism, English nationalism had been re-born.

3. The Settled View

> Conservatism is a settled view of the nature of human society in general and our own society in particular, which each succeeding generation does but re-express.
>
> (Enoch Powell,
> 'Conservatism and the Social Services',
> *The Political Quarterly*, 1953).

English nationalism has been travestied by romanticism and con-fused by imperialism. But no account of its calvary would be com-

[15] Speech at Hanwell, May 25th, 1967 (*Freedom and Reality*, op. cit.). De Gaulle had just administered another contemptuous rebuff to Britain's half-hearted desire to enter the Common Market, provoking near-universal resentment and wounded pride in Britain.

plete which failed to perceive how it has also been weighed down by
conservatism. The 'matter of its imagining' (in Powell's phrase) is
almost wholly conservative. This is not a question of the political
Conservative Party but of that profounder, ambient conservatism
which has marked the structure of English society for several centuries. The English national identity sags with the accumulated
weight of its symbols and traditions, and is in consequence perhaps
the least *popular* nationalism of any major country except that other
island, Japan. This is in fact why the nationalism of the English
appears so 'dormant' and 'unaggressive' (as *The English Race*
put it): simply because the 'people' had so little positive part in
creating it, or have forgotten the part they did play. On the whole,
they have been forced into the stereotype of the plucky servant who
'knows his place' and, when the trumpet sounds, fights with the
best of them. The fact poses a grave problem to would-be leaders of
English national revival.[16]

An unintentionally comic clue to the problem is provided by
Powell's own history of England, *Biography of a Nation*.[17] The
'Introduction' is a familiar, puzzled rumination on the subject:
'There is no objective definition of what constitutes a nation. It is
that which thinks it is a nation . . . self-consciousness is the essence
of nationhood . . . National consciousness is a sense of difference
from the rest of the world, of having something in common which
is not shared beyond the limits of the nation . . . This phenomenon
of national consciousness remains almost as mysterious as that of
life in the individual organism . . . This living thing, mysterious in
its origins and nature, is perhaps the most difficult subject of purely
human enquiry . . .'; and so forth. But, turning from this Idealist
prologue to the text, the inscrutable secret reveals itself at once as

[16] In this respect, the English right-wing dilemma is almost diametrically
opposed to the American one. In America there is a popular, vividly-felt nationalism *without* a corresponding deeper structure of conservatism. Hence, for example, the recent American obsession with Edmund Burke, the founding father
of modern English conservatism, and the interesting debate which surrounded
and followed the publication of Russell Kirk's compendium *The Conservative
Mind* in 1953 (see e.g. G. K. Lewis, 'The Metaphysics of Conservatism', *Western
Political Quarterly*, vol. VI, and 'The Toryness of English Conservatism',
Journal of British Studies, vol. I, No. 1).
[17] *Biography of a Nation: a Short History of Britain*, Enoch Powell and Angus
Maude, 1955.

all too simple: the shallowest imaginable montage of school-book clichés, wholly concentrated around the conventional symbols of conservative nationality (the Crown, Parliament, the Constitution, etc.). These are the unsurprising content of the national self-consciousness.

It is difficult to exaggerate the degree of Powell's symbol-fetishism. He literally worships every sacred icon of the great conservative past. Hence, for instance, his enraged opposition to the Royal Titles Bill of 1953, which did away with Elizabeth II's queenship of the Commonwealth. Faced with such desecration Powell was forced – to the dismay of his fellow-Conservatives in parliament – to identify himself with England's soul. Destiny had struck again: 'We in this House . . . have a meaning only in so far as in our time and in our generation we represent great principles, great elements in our national being . . . Sometimes elements which are essential to the life, growth and existence of Britain seem for a time to be cast into shadow, and even destroyed. Yet in the past they have remained alive; they have survived; they have come to the surface again and . . . been the means of a great flowering which no-one had suspected. It is because I believe that, in a sense, for a brief moment, I represent and speak for an indispensable element in the British Constitution that I have spoken.'[18]

[18] Speech in the House of Commons, March 3rd, 1953. Powell has also contributed two farther volumes to the glory of the Constitution, *Great Parliamentary Occasions* (1960) or 'authentic glimpses into the past of Parliament', and *The House of Lords in the Middle Ages* (with K. Wallis, 1968), a history which devotes as much space as humanly possible to ritual and trivia – 'Every institution has a local habitation . . . the peculiarities of the place affect the behaviour and life-story of the institution itself. No scrap of information therefore about the place and arrangements of sitting of the institution . . . is to be despised . . . This is one advantage, at any rate, which a working member of such an institution has . . .'. The criterion of selection of Powell's 'great Parliamentary occasions' is the 'pedantic devotion' which the Englishman accords tradition: 'With almost incredulous delight we find that . . . Humanity, as represented and revealed in Parliament, does not seem to change at all as the centuries pass.' Real history is of no significance. It will come as a surprise to most readers, for instance, that the only 'great occasion' of the 20th century was the debate over the revised Church of England Prayer-Book in 1927. But what mattered was the purely parliamentary drama it gave rise to. John Jones, a Labour member, objected to this trivial squabble 'on behalf of the great mass of the workers of this country (who) are more interested in the rent-book than the prayer-book'. Powell comments: 'The House of Commons, like a mediaeval court, has its licensed buffoons and tolerated jesters.' (pp. 117–18).

He was both right and (in a sense important for understanding his whole political line) quite wrong. In one respect he does indeed represent very well an indispensable feature of English Constitutionalism – its obsession with the safe, fossilized forms of past authority and legitimacy. Yet of course the obsession must never be given free rein: its whole point, in England's traditional consensus-politics, was its function as an instrument of adaptation, a way of absorbing and neutralizing *change*. When it becomes absolute, it becomes useless. But Powell has a taste for absolutes. His destiny-filled solitude often blinds him to the wider logic of the Party, and the historic cause, which he wishes to serve. Utterly devoted to English conservatism, he is nevertheless also driven by a blinkered fervour which is alien to its way of working. Hence – as on the occasion in question – he easily finds himself far to the right of political conservatism. By a revealing paradox, this ultra-English bigot is compelled to feel and act in the most surprisingly 'un-English' fashion – that is, in a fashion which contradicts the real essence of the conservative political hegemony.

The mainstream of English conservative consensus has always effectively captured or suppressed left-wing disruption. The left, painfully conscious of its own dilemma, has not noticed how conservatism also had to control the right. Now, a retrospective penumbra of false consciousness eliminates them both. Not only does it politely pretend that the conservative hegemony has survived without difficulty (a fact of English nature), and quietly bury the history of the left, like syndicalism, the workers' control movement, and the other forces beaten in the great defeat of 1926. With almost equal effect, it expunges the grisly history of the English right. Mosley (like the British Communist Party) serves merely to underline the message: 'extremism' and foreign ideas never find a toehold here. When, finally, nemesis returns in the shape of Powellism, England is convulsed with astonishment: is it possible to be 'English', and extreme?

Yet the miracle of this long-lived conservatism lies, after all, in one word: war. Modern English conservatism was forged out of its 22-year war against the French Revolution and Napoleon. This was no war of popular nationalism, having as its stake the casting of English society in a new form: it was the opposite, a patriotic war of counter-revolution which reinforced the conservative social structure, and channelled and moulded popular forces in a fashion

which made society able to bear the immense stresses of industrialization. It aimed to eliminate the people from history as other than
a subordinate force, and fathered precisely that non-democratic
nationalism which, now, Powellism is endeavouring to inject life
into from the right.

In old age, the imperialist system erected on this original basis
has received two massive infusions of vitality from the two farther
patriotic wars of the 20th century. Official legends regale the reader
with tearful accounts of the tragic economic 'sacrifices' and 'losses'
of 1914–18 and 1939–45. In fact, the First World War providentially
saved Old England from collapse and civil war, and prepared the
terrain for crushing the proletariat in 1926; while the Second World
War furnished the perfect restorative, in the form of a victorious
patriot drama where English conservatism could hardly avoid
looking, and feeling, like a St. George with one shining foot on the
Nazi dragon's tail. Fortunately, the feet of the U.S.A. and U.S.S.R.
were on its neck. In both wars, England was on the right side,
pursuing her long-established strategy of alliance with U.S.
imperialism. It is true that the war effort of 1939–45 produced much
more social egalitarianism in England than any other event in her
recent history, enough to result in the electoral defeat of Churchill
in 1945. Yet – paradoxically – it also contained the social upheaval
more firmly than ever in a renewed 'national' ideology of unity, a
sense of patriotic purpose and regeneration. Hence (given the
Labour Party's subordination to these myths) it led inevitably to the
stifling new conservatism of the 1950s and 1960s.

So Powell's inheritance as an English nationalist is a very strange
one. This stale, romantic, middle-class nationalism has survived
on the surrogates of imperialism and foreign war for nearly a
century. It is at the same time curiously under-developed (or
'submerged') because of its conservative, non-popular nature, and a
living anachronism in a Europe in which nationalism has begun to
assume new forms. How can it be made to live again?

4. The Logic of Prejudice

> The music sounded, and in my breast
> The ghosts of my fathers arose from rest . . .
> Like the priests in Aïda they danced on my head
> And sang savage hymns to the gods that are dead.
> (Enoch Powell, Poem XIX, *Casting Off*, 1939)

England needs another war. This alone would recreate the peculiar spirit of her nationalism, rally her renegade intelligentsia (as in the 1930s), and reconcile the workers to their lot. Unfortunately, war of that sort – like her empire – is a lost cause. The 'British' patriotic symbols are unlikely to receive farther transfusions of blood. Nelson, Wellington, Haig and Churchill will – with any luck – never arise from rest to dance on our heads again.

The true-blue nationalist's dilemma is a serious one, therefore. His sacred traditions are visibly withering. There is a new generation which finds them meaningless or comic. Even the schoolteachers – once high-priests of national conservatism – are no longer reliable. When not an international bore, England has become an international joke: her only claim to distinction in the 1960s was a mainly anti-national pop culture and a (largely unmerited) reputation for *dolce vita*. How can England's silent majority be got to return to the fold, before it is too late?

War was the great social experience of England in this century – yet war served only to confirm and re-validate the value of the past, to affirm the essential continuity of the national tradition. The only *new* experience, going sharply counter to tradition, has been that of the coloured immigration of the 1950s and 60s. Hence, as Powell realized, it has become possible to define Englishness vis-à-vis this internal 'enemy', this 'foreign body' in our own streets. This is exactly what he tried to do in the speech of April 1968. It was more than a case of locating a new scapegoat: this scapegoat was to have the honour of restoring a popular content to English national self-consciousness, of stirring the English 'corporate imagination' into life once more, by providing a concrete way of focussing its vague but powerful sense of superiority.

How strong the force is which Powell began to tap in this way has been demonstrated by the rapid series of rightward steps which the Establishment took to deal with it. At each successive phase of the racial storm in the 1960s, more strict immigration controls were imposed. Writing in *Crossbow*, the organ of 'liberal' young Conservatism, N. Scott remarks that these were no more than fearful 'reactions to public opinion' which 'rendered respectable racially-prejudiced reactions to fears of unemployment and over-population'. But the same writer can only end his plea for tolerance and 'constructive race relations' by conjuring up precisely the phoney, old-style nationalism which Powellism goes beyond: 'Intolerance and racialism present Britain with a challenge to the values upon which life in these islands have been built . . . It is not, I hope, unfashionably nationalistic to recall Milton's words: "Let not England forget her precedence of teaching nations how to live".'[19] The fact is, that intolerance and racialism did *not* present any challenge to national values, as long as (like military violence) they were comfortably located abroad; located at home, they represent a new situation to which rhetoric of this kind is irrelevant. As for the Miltonian precedent, it embodies very well a bourgeois moral high-mindedness which the English masses have never been particularly fond of. *Their* sense of superiority does not need them to pose as ethical models to an admiring universe.

Six months after his April 1968, speech, Powell told the London Rotary Club (enjoying a week-end in all-white Eastbourne) that his words had 'revealed a deep and dangerous gulf in the nation . . . a gulf between the overwhelming majority of people throughout the country on the one side, and on the other side a tiny majority with a monopoly hold upon the channels of communication, who seem determined . . . not to face realities'.[20] The populist intention is

[19] N. Scott, 'Constructive Race Relations', *Crossbow*, Jan.–March 1970. In fact, modern English nationality also preserves a kernel of older identity derived mainly from the 16th and 17th centuries, which there is not room to discuss properly here. It was associated with the experience of Puritanism and the 'Puritan Revolution' of 1660, and as a result – 'English nationalism . . . has always been closer than any other nationalism to the religious matrix from which it rose . . . (to) a religious life and sentiment . . . full of social activism, of a feeling of responsibility for the betterment of the world'. (H. Kohn, 'The Genesis of English Nationalism', *Journal of the History of Ideas*, vol. I, No. 1, 1940) Taine's lengthy account of this national high-mindedness in his *History of English Literature* is still unsurpassed. This strictly *bourgeois* element of English national feeling is of course also represented in Powellism. Indeed, his reputation for personal high-mindedness is such that, at the time of the Profumo scandal – 'The entire country waited for some time in suspense for Powell's judgement on his leader (Macmillan). He was already known to be a man of exacting conscience – some said a puritanical conscience – who would have no truck with lechery and lying. His positive affirmation that Macmillan had not erred was a powerful reinforcement to the Prime Minister in his distress' (T. E. Utley, op. cit., p. 88). Some of Powell's populist appeal comes from the fact that *such* a morally impeccable source should tell the people their instincts are sound, and need not be restrained by a middle-class morality.

[20] Speech at Eastbourne, November 16th, 1968 (*Freedom and Reality*, op. cit., p. 227).

unmistakable: the new national spirit is of and for the overwhelmingly and decently prejudiced majority of English men and women,
opposed by the 'aberrant reason' of a tiny minority who think they
know best (and which actually included, as Powell knew very well,
most members of both parliamentary parties and virtually the whole
politico-cultural élite of conservative England).

In another sense, however, England's coloured minority is not
such a fruitful choice for the New Right. It is quite a good scapegoat, and served to achieve a preliminary mobilization of popular
sentiment in the right direction. Yet there are inescapable limits
to its farther development. In this way, the English coloured population contrasts oddly with the traditional victim of European right-
wing nationalism, the Jews. It is, in fact, almost entirely proletarian
in character, and unlikely to be anything else for some time to
come – hence, it is impossible to pretend plausibly (as one could
with the Jews) that it *is* the oppressive 'tiny minority', or at least is
in league with it. England's Indians and West Indians can scarcely
be identified with 'the system' by which the majority feels obscurely
oppressed. They do not measure up to the task of re-defining England's destiny, as it were. In addition, they present the defect of
being geographically concentrated in a few areas (whereas it hardly
mattered where the Jews were, since they could so easily be imagined as everywhere). Above all, it should not be overlooked how
vital immigrant labour has become to the British economy, as to
the other West European economies. The Confederation of British
Industries itself has always opposed restrictions on immigration and
talk of repatriation.

Not only does the working-class composition of the new-immi-
grant population limit its potential as a political whipping boy. One
may even argue that, to date, it has been assimilated into the existing state structure with considerable success. In one of the most
radical commentaries on this issue, A. Sivanandan points out how
the 'philosophy of race relations' in England, dealing with the
problem of black labour, is 'like a barium meal . . . revealing the
whole organism of the state'.[21]

In the discussion of the British state above (Chapter 1) it was
noted that one of its outstanding historical traits was a domestic

---

[21] A. Sivanandan, *Race, Class and the State: the Black Experience in Britain*,
London 1976, pp. 347–8.

class strategy of absorption. This reposed typically upon the high degree of responsible self-activity by the intelligentsia, and the latter's co-option of emerging leaders from below. The effect was to reduce the pressures from underneath to manageable, quantitative demands. The more political, system-threatening side of these pressures (as in Chartism or pre-1914 Syndicalism) died away into fringe groupings and 'extremist' sects. To a remarkable extent the system has been able to repeat this feat in the case of the new internal minority created by black immigration of the 1950s and 1960s.[22]

In effect, this 'internal colony' of assorted newcomers amounted to a new bottom layer of the old class-structure. As Sivanandan says: 'The jobs which "coloured immigrants" found themselves in were the largely unskilled and low status ones for which white labour was unavailable or which white workers were unwilling to fill ... The indigenous worker would move upwards into better paid jobs, skilled apprenticeships, training programmes, etc.'. The new stratum soon occupied the worst housing, concentrated in the most decaying inner-city areas: conditions which of course reinforced stereotypes about them, and added to the already massive discrimination which they experienced.

In spite of its distinctive features (colour and external origin, strong cultural contrasts with the natives) this new class was not basically resistant to the old strategy. When it threatened to become troublesome and 'socially counter-productive', governments undertook a specially elaborated version of the technique involving stricter controls on black immigration and an apparatus of attack on discriminatory practices. Sivanandan's view is that these were designed to reconstitute migrant labour on a more European model, that of the temporary *gastarbeiter* rather than the black citizen who had come to stay. The climax of this integrationist philosophy was

---

[22] 'New Commonwealth' citizens numbered 1,157,170 in Great Britain, or 2.1 per cent (1971 Census figures, in *Ethnic Minorities in Britain*, Community Relations Commission, London, 1974). This compares with only 30,765 in Scotland, 0.6 per cent; and 13,730 in Wales, or 0.5 per cent of the population. The three essays in *Racial Conflict, Discrimination & Power*, edited W. Barclay, K. Kumar and R. Sims, 1976, as 'The British Case Study', give some idea of the economic basis of English immigration and racism. Michael Banton's *Racial Minorities*, London, 1972, attempts a sociology of the race problem in England. Ernest Krausz's *Ethnic Minorities in Britain*, London 1971, widens the perspective by comparing black to other minorities.

the formation of the Race Relations Board, which on the whole 'succeeded in what the state meant it to do . . . to create a class of coloured collaborators who would in time justify the ways of the state to the blacks'. Together with the Community Relations Commission (1968) it 'took up the black cause and killed it' in a widely successful operation of integration. As a consequence, the author concludes, the state in Britain 'has successfully taken politics out of the black struggle . . . taught the white power structure to accept the blacks and taught the blacks to accept the white power structure . . .' limiting the gangrene of racism.[23]

In the 1960s black militancy (like student power and womens' liberation) seemed a far more revolutionary movement than the tame nationalisms of Scotland and Wales. Yet in fact it proved relatively assimilable by the traditions of English social conservatism. Oddly enough, the black minorities were protected by the very conservative, hierarchical order which oppressed them. The constant barrage of petty humiliations and snobbish insults, the small change of 'discrimination' so many personal accounts bitterly relate, were the product of this inert, caste-conscious society. But its very backwardness was related (as always) to stability, and in these conditions the old strategy was still practicable. The intelligentsia formed the 'race relations industry' (as its opponents dubbed it), to put the new anti-discriminatory legislation into effect. Even against the much greater obstacles represented by a black, ghettoized sub-class this cooptive approach could still function. It could not remove the problem, and English racism will clearly always have a chronic source of exploitation. But its limits as a right-wing cause have been established too: no successful right-wing nationalism can mobilize *on this basis alone*.

Powell tried hard to extend the area and effect of the racial storm-area, first by his 'repatriation' proposals (offering himself with characteristic integrity as a future Minister of Repatriation), and then by new fantasies of a burgeoning, prolifically fertile coloured horde forcing the dried-up native stock off the island altogether. He has never ceased to return periodically to the subject, seeking to

[23] Michael Banton, op. cit., describes some episodes from the earlier history of political integrationism, like the 1960s Campaign Against Racial Discrimination (CARD) and the disputes surrounding its dissolution. These are particularly interesting in relation to the role of the intellectuals (white and black) in reformulating hegemony (see Chapter 1, above).

recreate the first major shock-success. Yet, aware of its limitations, he was forced to move to other ground. The new destiny was not emerging with the hoped-for speed. He turned to Ireland.

Powell showed a stirring interest in England's most ancient problem only a week after the Londonderry riots of 1969. A letter of elevated moral tone appeared in *The Times* in August, rebuking the British Army commander in Ulster, General Freeland, for his 'political' comments during the crisis. Then in February 1970, Powell addressed an Ulster Unionist rally at Enniskillen. He declared that 'The ultimate fact in human society, and in the world of states and nations, is belonging or not belonging . . . The belonging of Northern Ireland and the not-belonging of the Republic are at present obscured by the condition of the law . . . The fiction of the Ireland Act, 1949, must go . . . (and) . . . the entry, the residence, the settlement and the franchise of the citizen of the Republic of Ireland will have to be determined exactly as those of a Frenchman, a Russian or an Australian are determined . . . Nothing, in my judgement, would conduce so much to banish strife and disorder as the plain and open assertion, in legal and constitutional terms, that the people of these countries belong, uniquely and solely, to the United Kingdom and are part and parcel of this nation, which is in process of defining and recognizing itself anew . . .'.[24]

The same blinkered directness and inflexible 'logic' which had always marked his career took him to the farther shore of his new cause. When Conservatism returned to office in 1970 he found himself excluded. His 'extreme' notions were in disaccord with state strategy, so the High Priest of traditionalism was kicked out of the Temple. His disenchantment was vastly aggravated by the Heath government's main policy in the 1970–3 period: getting Britain into the European Community. The policy was strongly supported by the economic right and by most Tory militants. His irreconcilable nationalist hostility to the move forced him farther and farther away from them (and indeed, into the company of the Labour Party's left-wing nationalists, who were leading the anti-EEC crusade). Finally he resigned from his English constituency, and from the

[24] *The Times*, February 9th, 1970. On the day after this address, Powell said on television that his declaration was only 'logical', and something that needed saying. It was not at all calculated 'to increase animosity between those of different religions'. The Conservative shadow Home Secretary Quintin Hogg commented afterwards that 'Logic was not, perhaps, the friend of good politics.'

Conservative Party, still protesting that he was the only true Tory left in the country.

His main hope for a base now lay in Northern Ireland: the ultra-British province whose war (so he imagined) would serve as the regenerating focus, the inspiration of the reappearing Saxon ghosts. Here was the prophetic wilderness indeed: a mini-Armageddon, ravaged by Biblical warfare. The hero was now on the most distant shore, the frontier of his nationalist universe, as M.P. for Down (South). Sixty years before Tory nationalism had rallied on this soil, to threaten civil war and the destruction (disguised as the salvation) of the British state. Could the experience be repeated, and the threat this time made reality? A salvo of entreaties rained back upon the centre from outer darkness.

They were worse than pointless. It was argued above (Chapter Five) that the Ulster situation does not permit of an integrationist solution; on the contrary, it is far more likely to end in some kind of separate or semi-separate régime, and events have moved perceptibly in this direction in the very years of Powell's Irish retreat. He had assumed that, for all its darkness, the wilder shore *was* a bit of England. His idealism had misled him: because the Protestants had once proclaimed their eternal allegiance to the Crown, he thought this consciousness was effective reality. It is not: the reality crumbled away even as he thundered from the United Ulster Unionist benches. Far from revivifying the Union, and England herself, Northern Ireland began to join the general trend towards disintegration, or 'devolution'. The last outpost had abandoned the Motherland.

He will probably have to return to the centre, partyless and still more immured in prophetic isolation. His only hope is the collapse of the old state which he worshipped with such intensity: a new political desert in England itself, from which he may yet be called, in spite of (but at that moment because of) his severance from all the old system parties. However, this poses the question of the *social* content of this messianic project. Here one encounters farther difficulties.

5. The Oak Tree's Roots

> 'Often, when I am kneeling down in church,
> I think to myself how much we should thank

God, the Holy Ghost, for the gift of capitalism'.
(Enoch Powell, quoted in T. E. Utley.)[25]

Powell has indicated clearly what England's social future should be, in any number of perorations: 'Whatever else the Conservative Party stands for, unless – I am not afraid of the word – it is the party of capitalism, then it has no function in the contemporary world, then it has nothing to say to modern Britain . . .'.[26]

The capitalist market-place is another of the traditional fetishes Powell worships with total devotion, alongside the Crown and the Constitution. His view is a curious inversion of Fabian Socialism: the Webbs identified socialism with State ownership, control, and planning, while he identifies any form of State economic intervention (except currency issue and control) with 'socialism'. He cannot forgive his own party its corruption by 'socialism' in this sense. The modern Conservative Party has become a party of the State, it tolerates or even favours State power and bureaucracy almost as much as Labour. Powell even occasionally compares this State power to fascism: it represents, he claims, the true threat to our freedom – the inhumane, corporative dominance from above, from which only capitalism can preserve us. Hence, England must return as far as possible to the conditions of *laissez-faire*.

Two aspects of this odd rhetoric go some way to making it comprehensible, and help distinguish it from the ancient, over-familiar Conservative ideology of 'free enterprise' (a pedal which the Tories have had to lean on heavily ever since the Liberal Party died off, and they found themselves the main industrialists' party). Firstly, Powell's diatribes are not so much defences of the 'free market' as envenomed attacks on the mainstream of political consensus: the 'State power' against which he inveighs is no less than the tacit basis of agreement informing English political life, which (as always in the past) enables the two-party system to function smoothly and guarantees the peaceful evolution which is supposed to be the essence of English Constitutionalism. The slogan of 'laissez-faire' is the only economic one which distances his position sufficiently from the prevailing 'bad myths'. And, naturally, it appeals to at least one sector of the 'people' he is trying to galvanize into political

---

[25] op. cit., p. 114.
[26] *Freedom and Reality*, op. cit., p. 10.

life – the small business-man (still important in the West Midlands he represents) or the small *rentier* who feels oppressed and helpless in the face of today's great concentrations of economic power. This petty bourgeoisie is, after all, part of that historically absent or repressed English populism remarked on above – part of the historical 'people' kept in social servitude by the conservative hegemony.

Secondly, Powell's conception of the laissez-faire economy emphatically does not signify a *weak* or merely marginal State power – the State of classical English liberalism which was meant to do no more than 'hold the ring' for competing economic forces. Given what has happened in the past, a modern free-enterprise State must be *strong* (if only to cope with the much greater strength of business and financial organization today). Hence, Powell's economics are more compatible than they seem with his evident authoritarianism. The 'freedom' which his capitalist State would foster includes, quite logically, the 'repeal of the Trade Disputes Act of 1906'.[27] No less naturally, it includes repression of student agitation and of such infamous national scandals as the schoolteachers' strike of 1969–70. To let capitalism off the leash again in the way Powell envisages would need, in fact, the strongest State action against workers, students, and intellectuals (the 'tiny minority who control communications', etc.). And obviously this face of Powellism appeals to an even wider stratum of discontented middle-class and lower-middle-class natives, like the Conservative Party militants he travels the country addressing.

Both these facets of Powell's ideology are very much the daily bread of nationalist, right-wing reaction in the past. They represent no more than the classical formula established succinctly by Charles Maurras long ago: 'Authority at the top, liberty below'.[28] If the nation is ill and led astray, then it follows that the prevailing political force must be corrupt and incompetent. It cannot be cleansed or

[27] See *Freedom and Reality* ch. 10, 'Changing Trade Union Law', pp. 146–7. 'The evil of trade unionism', Powell states roundly, 'lies in the coercive power of combination which the trade unions possess, and which they use, either by threatening to withdraw their labour collectively or by actually doing so, in order to try to obtain more for their services than these would command in the open market without this coercion...'

[28] *Dictator and King* (1899), quoted in *The French Right* (selections ed. J. S. McClelland, 1970).

put to rights except by a strong, decisive leadership able to express the true national will. By definition, the nation is always being betrayed. It must, therefore, be *redeemed*.

Powell has always been riveted by the notion of the national destiny re-emerging from betrayal and ruin. One of his early poems is about the Portuguese national poet Camões (Camoëns), who was shipwrecked in the Mekong Delta in the 16th century:

> Black the mountains of Timor
> Sweeping from the sea
> Watched Camoëns drift ashore,
> Rags and misery . . .

But the poet was to be saved from death, to compose the great national epic *Os Lusiadas*, and even in the depths of his degradation held in one battered hand 'a jointed fennel-stalk' –

> Hidden in that hollow rod
> Slept, like heavenly flame
> Titan-stolen from a god
> Lusitania's flame.[29]

In 1953, amid the humiliation of the Royal Titles Bill, he imagined 'a great flowering' that might still come forth from destruction. In 1964, at the Royal Society of St. George, he compared England to Greece: 'Herodotus related how the Athenians, returning to their city after it had been sacked and burned by Xerxes . . . were astonished to find, alive and flourishing in the midst of the blackened ruins, the sacred olive tree, the native symbol of their country. So we today at the heart of a vanished empire, amid the fragments of demolished glory, seem to find, like one of her own oak trees, standing and growing, the sap still rising from her ancient roots to meet the spring, England herself . . .'. Even now England must not despair: in spite of Heath, Wilson, and the Rolling Stones – 'we know not what branches yet that wonderful tree will have the power to put forth.'

In spite of all these classical features of right-wing destiny-mongering, however, Powellism still contains a glaring weakness

---

[29] Poem VI, 'Os Lusíadas', *Dancer's End*.

at its heart: a far too overt identification with capitalism. This may appeal to capitalists, and particularly small entrepreneurs, but there is evidently a far larger area of the national soul to which it will never appeal at all. Most successful past brands of reaction have at least had the sense to conceal their links with capital from the public gaze. Powellism, by contrast, has its trousers down from the start: capitalism is nudely exposed as another cherished institution of Old England. When reminded by J. K. Galbraith at a Cambridge University Union debate that 'the competitive system was now an illusion, that the market was dominated by large monopolistic or semi-monopolistic concerns which have many of the attributes of the State and which . . . create rather than obey public taste,' Powell merely admitted that there was, indeed, much truth in this statement.[30] He knows perfectly well that his *apologia* for capitalist freedom are in practice justifications of existing, large-scale finance-capital.

It is all very well to say that 'capitalism is now the revolutionary cause', as Powell does. The English masses are not likely to see their destiny there – on the contrary. What odd naïveté is it that prevents Powell from perceiving the vital necessity to any counter-revolution of disguising its true nature, of pretending to be some kind of revolt *against* capitalism? As regards the prejudices Powellism works on, its power is (as we noticed) limited. Now, in its central social doctrine, it seems to present an inexplicable weakness, and to be manifestly incapable of furnishing the void of English nationalism. Why is this?

The most convincing explanation may lie in the peculiar faults of English nationalism itself (I have tried to examine these more directly below, in Chapter 7). Powell has tried to reformulate a viable English nationalism single-handed. Although there are many roughly comparable episodes in modern history, it is doubtful if any other political intellectual has undertaken quite such a Sisyphus-like task. In these situations the would-be hero claims to be merely the mouth-piece of a buried force, and that this is moulding him. There is always some pretence in the act. Yet there is usually a reality, too, or else his charisma would invoke no response. But where – as in the England of the 1960s and early 1970s – a structural identity-defect impedes this nationalist response altogether, the

[30] See T. E. Utley, op. cit., pp. 117–29.

shaman is left in peculiar isolation. The historical situation does make the man, but in a less flattering sense than the one he desires. In this case, it has deprived him of the effective, shaping pressures that his fantasy needed to become reality. Those pressures would have washed away his pro-capitalist naïveté. In their absence all his mono-maniac features – his slightly crazy rigidity, the taste for abstractions like monetarism, etc. – have become amplified. Reality itself should have ironed out his contradictions; but it has (so far) failed to rise to the occasion.

Powell's persistence along this track is all the more bizarre in the light of the implicit alliance with parts of the Labour Party which he has consciously cultivated for some years. In the anti-Common Market crusade he discovered that the Labour Left was closer to his heart than the Conservatism of Edward Heath. His recommendations to vote Labour in 1974 did more than anything else to arouse Tory anger and despair of him, and forced his exit from the party. This clear identification of Labour as the more national-minded of the ruling parties ought to have made him reconsider the capitalist chapters of his *Weltanschauung*. Yet he does not appear to have done so. On these matters he still occasionally grinds out the same old text-book homilies and Friedmannite nostrums, from an ever-deeper political loneliness.

6. English Authoritarianism

> Oh that this dull necessity
> And mastering force of sanity,
> This too strong texture of the mind
> That keeps me by its toils confined
>   In the world's badness,
> Would break at last and set me free
> Into the sunlit, halcyon sea
>   Of madness.
>
> (Enoch Powell, Poem XXI, *Dancer's End*)

The central problem of Powellism arises mainly from asking the wrong questions about the phenomenon – from considering Powell, his Conservative Party backwoodsmen, and his potential mass following as a tendency, or even a movement. Then one must ask what this movement may tend towards, and the question of 'fascism' inevitably arises.

Nothing could obscure the real issues more. In England, even the home-grown fascism of Mosley or the National Front is largely a distraction. The genuine right – and the genuine threat it represents – are of quite a different character. One of the few things in politics that may be confidently predicted is that J. Enoch Powell will never lead a column of blue-shirts into Parliament Square.

The ideological weaknesses and absurdities of Powellism matter little, simply because *in itself* it probably tends towards nothing at all. It is not, and probably never will be, a 'movement' in that sense. However, unlike English fascism, it is certainly not a distraction. It is, on the contrary, directly linked linked to and expressive of profounder changes of the utmost gravity. Intellectually – or in terms of the history of right-wing ideas – Powell may be negligible. This does not remove his political significance in the least.

Powellism is a symptom: the true threat lies in the developing disease of which it is a symptom. Powell has emerged apparently as an active challenge to the existing political consensus from the right. In fact, he and his repercussions are symptomatic of the growing paralysis and deterioration of the consensus itself. There *is* a national insanity in the air, but it did not originate in Powell's second-rate ruminations. It is located squarely in the mainstream of English politics and – beyond that – in the harsh contradictions of English capitalism which the political consensus has been struggling with in vain for a quarter of a century.

Powell – as we saw – attributes the chronic crisis and historical loss of nerve of the English governing class to *consciousness*. It has fallen foul of unfortunate myths, and acquired a false self-consciousness – whence its dithering, its narcissistic isolation from reality, its feeble losing battle against economic crisis. The truth is the opposite. The continuity of England's incredible myth-consciousness, and her political decay, are the products of a material history – the shrinking material basis of an imperialist order still trapped in its own historical contradictions. And Powellism, the would-be trumpet-blast to cleanse the national mind, is only a belated echo of this decline. Its importance is, precisely, that it enables us to perceive just how advanced the rot has become.

Powell's pathetic nationalist demagoguery can reverberate only within this peculiar environment of decay and isolation. Somewhat earlier in the history of his nation he would have passed unnoticed, an obscure classicist and political conformist glumly turning over his own garden. Yet now this fossil epitome of Old England looms across the national scene, a mushrooming caricature of patriotic destiny. European nationalism generally has assumed new shapes – not least in the British Isles. But England has become culturally and politically isolated, imprisoned within her dying imperialism, and here this archaic development can still have an impact. It can work upon the submerged nationalism of the English, trying at least to give a reactionary content to its uncertainty, and appeal to the (perfectly justified) national feeling of frustration and anger. Because this feeling is so inarticulate, and so divorced from the genteel clichés of the Establishment, the New Right can, at least, suggest convincingly that something is profoundly wrong and that something must be done about it, in a partly familiar idiom.

Yet what purchase it has is due to the fissure which has, slowly, opened up in the traditional mode of hegemony. The political Establishment has begun to lose its old grip on the nation, and on the masses. It has – so to speak – started to shrink out of contact with the social realities over which, traditionally, it exerted an all-embracing and conservative control. It is only from this new fissure in the socio-political structure that the stale fungus of Powellism has been able to sprout, so rapidly and with such effect. Where else could such mothballed platitudes resound so strongly, where else could fusty junk like Powell's produce quite such a sensation? Where, but in the stagnant, involuted atmosphere of a world near the end of its tether?

Because the political consensus lies within the area of rot, Powell understood intuitively from his solitude that it was necessary to go beyond and outside it, although it took him many years of groping to discover the way. Then, the new phenomenon of domestic racism – outside the grip of traditional hegemony *because* novel – suddenly disclosed the fracture which he needed. His destiny-fantasy at once acquired some leverage upon reality. This particular social problem has (as we noticed above) limits of exploitability, as does the Irish question to which Powell has now turned. But both are, nevertheless, deep running sores which the present English body politic can probably no longer cure. By thrusting a knife into them, Powell can quickly aggravate the patient's general condition; he already has.

It goes without saying that Powell, wrapped as ever in his conservative fetishism, does this in the hope of re-injecting life into the old political machine. He piously imagines that his words will send fresh red blood racing through the arteries of Westminster. It has probably never occurred to him that these aged organs may not be able to take the strain. He has often remarked, in his usual awed fashion, upon the amazing continuity which has characterized English political life in the past. He believes he is part of this continuity, engaged on giving it the new national basis it needs. It has never crossed his mind that he might be killing it. Yet there can be little doubt that this is the meaning of the astonishing spectacle that has begun to unfold itself: in Powellism, the English conservative Establishment has begun to destroy itself. Its secular hegemony has come to this: a solitary figure, solemnly and self-consciously identified with every fibre of the glorious past, who is nevertheless compelled to devour the patrimony he worships. His importance – and his seriousness as a phenomenon and as a political figure – is not intrinsic, but rather in his relationship to this wider process. It lies in his function as a ferment of disaggregation within a deeper contradictory movement. It is the logic of this movement that has carried him to where he is, and forced him to destroy his own idols.

To the left, absorbed in its own problems and the effect it is (or is not) having upon the social order, it comes as a surprise that this order should have begun to collapse in a different direction altogether. Now that Powellism has happened, however, the lines of force leading towards this result at least become more clear.

They radiate out from the underlying situation of stalemate, or irresolvable contradiction, in which British capitalism has been lodged since early in the century. This is not the place to try and analyze at length the main causes and features of the condition, or to distinguish specifically British traits from those which have also affected other capitalist States. In essence, the 'disease' is no more than the peculiar nature of British imperialism, or the complex of foreign and financial interests which the bourgeoisie acquired in its earlier development, which it preferred to the development of its domestic economy, and which – latterly – it has only been able to retain and develop *at the expense of* that economy. This contradiction has manifested itself in an 'economic crisis' lasting more than 20 years. It has become the near-exclusive concern of government in this period. Everything else has been made to depend on it. According to the time of year and the stage each politico-economic cycle has reached, the perennial British crisis is 'growing', 'grave', 'very grave', 'on the mend', 'looking up', 'turning the corner' or 'finally on the verge of solution'.

Throughout this period, both great political parties have accepted the same definition of the 'economic crisis', and struggled hopelessly to resolve it in the same ways (the Labour Party perhaps somewhat more consistently than the Conservatives). Since the definition was superficial and mythical (a genuinely 'bad myth' in Powell's sense) and the remedies were and are only palliatives, the result has been a staple political diet of boredom and irrelevance, incomprehensible to most of the population. For practical purposes, the national soul has been the Bank of England for two decades, and political life has been tied entirely to a number of economists' fetishes ('the Pound', the 'balance of payments', 'Britain's reserves', etc.) in the name of political realism and common sense. It is not surprising that the natives have become deeply, angrily, inarticulately restless.

What is surprising is that they have taken so long to react. During this era of decline and attrition, the political consensus has lost much of its earlier vitality. It was not designed for conditions like these – the two-party system and the English constitutional machine assumed their contemporary form, in fact, within the successful economic empire whose remains they have been wrestling to defend. Then it ensured mass adhesion and averted class conflict in much easier circumstances. In the last ditch where the political Establishment has now been labouring for so long, it has shrunk into a parody of its former self. Originally it functioned by securing a consensus around great national ideas and policies; since there have been no such ideas since 1945, it has had simply to avoid social conflict at any cost. 'Consensus' has become something like paralysis.

It is in this feeble, palsied world that Powellism can arise and produce its effect – it refuses to play the (debased) 'game' of consensus politics, and actively stirs up conflict instead of conspiring to stifle or ignore it. Talk of Powellite 'fascism' or of 'Tory counter-revolution' wilfully ignores the real conditions under which Powell and racism obtained their remarkable leverage over the system. The fact is, that there has been no 'revolution' to provoke the wave of reaction. It is true that at the same time as Powell has emerged there has been the beginnings of a challenge from the left: the nascent student movement, People's Democracy in Northern Ireland, and a rising tide of strikes.

That period of militancy culminated, and ended, in the winter of 1974. The climax of the mineworkers' strike and the defeat of the Heath government was followed by nearly three years of relapse into Labour-led 'consensus'. Economic depression provided the climate for both the Social Contract and a steadily-rising tide of reactionary thought and sentiment. The working class – contrary to so many predictions of the 1960s – lent its support to Labour's attempt at salvaging the old state. Behind this futile gesture, the economic and political crisis of the system continued to mature. Its temporary reprieve on the social front was annulled by the new challenges from Scotland and Wales. What would its situation be when – as will shortly happen – it was faced by both threats together? Not even the IMF will shore up a state undermined by nationalist secessions (one of which intends to take the chief assets with it) *and* social revolt against falling living standards. At some point, the rest of the capitalist world will simply be compelled to declare 'enough is enough', no matter what the consequences of British bankruptcy and upheaval.

Powell sits in unsplendid isolation, awaiting this day. It is his only hope. His career to date has been one of accelerating failure, a self-chosen voyage to outer darkness without precedent in recent politics. From there, he broods on each evidence of disintegration and collapse, every sign of Labour scission and Tory discomfiture, hoping that in the coming trauma the call will finally, unmistakably be heard. Amid the fragments of demolished glory, the 'blackened ruins', his sins and contradictions will be forgiven him. Still aware of his stature in spite of his tragi-comic mishaps, an English people will turn to this unmistakable native symbol. Around him the nationalists in all the old parties will reform an authentic 'National Government' of recovery – no mere coalition, but a new régime like de Gaulle's, presenting itself as the valid recreation of sacred traditions.

In that case, it would be seen that he was merely before his time. He produced the idea – and gave it an exaggeratedly racist definition – before the reality of England was ready, before the British *ancien régime* had sufficiently decayed. In the later phases of that fall, amidst the rapid changes forced by peripheral and class struggles, his moment could still arrive.

7. The English Enigma

Smile at us, pay us, pass us; but do
   not quite forget.
For we are the people of England, that never
   have spoken yet.
                                    G. K. Chesterton, *The Secret People*

Weston Park is one idea of England. A Tudor country-house, over-laid but not ruined by the fashions and follies of many later genera-tions, it lies comfortably in a fold of the Sussex Downs. On the southward exposure its great gardens settle through informal steps, flagged walks and topiary hedges into a wooded ridge screen-ing the bungalow-scrabble two miles away. Behind, Chanctonbury Ring gives a false impression of timelessness to the skyline.

This is not simply the Foreign Office view of English values. Weston Park belongs, as a matter of fact, to the Foreign Office. The outbuildings have been tastefully converted in a traditional style for foreign guests. *Préfets*, *Bürgermeister* and minor Eurocrats toast their feet at the log fires in the library. Outside, it is Junior Congressmen and *Deputati* who are being taught croquet on the lawn. In the Victorian dining-hall the Atlantic Alliance is fortified by claret, although the deplorable acoustics (not always unfortun-ately) make conversation difficult.

First used as a centre for re-educating captured German officers towards the end of World War II, the estate was turned by the F.O. into a permanent university of the British Way. Injections take place over periods of a week or so, under labels like 'The EEC and NATO: emergent problems', or 'Workers and Managers: towards fruitful relations'. These frank and civilized discussions are chaired by the House-master, a choleric German Tory. Under him a team of decent chaps smooths out the small snags of communal existence. Beneath them again, numbrous servants occupy their station with well-timed flashes of sardonic popular wit. There is even a 'pub' in a converted wash-house where, with suitable excitement and pleading, the guests are allowed to drink after hours.

Although never quite understanding it, the foreigners are in this way squeezed through a ten-day time-capsule equivalent of English education. While their minds focus on the Great Issues of the printed programme, England is quietly being sold them. Basking in her security, the middle-rank parliamentarians and officialdom of the Atlantic area can hardly avoid at least a twinge of those profound, infantile sensations of gratitude which hold the house up. Long after the debates are forgotten, one can see how this respectful feeling of 'England' will remain.

This is not idle speculation. There exists, in fact, an Old Boys' Association of Weston Park, with a tie, a coat-of-arms and re-unions. Its magazine *Friends of Weston* circulates quite widely over a new and synthetic British empire.

At one such conference ('The Problem of Identity: Region or Nation?') a Frenchman raised the question of English nationalism. There had been some talk of Corsica and General de Gaulle. Why, he demanded, did the English think they were immune from these questions?

There is no doubt they do. On this occasion the usual excuses and speculations were paraded. Unlike their Celtic fringe, the English are too vague and mixed-up to fit a nationalist stereotype. Nobody knows what an 'Englishman' is, in that sense. The standard jokes about 'An Englishman, an Irishman . . . etc.' juxtapose three racial clichés to an undefined (and hence superior) centre. Too internally differentiated for the vulgar measurements of nationalism, the English then spread themselves too far externally. Empire diluted the imponderable essence even farther, to the point where recapture has become impossible. This is why there is no national dress, an obscure and unresurrected folklore, and a faltering iconography ('John Bull', etc.).

Deep puzzlement was caused by these remarks. The guests were aware of being enclosed in one of the strongest, most distinctive identities of modern history. They were there to be impressed by its 'way of life'. There was even less doubt about the hosts busy deprecating their strange absence of nationalism, with such intolerable suppressed superiority: *echt* Englanders to a man. Later on, expeditions were planned to Westminster, Oxford and the other national shrines.

So the absence of nationalism was plainly a myth – some kind of counter-myth, presumably, set against the majestic body of customs and symbols displayed at Weston Park? But why? The crux of the problem lies in the uneasy truth which is there somewhere. The identity on display – one might say offensively, often obsessionally on display – in England *is* somehow different from the standards of modern nationalism.

To take only the nearest, most obvious contrast (the comparison was made at Weston Park) there are in the periphery of the British Isles three relatively ordinary examples of modern political nationality. Differing greatly among themselves, the national characters and movements of Ireland, Wales and Scotland can none the less be compared to standard cases elsewhere. This is why the jokes work. These marginal folk are more easily summed up in typifying commonplaces. The thinner atmosphere out there invites generalization. They behave more predictably (and so more humourously) like Slav enthusiasts, Jews, Basques, Bavarians, or the 'natives' who have constituted the nationalisms of the Third World.

Somehow, the English are different.

It is no answer to the puzzle, either, to point at England's racism. Nobody who has studied recent political history in the country will under-estimate the force or the significance of this factor. Yet it is not so easy to characterize.

'We were just completely shocked numb. It was predictable in so many ways and yet still quite shocking. You suddenly realized how little influence the Left really had, how the roots of the political organizations . . . had been rotting in the soil . . . It did more to me than the May events and Czechoslovakia rolled into one'. So writes David Widgery in his compilation of British ultra-left history, *The Left in Britain 1956–1968*. The event was the London dockers' march in support of Enoch Powell.

The common tendency is to amalgamate these phenomena to an English (or British) nationalism, or popular 'chauvinism'. Then the step is short to saying (or at any rate feeling) that this is the reality of society. The famous apparatus of constitutional liberties is a hypocritical sham; underneath it, here is what an imperialist people is really like.

Hence that familiar paralysis of views so often encountered in political England. On the one hand, disenchantment with 'the system', and recognition that the Labour Party was long ago irretrievably compromized by Weston Park; but on the other, a dismal sensation that the raw reality beyond the old order may be worse. In between, nothing except powerless utopian sects. Jokes or apocalyptic forebodings are the standard ways out of the cloud which often settles at this point.

There is something wrong with the logic. And the mistake is probably in the ascription of racist sentiment to an undefined mass 'nationalism'. It is much more the symptom of *an absence of* popular nationalism among the English. There is no coherent, sufficiently democratic myth of Englishness – no sufficiently accessible and popular myth-identity where mass discontents can find a vehicle. This is the source of the disconcerting lurch from a semi-divine Constitution and the Mother of Parliaments to the crudest racialism.

That this is so is illustrated by the career of Powell, as well as by the history of race-relations. His aim was the political redefinition of an English nationalism, along lines parallel to those of General de Gaulle. In this way, so he hoped, there would occur the long-awaited post-empire crisis and renaissance. Although personally equipped with the attributes of a nationalist demagogue, he found the task immensely harder than anyone imagined. The obstacle was an objective one. It lay in the fact that those rich English traditions he wanted to make ferment again are quite unadapted *to this sort of mobilization*. An element is absent from them; the catalysis does not take place.

It is this missing factor that explains the precipitous descent into racism. Failing to meet and fertilize a latent myth-body, his restless ego was impelled into darker (and ultimately hopeless) shores. All the surrogates he found were in the direst contradiction to his main search: the lunacies of Friedmannite monetary economics and an abstract reverence for pure capitalism; the wild belief that a route back to his goal might emerge from the dilemmas of Ulster Protestants; and the potential fascism of the anti-immigrant movements. The wanderings of this deranged Ishmael are so many paths round an absence.

What is this absence? The fact is that a mobilizable nationalism is not only a matter of having common traditions, revered institutions, or a rich community of customs and reflexes. England has more of all these than almost anywhere else. But then, so did feudal societies; so did slumbering despotisms which had never heard of democracy or the national state.

National-ism in the relevant sense is not a question of simple 'identity' (as is often thought). Being different from others, having a recognizable and articulate physiognomy, are necessary but never sufficient conditions of its development. The sufficient condition, the catalyst, is something more. And this something is precluded by the main characters of English history since 1688 – precluded, above all, by those features of which English ideology is most convinced and proud, her constitutional and parliamentary evolution.

The mobilizing myth of nationalism is an idea of the people. This must not be confused with an abstract concept of – for example – the virtue of The Working Class. It has to be a concrete, emotive notion anchored in popular experience or lore. This idea depicts the (supposedly) self-initiated action of the people: the Revolution, the Overthrow of Foreign Oppression, the War of Liberation (and so on).

It is of no importance that these actual events never happened as the mythology pictures them – that, for instance, only a minuscule part of the population actually took part in The Rising while the slightly larger number who knew of it stayed at home wagering on the result. What counts is the later mass beliefs. These are amplified into an inheritance, broadcast in ballads, written into elementary history text-books, novelized, sermonized, and institutionalized into street-names and statues. From the process there derives an always-latent conviction of popular will and capacity. The People could always do it again.

This is how the modern political principle of nationality works. It has little to do with democracy, as such. The French and American variants are strongly democratic in origin; the German and Italian are not. Representative or party-political democracy is only one way of conceiving the people-principle: there are myths of blood and spirit, as well as those descended from the Enlightenment. Populism is of its essence, while parliamentarism is decidedly not. Under the modern conditions that have prevailed since the French Revolution, reactionaries and progressives alike are forced to embrace some myth of the forceful entry of the masses into history.

So nearly all the modern nations have such a myth, the key to their 'nationalism', and the common source of their political upheavals and regeneration. England does not possess one. 'Modern conditions', in the pertinent sense, have never reached her. This is certainly one of the explanations of the astonishing resistance of a fossilized and incompetent political order, through thirty years of imperial defeat and economic degeneration. Were there an alternative in the sub-strata of that system, it would surely long ago have been summoned up to action.

In England 'modern conditions' were effectively reversed. The standard myth-pattern corresponding to modernity has been put on its head. The dominant *Gestalt* of political England is patrician, not popular: it perceives a grateful People, allowed to advance after making the proper representations at Weston Park.

Of course, this mythology is as false as many of its nationalist counterparts. As a matter of fact, the English people achieved the first great, forceful intrusion of the masses in modern times, during the Civil Wars of the 1640s. This event made 'modern times' possible. But the long, successful counter-revolution of the propertied classes obliterated the ideological potential of that upheaval, and substituted another.

Thus, England benefited from a great Revolution and – alone in this – contrived to suppress and eliminate the mythic side-effects. Through this inversion, her Totem became the contrary of populism. Not the self-action of the *Volk*, but the inexhaustible wisdom of Institutions and their custodians; not a belief that the People can do anything, in the last resort, but the conviction that popular aspirations will always, in the end, be attended to *up there*.

The concluding act of the English Revolution in 1688 established a pre-democratic constitutional state. This is the patrician machine which still exists and functions almost three centuries later. In the first half of this century, it bent universal suffrage into its own shape in the form of the British Labour Party: élitist, undemocratic, relic-worshipping, and gradualist. Not 'moderate' by bitter experiences of revolution and betrayal: moderate by obsequious and deeply-rooted national principle.

1789 and the other upheavals which constituted the contemporary nations of the world were all immoderate. They were in the name of abstract principles whose logic demanded immoderation: it was no use being half-heartedly in favour of Equality, Liberty or the People. But in England, mercifully, the great turnabout had occurred before these dangerous principles and myths were formulated. The ruling caste of the country and counting-houses instilled an insular counter-myth which most English democrats and socialists still believe: moderate, reasonable passion for Equality (and the other modern icons) achieves results. Let the fair case be put: a team of decent chaps up there will do the possible. The system may need a shove now and then; but They will always end by a compromise with Us.

So those phoney excuses proffered at Weston Park come down to this. Some vital elements in the modern principle of political nationality are diminished, or lacking in England. These relate to the populist side of nationalism, and affect the ability of left and right alike to inspire mass mobilization against the old state-system (it is of course in this context that the 'stereotypes' referred to usually get their importance).

Historically, the inward lack corresponded to an outward presence: it can be explained by the fortunate place England occupied in the world's political economy after 1688. The fact is that this role was so prominent and imperial for so long, that bourgeois society required no farther drastic transformations for over two centuries. The patrician political state and *mores* became permanent: an odd, transitional form petrified by primary and external success. The modern principle of political transformation (nationalism) was haltingly evolved everywhere else, until it became near-universal. For everywhere else was compelled to somehow react against the successful offensive of English commerce and empire (and later on, against the crusades of her imperialist rivals).

That principle will return to England, after this prolonged global detour and development. But it does so against great conservative resistances, which have survived the disappearance of imperial good luck. During imperialism, the English political world compensated to a certain degree for its static and hierarchic nature by successful external mobilization: aggression or defence against securely foreign enemies. But this substitute and its myth-deposits are fairly useless now. Neither England's immigrant population nor the Common Market were external foes in that hallowed sense (although a lot of steam has gone into the pretence that they are).

Now mainly sustained by Labourism, the English political universe is liberal, not democratic; constitutional, not populist; conservative, not radical in either a right-wing or a left-wing sense. It is probably the strongest national-political order of modern times; but this is a strength purchased at a specific and inadequately-understood cost. As the good fortune of the system has drained away, the cost has become crushing.

Patrician *grandeur* is incompatible with modern nationalism. The stronger it is, the greater is the contradiction. Where it has been buttressed by successful imperialism as well as by domestic culture, the resultant fixity is overwhelming. The illusion that this system can persist for ever, in unending accommodation, is absolute: the only absolute of English politics.

The Great-British state has been compatible – of course – with an overweening sense of superiority over other peoples. But one has to be careful here: whether institutional or racial in content, such vanity is not the same thing as vulgar nationalism. It covers the same range of objects as an English nationalism would, but does not arrange them in the same way or derive out of them an effective populist message. Just the opposite: it suppresses any hint of such a message, in spite of its grossness, bragging, foreigner-hating, and 'insularity'. The myth it always turns on is that of the British war film: a race of heroes who know their place, and tug their forelocks all the way to Hell and back.

The inner political nervelessness of Great-British chest-beating is what disqualifies it as 'nationalism'. It is this inertia which has become fatal to the system in its latter days. Open to endless tinkering, the evolutionary miracles of Constitution and Parliament cannot alter their own nature. In response to growing disasters – economic collapse, bankruptcy, the class struggles of 1968–74, Ireland, peripheral nationalism – the patrician state can only become more itself. After Heath had been jolted out of power by the miners' strike, the result was not a political struggle destructive of the state: it was a non-struggle, restorative of the state, in which all three parties united in a campaign of univocal moderation.

The contradiction between the form of the United Kingdom state and any would-be English nationalism can be resumed in a word: class. This is a state which has always intimately depended upon a hierarchical and élite social formation: as many recent studies have demonstrated, that dependence has been modified but never abolished. But as as an effective mobilizing myth nationalism relies entirely on a semblance of classlessness: equality in spirit, belief, blood, or whatever.

In England, that appearance is unattainable without a radical *political* break. That is, without a radical reform of the state and government amounting to revolution. The usual tenor of political debate in England inverts this concept. While in many countries political arguments always end by blaming the state, the English always blame society: debate on politics invariably becomes discussion of economics. This is felt to be sober island realism. Salvation lies with a better balance-of-payments and more moderate trade-union demands.

Wrong in so much, Powell was never mistaken on this point. Real English recovery depends on profound alteration of the inner political climate. But that is not possible while the old, rotting political constitution endures. Without such a change, however, the economic formulae and tactics occupying 90% of English political thinking are still-born: they will return to a dead centre of inertia. This has always been obscurely acknowledged in government appeals to Dunkirk spirits and ghostly 'teams' rowing in unison: the tribute of patrician vice to a missing nationalist virtue.

Both right and left have paid this tribute, and been sunk by it. The left, in particular, in its breast-thumping campaigns against the Common Market, committed two mistakes compounded from a third. A year after the EEC referendum – with the system back at inertia-point – it was submerged in impotence, everywhere but in Scotland. The 'national independence' of the Anti-EEC movement w.'s that of the Union Jack. It reflected a vestigial imperial patriotism close to expiry, not a new image of England. Thus might the Viennese social-democrats have defended Austria-Hungary – had it survived long enough – against a Danubian Common Market. Surely our Slavs see the point of the Hapsburg Road to Socialism!

With infallible aim, the Great-Briton illusion was then anchored to the most hopeless side of Vienna–London: the Ark itself, our Ancient Liberties, Two-Party System, Speaker, Monarch and metaphysical Sovereignty. Let these remain untouched by Balkan hands. A little more public ownership and enterprise and they will flower into Windsor Socialism. Confronted by this promise the Britons voted, mercifully, for Europe. They may have had little idea of what they were saying 'yes' to. Surely they knew what they were refusing.

The wish was that a noble and puissant left-wing nation would rouse herself like a strong man after sleep. But to have a leftish nationalism one requires the conditions of nationalism *tout court*. These conditions are annulled by the constitutional grovelling endemic to Labourism. For what is deferred to is a tri-secular caste state rooted – as the tri-secular instinct of the English people knows perfectly – in non-egalitarian, proprietorial ways. Save Our Parliament was a slogan for mass sedation, not mass mobilization. No wonder the strong man scarcely stirred.

A number of factors incline most commentators to foresee a reactionary resolution of the English enigma. The sheer social conservatism which sustains the Weston Park state; the Labour Party's deep complicity in the whole ancient system; the uncertain, ominous presence of Powell and a vocal racist Right; the abstraction and impotence of radical or revolutionary opposition, ranging from the Liberal Party to the Marxist groupings. Even at its gentlest and most liberal – so the argument runs – this remains a basically Tory society, cast in a stratified and deferential mould, too anchored in archaism ever to free itself by spontaneous effort or reform.

Hence, the break can only be more or less disastrous in nature. Only the combined pressures of external collapse (e.g. the break-down of the currency) and internal upheaval (whether as nationalist or as social revolt, or the two at once) will be enough to unseat this resistant system. The resultant emergency régime will confront an accumulation of problems – far more, far more serious, than those of the 'National Governments' in the 1930s. Drastic action will have to be taken immediately, against foreign creditors, against the Scots and the Welsh (possibly in Ulster as well), and against the organized working class. Since there is no left-wing movement or coalition able to undertake it, an improvized right-wing one will. This 'Gaullism', while of course manipulating the symbols of tradition and extolling the ancient virtues, will be forced to go beyond a transitional, or 'caretaker' role. It will desert the sacred continuities even as it hymns them.

Its principal purpose is laid down in advance: the forcible, break-neck achievement of that successful modernization which has eluded all United Kingdom governments in this century (except in time of war). For this, a new constitution and state are needed (even if they retain some vestments of the old). As in France, it is arguable that effective modern capitalism always required a second revolution: this will be that long-awaited 'revolution from above'. As in General de Gaulle's France it will be accompanied by a wave (in the English case one must say almost by the invention) of popular chauvinism, encouraging the rejection of that deepening sense of inferiority and defeat which has coloured the last two decades.

But whereas the French transformation occurred during an epoch of general capitalist expansion, while the European Economic Community was being formed, this English equivalent of Gaullism will experience an era of depression. Like everything else, this renaissance will be too late. The Common Market is in growing difficulties, whether or not it embraces some new members in the 1970s and 1980s. The General inherited a still united French territory, where neo-nationalism was politically invisible. His English successor will take over a realm already far on the road to disintegration. He will confront the real likelihood (it may be already the fact) of a land and sea frontier threatening to come between the new English state and its main economic asset in the world's eyes: North Sea oil. Internally, the 'strongest, most united trade union movement in Europe', which propped up the old régime's last years through the mid-70s 'Social Contract', will most probably be in open disaffection. To counter this, the new strong men will be driven to mobilize popular support separately, and nationalism will be the main vehicle for the effort: more specifically, a renascent 'great-nation' ideology directed against small-nation treachery and pretentions. Together with the anti-minority feeling already fostered by racism, this will furnish enough mobilizing energy (though of course other foreign perils may exist, or be whipped up in the campaign).

If Weston Park survives the alteration, there will be much less of that bland, superior puzzlement about English identity in a few years time. For England will have become a nation like the rest: belatedly, probably painfully, still retaining all sorts of garbled universal-mission ideas (like the French), but at bottom quite simply. In time, the rest of us will learn to live with the result, which will have some compensations as well as its bitterness and ultra-nationalist follies. So will the English themselves, severed at last from the internal and external burdens of their empire.

Modern methods of aerial survey can detect ancient foundations and sites located beneath recent roads and fields: shadow-plans visible only at this great distance. As I argued above (Chapter 1) the contemporary crisis of the British state reveals such an ancestral design in its heart: approaching its dissolution, the primal pattern becomes unexpectedly clear. This is the key nexus which must be definitively undone by whatever political upheaval descends on England.

'The English doctrine of the absolute, arbitrary, illimitable sovereignty of Parliament, born in the 17th century, carried into the new Parliament of the Union and reaching its full preposterous stature in the Victorian age, still holds', wrote Neal Ascherson in a telling comment on recent discussions of reform.[1] The transitional bourgeois state retained at its core certain features of the *real* 'ancien régime', absolutism. While continually adapting and modifying these in its long voyage into modern times, it never discarded them: its great boast, and (ultimately) its great failing. 'Great political changes follow changes in the way society produces and earns and consumes', he goes on, 'But the condition of institutions may decide whether those changes come easily or with agony. The absolutism of Parliament has become as much a Leviathan as the absolute right of kings, because it has prevented the emergence in Britain of the doctrine of popular sovereignty as the true source of power. Scotland before the Union never admitted the divine right of Parliaments, any more than modern European states do. But in Britain, the political peasants still wait for their charter . . .' Thus, devolution was conceived as a charitable dispensation within that absolutism: through it, the Crown in Parliament Assembled awarded certain powers and functions to some among Its subjects, and retained Its general lordship over them all. The immigrant minority, the Scots and Welsh perceive this as the power of the English people over them; the archaic Constitutional myth sees only the Sovereignty of Parliament. For its upholders, notes the same writer, 'Imagining a House of Commons which was limited, which could be defied, was as impossible . . . as imagining the world the morning after one's own death'.

The morning after death need not be as grim as the triumph-of-

---

[1] *The Scotsman*, Edinburgh, Feb. 18th, 1977. He was commenting on a Rowntree Trust conference on the 'Future of Parliament', devoted to imagining political changes needed to cope with the nationalist and other crises.

reaction argument states. It foresees an English iron age of belated, and hence draconian, capitalist restoration. In reality what is foreseeable is a contest. While at this time the forces and moods of the Right are stronger, the opposition is not negligible. A new grouping of right-wing forces may try to impose the conditions of the change; but new groupings of left-wing forces will also be possible once Leviathan has foundered, and taken down Labourism with it. There will be a new left-nationalism, as well as the rightist variety that figures so prominently in the forecasters' minds. The concept of 'Tory England' is also a myth.

From the late 1950s onwards there has emerged – at the same time as racism, Powellism, and the chain of governmental debacles – a gathering movement of historical revision and socialist culture. Much wider, and deeper, than the spectrum of organized left-wing bodies, this tendency extends in influence from Labour and even Young Liberalism to the different Communist parties and embraces many 'non-aligned' intellectuals. It was originally associated with the early phases of *New Left Review* and the Campaign for Nuclear Disarmament, and its major intellectual inspiration has arisen from the work of Edward Thompson (above all *The Making of the English Working Class*) and Raymond Williams (above all *Culture and Society*). In the 1960s it expanded on to the scale of a national movement, above all through the influence of Raphael Samuel's 'History Workshops' in Ruskin College, Oxford. Expressed in the Workshop's *Journal* and many other publications, this seminal movement has fostered a new general culture and outlook to some extent balancing the simultaneous growth of sectarian Marxism in England.

The kernel of the movement was from the start 'history from below'. I noted previously the quite distinctive problems this concept faces in the historical context of the Anglo–British state. But of course it is just these problems which have constituted the legitimate raison d'être of the movement itself. Intellectual opposition to such an essentially non-populist structure, to a tradition so overwhelmingly 'from above', must necessarily lean very hard in the contrary direction. In the direction, that is, of eliciting every possible popular or mass contribution to the fabric of English development, emphasizing every discoverable heroism or neglected workers' initiative. The result is something like a collective, endless 'epic poem' of popular and radical achievement (to use the term

Edward Thompson employed in his earlier biography, *William Morris*).

As a broad intellectual and ideological trend, this has gone under the banner of populist socialism. Yet it is not difficult to perceive it in another perspective, deriving from the comparative history of national movements. All such movements have adopted analogous populist aims, and sought in a similar way to ascribe the nation's real or hidden history to folk initiative. Romantic excess and indiscriminate empiricism have also been common aspects of these schools. Making due allowance for the different circumstances of the British Isles (an established conservative state and culture, rather than a 'new nation' contesting alien dominance) it is possible to appreciate the common traits. Odd as it may seem, the deformation of Englishness by her state-history has generated a late but unmistakable variety of left-nationalist popular culture.

Equally naturally, this is a cultural nationalism which has not yet come to consciousness of its own nature and purpose. Hence it has remained closer to ideas of a rather undefined socialism, politically, rather than to ideas of England. But this may not be for long. It is none the less an English phenomenon, and the seed-bed of a national future being gestated by the decline of the old state-system every bit as much as Scottish or Welsh nationalism. To acknowledge it in this way is not to diminish its character. On the contrary, one can then detect a much more concrete hope in the British political future. The latter depends mainly on the English people. Here, in this progressive and generous cultural movement, they have at least part of what corresponds to the usual model of nationalist revival – the attempt to find strength for a better, more democratic future by re-examining (on occasion re-inventing) a mythic past. Marxism by itself could never furnish this, however important its intellectual and political contribution to the end-product.

To those who care for England and strive to see her free of the old harness, this hope is critical. It means there is a romanticism not infallibly Tory in its results, and a national-populism distinguishable from the habit of authority and the sink of deference. Much more than a scholarly rediscovery of *Volksgeist* is at stake. This rediscovery of the past is political contestation, as well as bookish populism. It restores the People to the liberal-constitutional universe of the patriciate, labouring to supply the data and conviction which popular mobilization against the old state will one day need.

Its centre of gravity lies in this future political process, where it may one day serve as a cultural bond between sectarian Marxism and a wider popular movement.

All this depends on some restoration of the English political identity, after centuries of Weston Park. The English revolution is the most important element in the general upheaval of British affairs described in this book. It is also the hardest to foresee, and will take longest to achieve. Upon its character – conservative-nationalist reaction or socialist advance – will depend the future political re-arrangement of the British Isles, as federation, confederation, or modernized multi-national state.

Post-script, February 23rd, 1977. At the moment of going to press, the failure of the Labour government's Devolution Bill in the House of Commons has rendered the break-up of Britain more imminent, and its form more predictable. The collapse of a negotiated, gradualist solution will drive the Welsh and Scottish national movements into sharper opposition to the state. The state will be riven and dragged down by the additional burden of this debacle, and it seems improbable that the old party-political system will re-emerge from the crisis. In this sea of troubles, the end of Leviathan will almost certainly come about with agony, rather than easily.

8. Supra-Nationalism
and Europe

All students of the subject soon become aware of one important fact: the monumental sterility, pretension and evasiveness of most theoretical discussion of the European Community. This is the topic upon which modern 'political science' has concentrated much of its effort, and done its very worst.[1]

There is one great exception to this rule of abstraction and banality, one work by a European professor which – even though still couched in terms of abstract social science – nevertheless propounds an intelligible historical and political thesis about the Common Market. This study locates the last twenty years of Western European history in a larger historical and developmental perspective. It relates that history to the grand themes of imperialism and anti-imperialist struggle in modern times. And it takes up a definite, provocative and highly stimulating political stance to-

[1] Most of it fulfils Alfred Cobban's description of political science as mostly a device for avoiding politics without achieving science'. See 'The Decline of Political Theory' in *Political Science Quarterly*, vol. LXVIII No. 3 (Sept. 1953). This is no place to explore the ferro-concrete avenues of Pluralism, Functionalism, Neo-Functionalism and Federalism; a competent town-plan can be found in (e.g.) Charles Pentland's *International Theory and European Integration* (1973). In his Preface the author says with great accuracy that 'the prevalent state of mind among students of integration . . . is the feeling that this literature lacks theme, pattern and direction', (p. 11). Another leading integration theorist has written, more movingly: 'As a contributor to the European integration literature I have more and more come to feel as if I were excavating a small, isolated portion of a large, dimly-perceived mass, the contours of which I could not make out . . .' L. N. Lindberg, *Journal of Common Market Studies*, vol. 5 no. 4 (1967), p. 345. The novelty of many aspects of the EEC, plus the absence of a genuine 'European' or cross-frontier intelligentsia, allowed American political science to invade and expand into somewhat monstrous forms. There are obvious analogies to other aspects of history here.

wards its subject – in fact, it is something like the Bible of those parts of the European Left hostile to the EEC.

For all these reasons, we must be grateful to Johan Galtung and his book *The European Community: A Superpower in the Making* (1973). It is an obligatory starting point for farther radical and critical approaches to the subject. Yet it is also very incomplete as a starting point, and – or so I shall go on to argue – this incompleteness leads to serious distortions in the picture of Europe which Galtung finally presents. And it is this conjunction of importance and error which makes it so important to consider the argument closely.

Galtung's leading contention is that in Common Market Europe 'a new superpower is emerging'. This may not always seem so, the author concedes at once. The difficulties and contradictions of its formation are – to put it mildly – as much in evidence as its successes, in an everyday, journalistic sense. However, we must not trust to such short-term views. This is the principal (and most valuable) methodological point Galtung holds to: proper understanding of what is happening in Western Europe requires a much longer and deeper historical perspective.

This larger view leads one to perceive the superpower's slow, if difficult, emergence. The European Community is no less than an attempt 'to recreate (1) a Eurocentric world, a world with its center in Europe, (2) a unicentric Europe, a Europe with its center in the West' (p. 12). The EEC stands therefore for a new imperialism. As the author goes on to state: 'Our thesis could also be formulated as saying that the community is an effort to turn history backwards, only adding a dimension of modern technology, a logical effort, easy to explain and foresee with elementary knowledge of Western European history and some social theory'. What is the formula? 'The basic formula for understanding the Community is: "Take five broken empires, add the sixth one later, and make one big neo-colonial empire out of it all"' (p. 16). The five broken empires: Germany, France, Italy, Belgium and the Netherlands; the sixth one is Great Britain, the largest, most recent and least repentant ex-imperialist of the whole gang.

The break-up and humiliation of these old great powers, during and after World War II, has led to this attempt at regeneration – to a difficult re-formation of ranks, as it were, and a renewed march to world power. The 'Market' aspect of this new Europe should not deceive us. It is meant to deal in 'power units more than in economic units alone. Hence an analysis of power is indispensable to understanding the European Community' (p. 17).

Such reborn power is to be exercised on the outside world – on Eastern Europe and the 'Third World' of less developed countries. Galtung is frankly preoccupied with these external relationships. They are what the process is really directed towards, and the 'neo-imperialism' which they amount to defines his concerns. As he says right at the start, the question that really matters is 'What does the European Community mean to the masses of the world, to the world proletariat? And what does it mean to the world community in general?' (Preface, p. 5). His main examination of EEC-Third World relationships (Ch. 6, pp. 68–85) leads him to the conclusion that the new empire is a continuation of the old. Uniformed, settler-and-soldier imperialism has of course given way to more veiled and economic modes of exploitation, and these were defined for the EEC by the Yaoundé Convention with 18 African states (1963). But the question remains: *What, then, has changed?* – essentially, that European countries now do collectively what they used to do singly and in competition regulated by the division of the world into empires, or "spheres of influence". As Nkrumah has pointed out, this is "collective colonialism"' (p. 73).

Although the critique deals with Yaoundé, it is easy to see that the author would extend it to the more recent, still more extensive, Lomé Convention (January 1975). The 46 states covered by the latter agreement have also been hoodwinked into collective neo-colonialism – into 'old policies pursued with new means. The old policies left these countries exploited, fragmented, and penetrated. There is nothing in the new joint policy so diametrically different that the result should be qualitatively different from what today's E.C. member countries obtained separately during the last centuries. On the contrary the giant size of the E.C. empire may make the struggle for equity even more difficult. Conclusion: trade with the E.C. is unavoidable. But *close* participation in this system is not in the interest of the less developed countries and should be avoided' (pp. 84–5).

The outlook is almost as bleak for Eastern Europe. Here the EEC's economic assault will, in conjunction with the crushing weight of the U.S.S.R., bring about ever greater dependency. The smaller Eastern states will be 'squeezed' more and more, until

'Europe becomes split in a much more fundamental manner than by the Cold War' (p. 97). Comecon will never develop into a comparable, valid association of states and peoples, able to resist the three lines of neo-imperialist attack: 'exploitation, fragmentation, and penetration'.

Not surprisingly, therefore, Galtung looks forward with some eagerness to the demise of the European Community. Although it will become a superpower, this power will not last long. Mercifully, certain 'counterforces' will arise against it and set the clock forward again. The main source for these forces is – again not surprisingly – the under-developed lands. The argument here is that a strong reaction from the Third World may be what will eventually save Western Europe from itself . . .' (p. 151). Its techniques of neo-colonial control will not prevent further social revolution in Africa and other parts of the Third World. It will not be able to win over its own youths to the European cause, since they are increasingly Third Worldist, anti-growth and anti-bureaucratic in outlook. Both externally and internally, the very expansion of the E.E.C. will generate counterwaves, of which the first was the Norwegian referendum in 1972 – the first important rebuff suffered by the European Community . . . Other such counterwaves will come', as the 'progressive forces and progressive countries' of the periphery, the radical, the outlying and the down-trodden learn to unite their efforts against the new imperial menace (pp. 157-9).

II

The impulse to this diagram of the E.E.C.'s significance came from Galtung's realization of the need for a larger historical perspective. But there is one immediate and very important qualification to be made. His impulse is wholly correct; but it does not go nearly far enough. He employs as principal reference points the recent imperialist past of Western Europe (approximately 19th–20th centuries, to 1945 or the 1950s), and the still more recent relationship with the 'Third World'. These are unquestionably key factors, which find a place in any intelligible interpretation of the E.E.C. Yet *in themselves* they are so inadequate as a basis for theory that the result is bound to be (at least) extremely one-sided.

A first clue to what may be missing is provided by a curious list of Europe's 'ideological powers' (p. 53). This is where Europe really has it over the U.S.A. and other competitors, the author claims, since 'in terms of . . . culture or ideology Western Europe has always remained the center of the world . . . and the cradle of the major ideologies of conservatism, liberalism, and marxism.' This exporting of ideas was indeed one of the natural functions of the older imperialisms. But there is an absent guest in the list: by far the most important and influential mass cultural by-product of 19th century Europe, eclipsing the other three in significance to this day.

Europe invented *nationalism*. So central was the diffusion of this commodity that one can (e.g.) show quite easily how the other cultural forms, conservatism, liberalism and marxism, were in practice exported always in association with it, or even in terms of it. Intra-European uneven development in the 19th century led to the formulation of nationalism, to this new and distinctive complex of political and philosophical notions – a complex both different from, and far more dynamic than, the older conceptions of nationality and state. Then the explosive outward surge of industrial-based capitalism carried it very rapidly to every part of the globe. Implanted by imperialism, it nevertheless became (just as it had previously done in Central and Eastern Europe, and in Latin America) the main vehicle of anti-imperialist struggle, the ideology of independent development.

This original formation of nationalism took many centuries. It is a process so deeply rooted in Europe's history – and above all in the western areas of the continent – that it is no mere cliché to say one hardly knows where to begin. In one recent study of early modern history Immanuel Wallerstein states that European development had 'a peculiarity that is the secret of its strength. This peculiarity is the political side of the form of economic organization called capitalism. Capitalism has been able to flourish precisely because the world-economy has had within its bounds not one but a multiplicity of political systems.'[2] It was this 'peculiarity' that made north-western Europe into the original 'core area' of the capitalist world-economy, the source of its devastating expansion.

The reason is that from the very start this process – the process which made the 'modern world' of industrialized development –

[2] I. Wallerstein, *The Modern World System: Capitalist Agriculture and the Origins of the European World-Economy* (1974), p. 348.

demanded competitive differentiation and inequalities. It rested upon a distinction between core areas and the 'periphery' (or 'semi-periphery') round about them. As the same author has said in another context: 'The key fact is that given slightly different starting points, the interests of various local groups converged in north-west Europe, leading to the development of strong state mechanisms, and diverged sharply in the peripheral areas, leading to very weak ones. Once we get a difference in the strength of the state-machineries, we get the operation of "unequal exchange" which is enforced by strong states on weak ones, by core states on peripheral areas. Thus capitalism involves . . . an appropriation of the surplus of the whole world-economy by core-areas. And this was as true in the stage of agricultural capitalism as it is in the stage of industrial capitalism.'[3] The process could never be started or kept up effectively within the older world-empires. Only a multiplicity of unequal political units allowed this 'unequal exchange', this appropriation of surplus, to expand towards the breakthrough of the industrial revolution. And European diversity provided the original conditions for it to get going.

Wallerstein relates the emergence of this modern state-system to the 16th century. But the story can be taken back even farther. In his *Lineages of the Absolutist State*, Perry Anderson describes how 'The haphazard multiplicity of political units in late mediaeval Europe became an organized and inter-connected state-system . . . a plural *set* of partners – for war, alliance, trade, marriage or propaganda – within a single political arena, whose bounds and rules became ever clearer and more definite. The cross-cultural fecundity that resulted from the formation of this highly integrated yet extremely diversified system was one of the peculiar hallmarks of pre-industrial Europe . . . No comparable set existed anywhere else in the world.'[4] He then goes on to argue that the emergence of this state-system of the Renaissance can only be explained with reference to the traits of European feudalism *and the whole inheritance of Mediterranean Antiquity*.

There is no space here to consider these fascinating theses in more

[3] I. Wallerstein, 'The Rise and Future Demise of the World Capitalist System: Concepts for Comparative Analysis', *Comparative Studies in Society and History*, vol. 16, No. 4 (Sept. 1974), p. 401.

[4] Perry Anderson, *Lineages of the Absolutist State* (1974), p. 428; the argument continues from the same author's *Passages from Antiquity to Feudalism* (1974).

detail. But the point is obvious. Whatever else it is about, the European Community is an effort to reconcile and somehow fuse together a collection of nation-states and nationalisms. And in Europe – above all in the West – the historical roots of nationalism are extremely far-reaching. 'Nationalism' in the now historic sense of the 19th and 20th centuries was the crystallization, the harder and more definitive form, of a process of societal and state formation extending through centuries. As Wallerstein observes, the process is synonymous with 'capitalism': the latter's uneven development progressed through a multiplicity of political units, and forced them all alike – whether aggressively or defensively, whether as 'core-areas' or as 'periphery' – into this armoured cultural form. This form was then generalized and strengthened still farther by being exported to the rest of mankind, on the successive waves of imperialism. It has become part of the universal climate, part of the capitalist world-system – 'the gift and malediction of Europe to the globe'. in Anderson's phrase.

So Professor Galtung's categories are not ample enough. He says little about the 'internal' constitution and affairs of the European Community, preferring to concentrate upon its external impact and aims. Yet his theses on the E.E.C. and the Third World presuppose an image of an emerging superpower – of an effective new state, therefore, a centralized power that will succeed in somehow rising above or gathering together the ancient, tenacious, millenary diversity of the continent. And if one pays the least attention to the underlying historical problem *this* involves, the whole argument looks different. For of course 'internal' and 'external' really hang together. The internal constitution of Europe in the past – nationalist and imperialist Europe – was obviously inseparable from its relationship to the other continents. This has not ceased to be true. Hence a study which is mistaken or defective on one side is likely to be mistaken on the other as well.

III

The mistake is as follows: a larger historical perspective on the internal difficulties of 'European integration' (to employ the standard political-science euphemism) makes it look very unlikely indeed that a powerful state will emerge – an effective, 'super-power' state of the sort Galtung envisages. Hence his thesis of a 'second round' of European imperialism will not be fulfilled – the historical clock can never be put back in the way he suggests, even temporarily. If this is so, the predictions about Europe's future relations to the 'world proletarians' are wrong. And most probably, the diagnoses of the current situation (the Lomé agreements, etc.) are mistaken also.

The European Community of national states has emerged in the last twenty-five years. The official goal of its founders, and of the generation of idealists who have laboured in it, has always been (as Galtung says) a new multi-national political state. The official literature of the Community has always insisted upon the remarkable novelty, the historical originality of the venture. However, the historical reference justifying the claims is normally very limited. It is nearly always the same: after centuries of murderous fratricide, the Europeans have at last found a formula for permanent cohabitation. Peace and ever closer co-operation, instead of the wars that ended for good in 1945.

As far as it goes, this is of course an edifying vision. But, like most of the moral idealism so prominent in European-Community affairs, it hides a different, less reassuring historical reality. Like nationalism, warfare was endemic in modern European history. But this means that – again, like nationalism – it was part of the very structure of the continent's development. It is not the case the Europeans were misguided for centuries until finally, chastened by the disasters of 1939–45, they saw the light and decided to behave rationally.

It *is* the case (as we are now coming to understand the history of capitalism) that the strains and contradictions of uneven development tore the continent apart for four centuries, with increasing violence, until the locus of the process (the 'core area' in Wallerstein's schema) was removed from Europe altogether by the result of the Second World War. After that – with the mainspring of conflict taken out, as it were – the European powers had nothing to fight about. They were reduced to a situation of common dependency and semi-marginality, in terms of world power relations. *Power* relations are not secondary, extrinsic aspects of the capitalist world economy, not something to write a footnote about once the gist of the matter is understood. They *are* the substance of the matter!

With only minor attempts to 'recreate the past' – the Suez fiasco of 1956, the ten years of Gaullism, Germany's timid effort at a new *Ostpolitik* – Europe has remained in this historical limbo since the late 1940s. It dared not do anything else. The violence it had exported so consistently to the rest of the world had, finally, recoiled upon European heads with an irresistible force. The transfer of power to the new victors east and west of it, the division into blocs, the nuclear stalemate – in the face of these familiar circumstances it was simply impossible for them to continue the old ways. This impossibility was a question of structure, not of will, a question of Europe's new place in the world economy, not of its reformed character and wish to change (important, and genuine, as this may have been in the building of the Community).

As well as 'core-areas' like the United States, and the 'periphery' of exploited or powerless lands, there is also the category of the 'semi-periphery' in Wallerstein's analysis. 'The semi-periphery is needed to make a capitalist world-economy run smoothly . . .' he points out, for it is this intermediate stratum which prevents the radical polarization of the whole system. 'Why do not the majority who are exploited simply overwhelm the minority who draw its disproportionate benefits? . . . The existence of the third category means precisely that the upper stratum is not faced with the *unified* opposition of all the others because the *middle* stratum is both exploiter and exploited . . .'[5] So one might say that Europe has been relegated by the war from core-area to semi-periphery, above all *politically*. This relegation in terms of power has been much greater than economic considerations alone would warrant. The European revival of the 1950s and '60s led to the notorious discrepancy between the continent's economic weight in the world, and its politico-military feebleness. But even this great material renaissance has of course been mined by 'exploitation' from the core-area across the Atlantic, of the sort publicized by books like *Le Défi americain*, and most recently and magisterially documented by Barnet and Müller's *Global Reach: the Powers of the Multi-national Corporations* (1975).

The function of the middle stratum is to play it both ways. It has a significant margin of manoeuvre, and is not just a tool in the hands of the new imperial centre. However, the margins are circumscribed pragmatically, as the system is built up: new precedents are set, new customs established, new power-boundaries are

[5] Wallerstein, 'The Rise and Demise', etc., op. cit., pp. 404–5.

recognized. We know the name of this system: Atlanticism. The other side of it is that which Galtung's analysis devotes so much attention to: the new relation to the periphery proper, which Europe was forced to arrive at through de-colonization.

At the same time as the former central powers were relegated by defeat into a common servility, they were forced to abandon their old grip on the periphery. The generalized rebellion of peripheric lands put an end to uniformed imperialism, during the twenty-three years from the British abandonment of India to the collapse of Portuguese Africa. It did not put an end (how could it?) to the underlying conditions of uneven development and unequal exchange. But it did impose a new order in which these conditions were openly, straightforwardly displayed. It imposed a more 'rational' system of appropriation, one which functioned through political independence and agreement. Although it maintains (inevitably) many of the old economic and cultural relations built up by centuries of 'development' on the back of 'underdevelopment', it is in any larger sense mistaken to see this system as merely the old one disguised or 'recreated'. Since the Suez expedition the only real threat in the latter sense has been the possibility of a military occupation of the Middle Eastern oilfields in response to OPEC's recent assault upon the mechanisms of 'unequal exchange'; and this is an American threat. No-one even imagined Europe capable of such an action (and the likelihood is they would act, somewhat half-heartedly, to prevent it).

Atlanticism was one aspect of the post-1945 re-ordering of the world capitalist economy. It concerned the new relationship between the indisputable core-area, the United States, and the now relegated middle stratum. The two primal core-area states, England and France, found this relegation particularly hard to digest, for evident historical reasons. The U.K. 'special relationship' and Gaullism were their ways of protesting; it is hard to say which of these involved the greater delusion, or the more obvious political pathos.

But that aspect implied the other: Atlanticism with its free economy and 'free world' orientation demanded the progressive liquidation of the archaic vestments of an older imperial world. It envisaged the spread and strengthening of capitalism, through 'national' movements and new states. If only rebellions could be kept nationalist, not nationalist-communist, then why should capitalism not develop across the Third World in time? Why should not the 'middle stratum', the semi-periphery, be expanded as successful capitalist nations arose out of the old conditions of colonial or semi-colonial dependency?

This is not the place to discuss the extent to which this re-ordering has worked, or not worked.[6] The point which concerns us here is this: the European nations occupy a determinate, intermediate place in the overall machinery of world capitalism. This position largely regulates their existing relationship both to the U.S.A. and to the Third World, and it cannot be changed at will. Even supposing there was a will to develop into a new core-area, to become a super-power (and it is very doubtful whether there is such a *will*, as distinct from a lot of imprecise notions and rhetoric), they could not do it. Or rather, they could not do it without a really drastic, fundamental change in the very structure of the world-economy. That is, without something like a complete *volte-face* by America – or, of course, a war.

Galtung's thesis, by contrast, is that the European community is indeed moving – on the plane both of ideal and socio-economic reality – towards this goal. That is, towards undoing the 'relegation' of post-World-War II, the subservience of Atlanticism, and the more modest relationship to the periphery it now enjoys. We have seen something of the external implausibility of the idea. But there is an even more striking *internal* difficulty – indeed, a problem which must be reckoned quite decisive – and we should look at this next.

IV

The plan of the European Community is not only a novelty, an original and unpredictable direction of events. Looked at in a wider scale of reference, it appears as startlingly – one is tempted to say, incredibly – different from everything at all resembling it in the past.

[6] The question of whether Nigeria, Brazil, Iran, etc., do represent the emergence of a genuine 'non-dependent' capitalism, and the significance of this for the Third and Fourth Worlds, is currently being very actively debated. See especially Bill Warren, 'Imperialism and Capitalist Industrialization', in *New Left Review*, No. 81 (Sept.–Oct. 1973). This provocative analysis gave rise to an interesting discussion in *NLR* No. 85 (May–June 1974), by Arghiri Emmanuel, and the U.S. marxists P. McMichael, James Petras, and R. Rhodes.

There are many historical phenomena similar in the broadest outline to what it is trying to become (although they seldom if ever figure in the apologetics of the E.E.C.). The Community should turn eventually into a pluri-national state of some sort: whether a kind of super-nation-state founded on 'European chauvinism', as Galtung suggests, or a 'supra-national' body presiding over existing states – or whatever. Multi-national states in the generic sense were very much the staple of human history. Tsardom, the Chinese Empire, the various empires of the Indian sub-continent, the empires of Mediterranean Antiquity, the Ottoman Empire, the Hapsburg dynastic state of Central Europe – and so on. Large pluri-cultural and pluri-linguistic 'empires' in this sense (empires not to be confused with those of imperial*ism* in more recent times!); and on the other hand small city or provincial states, petty dynasties and communes like those which constituted 'Italy' and 'Germany' until just over a century ago. Most societies conformed to these types, until capitalism's invasion of the world produced the nation-state. That is, produced the relatively mono-cultural, homogeneous, unilinguistic entities that have become the U.N.O. standard pattern of this century.

In these ancient social structures, Ernest Gellner notes, 'nationalities are mixed up horizontally . . . (and) . . . the language and culture of the partners is a matter of considerable indifference to them; the lord may be concerned with the peasant's delivery of produce, the peasant with protection and freedom from oppression, but neither spares much thought for a matter as trivial as the other's speech and accent.'[7] Dynasties were usually of foreign origin, he goes on to point out (and there are quaint relics of this tradition in, for example, the present royal houses of Great Britain, Belgium, and other countries). Various nationalities and cultures could co-exist under those conditions, and one could rule over another, or over many others. Or one religion could rule over others, as (notably) in the Ottoman Empire. Alien rule was not intolerable, but quite normal, as was rule from great distances, through complex bureaucracies (and many other sins the E.E.C. is commonly reproached with).

So – one might be tempted to conclude – what *is* really so novel about a new multi-national state in Western Europe? The answer

[7] Ernest Gellner, 'Nationalism', in *Thought and Change* (1964), pp. 152–3.

is that, judging by everything we know about the old multi-national states, the venture must be not novel but impossible. For, as the same author goes on to say most forcefully, these older empires were doomed. They were doomed to disintegrate into nation-states on the western model, not by some law of decay or incapacity, but by the nature of capitalism.

Multi-nationality was unimportant, or quite tolerable, in a society of lords and peasants. Its real condition of historical existence (which is of course the condition of most history) was a settled, relatively changeless, agrarian social order. It goes without saying that all the great states of that type tried to encourage 'trade', a certain amount of industrial urban activity, and so on. But the advent of capitalism meant something profoundly different. It meant 'development' in that contemporary sense we now take for granted. It meant the dominance of cities over the countryside, the destruction of the old agrarian order itself, new and vast movements of population . . . and so to Marx's famous litany of bourgeois achievement: 'The bourgeoisie, wherever it has got the upper hand, has put an end to all feudal, patriarchal, idyllic relations. It has pitilessly torn asunder the motley feudal ties that bound man to his natural superiors, and has left remaining no other nexus between man and man than naked self-interest, than callous "cash-payment".' (*Communist Manifesto*).

If capitalism had grown up in an even, slow fashion over these territories, then its changes might have been less apocalyptic than Marx's description. Being slower, they might have been more controllable. The dynastic states might have been able to adapt, or at least to endure longer in history. However, all these 'ifs' and 'mights' are mere abstractions: for capitalism's impact was ininvariably uneven, rapid and disruptive. It was uneven on the world scale, establishing and re-establishing that hierarchy of core and peripheric regions Wallerstein describes. And this unevenness was duplicated within each traditional territory as well. One area, one nationality, one well-situated urban region always obtained the upper hand – found its centrality, its powers of domination, magically augmented by the new forces of production. The others found themselves, by the same token, 'deprived' (under-developed) in a dramatic sense quite distinct from the customary miseries of the *ancien régime*. Hence, the new developments forced open fissures between those cultures which had previously lain together peace-

ably. Angry consciousness of these splits quickly developed, constituting a dynamite which exploded them apart – into the new
national states, the inheritors of empire.[8]

The paradox can be briefly stated. Capitalism was uneven in its
development, this unevenness tore apart the essential fabric of the
old multi-national states, forcing the formation of a multitude of
nationality-states instead. The European Community is an attempt
to erect a multi-national state *on the very basis which proved fatal
to the old ones* – rapid capitalist development. And it is trying to do so
with, as its building bricks, not politically unstructured nationalities,
not 'historyless peoples', but formed and hardened nation-states
produced by an earlier phase of capitalist history. These states include four of the world's original national states, England, France,
Denmark and the Netherlands; three 'late-comers' who are still
fairly ancient by world standards, Italy, Germany and Belgium;
and only one relatively new state, the Irish Republic.

There is an outstanding *cliché* which almost always emerges at
some point in discussion of problems like these. It is: the nation-
state is obviously far too small for the needs of modern economic
organization. In the marxist version it goes: capitalism must over-
ride the boundaries of the nation-state – or, the internationalization
of capital has rendered national frontiers archaic. Statements like
these have been made for a long time now (e.g. they featured in
debates on imperialism around 1900). Few would deny that some
truth attaches to them, that the scale of economic development has
increased since 1950, or that multinational firms play a bigger part
in economic and political life today. The trouble is, that this truth
really lies in the shadow of another, more awkward, less obvious
verity. Capitalism has always had problems with nation-states
and nationalism. But it has also created, needed, and depended upon
nation-states and nationalism. In purely economic terms, it has
always tended towards larger scale, and a utilitarian *rationale*
indifferent to pettifogging customs and ethnic colorations. But in
social terms – that is, in the historical reality of its implantation – it

[8] There is a classical description of the process and its dialectic in *The Dissolution of the Hapsburg Monarchy*, by Oscar Jaszi (1929), Ch. 9, 'The Tragedy of
Free Trade'. Its theme is that: 'Only a constant economic growth of all the peoples
of the monarchy could have been the real unifying force of the customs union
and which could have filled, with a real content, the economic framework created
by the despotic will of the Emperor' (p. 194).

has always been forced into organic compromise with these very same things.

In one sense a 'world system' from the beginning, and equipped with an innate universalism, capitalism has *also* been consistently incapable of realizing this potential. For the shock of this system's impact upon world society has invariably provoked the defensive reactions we know as 'nationalism'. There was no other possible way for human relations to sustain the colossal, accelerated, uneven impact of these changes. This is why 'capitalism' in the abstract always meant capitalism-in-one-nation, in the concrete. As the shock-waves of development spread out from the original core-area, western Europe, they forced the formation of one series of national states after another – from central and eastern Europe in the 19th century, to the remotest areas of Asia and Africa today. Developmental 'progress' as the world has actually experienced it has been from this point of view like an earthquake; and the lines of stress and fissure which its forces have found are, almost always, those supplied by ethnic nationality and culture. Hence it is along such lines that society has to re-group, and adapt to the new conditions of the 'world system'.

Can capitalism exist, and go on developing, *without* this accompanying process? Can it ever leave 'nationalism' behind? Can it rise above the 'irrational', cohesive community of the nationality-state? Can it do this, above all, in the original core-area, the matrix of the whole existing world economic system – where, clearly, such states have an older, harder armature than anywhere else?

These questions are deeper than the ones posed by European *idéologues*. But it is only to be expected that the latter's idealism would evade them. More surprisingly, one finds Johan Galtung to some extent in agreement with them, in spite of his hostility to the E.E.C. He too seems to think it is enough for European leaders to *will* the transcendence of these structures for a new 'superpower' to arise.

But really it is not, if one poses the question in the larger, more historical perspectives of capitalist development. For there are certain laws of that development. And there are no signs that the present European capitalist régimes have escaped from these laws.

V

Professor Galtung's case rests upon a remarkably abstract agrument about the nature of power (Ch. 3 – 'On Power in General'). It is in terms of these abstract definitions of 'power', summed up in a number of diagrams and tables, that the E.E.C. turns out to be such a Leviathan. As a matter of fact, one can hardly help noticing uncomfortable similarities between his style of argument here and that so popular among Brussels propagandists. They too are excessively fond of lists of resources, world-trade percentages, GNP projections and so on – as if it followed from these that the Community was a *power*, in the political sense.

The historical argument I have counterposed, in terms of uneven development, can also be applied to the present, to see if it fits. Let us suppose it is right: a number of things would follow. It would follow, for example, that by far the most important sector of E.E.C. policy internally must concern 'regional development'. Because it is only if the governing centre of the Community keeps control of the constant tendency towards uneven development that unity can be preserved at all in any political sense – let alone be used as the basis of a new state-form. If it cannot do this, then the social fragmentation accompanying capitalist progress will go on too – the old contradiction will continue, in one form or another. One can go farther – it is virtually certain that the centre *will* fail to maintain control, because the socio-economic forces at work creating the disparities are very powerful, and it is still weak. It is no secret that the Community *as such* has no effective regional planning or developmental powers, and simply assists various national programmes (all of them deeply defective in different ways). Consequently, one would expect to see new patterns of uneven growth arising in the E.E.C. area – new fissures, partly coinciding with the old frontiers and partly independent of them, and a demand for new political forms related to them.

This is, surely, precisely what we *do* perceive in the Common Market free trade area today. Today, of course, profound North-South scission is undermining the original ideal of E.E.C. even development. Compared with Germany, the Netherlands, Belgium and Scandinavia the 'southern' countries have been unable to liquidate their more archaic sectors; as a result they remain tied to quite different, less stable political forms, and in any generalized crisis like the present one the difference is sure to become more acute.

This large regional disparity is increasingly riddled by smaller ones. And – as one would expect – these pressures have sought out and found the old, buried fault lines of the area. That is, the ethnic-cultural divisions which were originally fused together in com-pounding the larger European states. From this has come an explosion of new 'nationalisms': Breton, Occitanian, Scottish, Welsh, Walloon and Flemish. In Italy, it is probably only the early adoption of an advanced pattern of regional self-government which has prevented more striking expressions of the trend there. Spain is not at present a member of the E.E.C. But if a future democratic régime does enter, it will almost certainly bring with it more prob-lems of this kind, in the shape of Basque and Catalan separatism. Surrounding these revived nationality-movements and ideologies, there is also a perfectly recognizable *malaise* of regional discontent, demands for forms of 'decentralization', grumblings at the 'metro-polis', and so on. Even regions which do not have a nationalism at hand to crystallize their grievances are forced to find some voice. It should not be forgotten that Europe's last great-power Prince did not fall, finally, in the name of any of those grand visions of international prestige which had filled his life. He was not even overthrown by the upheaval of 1968. General de Gaulle was de-feated over his plans for an administrative 'regionalization' of France.

If one now adds these factors to the well-known ones appearing in European-Community politics – the daily rivalries of the national states, the petty horse-trading, the painful slowness of real 'in-tegration' in these circumstances – then the prospects for the new super-power look very dim. One is tempted to embellish a cele-brated metaphor used by Walter Hallstein: 'integration' is like riding a bicycle – the choice is between going forward or falling off.[9] It has become more like riding a bicycle (the machine bears no resemblance to a BMW 500) on an uphill slope while one part after another falls off. In addition, the rider has begun to suffer from severe arthritis; he stops more and more often to get his breath back, and finds it harder and harder to imagine the view from the top. It is difficult enough to wobble round the next bend.

[9] As quoted in G. Smith, *Politics in Western Europe* (1972), p. 302.

Community apologists have recognized and lamented often enough the absence of a motor in the process. There is no mass popular enthusiasm behind it – no great force, therefore, which compels the politicians and parties to give it the urgent priority that it merits (according to the propaganda image). There is no equivalent of European 'nationalism', except to a very limited degree among intellectuals and élites. So it is usually concluded (with that weary hopefulness marking so many Community debates) that the phenomenon will grow up in time, given the right education and much patience. It will 'develop', like Europe itself.

This is a mistake. Nationalism is not only a persistent function of capitalist development, informing the process from within. It is also, notoriously, a set of popular feelings and ideas (and this subjectivity *is* its mode of functioning, its efficacy as a mobilizing power). It never grows *only* as a response to cultivation from above, because certain élites believe that people ought to see themselves as 'so-and-so's' (rather than whatever they thought they were before). The growth occurs when real socio-economic forces erupt into people's lives and show them the concrete meaning of identifying as 'so-and-so's' – when they begin to see, or think they see, there is something in the ideology for their own life-prospects. Anyone who wants to see the process at work today only has to spend a few days in Aberdeen or Nantes.

But it will probably never be seen at work, *in the required sense*, in 'Europe'. Nationalism in the real sense is never a historical accident, or a mere invention. It reflects the latent fracture-lines of human society under strain. And in the case of Europe as a whole, these lines are very large ones: they pass between Western Europe and the U.S.A., on one hand, and along the traditional Elbe-Trieste frontier on the other. It might not be theoretically impossible for a large-scale West-European nationalism to evolve, in the case of really serious conflicts along these divisions, conflicts amounting to economic or military warfare.

In the world economy as it is, this dramatic development is obviously extremely unlikely, unless there is an as yet unforeseeable aggravation of the crisis in course.

VI

In this context I must leave a more informed critique of Professor Galtung's views on Euro-African relations to others. The point relevant to the above argument is that the relationship – and above all the transition this year from the old agreements to the new Convention of Lomé – hardly makes sense if interpreted as the tightening grip of an aggressive new superpower. It does not present a picture of a strengthening state imposing a new-imperialist stranglehold (were this the case it would be very hard to understand why states like Tanzania or the new revolutionary régime in Guinea-Bissau had chosen to sign). Rather, the impression given is that of the relative advantages which a group of less-developed countries can extract *from a weak capitalist state*.

In purely economic terms the E.E.C. is strong, and naturally this inequality remains predominant in exchange with the very poor making up a majority of the Associated States. But politically it is feeble. And in Third World relations, as in relations with the U.S.A., the U.S.S.R. and Japan, it is this chronic *décalage* which is really important. Unfortunately, Galtung has also accepted some of the new conventional wisdom of international relations. That is, the myths about the end of bi-polarity that emerged in the Nixon-Kissinger years; 'It is in relationship to the outside that the super-state aspect ... will become evident ... a more adequate geometrical figure (of world politics) would be a *pentagon*, with Japan as the fifth corner – already alluded to by President Nixon in July 1971, and worked into the plans for the reorganization of the British foreign service' (p. 26).

The British Foreign Office is a poor guide to the realities of world power these days. And if it reposes the same sort of belief in *Pax Bruxellana* as Galtung apparently does, it is due for some more disenchantments. The Community is, and is likely to remain, the weak side in any such power game, for these historical and structural reasons we have looked at. Among the five great-power candidates, it alone is not a 'nation' nor likely to evolve into one. Three of the other four are indeed, in very different ways, pluri-ethnic communities occupying great tracts of the globe. But this only reinforces the point. For they have succeeded in imposing a unified nation-state structure and a supporting mass nationalism on their heterogeneous basis (more or less as England and France did in earlier modern times). And two of them, of course, have done this in terms of new modes of collective economic development diverging from the capitalist forms described above.

All this is not to say that the Common Market is either meaningless or doomed. The peculiar ambiguities of 'integration' (to say nothing of theories *about* integration) have always made it all too easy to be either over-optimistic or over-pessimistic. It has always been too easy to draw up one-dimensional lists which 'prove' these visions: achievements and hopes on the one hand, palpable short-comings and absurdities on the other.[10] And a great deal of 'debate' on the subject always consists of inconclusive duelling with these paper swords.

The European Community will not disintegrate from one year to the next. Although the panting bicyclist will undergo no magical, butterfly-like transformation into a super-machine, he is not likely to slide back too far downhill either. The mass of real interests involved in the process are likely to prevent any such collapse. It may never be a world super-state; it is unlikely to cease being a real force in the world either.

So, even if one adopts the relatively disabused and sceptical conception of it I have been arguing for, the question of a political judgement of the E.E.C. remains. From any radical point of view (and above all any point of view related to marxism) there is a duty to attempt some overall judgement about the phenomenon – on what it means as a whole, in terms of the longer perspective of progress or development which one is championing. Galtung's ideas lead him to a simple conclusion in this sense: he is against it. Is it really as simple as this?

VII

It is interesting and relevant here to note that, in spite of his general hostility, Galtung cannot avoid finding at least a few words to say in favour of the E.E.C. After one of his structuralist's tables of relationships (p. 57), he admits there can be no doubt that – 'the E.C. member states have been building for themselves a *peace* structure' which amounts to more than mere equality. For this is a peace '. . . *built by associative means*', and as such, 'from a peace theoretical viewpoint, almost ideal where relations among states

[10] Critiques of Galtung's position on this issue have also appeared in the *Journal of International Studies*, vol. 3, no. 2 (Autumn 1974), 'Africa and the Enlarged EEC', by James Mayall; and vol. 3, no. 3 (Winter 1974–5), 'The European Community and the Third World', by R. Marwood. See also the recent survey carried out by *Le Monde diplomatique* (April 1974), M. Paunet, P. Lemaitre, P. Cheysson.

are concerned ... Also, it is a structure that Third World countries and socialist countries might look to to get ideas as to how a group of countries can defend itself effectively against economic aggression from a giant. What the E.C. has done relative to the U.S. may well turn out to be what other countries will have to do relative to the E.C. . . .' (pp. 58–9).

Indeed it turns out that Galtung is strongly in favour of a 'European Community' of his own, which he defines as follows: '. . . consisting of small, social units, like cantons. These would be bigger than municipalities but smaller than regions, free to choose their own social structures within a basically socialist and humanist framework, with a high level of mobility between them – interdependent, but also self-sufficient so that they could survive a crisis among themselves' (p. 131). Thus, his ideas rejoin on one side what has always been a mildly influential current of thought within Europeanism itself: the French-style 'federalism' deriving from a 19th century Proudhonist tradition and represented today by (e.g.) Alexandre Marc and his school.

It would be unfair to criticize this vision just for its Utopianism. Utopianism has always abounded in this area of thinking, and it is the habit of thought itself which merits critique rather than this or that specimen of it. However, it is significant that Galtung's style of argument about Europe leaves space for it. The argument as a whole might be defined as: structuralist in method (though with some historical reference-points) – Third-Worldist, New Leftist and small-community romantic in outlook. Utopianism attaches to it both as regards this latter aspect, and also as regards its general conception of uneven development and developed-underdeveloped relationships. For, once the evils of E.E.C. neo-imperialism are denounced, the solution to the malady of the world order is seen as '. . . a central authority, distributing important processing industries more evenly between countries just slavishly copied or adapted . . .' (p. 69). What is such a 'central authority', impartial and omnipotent, reminiscent of but the world socialist government of many past visionaries?

The E.E.C. is associated with a distinctive brand of bourgeois idealism, containing elements of liberalism, Christianity, cultural vanity, and social-democracy. Socialists have frequently been tempted to reply with a contrary brand. Denouncing the capitalist or imperialist realities behind this smokescreen, they have however no wish to fall back into simple nationalism. So they project an idea of 'their' Europe, the non-toxic variety which will consist wholly of non-antagonistic relationships, cooperation towards even, all-round development, and so on. This is the 'United Socialist States of Europe', or 'L'Europe des peuples' as distinct from 'L'Europe des monopoles'. This alibi then allows them to oppose the E.E.C. *de facto*, while retaining a good conscience in reserve: when the chance comes, they will show how much better *their internationalism* is.

Perhaps equally important, the stance allows them to ignore the subject most of the time. Here one can only agree most warmly with Galtung's verdict: 'The E.C. is an instrument . . . used by the conservatives, and largely ignored by the radicals' (pp. 146–7). More generally, he says, discussion of the ideas in his book all over the continent showed him that 'the European Community still operates largely in a vacuum where political consciousness is concerned, even to the point that there seems to be more interest concerning the Community outside than inside the Community itself . . .' (p. 6). It should have been the left that formed this political consciousness, of course; instead of which, its gaze is fixed on other parts of the world, betraying 'in the present generation of European leftists a blindness not dissimilar to the preceding generation . . .'

Any more realistic focus surely demands a more complex, less facile attitude towards 'capitalist Europe'. A future 'Socialist Europe' may be very different from and far better than all this. But it cannot be credibly visualized as having *no real connection with* the bedraggled, sordid reality. No one would think that (e.g.) Italian socialism or French socialism would emerge unmarked from these particular capitalist moulds (any more than the Soviet State could literally 'free' itself from Mother Russia or Maoism from Chinese traditions). So one should at least employ a comparable critical intelligence towards the European quasi-state as towards these old enemies. Uncritical 'acceptance' carries one unerringly to the extreme right-wing of the left (if not into the pockets of the right itself); uncritical 'rejection' carries one to the nowhere of Utopia. And discussion towards discovering what ought to be our dialectic rapport with it has been impossibly hampered by basic confusions on what it is.

In spite of the mountains of words, radical discussion about Europe is still in an elementary state. For the sake of that discussion, and in riposte to Johan Galtung's bold position, here is the stance which might emerge from some of the above reflections: because he is wrong, and there is no E.C. super-nation on the horizon, the left can afford to be much more matter-of-fact about 'Europe', including the institutions, personnel and some of the purposes of integration. Since it is founded on a historical and theoretical analysis, this is more than mere pragmatism *à l'anglaise*. It reflects the perception that the purely economic reinforcement of capitalism simply does *not* entail a corresponding reinforcement of bourgeois *power* in the crucial state-ideological sense. The fog-machines of Europeanist ideology work overtime partly to conceal the fact. In reality, the strengthening of capitalism in its new cross-frontier dimension may be leading to an enfeeblement of this crucial authority – for it is weakening the old nation-state machines without putting anything likely to be as effective in their place. There can be no equivalent of the god-like dynasties which ruled over past multi-national societies here. It is quite difficult to see why radicals should grieve over this. The reality of integration in Western Europe is working for them, as well as against them: it is built round a contradiction ignored by European *idéologues*. Do we have to ignore it as well?

9. The Modern Janus

The theory of nationalism represents Marxism's great historical failure. It may have had others as well, and some of these have been more debated: Marxism's shortcomings over imperialism, the State, the falling rate of profit and the immiseration of the masses are certainly old battlefields. Yet none of these is as important, as fundamental, as the problem of nationalism, either in theory or in political practice. It is true that other traditions of western thought have not done better. Idealism, German historicism, liberalism, social Darwinism and modern sociology have foundered as badly as Marxism here. This is cool comfort for Marxists. The scientific pretensions and the political significance of their ideas are greater than those of such rivals, and no one can help feeling that they ought to have coped better with such a central, inescapable phenomenon of modern history. My thesis is that this failure was inevitable. It was inevitable, but it can now be understood. Furthermore it can be understood in essentially materialist terms. So as a system of thought historical materialism can perfectly well escape from the prolonged and destructive impasse in which it has been locked on the issue. However, the cost of doing so is probably 'Marxism'. Materialism cannot escape unmarked and unchanged from the ordeal, for an obvious reason. The reason is that to perceive the cause of *this* failure is to see something of Marxism's real place in history, some of its limitations, some of the unconscious roots which tied it blindly to the course of modern historical development. It means seeing Marxism itself as a part of history in a quite uncomplimentary sense, one which has nothing to do with the holy matrimony of theory and practice. It means losing for all time that God-like posture which, in the guise of science, Marxism took over from Idealist philosophy (and ultimately from religion).

Marxist 'failures' over nationalism appear to us in the first instance as philosophical, conceptual ones. The great names from Marx himself to Gramsci did not pay sufficient attention to the subject, dealing with it incidentally or tangentially rather than head-on. Those who did tackle it more directly, the Social-Democrats of Tsardom and the Hapsburg Empire, disagreed wildly among themselves. After the trauma of 1914 Marxists never had the stomach to return to this debate on anything like the same level. Had they desired to after 1925, the complete fetishization of Lenin's supposed positions on the question made it both politically and psychologically very difficult.

The *coup de grâce* to their dithering was administered by Stalin's essay on *The National Question* (1912). By the most sinister of coincidences, the one text most suitable for canonization in the new creed was by the great dictator himself. That this essay was one of the more modest relics of the great unfinished pre-1914 debate mattered little. Under the new conditions it riveted Stalin's name to the halo of Lenin. This is why it is still almost universally parroted by every brand of party Marxism. For half a century, organized Marxism has relied almost entirely upon this inadequate instrument in grappling with this most baffling and dangerous historical opponent – whose force seemed set fair to annihilate it altogether until the turning-point of Stalingrad.

This is a sad chapter in the history of ideas. But in itself it explains nothing. If one thinks it does, then the temptation will remain to say that surely, somewhere or other in the prodigious variety of revolutionary talents Marxism assembled, there *must* be a theory of nationalism. We are not cleverer than Rosa Luxemburg or Otto Bauer. We are not more painfully conscious than them of the critical and devastating nature of this phenomenon for socialism. So if we excavate assiduously enough the theory will surely emerge, like a crock of gold, from between the lines of the classics, maybe even from the scattered remarks and letters of Marx and Engels themselves.

In other words, if one believes that the 'failure' was essentially a conceptual, subjective one, the temptation remains to lend a retrospective helping hand. This exercise appeals strongly to the devotional side of Marxists. 'What so-and-so *really* meant was of course such-and-such, bearing in mind the following (commonly overlooked) texts . . .'; 'the insights of Lenin-Stalin or Engels-

Marx must be complemented by Luxemburg's observations on ...'; and so forth.

Real respect for our forebears demands we recognize the futility of these rituals. Their 'failure' was not a simply conceptual or subjective one. No amount of brass-rubbing will compensate for it. The fact is, that if they could not put together a tolerable theory about nationalism, nobody could, or did. Historical development had not at that time produced certain things necessary for such a 'theory'. The time was not ripe for it, or for them. Nor would it be ripe until two further generations of trauma had followed 1914. There is nothing in the least discreditable to historical materialism in the fact, although it is naturally lethal to 'Marxism', in the God's-eye sense.

The philosophical failings lead us back in turn to real history. They lead us back to the material conditions under which the enigma of modern nationalism presented itself to these past generations. Lacking angelic perspicuity, they had to confront it under very severe limitations. Nationalism is a crucial, fairly central feature of the modern capitalist development of world history. Time-bound like other systems of speculation, Marxism did not possess the power to foresee this development, or the eventual, overall shape which capitalist history would assume. As regards nationalism, the trouble is that not much less than this is required for approaching the problem.

Idées Reçues of Nationalism

So much by way of introduction. To go farther let us remember how most Marxist (and other) thinking about the subject oscillates between the horns of an over-familiar dilemma.

On one hand nationalism can hardly help seeming a good thing, a morally and politically positive force in modern history. It has been the ideology of weaker, less developed countries struggling to free themselves from alien oppression. From the time of the Greek and Latin-American independence wars up to the recent struggle in Indo-China, it appears as in this sense an aspect of progress. But on the other hand we know quite well that the term applies, and applies no less characteristically, to the history of Italian fascism and the Japanese military state of the 1930s, to the careers and personalities of General de Gaulle, General Amin and the Shah of Iran.

The task of a theory of nationalism – as distinct from a stratagem for living with the contradiction – must be to embrace both horns of the dilemma. It must be to see the phenomenon as a whole, in a way that rises above these 'positive' and 'negative' sides. Only in this fashion can we hope to escape from a predominantly moralizing perspective upon it, and rise . . . I will not say to a 'scientific' one, as this term has been subjected to so much ideological abuse, but at least to a better, more detached historical view of it. In order to do this, it is necessary to locate the phenomenon in a larger explanatory framework, one that will make sense of the contradictions.

The question arises of what this framework is. My belief is that the only framework of reference which is of any real utility here is world history as a whole. It is only the general process of historical development since (at least) the end of the eighteenth century which can serve to give us the focus we need on such a huge and complicated problem. Most approaches to the question are vitiated from the start by a country-by-country attitude. Of course, it is the ideology of world nationalism itself which induces us along this road, by suggesting that human society consists essentially of several hundred different and discrete 'nations', each of which has (or ought to have) its own postage-stamps and national soul. The secret of the forest is the trees, so to speak. Fortunately, this is just the usual mangled half-truth of commonsense.

No – it is the forest which 'explains' the trees, in the sense which interests us today. It is certain general conditions of geography, topography, soil and climate which determined what trees should grow, how thickly, how far, and so on. In other words, 'nationalism' in its most general sense is determined by certain features of the world political economy, in the era between the French and Industrial Revolutions and the present day. We are still living in this era. However, we enjoy the modest advantage of having lived in it longer than the earlier theorists who wrestled with the problem. From our present vantage-point we may be a little more able than they were to discern some overall characteristics of the process and its by-products. Indeed it would not say much for us if we were not able to do this.

Next, we must inquire what are those features of general historical development which give us some clue about nationalism. At this point it may help to dip briefly into the mythology of the subject. If someone were producing an up-dated version of Gustave

Flaubert's *Dictionnaire des idées reçues* for the use of politics and
social-science students, I think the entry 'Nationalism' might read
as follows: '*Nationalism*: infrequently used before the later nineteenth century, the term can nonetheless be traced back in approximately its contemporary meaning to the 1790s (Abbé Baruel, 1798).
It denotes the new and heightened significance accorded to factors
of nationality, ethnic inheritance, customs and speech from the
early nineteenth century onwards. The concept of nationalism as a
generally necessary stage of development for all societies is common
to both materialist and idealist philosophies. These later theoretical
formulations agree that society must pass through this phase (see,
e.g., texts of F. Engels, L. von Ranke, V. I. Lenin, F. Meinecke).
These theories also agree in attributing the causes of this phase to
specific forces or impulses resident within the social formations
concerned. Nationalism is therefore an internally-determined
necessity, associated by Marxists with, for example, the creation of a
national market economy and a viable national bourgeois class; by
Idealists with the indwelling spirit of the community, a common
personality which must find expression in historical development.
Both views concur that this stage of societal evolution is the necessary precondition of a subsequent, more satisfactory state of affairs,
known as "internationalism" ("proletarian" or "socialist" internationalism in one case, the higher harmony of the World Spirit in
the other). This condition is only attainable for societies and individuals who have developed a healthy nationalism previously.
While moderate, reasonable nationalism is in this sense praised, an
immoderate or excessive nationalism exceeding these historical
limits is viewed as unhealthy and dangerous (see entry "Chauvinism", above).' The gist of this piece of global folklore (which unfortunately embraces much of what passes for 'theory' on nationalism) is that nationalism is an inwardly-determined social necessity,
a 'growth-stage', located somewhere in between traditional or
'feudal' societies and a future where the factors of nationality will
become less prominent (or anyway less troublesome in human history). Regrettably, it is a growth-stage which can sometimes go
wrong and run amok. This is mysterious. How can adolescence
become a deadly disease?

Whatever the doctors say about this, they agree on the double
inwardness attaching to nationalism. It corresponds to certain
internal needs of the society in question, *and* to certain individual,

psychological needs as well. It supplies peoples and persons with an important commodity, 'identity'. There is a distinctive, easily recognizable subjectivity linked to all this. Whenever we talk about nationalism, we normally find outselves talking before too long about 'feelings', 'instincts', supposed desires and hankerings to 'belong', and so on. This psychology is obviously an important fact about nationalism.

The Maladies of Development

The universal folklore of nationalism is not entirely wrong. If it were, it would be unable to function as myth. On the other hand, it would be equally unable to function in this way if it were true – that is, true in the sense that concerns us in this place. It is ideology. This means it is the generally acceptable 'false consciousness' of a social world still in the grip of 'nationalism'. It is a mechanism of adjustment and compensation, a way of living with the reality of those forms of historical development we label 'nationalism'. As such, it is perhaps best regarded as a set of important clues towards whatever these forms are really about.

The principal such clue is the powerful connection that common sense suggests between nationalism and the concept of development or social and economic 'growth'. It is true that the distinctively modern fact of national*ism* (as opposed to nationality, national states and other precursors) is somehow related to this. For it is only within the context of the general acceleration of change since about 1800, only in the context of 'development' in this new sense, that nationhood acquired this systemic and abstract meaning.

However, it is not true that the systemic connotation derives *from the fact of development as such*. This is the sensitive juncture at which truth evaporates into useful ideology. It is simply not the case (although humanity has always had plenty of reasons for wishing it were the case) that national-ism, the compulsive necessity for a certain socio-political form, arises naturally from these new developmental conditions. It is not nature. The point of the folklore is of course to suggest this: to award it a natural status, and hence a 'health' label, as if it were indeed a sort of adolescence of all societies, the road we have to trudge along between rural idiocy and 'modernity', industrialization (or whatever).

A second significant clue is that pointing towards social and personal subjectivity. It is true that nationalism is connected with typical internal movements, personnel and persons. These behave in similar ways and entertain quite similar feelings. So it is tempting to say (e.g.) that the Italian nationalism of the 1850s or the Kurdish or Eritrean nationalism of the 1970s rest upon and are generated by these specific internal mechanisms. They express the native peculiarities of their peoples, in a broadly similar way – presumably because the people's soul (or at least its bourgeoisie) needs to.

However, it is not true that nationalism of any kind is really the product *of these internal motions as such*. This is the core of the emprical country-by-country fallacy which the ideology of nationalism itself wishes upon us. Welsh *national*ism, of course, has much to do with the specifics of the Welsh people, their history, their particular forms of oppression and all the rest of it. But Welsh national*ism* – that generic, universal necessity recorded in the very term we are interested in – has nothing to do with Wales. It is not a Welsh fact, but a fact of general developmental history, that at a specific time the Welsh land and people are forced into the historical process in this fashion. The 'ism' they are then compelled to follow is in reality imposed upon them from without; although of course to make this adaptation, it is necessary that the usual kinds of national cadres, myths, sentiments, etc., well up from within. All nationalisms work through a characteristic repertoire of social and personal mechanisms, many of them highly subjective. But the causation of the drama is not within the bosom of the *Volk*: this way lie the myths of blood and *Geist*. The subjectivity of nationalism is an important objective fact about it; but it is a fact which, in itself, merely reposes the question of origins.

The real origins are elsewhere. They are located not in the folk, nor in the individual's repressed passion for some sort of wholeness or identity, but in the machinery of world political economy. Not, however, in the process of that economy's development as such – not simply as an inevitable concomitant of industrialization and urbanization. They are associated with more specific features of that process. The best way of categorizing these traits is to say they represent the *uneven development* of history since the eighteenth century. This unevenness is a material fact; one could argue that it is the most grossly material fact about modern history. This statement allows us to reach a satisfying and near-paradoxical conclusion: the most notoriously subjective and ideal of historical phenomena is in fact a by-product of the most brutally and hope-lessly material side of the history of the last two centuries.

The Metropolitan Fantasy

Uneven development is the verbal opposite of even development. The opposition is verbal, not real, since all the actual 'development' human society has been forced through since the Industrial Revolu-tion is uneven. Nevertheless, the notion and aspiration of even development is so powerful that we ought to start from it. It is, after all, close to being the nerve of a Western or 'Eurocentric' world-view – the *Weltanschauung* which still tends to govern the way we think about history, and so (amongst other things) about nationalism. It is noticeable, for instance, that the mythology re-ferred to previously is a way of pretending that nationalism is somehow part of an even, natural evolution of social events.

The idea of an even and progressive development of material civilization and mass culture was characteristic of the European Enlightenment. It reflected a forward view natural to the élites of that time and place. Like their predecessors in eras of high cul-ture they still thought in terms of civilization versus 'barbarians' in the outer mists. But the new convictions of Progress made the outlook for the barbarians more favourable: given time, and help, they might catch up. This redemption was conceived of as a process of steady acculturation, both outwards and downwards. Outwards from the centre to these peripheric regions, and sociologically downwards, from the cultivated classes to the servants and labour-ing people.

Capitalism was to be a powerful instrument in this diffusion. As regards the nationality factor, Kant put it very clearly. The national divisions of mankind were an excellent thing in themselves: in Europe, for example, they had helped prevent the formation of a universal despotism, an Empire of the Eastern sort. In the future, it was middle-class trade which would ensure they did not get out of hand. 'The spirit of commerce, which is incompatible with war, sooner or later gains the upper hand in every State', he wrote, and 'the power of money' (which he thought the 'most dependable of all powers') will compel ruling classes to see sense. That is to get rid of their atavistic urges and make peace at all costs (*Perpetual Peace, a Philosophical Sketch*, 1795).

As we now know, the real developments implicit in the ideas and forces Kant was counting on were quite different. Nor could they possibly have been foreseen by the grand universalizing tradition Kant represented, a tradition still Christian even in its new secular forms. In reality, the spirit of commerce and the power of money, as they invaded successive areas of the globe, would lead to the renewal of atavistic urges. They would produce an intensification of warfare. Instead of growing less significant *as* barriers, national divisions would be erected into a new and dominant principle of social organization. History was to defeat the Western Philosophers.

The defeat has been permanent. This is perhaps the true, longer meaning of Marxism's 'failure' over the National Question. Unable to foresee the real contradictions of Progress, its catastrophic side, this tradition of thought has also thereafter found it consistently impossible to apprehend and digest the fact properly. In turn, this blind spot has consistently become the fertile source of all modern irrationalism. It is the complex of refractory, unassimilable phenomena linked to nationalism and its many derivatives (racism, anti-semitism, etc.) which time and time again appeared to undermine and thoroughly discredit Western rationality. This opened the door to anti-rational and pessimistic philosophies – that *série noire* which has so closely counterpointed the march of Western Progress over the globe, and occasionally threatened to break it up for good.

The unforeseeable, antagonistic reality of capitalism's growth into the world is what the general title 'uneven development' refers to. It indicates the shambling, fighting, lop-sided, illogical, head-over-heels fact, so to speak, as distinct from the noble uplift and phased amelioration of the ideal. Modern capitalist development was launched by a number of West-European states which had accumulated the potential for doing so over a long period of history. The even-development notion was that this advance could be straightforwardly followed, and the institutions responsible for it copied – hence the periphery, the world's countryside, would catch up with the leaders in due time. This evening-up would proceed through the formation of a basically homogeneous enlightened class throughout the periphery: the international or 'cosmopolitan' élite in charge of the diffusion process. But no such steady diffusion or copying was in fact possible, and neither was the formation of this universal class (though there have been and are caricatural versions of it, in the shape of comprador bourgeoisies allying themselves to metropolitan capital instead of to their own people).

Instead, the impact of those leading countries was normally experienced as domination and invasion. The spirit of commerce was supposed to take over from the traditional forms of rapine and swindle. But in reality it could not. The gap was too great, and the new developmental forces were not in the hands of a beneficent, disinterested élite concerned with Humanity's advance. Rather, it was the 'sordid material interests' (as Marx and Engels relished saying) of the English and French bourgeois classes which were employing the concepts of the Enlightenment and classical political economy as a smokescreen. Even with the best will in the world (which they did not have), Progress could not help identifying herself to some degree with these particular places, classes and interests. And in this way she could not help fomenting a new sort of 'imperialism'.

On the periphery itself, outside the core-areas of the new industrial-capitalist world economy, people soon needed little persuasion of this. They learned quickly enough that Progress in the abstract meant domination in the concrete, by powers which they could not help apprehending as foreign or alien. In practice as distinct from the theory, the acculturation process turned out to be more like a 'tidal wave' (in Ernest Gellner's phrase) of outside interference and control. Humanity's forward march signified in the first instance Anglicization or Frenchification, for as long ahead as the people most conscious of the change could see. As was said later on, more globally: 'Westernization' or 'Americanization'.

There was never either time or the sociological space for even development. The new forces of production, and the new state and military powers associated with them, were too dynamic and uncontrolled, and the resultant social upheavals were far too rapid and devastating for any such gradual civilization-process to take place. There was to be no 'due time' in modern history. All time was undue once the great shock-wave had begun its course. For those outside the metropolis (where in unique and unrepeatable circumstances things had matured slowly) the problem was not to assimilate culture at a reasonable rate: it was to avoid being drowned.

The Enlightenment was borne into wider reality by bourgeois revolutions which shook the older social world around them to pieces. In these less-developed lands the elites soon discovered that tranquil incorporation into the cosmopolitan technocracy was possible for only a few of them at a time. The others, the majority, saw themselves excluded from the action, rather than invited politely to join in; trampled over rather than taught the rules of the game; exploited rather than made partners. It was no consolation to be told that patience was in order, that things would even up in the next generation, or the one after that. Was this true at all? Would not the actual configuration of the new forces of change merely put the English even more firmly in charge of an even more un-Indian India; the Germans even more in control of second-class, Slav lands? True or not, the point came to seem academic. Given the violence and rapidity of the changes in act, patience and time were no longer human possibilities anyway.

The Necessary Resort to Populism

Huge expectations raced ahead of material progress itself. The peripheric élites had no option but to try and satisfy such demands by taking things into their own hands. 'Taking things into one's own hands' denotes a good deal of the substance of nationalism, of course. It meant that these classes – and later on sometimes the masses beneath them, whom they felt responsible for – had to mobilize *against* 'progress' at the same time as they sought to improve their position in accordance with the new canons. They had to contest the concrete form in which (so to speak) progress had taken them by the throat, even as they set out to progress themselves. Since they wanted factories, parliaments, schools and so on, they had to copy the leaders somehow; but in a way which rejected the mere implantation of these things by direct foreign intervention or control. This gave rise to a profound ambiguity, an ambivalence which marks most forms of nationalism.

Unable to literally 'copy' the advanced lands (which would have entailed repeating the stages of slow growth that had led to the breakthrough), the backward regions were forced to take what they wanted and cobble it on to their own native inheritance of social forms. In the annals of this kind of theorizing the procedure is called 'uneven and combined development'. To defend themselves, the periphery countries were compelled to try and advance 'in their own way', to 'do it for themselves'. Their rulers – or at least the newly-awakened élites who now came to power – had to mobilize their societies for this historical short-cut. This meant the conscious formation of a militant, inter-class community rendered strongly (if mythically) aware of its own separate identity vis-à-vis the outside forces of domination. There was no other way of doing it. Mobilization had to be in terms of what was there; and the whole point of the dilemma was that there was nothing there – none of the economic and political institutions of modernity now so needed.

All that there *was* was the people and peculiarities of the region: its inherited *ethnos*, speech, folklore, skin-colour, and so on. Nationalism works through *differentiae* like those because it has to. It is not necessarily democratic in outlook, but it *is* invariably populist. People are what it has to go on: in the archetypal situation of the really poor or 'under-developed' territory, it may be more or less all that nationalists have going for them. For kindred reasons, it had to function through highly rhetorical forms, through a sentimental culture sufficiently accessible to the lower strata now being called to battle. This is why a romantic culture quite remote from Enlightenment rationalism always went hand-in-hand with the spread of nationalism. The new middle-class intelligentsia of nationalism had to invite the masses into history; and the invitation-card had to be written in a language they understood.

It is unnecessary here to explore the process in detail. Everyone is familiar with its outline, and with much of its content. We all know how it spread out from its West-European source, in concentric circles of upheaval and reaction: through Central and Eastern Europe, Latin America, and then across the other continents. Uniformed imperialism of the 1880–1945 variety was one episode in this larger history, as were its derivatives, anti-colonial wars and 'de-colonization'. We have all studied the phenomena so consistently accompanying it: the 'rediscovery' or invention of national history, urban intellectuals invoking peasant virtues which they have experienced only through train windows on their summer holidays, schoolmasters painfully acquiring 'national' tongues spoken only in remote valleys, the infinity of forms assumed by the battle between scathing cosmopolitan modernists and emotional defenders of the Folk . . . and so on.

But before we go on, let me try to sum up this part of the argument. Real, uneven development has invariably generated an imperialism of the centre over the periphery; one after another, these peripheric areas have been forced into a profoundly ambivalent reaction against this dominance, seeking at once to resist it and to somehow take over its vital forces for their own use. This could only be done by a kind of highly 'idealist' political and ideological mobilization, by a painful forced march based on their own resources: that is, employing their 'nationality' as a basis. The metropolitan fantasy of even development had predicted a swelling, single forward march that would induct backward lands into its course; in reality, these lands found themselves compelled to attempt radical, competitive short-cuts in order to avoid being trampled over or left behind. The logistics of these short-cuts brought in factors quite absent from the universalizing philosophy of Progress. And since the greater part of the globe was to be forced into detours of this kind, these factors became dominant in the history of the world for a long period, one still not concluded.

In the traditional philosophical terminology, this amounts of course to a 'contradiction'. The contradiction here is that capitalism, even as it spread remorselessly over the world to unify human society into one more or less connected story for the first time, *also* engendered a perilous and convulsive new fragmentation of that society. The socio-historical cost of this rapid implantation of capitalism into world society was 'nationalism'. There was no other conceivable fashion in which the process could have occurred – not, that is, unless one resorts to the metropolitan fantasy of a gradual, secular, contradiction-free 'development' imagined in purely economic or statistical terms. It is a matter of everyday observation that apologists of developed-country Progress still do resort to arguments like this; and that the protagonists of under-developed country nationalisms still do passionately rebut them with talk about human nature, sturdy popular wisdom, and all the rest. The world market, world industries and world literature predicted with such exultation in *The Communist Manifesto* all conducted, in fact, to the world of nationalism. They were supposed to lead to a contradiction much more palatable to the Western-philosophical taste: that between social classes, a proletariat and a bourgeoisie essentially the same everywhere – two cosmopolitan classes, as it were, locked in the same battle from Birmingham to Shanghai.

The Anti-Imperialist Theory

It is only too easy to deduce from this picture a certain theory of nationalism. I will call this the anti-imperialist theory. It lays primary emphasis upon the successive waves of peripheric struggle, from the early nineteenth century up to the generalized Third World rebellion of the present day. And, of course, it views the phenomenon in a highly positive moral light. There may have been aberrations and excesses, but nationalism is mainly with the angels of progress. This point of view is given its most cogent expression at the end of Gellner's celebrated essay on nationalism. 'By and large this does seem a beneficent arrangement', he argues, because if the nationalist response to development had not occurred then imperialism would have simply intensified, and 'this politically united world might well come to resemble the present condition of South Africa . . .'[1]

The anti-imperialist theory is better than stories about demonic urges and irrepressible atavism. It does relate nationalism to the wider arc of historical development (in the way we saw was necessary), and it does encompass some of the mechanisms of that process. It combines a degree of theoretical consciousness with its strong practical and political impulse, the impulse of solidarity with the under-development struggles which are still proceeding over most of the globe. Yet it is really incorrect. In effect, it is a sort of compromise between historical materialism and commonsense: between the much more ambiguous truth of nationalism and those mythologies I mentioned previously. As such, it renounces the difficult task of gripping both horns of the dilemma and – for the most sympathetic of motives – clings aggressively to one of them. In many cases (though not in Gellner's), it comes down to little more than a more sophisticated justification of romantic nationalism, now transformed into 'Third Worldism'.

The truth is less palatable. Anti-imperialist theory lets go of the real logic (or illogic) of uneven development, because it lets go of the totality of the process. It forgets or disguises for its own purposes what the central drive, the main dynamic of this whole contradictory movement has been. That is, the irresistible and transforming impact of the developed upon the under-developed, of the core-areas upon the world's countryside. Nationalisms do 'resist' the impact, true, and with some success – but only to be transformed themselves, as they adopt the forces which attacked

[1] Ernest Gellner, *Thought and Change*, London 1964, pp. 177–8.

them. And this whole pattern of resistances could not avoid changing and informing the entire developmental process – it could not help making nationalism a kind of world norm, a standard for the advanced and industrialized countries as well as for the awakening ones.

From the very outset, part of the 'superiority' of the development leaders lay in their political and state systems. It lay in the fact that they had invented the national state, the real proto-type of the national*ist* ideal, by quite empirical processes extending over many centuries. They discovered and proved its power long before nationalism had been formulated as the general, systemic response to that power's incursions throughout the world. When it came, that response could not help being highly overdetermined ideologically.

In this general sense, nationalism was obviously generated as a compensatory reaction on the periphery. Its ideal intensification corresponded to the absence of a material reality: the economic and social institutions of modernity, those developmental arms now being wielded with such effect by England, France and later on by by the other territories that achieved them. It was the absence of these arms, and despair about getting them, which made the compensating ideological weapon of nationalism a necessity: the idealist motor of the forced march out of backwardness or dependency.

Hence, as the most basic graph of nationalist history will demonstrate, the ideology has always been produced on the periphery (or at least, by people thinking about its dilemmas, whether they are themselves in it or not). The *locus classicus* was in Germany and Italy, during the era when these were march-lands endeavouring to re-order themselves to face the threat from the West. And the rhetoric and doctrine of nationalism have been constantly re-formulated and replenished by spokesmen of the periphery ever since, up to the time of Amilcar Cabral and Che Guevara. The power and omnipresence of this ideology require no emphasis here.

However, this very influence has also meant that the ideological dimension of nationalism has always loomed too large in reflection about the phenomenon. There is a distinct sense in which this dimension has been far *too* important for theorists. The point is that the ideological over-determination is itself a forced response, and what forces it is a material dilemma – the crudest dilemma of modern history. That is, 'under-development', the fact of not having and the awareness of this intolerable absence.

But then, this being true, something else follows. The march-lands and the countryside may have formulated the ideology of nationalism. In the nature of things, it was unlikely to be they who translated this rhetoric into fully-functioning reality. They did not have the power to do so: this is the entire *material* point of the dilemma around which nationalisms revolve. On the contrary, once the advanced states and economies took over the doctrines of 'nationalism' they were certain to give these ideas real muscle. England and France and the United States did not invent 'national-ism'; they did not need to, originally. They were in front, and pos-sessed the things nationalism is really about (as distinct from the things its ideology displays). The Enlightenment and classical political economy were great statements about being in front. But – precisely – statements of a type utterly different from what came into fashion with the age of nationalism.

'Uneven development' is not just the hard-luck tale of poor countries. It dragged the wealthy ones in as well. Once the national state had been ideologized into 'nationalism' and turned into the new climate of world politics – the new received truth of political humanity – the core-areas themselves were bound to become nationalist. As the march-lands caught up in the later nineteenth century, as Germany, Italy and Japan emerged into the extra-rapid industrialization made possible by their 'revolutions from above', was it surprising that England and France developed their own forms of 'nationalism'? There resulted a struggle between founder-members and *parvenus*, where great-power nationalism was forged from the new notions and sentiments. Forged, naturally, with far greater efficacy than on the periphery, for the simple reason that these societies had the media and the abundant human and material resources to do so.

In other words, 'uneven development' is a dialectic. The two sides involved continuously modify each other. Nationalism may have originated as a kind of 'antithesis' to the 'thesis' of metropolitan domination. But it was rapidly, and inevitably, transmitted to the whole process. However, the term 'dialectic' should not be allowed to mislead us any more than the inebriants of romantic-nationalist ideology. It does *not* mean (as Gramsci once put it) that history is a boxing-match with rules, where we can be secretly sure what kind of 'synthesis' is going to emerge. In the quite un-Hegelian reality, for which 'uneven development' is merely an approximate label, there has never been any certainty as to who would win. As a matter of fact, the 'antithesis' came near to destroying the 'thesis' altogether; and the states denoted by the latter term only won in 1945–6 by the development of powers so enormous as to threaten the annihilation of historical humanity itself. It is not impossible that in some later stage of the same struggle they will be employed.

Nationalism and the Irrational

'Uneven development' is a politely academic way of saying 'war'. The process it refers to is warfare – that 'development war' (as one might call it) which has been fought out consistently since the eruption of the great bourgeois revolutions. The causes which disproved Kant's predictions about national divisions also disappointed his dream of a Perpetual Peace. For much of the time, naturally, the struggle has been conducted in socio-economic or diplomatic terms. But this essentially conflictual process has always tended towards real warfare. And we all know, it is the simplest matter of historical fact, that from the Franco-Prussian war to the present day, modern history has degenerated into military conflicts of a type and scale unimaginable previously. Instead of the social revolutions forecast by the men of the 1840s, there have been World Wars. Instead of civil strife, there has been imperialist and nationalist slaughter; and the social revolutions which have occurred have done so as by-products of these wars – so intertwined with nationalist motifs as to have a sense quite different from the one envisaged by Marxist universalism.

In this world at war, it is absurd to award 'nationalism' a sort of patented right on one side. This moralizing perspective not only prevents one from grasping the importance of great-power nationalism in the unfolding of the whole process. It fatally impedes one's view of what must be considered a central sector of the phenomenon: fascism. Beyond this, it deforms any theoretical effort to approach the problem of nationalism's so-called 'irrationality'.

I pointed out already that core-area nationalism was, in the long run, as inevitable as peripheric nationalism; but likely to be more effective. The most potent versions of all were to be found in a distinct location within the larger history we are analyzing. That is, in nationalities which to some degree combined both factors: a painful experience and fear of 'under-development', *and* modern socio-economic institutions enabling them to mobilize and indoctrinate their masses effectively.

There is no doubt where this explosive combination was found: in the notorious 'late developers' of this century's history. What were the factors that Germany, Italy and Japan combined together in the trajectories which made them the Axis Powers of 1939-45? All three were societies with a relatively recent experience of 'backwardness' – a deprivation and impotence suddenly made humiliatingly evident to them by the impact of outside powers. All three reacted to this dilemma with particularly strong, compensatory ideological mechanisms – mechanisms which, as far as the two Western members are concerned, comprise virtually the whole panoply of nationalist beliefs and sentiments. Then they rapidly evolved some of the real substance of nation-state power, through break-neck industrialization and State-imposed societal regimentation. Their capacity to do this arose, of course, from their general position in the world political economy: they were not in the real periphery, and occupied an intermediate place between it and the centre – the march-lands or semi-periphery of the process.

In this way these societies were able to realize the ideology of 'nationalism' with unprecedented force. How effective this embodiment was would be shown by the subordination of the German working class – once the vanguard, the great hope of European socialism – to Hitler. However, in spite of these successes, the latecomers' position remained precarious. In the first half of this century all three were confronted with the fact, or the immediate likelihood, of breakdown. For all of them this implied relegation: permanent confinement to the secondary, semi-peripheric status, exclusion from the core-area's 'place in the sun'. Physical or moral defeat, the menace of internal collapse, or (as they saw it) continued or renewed aggression by the central imperial powers – these were the motives that impelled them into a still more intensive form of nationalist mobilization. It is not surprising that the country weakest in those real developmental factors I indicated, Italy, should at this point have generated the especially strong and influential 'ideological' response of the first fascist movement. Nor that this ideology should have been rapidly appropriated and turned into effective power by the late-developer with the real sinews of imperialist force, Germany.

What counts in the present argument is a simple recognition of fact. It was these countries, that location in the uneven-development process, which engendered the full historical potential of 'nationalism'. In a perfectly recognizable sense, it was here that nationalism was carried to its 'logical conclusion', as an autonomous mode of socio-political organization. To theorize about nationalism without seeing this is worse than Hamlet without the Prince of Denmark. Nationalism is such a Protean phenomenon, it informs modern history to such a large extent, that one may of course maintain there is no such thing as an 'archetype' for it, no one single form which displays its meaning. Still, if forced to pick out one specimen in a compressed history lesson for some inter-galactic visitor, one would have little choice. Seen in sufficient historical depth, fascism tells us far more about nationalism than any other episode.

There is a larger theoretical issue behind this. As I said earlier, nationalist folklore has an easy answer about the more evidently disastrous aspects of modern history: they represent accidental aberrations or excesses. The anti-imperialist mythology adds something to this. For it, these catastrophes arise from the appropriation of nationalism by the imperialists and its abuse. Great-power chauvinism, or 'reactionary nationalism', is a metropolitan ruling-class conspiracy that borrows the ideas and feelings of the world's national-liberation struggles and employs them to dupe the proletariat. Regrettably, this often seems to work.

So, there are two kinds of nationalism. The main, essentially healthy sort we applaud in Indo-China and Mozambique; and the derivative, degenerate sort we oppose in, for example, the American working class, Gaullism, the Chilean *Junta* and so on. It is this difference which explains the 'irrationality' of some nationalist phenomena. While the mainspring of nationalism is progressive, these abusive versions of it are regressive, and tend towards the encouragement of social and psychological atavism, the exploitation of senseless fears and prejudices, and so towards violence.

Without for a moment denying that these political and moral distinctions are justified, and indeed obvious, one is none the less forced to point out that the *theoretical* dimension attaching to them is quite mistaken. The distinctions do not imply the existence of two brands of nationalism, one healthy and one morbid. The point is that, as the most elementary comparative analysis will show, all nationalism is both healthy and morbid. Both progress and regress are inscribed in its genetic code from the start. This is a structural fact about it. And it is a fact to which there are no exceptions: in this sense, it is an exact (not a rhetorical) statement about nationalism to say that it is by nature ambivalent.

The Collective Unconscious

This ambiguity merely expresses the general historical *raison d'être* of the phenomenon. Which is the fact that it is through nationalism that societies try to propel themselves forward to certain kinds of goal (industrialization, prosperity, equality with other peoples, etc.) *by a certain sort of regression* – by looking inwards, drawing more deeply upon their indigenous resources, resurrecting past folk-heroes and myths about themselves and so on. These idealistic and romantic well-springs adhere to every form of nationalism. It is a perfectly banal fact about nationalist history that such soul-searching quite easily becomes sheer invention, where legends take the place of myths. Indeed, this fabrication of an imaginary past was a prominent feature of that original 'progressive' national-liberation struggle, the Greek War of Independence of the 1820s.

Again, this is emphatically not to say that all forms of nationalism are as good, or as bad, as one another. It *is* to say that the huge family of nationalisms cannot be divided into the black cats and the white cats, with a few half-breeds in between. The whole family is spotted, without exception. Forms of 'irrationality' (prejudice, sentimentality, collective egotism, aggression, etc.) stain the lot of them. Hence, while we must, of course, distinguish among different national movements and ideologies to make any kind of political sense of history, these judgements do not really mark out one sort of nationalism from another. They repose upon different criteria: for instance, the supposed class character of the society in question, or its supposed rôle in the unfolding of international relations.

In short, the substance of national*ism* as such is always morally, politically, humanly ambiguous. This is why moralizing perspectives on the phenomenon always fail, whether they praise or berate it. They simply seize upon one face or another of the creature, and will not admit that there is a common head conjoining them. But nationalism can in this sense be pictured as like the old Roman god, Janus, who stood above gateways with one face looking forward and one backwards. Thus does nationalism stand over the passage to modernity, for human society. As human kind is forced through its strait doorway, it must look desperately back into the past, to gather strength wherever it can be found for the ordeal of 'development'.

This is also the situation which helps us understand why, in a quite general sense, the 'irrational' could not help arising into the process. Because, so far from being a 'natural' growth-phase, this is a *rite de passage* so terrible, so enforced by outside power, so fiercely destructive of all custom and tradition that there could never in the nature of things be any guarantee it would succeed. Let me put this in terms of a personalized metaphor. In mobilizing its past in order to leap forward across this threshold, a society is like a man who has to call on all his inherited and (up to this point) largely unconscious powers to confront some inescapable challenge. He summons up such latent energies assuming that, once the challenge is met, they will subside again into a tolerable and settled pattern of personal existence.

But the assumption may be wrong. In the social trauma as in the individual one, once these well-springs have been tapped there is no real guarantee that the great forces released will be 'controllable' (in the sense of doing only what they are supposed to do, and no more). The powers of the Id are far greater than was realized before Freud exposed them to theoretical view. In the same way, the energies contained in customary social structures were far greater than was understood, before the advent of nationalist mobilization stirred them up and released them from the old mould. Unfortunately Marxism – which should have accomplished a 'Freudian' analysis of the historical case, and still must do so – remained on the level of myth and guesswork here.

Extreme difficulties and contradictions, the prospect of breakdown or being held forever in the gateway – it is conditions like those, surely, which may lead to insanity for an individual or nationalist dementia for a society. Given the colossal strains of industrialization, and the variety and intensity of forces which this challenge unchained into more conscious activity, there is *in a general sense* nothing amazing about the emergence of irrationality in modern history. It would have been really amazing had there been *no* temporary triumphs of the anti-Enlightenment like Nazi Germany. But the forces behind its imperialism and genocide were 'demonic' only in a manner of speaking. To be exact, in the manner of speaking of those unable, or perhaps sometimes rather unwilling, to locate them intelligibly within the general framework of modern developmental history. It was easier to pretend the Germans had been assailed by some a-historical propensity – a natural (or even supernatural) *Geist*.

I cannot refrain from at least mentioning the alternative superstition now more common, though only *en passant*. If one rejects the *Doktor Faustus* mythology then it becomes hard to deny that fascism and genocide are somehow part of the 'logic' of modern history. Then it becomes all too easy to assert that they *are* the logic of modern history. That is, modern capitalist institutions, even industry and democracy as such, are all intrinsically fascistoid and evil: the totalitarian nationalist states of the 1930s show where we are all heading. There is no call to say more about this here. As a sort of lay diabolism, I suppose it must be considered one of the odder by-products of the defeat of Western Philosophy by nationalism.

Nation Triumphs over Class

I have said nothing about the sacrosanct subject of class so far. This has been deliberate, of course. In any materialistic approach to a problem like this, one does not only find the road blocked by the abundant mythology of commonsense; Marxism has its own cottage industry working away. We have our own half-truths, our own garbled ideology, our own glib evasions to distinguish us from the common herd. And our speciality has always been 'class'.

As I said before, the bourgeois Enlightenment had its own comforters in this field. The *philosophes* thought that war and blind patriotism were by-products of the rule of the landowning classes. Dynasties were supposed to have a vested interest in conquest and bloodshed. It was they who maintained the archaisms and irrationalities of human life in being – so, get rid of aristocracy and this would wither away also. Feudalism would be replaced by the rule of a genuinely universal class, a class whose interests coincided with those of humanity in general: the bourgeoisie. As Kant said, *this* class's vested interest seemed to be promoting peace and lowering barriers among peoples, in the name of economic and cultural development.

The radicals who lived into the earlier stages of this promised land, and realized that it was going to be extremely different from the blueprints, quickly formulated a new edition of the idea. The middle classes were far less than 'universal' in their interest. They too had an inescapable stake in chaos and warfare; indeed this would get worse, if only because of the superior means of destruction science now made possible. So nationalism became 'bourgeois nationalism': and it followed that if only one got rid of this class and its forms of economic and social organization, then nationalism too would disappear. Again, narrow folly and blind sub-rational instincts were kept alive and fed by those forms. Once the class whose aims really *were* consonant with those of humanity, the proletariat, acquired power then chauvinism would no longer have any *raison d'être*.

Naturally, the myth was modified later on. Narrow folly and revived archaism proved so popular that it had to be. It was diluted down into uncertain compromises of the sort that infuriated Rosa Luxemburg. Mass nationalism was good up to a point, in certain specific conditions, in the fight against alien oppression, and so on. Beyond that point it immediately degenerated again into a morbid delusion and an instrument of bourgeois reaction. In effect, the essence of the myth was saved by tactical retreats and manoeuvres. Lenin was the most brilliant exponent of these.

The basis of the belief here being defended was that class is always far more important in history than the petty *differentiae* nationalism seems to deal in. Class struggle was invariably the motor of historical change, nationality a mere epiphenomenon of it. Hence, it was literally inconceivable that the former should be eclipsed by the latter. Exceptions to the rule demanded exceptional explanations – conspiracy theories about the rulers, and 'rotten minority' speculations about the ruled. Finally, these exceptions blotted out the sun in August 1914.

I suppose this ought to have led to a radical investigation into what was wrong with Marxism's theory of history. But it did not, for reasons I hinted at earlier and cannot explore further here. Instead, after the revolution in Russia, the Third International engendered what was really an extreme intensification of the myths: internationalism had failed through lack of will-power and organization – for subjective reasons. The conspiracies and rotten apples had not been exposed and fought with enough determination. Had they been (the implication was) then the factors of class might well have triumphed over those of national division, there might have been a great social revolution instead of the war. This was the patched-up mythology with which Marxism moved towards its encounter with the fascist revolutions of the twenties and thirties.

When an ideology is preserved and defended with such intensity, against such enormous odds and evidence, it can only be because what is protected is felt as of incalculable worth. What was at stake in this long defensive battle was, clearly, Marxism's conviction of being the true heir to the positive or universal aspects of the Enlightenment. Unable yet to come to terms with the new world of nationalist development, Marxism clung with all the greater determination, with a practically religious faith, to this basic part of its creed. 'National frontiers have long been anachronistic for capitalism itself . . .': in the last century, how many exercises in justification have started or ended with these words!

It must be obvious from the tenor of these remarks that I share the conviction which always lay behind all this mass of sophisms. Socialism, whose intellect and heart lies more in the Marxist tradition than anywhere else, *is* the heir of the Enlightenment. The defensive battle was right, in spite of all its obscurantism and piety. Socialism was a premature birth. So far from being 'ripe' (or even 'over-ripe') for it, as its protagonists told themselves, conditions in the earlier half of this century were to remain locked in the vice of primitive, uneven development and nationalism. Hence, the faith could probably only have been defended in this way.

It does not in any sense detract from the honour of that fight, or from the ultimate value of what is protected, to point out that it involved theoretical errors. The main such error concerned class. A defective grasp of the overall nature and depth of capitalist development implied certain mistakes. It meant that it was not yet possible to employ the concepts of historical materialism in relation to their proper object, the only object which gives them genuine meaning: that is, the world political economy. This is the only genuine 'structure' which can be held to explain the assorted 'superstructures' of capitalist reality (including nationalism). The lacuna was only very partially remedied by the Marxist theory of imperialism, and the initial use this made of the notion of uneven development.

The Functionality of Nationalism

Unable to perceive the dominant contradiction of capitalism's growth during so much of this century *as* dominant, Marxism insisted it represented a chain of accidents. The real, basic contradiction still at work everywhere was, therefore, the class struggle. The more hidden it appeared to be, the more it was necessary to insist. The cloud of accidents was always on the point of dispersal. The social struggle was always just about to shed its irrelevant national or patriotic form and let the universal meaning show through.

There is no need here to explain the elements of exorcism and bad faith in all this. No need either to show how such attitudes colluded (as they really could not help doing) with the nationalism of the era, by counterposing quite abstract internationalism to a pragmatic support of nationalist struggles and wars over half the planet. This is not past history. It can be studied fairly exhaustively by anybody who can read a newspaper.

In the present context it is more important to say something about the underlying theoretical issue. The story of uneven development is one of how the unheralded contradiction I have tried to outline has enveloped and repressed the other antagonism upon which Marxism laid such stress: the class struggle. As capitalism spread, and smashed the ancient social formations surrounding it, there always tended to fall apart along the fault-lines contained inside them. It is a matter of elementary truth that these lines of fissure were nearly always ones of nationality (although in certain well-known cases deeply established religious divisions could perform the same function). They were never ones of class. Naturally, in innumerable cases the two things were inextricably confused, where an upper class of one nationality ruled over peasants and workers of another. But the point is that the confusion could only be regulated in terms of nationality, not in terms of class. As a means of mobilization, nationalism was simply incomparably superior to what was contained in a still rudimentary (often, one should say, a merely nascent) class consciousness.

The superiority was not accidental – a sort of unfair advantage temporarily won here and there, but soon to recede before the truth. It derived from the very structure of those 'modern' societies cast out of uneven development. There was never any chance of the new universal class which figured in Marxist doctrine emerging *as* 'proletarians', rather than as 'Germans', 'Cubans', 'Irishmen' and so on. The most serious difficulty the new western philosophers faced here was something entailed by this fact.

There is, after all, a sense in which it is manifestly true to say that class is crucial to an understanding of nationalism. Nationalist regimentation was to a very large extent determined in its actual form and content by the class nature of the societies it affected. Their social stratification posed certain problems which it had no alternative but to solve; and the 'solution' lies in the crudity, the emotionalism, the vulgar populism, the highly-coloured romanticism of most nationalist ideology (all the things intellectuals have always held their noses at). So what is actually being exorcized by the draconian insistence that class is more significant than nationality is a larger maleficent spirit than appears at first sight. It is, if you like, the fact that the 'solution' worked.

Nationalism could only have worked, in this sense, because it actually did provide the masses with something real and important – something that class consciousness postulated in a narrowly intellectualist mode could never have furnished, a culture which however deplorable was larger, more accessible, and more relevant to mass realities than the rationalism of our Enlightenment inheritance. If this is so, then it cannot be true that nationalism is just false consciousness. It must have had a functionality in modern development, perhaps one more important than that of class consciousness and formation within the individual nation-states of this period.

Marxists (and other internationalists) have the old way out of this dilemma, I know. It can be deduced from the central myth-store we have dipped into several times already. But of course – it can be repeated, in the tone of down-to-earth heartiness appropriate for unbearable contradictions like this – any fool knows that the struggle of the proletariat is in the first instance against its own national bourgeoisie, and is, to that extent, itself national (*Communist Manifesto*). So *of course* workers are first of all Germans, Cubans, etc., nor will they cease to be so at the Last Trump. There is no real contradiction between the attributes of nationality and those of proletarian or socialist internationalism: the former is only a phase on the way to the latter (etc.).

This is where the bite is. What these rotund platitudes exorcize is the truth that there *is* such a contradiction. Under the actual conditions of capitalism's uneven development, with the actual frontier-delimited class consciousness which that process threw up, there is a deadly contradiction at work. Had 'even development' taken place in the world, then presumably national awareness would have evolved also, as peoples became literate and politically conscious; and presumably this would have been the placid, non-antagonistic awareness, the 'natural' fact which still haunts the mythology of the subject – that should-have-been history which to a surprising extent still governs reflection on what there has been and is. In the world of national*ism* things are different. Its war-like circumstances constantly engender real antagonisms between nationality and class. And in these conflicts – as long as the primary contradiction of the world economy dominates it – the position of nationality will remain stronger.

At this point let me return to the original suggestion I made. That is, to the idea that the 'failure' of Marxism over this problem was inevitable, not an unfortunate accident which could have been overcome by trying harder.

The inevitability lay in the fact that, during the era when Marxists struggled most desperately and brilliantly with the enigma – before the onset of Stalinism – the general process of capitalist development had not gone far enough. The overall characteristics of 'uneven development' had not yet been sufficiently delineated by history itself. Only partially aware of this emerging framework, socialists continued to believe they were living in the Latter Days of capitalism's progress. Their conviction remained that the process *would* straighten out and become more logical, sooner rather than later. A great social revolution where it ought to occur, in the developed heartland, would ensure this – thus restoring the basis for even development, and vindicating western philosophy in its Marxist variant.

It took the great fracture of 1914 to begin to destroy the conviction. And this was only the start of the demolition process. After the war itself came the renewed failure of revolutionary class struggle in the west, the eruption of fascism in its stead, and still another imperialist Armageddon. Ever more clearly, socialism became the main ideological arm for the forced march of a whole new range of under-developed territories. It fused effectively with their new nationalism, rather than with this class-consciousness of workers in the developed countries. As uniformed imperialism was swept away by the generalized revolt in the Third World, the cumulative sense of uneven development began to become clearer.

Only then, perhaps – i.e. only in the past decade or so – has it become more possible to perceive the general outline and structure of the process. Until it had really extended everywhere on the globe and reached even the remotest areas of Africa and Asia (as it is now doing), the possibility remained an abstract one. But today the 'end' (in one sense) of development has begun to render it concrete. Capitalism has indeed unified humanity's history and made the world one. But it has done so at the cost of fantastic disequilibria, through near-catastrophic antagonisms and a process of socio-political fragmentation (numbering 154 states at the latest count) still far from complete. The momentum of the conflictual phenomena denoted by 'uneven development' has so far proved greater than the other, more unitary and rational tendencies of capitalism's growth. They and all their ambiguous progeny have become lodged in the resultant global order. Those national frontiers that have been 'anachronistic' since an early stage of capitalist expansion continue to multiply. In the 1970s there has even reappeared some likelihood of new barriers inside some of the oldest, most stably unified states of western Europe: France, the United Kingdom and Spain.

But there is a consolation in this picture for the theorist. For it is in admitting and looking at it more steadily that it does, at least, become possible to get some bearings on the question of nationalism. It is in relation to this framework that a better theoretical orientation towards the phenomenon may arise. One can start locating and defining it more clearly – because there is, at last, a more settled and inescapable landscape which it can be related to. We can at least glimpse something of the forest – it might be more accurate to say the jungle – and of those wider, outer conditions which have precipitated its fierce internal growths.

Nationalism and Philosophy

The task of making such a plausible theoretical definition is of course a huge one. I am not trying to do this here, only to indicate in the scantest outline how it might be done. Even among the few signposts I have sketched in there are great gaps I can only refer to *en passant*.

For example, I have said nothing about the economics of uneven development, a topic essential from the point of view of historical materialism. There is little I can do to remedy this omission here, except mention some notable contributions to it, like those of Arghiri Emmanuel and Samir Amin.[2] Nor is there time to even touch upon the problem of socialism's place in the dialectic of unbalanced development, although this also is a key topic in any effort to grasp the process as a whole. One might say, for example, that the displacement of socialism from metropolis to periphery has been in many ways the most significant sign of the triumph of uneven development. Of all the weird mixtures and alliances engendered by 'combined development' – the direct transference of advanced ideas or techniques into under-developed lands – this may be the most important. Nationalism defeated socialism in the zone of high development, forcing it outwards into successive areas of backwardness where it was bound to become part of their great compensatory drive to catch up – an ideology of development or industrialization, rather than one of post-capitalist society. In this position within the world economy, it has of course become a subordinate ally of nationalism. Yet this defeat has also implied the worldwide diffusion of socialism, at a tempo far more rapid than that imagined by the founding fathers – it has meant that capitalism could not, finally, unify the world wholly in its own image. Even in its American age of unprecedented prosperity and power after the Second World War, it was forced to confront its own end from a direction quite different than the one envisaged by theorists of even development.

As I say, the task of framing a 'theory' of nationalism is that of understanding the destructive mechanisms and contradictions of uneven development – and this, in turn, is the task of re-interpreting modern history as a whole. In this sense the puzzle of Marxism's 'failure' over nationalism is simple: the problem is so central, so large, and so intimately related to other issues that it could not be focussed on properly before. History itself is now helping us towards a solution. It would be presumptuous and unnecessary to

[2] Arghiri Emmanuel, *Unequal Exchange*, NLB, London 1971; Samir Amin, *Le développement inégale*, Paris 1973.

say much more about the problematic itself here.

But there are certain wider, more philosophical implications of it which may be briefly mentioned. The most striking of these concerns the ancient, archetypal opposition of idealism and materialism. It is not quite true that the real subject of modern philosophy is industrialization (as Gellner has said). But I think it is true that the real basis of philosophical speculation is the complex of issues surrounding economic development: more or less those indicated previously, uneven development and all its implications of nationalism, 'irrationalism', inescapable ambivalence, and so on. In this context it is important to note some things about the way reality now re-presents itself.

It is not true that the conception of nationalism outlined earlier is reductionist in character. It does not wish or think away the phenomena in question (political romanticism, the idealism of underdevelopment, subjectivism, the need to 'belong', etc.) by asserting that these are merely manifestations of economic trends. It does exactly the opposite. It awards them a real force and weight in modern historical development – one quite distinct from the groanings of metaphysical irrationalism – by explaining the material reasons for this newly-acquired leverage. It locates them in relation to the material dilemmas of backwardness, and so makes of them an objective fact, not a demonic mystery; but the objective facts of nationalist passion, the awakened mass of modern instincts, and the organization of these into total or racial warfare have their own decisive impetus. To show they are the other face of capitalism's invasion of our world does not entail their demotion to mere appearance or epiphenomenon.

'Materialism' in this sense does not indicate a mechanical or metaphysical pseudo-explanation of what we have been talking about. It does not indicate another battle in an ancient philosophical war which (precisely because of its 'philosophical' character) can never be won or lost. Rather, it points the way towards leaving this war behind. It is the 'real' or historical explanation which enables us to understand the modern war of words – that is, the inability of 'Marxism' to escape from the level of philosophy in the past, its own erection into the aberrant philosophy of 'dialectical materialism' and the consequent renaissances of philosophical idealism.

In discussing the question of irrationalism earlier, I suggested that Freud's mode of explanation was in some ways applicable. Let me

extend this analogy a little. To say that the assorted phenomena and
bric-à-brac of nationalism have a 'material' basis and explanation is
akin to saying that individual neurosis has a sexual explanation.
We all know the generations of indignant evasion which have now
gone into denying and disguising the latter theory (degrading, reductionist, undervaluing consciousness, etc., etc.). These evasions
were largely ideological misunderstandings of Freud. His theory
does not really 'dismiss' the higher things of human consciousness
at all: it enables us to appreciate their genuine weight, their true
function in the individual's history, by relating them to the unconscious and buried segments of that history – to the underlying,
forced dilemmas of personal development which have been willy-
nilly 'solved' in neurosis. Following the metaphor in our own
terms, one might say: 'nationalism' is the pathology of modern
developmental history, as inescapable as 'neurosis' in the individual,
with much the same essential ambiguity attaching to it, a similar
built-in capacity for descent into dementia, rooted in the dilemmas
of helplessness thrust upon most of the world (the equivalent of
infantilism for societies), and largely incurable. Socialism over a
sufficiently large part of the world *may* represent the necessary condition for a cure one day. But this is hazardous speculation.

The Angel of History

The failure I have been talking about has always engendered pessimism in the West, as well as regurgitations of Hegel and Spinoza.
These philosophies of defeat and anguish increasingly informed
western Marxism after the First World War. Their most impressive
and sophisticated formulation was of course that given by the Frank-
furt School. Theodor Adorno's *Minima Moralia* is the masterpiece
of this dark intelligence: with its reflections on life in the United
States, it also provides the most interesting connection with the
great revival that Frankfurtism is now enjoying there. But the single
most extraordinary image of their world-view (which I make no
apology for quoting once more here) was Walter Benjamin's angel
of history: 'His face is turned towards the past. Where we perceive
a chain of events, he sees one single catastrophe which keeps
piling wreckage upon wreckage and hurls it in front of his feet. The
angel would like to stay, awaken the dead, and make whole what has
been smashed. But a storm is blowing from Paradise; it has got

caught in his wings with such violence that the angel can no longer close them. This storm irresistibly propels him into the future to which his back is turned, while the pile of debris before him grows skyward. This storm is what we call progress.'[3]

In the last quarter of Benjamin's century, the storm has blown into the most remote areas of the world. Beyond the wreckage it has aroused the great counter-force of anti-imperialist struggle. But – as I suggested before – the theoretical truth of the angel's strange trajectory does not lie only here. The terror of his vision comes from the whole process of which Third World nationalism is a part, from the original west-wind of progress as well as the multiform reactions it has produced in the east and the south. The defeat suffered by imperialism was a precondition of philosophical advance, but only a precondition.

In that advance itself, what was 'Marxism' must become for the first time an authentic world-theory. That is, a theoretical world-view (the successor of religion and philosophy) which is actually founded upon the social development of the whole world. This is the meaning to be attached to a statement I made earlier on, concerning Marxism and historical materialism. In itself the announcement of the umpteenth forecoming transcendence of Marxism into something else would be meaningless. Has a month passed since 1890 without the solemn announcement of this quasi-divine rebirth? But philosophy alone would never have accomplished this act. It is history itself which has slowly created the real, new conditions for the change I am referring to. And it is these conditions which in turn allow us a better understanding of historical fate, and prepare the way for theoretical reformulations upon a basis far sounder than those of the past.

It is in dealing with the enigma of nationalism that 'Marxism' is inexorably thrust against the limits of its own western origins, its Eurocentric nature. Yet it could never overcome these limits in theory, until they had been thoroughly undermined and broken down in practice – that is, by the events of the past decades, where the reflorescence of western capitalism was accompanied by its persistent defeat and degeneration on the periphery. It is in this sense perhaps much less fanciful than may appear at first glance to suggest that the years that witnessed the end of the great struggle

[3] Walter Benjamin, *Illuminations*, London 1970, p. 259.

in Indo-China, the oil-producers' revolt and the revolution in Portugal will appear in retrospect to mark a turning-point in the history of ideas, as well as in American foreign policy or international relations.

What actual course will the thought of historical materialism follow, as it tries to build beyond these over-narrow Enlightenment foundations? In seeking a stronger and worldwide basis (as distinct from claiming it in the abstract, as Marxism always did) it would seem to follow from the argument advanced above that an essential step must be a return to sources. That is, to the real historical sources of Benjamin's single catastrophe, the home of the wind that has propelled us so far and so erratically. This means the history of western-founded 'progress'. It is only now that a distinctively non-occidento-centric version of this story is becoming possible, a version which will be something like the world's picture of modern development – a picture in which the Enlightenment, and the bourgeois and industrial revolutions of the West figure as episodes, however important.

This reflection permits me to try and situate the theory I have been schematically outlining. It should be seen as belonging within the same broad current of thinking as – to take the most evident examples – Immanuel Wallerstein's *The Modern World System* and Perry Anderson's *Passages from Antiquity* and *Lineages of the Absolutist State*. These are works by scholars originally concerned with Third World questions, impelled subsequently to a general reinterpretation of the origins of capitalist development itself. They do not arise from Eurocentrism but from the reaction against Eurocentrism – a reaction which has, nonetheless, the achievement of a better understanding of the European sources of modern development as one of its main responsibilities. In dealing with nationalism, we have of course been examining later stages of the process, the colossal chain-reaction set up by the fuller impact of the West upon the body of older world society in the later nineteenth and twentieth centuries. But this is recognizably part of the same broader task.

The 'sources' referred to in this conception are different from what has normally hitherto been meant by the term in the polemics of Marxism. They do not lie within Marxism itself, as a system of doctrine and belief. The movement of thought in question is outward-going, not inward-looking. It is a motion made possible by the new matter of history itself – a reflection of that matter, therefore, and not the expression of our own iconoclastic will, of a more intensive meditation upon ideas and data already in existence. It is for this reason that it cannot assume the form typical of so many past 'revisions' and counter-revisions in Marxist history – that is, prescient re-readings of texts, more rigorous and unassailable editions of old concepts.

I do not mean to imply that the internal re-exploration of our thought-world is futile, or uninstructive. This would be to dismiss too much of the French Marxism of the past decade as worthless. It is reasonably obvious that such re-exploration should accompany and complement the *external*, historical critique of Marxism. The two tasks ought to be one. The problems connected with what Marx and his disciples 'really meant' by their ideas and actions should issue into the consideration of what these actually did mean, as the actions of distinct generations of intellectuals in determinate historical circumstances. But the dilemma consists in where one puts the centre of gravity. If it is placed internally, the result is bound to be the perpetuation of sectarian theology in some form, however refined. This is the main, indispensable commodity in Marxism's corner of the world market in ideas, and there are bound to be buyers. If by contrast one's primary focus is external, and perceives one time-bound (though still unconcluded) chapter in the history of ideas, then the exegesis of ideas is serving a different purpose altogether.

I do not know what that purpose is. Like everyone else my back is turned to the future, and like most others I am chiefly conscious of the debris reaching skywards. However, there is no point in fabricating new totems for history to hurl in front of our feet after desacralizing the old ones. This is not a pessimistic stance, though I suppose there is a degree of wilful disenchantment about it: I would like to believe that it is no more than being compelled at last to face with sober senses our real conditions of life, and our real relations with our kind. Marxists have often been secretly afraid that they were wrong, and the reactionaries were right, on this crucial subject: that the truth behind the sphinx's riddle of modern nationalism might really destroy them for good. Then the wreckage would end by burying us all and the angel will never close his wings.

This fear is as unfounded as the instant-formula utopias of proletarian internationalism. A better decipherment of the riddle can only serve to separate out the durable – the 'scientific', or as I chose to call it above 'historical materialism' – from the ideology in our *Weltanschauung*, the grain from the husks represented by the defeat of Western Philosophy.

Into Political Emergency

A Retrospect
From the Eighties

When these essays were first put together as a book in 1977, some anxiety was expressed about the title. Might it not be more prudent, the publisher asked, to insert a question-mark after it . . . just in case? After all, the old gentleman's demise had been forecast in the past, all too often and loudly. He had shown an embarrassing capacity to pull round, outliving many would-be grave-diggers.

Four years later, I am more convinced than I was then that we were right to omit the question-mark. During this time the process of break-up has advanced so perceptibly that we now know a lot more about it. And indeed this is why it is possible, so relatively soon, to return to some of the ideas in the book and try to re-evaluate them.

Insufficiently confident about the immediate future of United Kingdom disintegration, the first edition was, by contrast, over-confident about one aspect of it – the role of peripheral nationalism. In part this reflected the author's personal involvement in the Scottish national movement (of which more below); and in part it echoed the preoccupations of the decade, in which events in Northern Ireland, Wales and Scotland appeared to be accumulating into an intolerable burden for London government. Westminster began by deriding the threat (when Lord Kilbrandon's Report on the Constitution came out) and ended by devoting most of its time to it, between 1976 and 1979. Finally, the Labour government fell because of it. The state had weathered the social and economic tumults of 1973–74 well enough, at the cost of a mere change of governments; 'devolution' seemed a far more accident-prone device liable to embarass all future regimes – and of course, even it stood no chance in Ireland, where the state might collapse in a literal sense if the tensions grew marginally worse.

There was something else behind this vision of territorially-led disintegration, however. There was what one might call the need of the post-war British left to discover – or occasionally invent – a way out and forward from its peculiar impasse. For over a generation, socialists had endured a wasting British world where no break gave relief. Overall decline and repeated economic crisis led to no rupture in the prevailing order. The downward spiral of UK industry and the periodic mutinies of sections of the working class suggested that an end must come; yet these factors were compensated for, again and again, by both economic and political strengths inherited from successful anterior development. The oldest of continuously existing states had more than simple chronology behind it. Its long evolutionary arc – the pride of all apologists for the Constitution – had accreted a variety of resistant supports, enabling strains to be transferred from one to another.

Such frustration and deferred hope were not, of course, unique to the British left during this period. However, no other nation in the European–North American ambit fell so far (from victorious empire to 'sick man' of the Atlantic) or reacted to defeat with so much fortitude and indifference. An unparalleled retreat into under-development, more and more like a collapse; yet accompanied by augmented political stability, and an intensified popular complacency shown, for example, in adulation of the monarchy. Incompetent governments succeeded one another, pitifully incapable of reversing the trend; but somehow the *system* seemed stronger than ever. It was in this mysterious vice that the search for ways out assumed an especially impassioned character.

The first and most common form looks to economic class conflict as the key. At its crudest, this view has imagined each major strike or dispute between the TUC and government as incipient breakdown. Such episodes have not been lacking in post-1950 history. Now and then, as in the battles over industrial legislation between 1969 and 1972 or in the miners' strike of 1973–74, they have in fact created a short-lived climate of apocalypse. More generally, industrial agitation in Britain always occurs against a backdrop of strong *social* class awareness: the inveterate, archaic, concretely articulated totality of 'us and them' inherited from England's patrician revolution. It has always been tempting to believe that a strike, or a 'winter of discontent', will generate a short circuit into this latent resentment. Class struggle will then replace class cohabitation: crisis at state level will spring straight from the elemental conflict.

The scenario has been disappointed so often in Britain there is evidently something missing. Aware of this, a second tendency in the 1960s and 1970s sought the fracture-point higher up in the social order. Not the working class alone, but workers in some kind of new alliance with intellectuals would make the leap forward. Hence, some degree of intellectual reformation was in order – a big, autonomous task in a society where the intelligentsia had in the past been both important and very conservative. The student movement of the later 1960s was of course the chosen vehicle for this outlook – the place where for a moment philosophy appeared to have discovered its own mass movement, capable of directly modifying social structures. But though the moment did not endure the larger trend did. Translating Gramscian, Althusserian and other ideas into British terms, a new and less conformist intellectual class certainly arose in those decades.

The 'reformation' occurred. It did not, however, show the slightest signs in the later 1970s of achieving the fertilizing, disruptive union with practice which theory demanded. Marxist sectarianism swelled its ranks, but affected the labour movement very little. Here was the context in which a third avenue of advance began to look appealing. The alliance of workers and alienated intellectuals was indispensable – so the key argument of *Break-up of Britain* went – but such forces can come together in reality only upon a *national* terrain. Workerism and intellectualism shared an internationalist philosophy rooted in a pre-nation-state inheritance. But all actual examples of revolution are necessarily national in origin and effective scope. Common cause between a restive proletariat and a dissident intelligentsia can be made only in that dimension – hence, exploration of the latter had become a precondition of farther progress.

This thought naturally raised all the problems of United Kingdom territoriality – problems habitually demoted from the socialist problematic, if not effaced altogether. Exactly like the ruling élite, the left took a sort of all-British homogeneity for granted. It duplicated the airless universe of 'this small, crowded island of ours' with its crushing metropolitan dominance, pervasive media control, and ideologically obscure 'regions'. But clearly such cohesion was a myth. The political and civil strength of British unity had been such that the myth was rarely seriously challenged – in the sense of opposed, or attacked. At the same time, however, nobody denied that there were at least four nationalities included in the British state territory, together with a number of fragmentary or marginal cases like Cornwall, the Isle of Man, and Shetland. Less acute and confused than the similar situation afflicting the Hapsburg empire in its later days, the question was still the same: what does 'national' *mean*, in this context?

Metropolitan-minded socialism saw no sense in the question (the most aggressive of 'metropolitan socialists' are found, of course, in the periphery itself). If any form of nationalism was to be involved in the new society, 'British' would do. All the essays gathered here contested this oddly complacent assumption. The strong but synthetic Anglo-British nationality, it was argued, was *uniquely* stamped by collusion with imperialism. Other big-stick patriotisms of the modern world had certainly been defiled by the same attitudes, but none was *entirely* constructed from the materials of colonialism, domination and civilizing mission but the British. The French, Russian, American, Chinese, Japanese and German nationalisms of this century have all incorporated elements of revolution, or justifiable mass reaction against defeat and inferiority. Although with a revolutionary origin of its own, the contemporary UK monarchical state had subsequently evolved through over two centuries of capitalist leadership. The mass political reflexes it rested upon were unbroken by revolution, and untested by defeat and national humiliation.

These political instincts are, therefore, overwhelmingly conservative. As the inescapable spiral of decline bears the old state form into break-down, it appears entirely unlikely that they will simply be transposed into a new British world of overt crisis and upheaval. 'British Socialism' was founded on this belief. But if one discounts that creed – forged in high-imperial times and given authority by the military victory of 1945– then a political and ideological transmutation must be more probable. A search for renewal will ensue. Whatever its eventual political colour, this is bound to try for more effective political mobilization – and in doing so, call into being some new community spirit, some new form of popular political identity. But in the latter, national factors are crucial: the new interpellation is certain to give them a salience quite different from the *ancien régime*.

The husks of the old British identity are more likely to be cast aside than incorporated. Failure is undiscriminating. Liberality, tolerance and pragmatism will probably share the fate of civil élitism, the 'amateur' state and the City. Some myth of popular sovereignty must replace the old one of 'parliamentary sovereignty', the Crown-in-Parliament. But *which* 'people' will be awakening, and claiming its rights? United Kingdom doctrine was always ostentatiously vague on the point: there have never been 'Britons' except in newspaper disaster lists ('Indian Air Crash, 8 Britons Feared Lost'), any more than there were 'Austro-Hungarians' before 1917.

'Peoples' in the relevant sense can be made through revolutions and wars, true enough – as perhaps Yugoslavia was transformed by its struggle against German occupation into something more than a state assemblage of nationalities. However, in the 1970s the Hapsburg model of dissolution through crisis looked much more likely. In Northern Ireland an armed movement had forced an end to the old form of 'indirect rule' by a Protestant-dominated assembly. Overt separatism had made striking electoral progress in both Scotland and Wales, and seemed likely to be rewarded with some kind of (admittedly weak) autonomy. In the Austria of this multi-national state, England itself, things were more unclear – as unclear as one might expect from a dominant nationality afflicted with a uniquely inflated official identity, the crowned Fatherland of Anglo-Saxondom. Even there some cracks were showing between reality and state-ego, however. The Messiah of a right-wing little England, J. Enoch Powell, had been driven into the shade; but nobody believed the immigrant ghettos would cease to be a problem. A kind of dry rot seemed to be rising into parliamentary and other institutions (except the monarchy), the product of cumulative failure, apathy and attrition. Ignominiously unable to solve the Fatherland's 'economic problem', the European Community had become the focus for this mood of sour contraction – and so the object of the most pernicious sort of foreigner-hating, scapegoat nationalism.

The Political Realm

It is important to note – albeit with the prescience of retrospect – that each of these three ideological exits had something true in it. It was not mistaken to believe that the class struggle, intellectual emancipation and the national question respectively posed growing threats to the old regime. The error lay only in attributing too leading or exclusive a role to one or the other battle.

Extending the view one could show equally how two other significant trends of the same period suffered the same kind of bias: single-cause crusades like CND and its successor, END, and women's politics. These movements differ from the more conventional tendencies mentioned above in having vast aims: saving the species from self-extinction, and the true liberation of one half of it. However, in the state arena we are concerned with here, the effect of such universality is, if anything, magnification of bias. Causes of *such* weight must self-evidently be decisive upon a less momentous stage – must be 'key' therefore, in any political assault on the British state formation. They *must* be able to furnish the rallying point, the connective tissue for forces and ideas otherwise disparate and fragmented.

What underlies such a consistent optical error? No doubt many reasons could be adduced to fit the different cases. As far as my own goes, events since around 1977 make me think now that two distinct failings were involved. One is very general, amounting to something like a structural deficiency in the inheritance of Marxist socialism; the other is more specific, and relates to what one might call the special inscrutability of the British state system. At the grander level, Marxist tradition is chronically hazy about politics and the state; and in our insular United Kingdom dilemmas the haze tends to be thickened to impenetrability by some contingent features, features owing little to philosophy and everything to the past history of one state formation.

Pitting itself historically against idealism's reverence for the state, conceived as a spiritual motor of peoples and their development, Marxism demoted the political realm. The state became not merely secondary – a demotion justifiable in itself – but curiously adrift from society's dominant structures. Different theories about it may notoriously be read off from different works and phases of the Marxist canon. Such differences fuelled the great historical disputes between revolutionaries and reformists, and were still unresolved by the time of the onset of Soviet dominance of Marxism's problematic, between 1920 and 1960 – during which theoretical initiatives largely dried up altogether. Lenin's peculiar reaffirmation of the political had been mightily underwritten by history. Nothing else mattered, or at least mattered *much*. Feuds over the true reading of the scrolls and ritual recantations of them scarcely count, in the annals of genuine theory.

Dealing with a mounting crisis in one of the world's major state formations, *The Break-up of Britain* remained oddly (yet characteristically) oblivious to that dimension of the question. The blank seems all the stranger in retrospect, because of the roundabout way in which the book *did* connect to it. It saw, quite correctly, that Marxism suffered from a kind of congenital defect in its inability to appraise *nationalism* properly. This was the recognition that accorded with the particular ideological bias of most of the studies in it. The obverse of that awareness, however, was failure to perceive how Marxist obtuseness over nationality is related to the wider uncertainty about politics and the nature of the state. The problem was the nation-state, its persistence and resurgence. But this puzzle resides as much in the second half of the description as in the first – not only in why 'nationalism' remains a stubbornly defining aspect of the human condition, in other words, but also in why ethnically demarcated territorial statehood continues to be inescapable, as the political structure of all foreseeable development.

On the side of nationalist evolution, a lot of black water has flowed under the rudimentary bridge of theory since 1977. It became a torrent as soon as the book was published. While we worried over the mild resurgence of ethnic realities in the British Isles, an epoch of national wars among socialist states was beginning. In East Africa and South-east Asia new regimes, all proclaiming themselves revolutionary and Marxist, plunged into open aggression against one another. Conquest, border wars, the liquidation of minorities, and hymns to the motherland's 'sacred soil' were again front-page news. Once dismissed as 'Balkan' memories, these relics were restored to life by the state-triumphs of Marxism. In Cambodia a Communist government briefly imposed what may yet be seen as the most terrible example of *Gleichschaltung* in modern history – before being swept away by invasion from a neighbouring Communist state (itself shortly to suffer the same fate from a third).

These and other events of the last four years – including aspects of the Iranian revolution, and the occupation of Afghanistan –

would appear to have validated parts of the perspective drawn out in the concluding essay, 'The Modern Janus'. Janus has acquired a violent new lease of life. Not long ago, some sanguine theorists consoled themselves with the belief that 'nationalism' in the deplorable sense was really a European – and indeed a specially *East* European – phenomenon. Though exported by empire and (often artificially) established in the post–Second World War system of nation-states, it had no real roots there. The Third World's short-circuit to socialism and revolution would cure it of the virus.

The later 1970s have indicated the uncomfortable shadow of that argument. If the 'cure' fails, then the Third World choice of socialism as a path of development will simply weld that ideology with nationalism into a new combination. Competing national socialisms could be as bad as, or worse than, competing bourgeois nationalisms. The evident weakness of nationalism in many regions of the globe was early growth, not imminent demise. Communism may indeed be the most effective mode of popular mobilization in such regions. However, the very energy and totality of this 'real' national liberation makes it impossible *not* to harness ethnic-cultural factors to the utmost. The ideology of Marxist-Leninist and other socialisms remains 'internationalist', naturally (subscribed to as such by most if not all of the warring regimes mentioned). But then, so was that of Christianity across centuries of religious warfare.

While this recent shooting-gallery has underwritten the thesis of culpable theoretical blindness on nationalism, it has not – as I now perceive it – confirmed the pessimism, or even despair of reason, that often accompanied that thesis in the past. This nice but all-important distinction was not drawn forcefully enough in the original material of *The Break-up of Britain*. The force of nationality in history, its persistence in and beyond any revolution now in gestation, implies no triumph of the 'irrational'. Such facile diabolism is merely the paper contrary of naive internationalism. What *is* entailed is the inescapability of state-led, state-informed development under conditions of relative (and perhaps growing) scarcity and inequality – a process that can hardly fail to be often conflictual. Recent happenings have rubbed home the message that there is no transcendental 'escape' from such circumstances; but this should be accepted as a sobering increase of reason, not an occasion for hysterics.

The constant penchant inclining socialists in the latter direction was located, essentially, in political primitivism. 'Was' cannot be straightforwardly converted to 'is'. This is thanks to the Marxist reawakening after the mid century, increasingly focused upon the political and state dimension. Together with Gramsci's tortuous explorations of the 1920s and 1930s (rediscovered in the same period), this renaissance of ideas is overcoming Marxism's political blind-spot. It is doing so – I confess ruefully but not over-abjectly – too late to have had enough influence on *The Break-up of Britain*'s arrival on the scene. Like the enthusiasts for the assorted 'keys' and 'crucial' rupture-points referred to previously, it failed to see there is no 'crisis' in the important sense *except in the state formation itself*; no break-down that counts, save in the hegemonic structure of political domination; and hence, no break-up of the United Kingdom but a process that passes through this 'central nervous system' and destroys its tenure of power.

Insufficiently alert on the philosophical plane, my ideas were to receive however their hardest rebuke from practice itself. The process of break-up was to accelerate and reveal its true character not long after reviews of the first edition appeared. As well as askew on theory, it was faltering on the more concrete terrain advertised in the title, that of British politics and the state.

Actual Twilight

The 'twilight of the British state' began to fall all right. We are farther into the uncanny region *entre chien et loup* than anybody imagined in 1977. However, while the original analysis saw the wolves coming, it did not delineate the end of the dogs' day with sufficient focus. That is, it failed to grasp how in the United Kingdom the degeneration and failure of 'the state' could proceed only via an overt crisis of 'politics' in the sense hallowed by constitutional traditions. It was in this way that British fog fatally aggravated a larger Marxist imprecision over the political realm.

The broad picture in chapter 1 did delineate the reasons for the peculiar absences and limitations of British statehood. It suggested their historical causes, and gave some explanation of why such an odd state had been able to survive into the present. What it did not do was fill in the obverse of the condemnation: the *presence* of the UK state, how such a pitiable historical specimen in fact occupies the power-spaces of its society, exerts its hegemony and ensures the reproduction of the vital forces. From this failure stemmed an inability to perceive just which course would be taken towards the grave and which foot would go in first – and so, inevitably, inability to weigh up the importance of factors like Ireland and peripheral separatism.

One aspect of such paralysis will be familiar to – and, I trust, pardonable by – all genuine foes of the United Kingdom Establishment, or at least those exposed to that régime's incessant self-justifications. The latter exhibit nothing but 'politics' in the most banal and parliamentarist sense. TV news-watchers and newspaper-readers are treated to an exclusive diet of reverential scrutinies of Westminster doings and electoral chances. Occasional irreverence or criticism of 'our system' serves principally to emphasize the underlying grandeur. This tends to be more than the proper concern of a democracy with its own form of government. It is as if, somehow, Great Britain revolved around 'the House' and a semi-religious posture towards its rituals was in order. Other nations may be more obsessed than the British with 'politics' in one sense or another; but is there any other where such an institution has become the national soul?

Sceptical reaction to this permanent ideological display tends to be extreme. Rejection of its basic imposture carries one, almost inevitably, to some sort of wholesale dismissal. An 'executive committee of the bourgeoisie' is bad enough; this committee-circus-shrine-symbol is perfectly intolerable. At the more studious level, rationalistic reflexes are of course encouraged by the way in which well-known analysts of the system, like Bagehot, Crossman and Mackintosh have themselves been unable to avoid profound cynicism. Thus the educated disparagement of those 'in the know' can be made to support more genuine, revolutionary hostility. The result is intellectual deletion of established 'politics'. They are a bourgeois charade with which *real* politics can have nothing to do; hence what happens at Westminster is unimportant; the reality of the state and the exercise of power are by definition different, and to be unmasked.

The truth inherent in such a reflex may return one unwittingly to political primitivism. What it blots out, of course, is the sense in which the state and real hegemony *are* the ostensible, sacralized apparatus of government (though not necessarily in the way described by its own lackeys). It remains true that the latter is not *all* they are. However, this is another question. One need not possess a complete chart of all the articulations of power to understand the special prominence of one of them. In British conditions, parliament occupies such a prominent – indeed pre-eminent – position.

Such a forward and frontal hegemonic place is the reflex of the (now equally celebrated) 'backwardness' of the British state form. *The Break-up of Britain* joined other critics in emphasizing the second aspect, and stressed the decrepit features of an early bourgeois régime maintained too long in evolutionary existence by its external good fortune. For well over a century – since the loss of Britain's brief industrial leadership – the dominant problem for it had been apparently to assume a more positive and interventionist role in economic development. State-led reindustrialization was the only way of retaining power, just as all over the world state-fostered industrialization had become the norm for gaining power and prosperity. Important in the self-consciousness of British rulers since the 1860s, this motif became all-important after the Second World War. And yet, clearly, the old régime had utterly failed to effect such a self-transformation. In war conditions it was capable of galvanic, almost revolutionary efforts in this direction; but peacetime invariably saw the resurfacing of old structures, and of a concomitant social conservatism and decline.

However, the absence of a typical modern state form with such 'modernizing' potential was the presence, consistently and success-fully asserted against 'failure', of a civil élite. The state never acquired sufficient distance from civil society, and so lacked the prerequisites for technocracy: autonomy, professionalism, powers of sustained initiative. But the other face was an unusually commanding hegemony of civil society itself. Exerted in in-numerable Gramscian modes which resonate throughout the social fabric, the crucial focus of this authority remains the parliamentary apparatus. Many studies have revealed the twentieth century mutations of Westminster parliamentarism – notably the rise of party-machine politics, and the ascendancy of the Cabinet and the Prime Minister's personal power – but none have demonstrated any important *displacement* of hegemony outside its orbit. Occult, manipulative forces like the Civil Service, the Security Services or the Army may have extended their domain; they have not overtaken the ostensible centre of ruling-class dominion.

The earlier analysis perceived how this mode of power rested in turn upon a peculiar configuration of United Kingdom capitalism (of which more below). But it did not adequately deduce either the *strategy* of state power inherent in it, or the indispensability of 'civil hegemony' for that practice. 'Parliamentarism' is so vital to this specific kind of hegemony that break-down, systemic failure, *must* proceed through the former. The book's optic had seen hegemony challenged, perhaps broken, by the exit-politics of the nationalists and the fissile state of Northern Ireland. In fact, the regime was teetering towards a more authentic, internal crisis, one promoted by the hopelessness of its two-party politics and aggravated by an international economic recession. The parliamentary-political order was entering into ferment – which means, in United Kingdom conditions, an incipient crisis of state strategy, a possible break-down so serious that emergency measures are required. These must be, in the first instance, parliamentary in nature. Far from indicating the superficiality of the rupture – as might be true in other, more friable political structures working via constant 'crisis' and party shifts – the changes signal the depth of what is happening.

The Phoney Counter-revolution

The political events of 1979 seemed at the time to mark a return to constitutional order. After years of danger signals, stability had returned. Edward Heath's trade union agonies and his final crucifixion by the miners, the great inflationary wave and the near-collapse of the currency in 1976–77, two indecisive elections producing an uneasy quasi-coalition of Labour and Liberals, the ascent of separatism and stalemate in Ireland – all this had culminated in the sour winter of 1978–79, against a backdrop of inexorable recession and growing unemployment. The electorate rushed for some sort of conservative security.

True, it rushed in different directions, depending upon how recent history had defined 'security'. In the industrial regions and Scotland this still meant Labourism, in spite of 1974–79; in the southern heartland, metropolitan England, it meant a reclothed Toryism. The divergence was noted as ominous even then. But for a while the effects were outweighed by the sense of returning familiarity. Separatism had been exorcized by the March referenda.

Liberalism suffered an equally sharp reverse at the general election in May. Third-party diversions dwindled, in spite of several years of innuendos about 'the end of the two-party system'. Mrs Thatcher's large, safe Tory majority would surely be followed by a swing back to the other pillar of constitutional *Ordnung und Recht*, Labour? Acutely miserable as many of her opponents were on 4 May, they could hardly avoid consoling themselves with the underlying feeling that the stars were, nevertheless, in their courses once more.

They were not. What we saw was merely a brief simulacrum of the formerly existing order. The Kingdom's constitutional countenance was able to recompose its battered features into a semblance of the old equilibrium. Then, in a time far shorter than anyone imagined, it was gone forever. Beneath the surface the currents of the previous decade had never ceased to run. They had simply altered course a little, and now they were eating their passage into the inner sanctum of the regime, the House of Commons party-game. In its moment of restoration, Westminster's *ancien régime* was about to be extinguished, as the state was forced into another era. It is in that transition that the break-up, no more than adumbrated in the 1970s, will be defined and rendered concrete.

While the illusory moment endured it was heightened by two other factors, one short-term, the other a deeper misunderstanding of Britain's post-war 'consensus'. On the former count, the Conservative Party's victory was hailed on most sides as a kind of outright bourgeois achievement. Socialists evoked bare-fanged reaction; *Daily Telegraph* readers saw a definitive end to nonsense over slackers and trade unions. For a while an ideological Punch-and-Judy spirit reigned, heightened by the evidently bellicose personality now in charge of the new government, and her reiterated expressions of intransigence. A genuine right-wing 'radicalism' had, according to this view, thrown away the gloves of liberal consensus. The result could not fail to be open class warfare and political polarization. Labourists had, of course, a special stake in such hysteria, since it directed attention away from the lamentable recollections of 1976–79 and made them the natural heirs of the coming swing-back to 'moderation'.

In 1984 – so went the short-lived tale – it would be like 1974. Labourism would repair the consensus damaged by rash reactionary meddling, most probably without third-party diversions. Shame-faced relief would again be felt by industrialists and *Times* leader-writers, even if the cost was a slight leftward displacement of the system. Trade-union antics are in the end more acceptable to the bourgeoisie than civil war and four million unemployed. Now as then, Labour's future front bench were a pretty responsible, moderate lot (Dr Owen, Mrs Williams, Denis Healey, and the rest) and the displacement would be minimal, perhaps not even noticeable. Another instalment, in short − for the philosophical supporters of Labourism (many of them far outside the party itself) one more inch leftwards, better than the opposite and all that can realistically be hoped for; for the custodians of twentieth-century state strategy, one more petty overhead to be fulminated over but paid.

Fortunately, this was largely ideological habit, now divorced from the real development of Britain's politics. What the mood of the moment overlooked was the larger pattern, which had arrived at its point of rupture almost unnoticed behind the brief outer spectacle. The danger signals had not been false. From the collapse of Wilson's heady modernization plans after 1965 up to 1979's 'winter of discontent' the symptoms had in fact accumulated, each one leaving some further weakness or fault in the structure. Now, a political load-bearing wall was about to collapse. It was Labourism that had reached the end of its tether, and become incapable of sustaining the old consensus.

Why did this happen to the secondary, alternative political formation in the system, rather than to the 'party of the ruling class'? Why to the reforming movement, rather than to the guardian of the status quo? A full understanding of this demands some appreciation of longer-term continuities in British state interests, which I will return to later. However, it is clear that the Labour Party, without becoming hegemonic ('the natural ruling party'), had a special custodial interest in certain vital areas of the modern UK. It was identified with the public-sector economy and the untidy range of social services labelled, from 1945 onwards, as 'the Welfare State'. These represented at once its practical achievement as a reform movement, and the basis of its lasting appeal and power. Wilson's 1964–66 government had endeavoured to transform Labour into the party of state-propelled modernization, and failed abysmally.

After that, it became ever more the party of *defence* for such past achievements. The power of initiative and attack was delivered over to the right. Between 1966 and 1979 the UK political stage ceased to be one where progressive forces advanced to wring concessions out of a reluctant and conservative Establishment. Instead, the left was thrust into an increasingly difficult rearguard action on behalf of the existing balance, against a right-wing reaction growing in fervour and ideological authority. There was a shift in the centre of gravity. Insufficiently registered in party propaganda or media commentaries – where of course the dead generations continued to reign – the effect of this was to render Labour what one can only define as a movement of pseudo-conservatism.

Genuine conservatism is the fight to preserve a given economic, social and state system with the minimum of concessions and compromises. It is carried on, naturally, by political groupings organically connected to the élites enjoying the advantages of that arrangement. Now, it is only on the wilder shores of sectarian abuse that Labour governments could be dismissed as mere 'conservatives' in that sense. However, under the conditions of inversion referred to, they were undoubtedly driven into a parody of conservatism. They turned into guardians of a social contract previously made, and now under assault both from circumstances and from political opponents. They assumed, therefore, the posture of a feeble, avuncular paternalism, as the would-be stewards of moderation and the British way. In policy this was perhaps best exemplified by the ludicrous 'Social Contract' of 1977–78, when the trade unions were lured into support for Healey's deflationary economic programme (in reality a weak variety of monetarism). In personalities, it was embodied successively by the two resoundingly hollow father-figures of Harold Wilson and James Callaghan.

In Scandinavia, given the special regional conditions of a historically weak right wing and an early-established and united left, social democracy has been able to establish an authentic hegemony (only now under threat). What was seen in Britain over the last political generation was, by contrast, the unsavoury pretence at hegemony from a movement defending its own sector of the social arena in the name of the whole. Where sectoral and class interests have been made *effectively* dominant, where through the state they have become the 'national interest', things are different. In the United Kingdom, where not even the most naïve apologists of the 'post-war social revolution' would now maintain anything of the kind had happened, the experience of the 1970s was the opposite. The working class was isolated and disaggregated politically. Its stake in the old regime (the 'welfare state') was exposed as merely corporate and clientelist in character, when defended by an absurdly vacuous and pseudo-national rhetoric. The steward had put on the laird's clothes and ruling manner, after giving up the idea of actually expropriating him and freeing the farm-labourers. Nobody who mattered believed the charade for a moment. As Crossman noted repeatedly in his *Diaries*, the fellow couldn't shake off his cringe or his petty-bourgeois snobbery.

Pseudo-conservatism derived from the exhaustion of the previously existing material conditions which had made reform possible, and tolerable to the rulers. Serious improvement and extensions of the welfare state depended on economic expansion. But after the failure of Wilson's 'technological revolution' there was no chance of the latter – at any rate on a scale sufficient to support a 'new advance towards socialism'. Instead, Labour governments were coerced into the position of being primarily managers of the economy: all too obviously, renewed and consistent growth had become the precondition of progressive reform. But, lacking the state apparatus capable of provoking the longed-for 'dynamism', they could only be bad managers. In the 1970s the decline intensified into 'de-industrialization'; bad – in the sense of unsuccessful – management turned into the desperate effort to stand still and avert retreat. The forces of 'British Socialism' found themselves not merely running capitalism, but endeavouring (vainly) to stop the run-down of welfarism.

Such hopeless stalemate poisoned everything. It rendered the old ideology of British Socialism absurd, naturally. But the effects upon the polity as a whole were much worse. Aided by the evolution of a more reactionary cultural climate, the right was able to project itself in new ideological vestments – as a liberating, 'radical' alternative. Here, the inversion was giving a new lease of life to the authentic ruling class. Twice in a decade – in 1970–72 and again in 1979 – it drew easy benefit from Labour decay and paralysis, as governments won majorities for programmes of shrieking counter-revolution. Thus, the political burdens of national decline were shifted on to the shoulders of the left; relieved of its responsibility, the right could pose as liberator and preach deliverance from the 'intolerable system' essentially its own.

Concealed behind the day-to-day rhetoric of British adversarial politics (where equal parties contend for office) this fifteen-year-long slide was simply a recipe for gathering reaction. Socialism, parliament, the state, traditional Toryism and the previous consensus were all discredited by it. The longer it persisted, the more violent the spasms of right-wing 'renewal' were certain to become. The two we have witnessed so far have been phoney counter-revolutions, as I will argue below; yet they presage something more ominous. They have been rehearsals for action still to come, at a later and more acute phase of the crisis. The longer Labourism in the old form lasted, the worse the decay of politics was bound to become, and the more devastating the eventual rightist *revanche*. Fortunately, its time was nearly up in 1979. In opposition Labour's break-up soon began, releasing both the good and evil genies of a quite different epoch.

Long-term State Strategy

Left pseudo-conservatism and right pseudo-radicalism have gone together – alternative political visages of the same long moment of decline. They are the increasingly diseased versions of the older two-party system, marking the latter's decreasing legitimacy and the crisis of the Keynesian political economy. But to understand why, around 1980, the slide became an actual drop into substantial political change we ought to look even more widely at the British context.

The 'economic problem': this has been the ostensible dilemma of UK party politics throughout its twilight. Governments, newspapers, television, conferences, innumerable books and articles have explored every facet of each recurrent crisis. All manifestos are obliged to advertise a solution; all administrations pass much of their time wrestling with the too-well-known symptoms, and failing even to begin serious therapy. The ideological assumption is of a nation faced with an intractable question to which any answer is extremely difficult: differing approaches are possible, yet *the* solution eludes one after another.

No-one would deny the existence of such a 'problem'. However, longer historical perspective will quickly reassure one that neither the 'problem', the 'solutions', nor the underlying consensual strategy of the state towards its economy are quite what they appear in current political rhetoric. To put it bluntly: there is a very long-term problem of economic adaptation and reordering, but there is also a (similarly long-term) British state strategy for coping with it and eventually solving it. The problem, in this alternative sense, is the inheritance of a predominantly archaic industrial sector tied to early development and imperialism; the solution, since early in this century, has been *to press towards internationalization of the UK economy* as the answer doing most good to the flourishing parts of the system and least damage to the ailing ones. It is not the case that no 'solution' has been practicable. The civil elite guiding the larger destiny of British capitalism has had a perfectly sound strategy which it has been able to pursue through the common ground or consensus of the political order. Had this not been so, the latter could never have endured with such stability and confidence.

Although possible and (of course) practically tested by ex-perience through various forms of party government, this strategy has one peculiar feature serving to distinguish it both from the economic formulae of politicians and the comparable grand designs of other capitalist states. It is largely *unavowable*. A national state formation cannot overtly embrace a goal which, by obvious implication, undermines and discredits its own separate existence and power. Internationalization is the trend – indeed, the only real tendency conforming to the special deformations of the British economy – but it can be followed only in the guise of ostentatiously *national* policies for rebirth, 'modernization', re-industrialization (and the other panaceas). Such programmes must be visible – they fill the daily political space – hollow, unsuccessful, and repetitive (so that 'failure' is never truly failure, and another effort may do the trick).

In modern bourgeois power-systems there has to be some distinction between state interest (presented ideologically as a true or essential 'national interest') and the programmes of parties or leaders. Under UK conditions, however, distinction has turned into wide discrepancy – and finally into an apparently irreparable divorce. This structural fissure is what explains the superficial paradox of an immensely strong politico-ideological order that, notoriously, has become incapable of achieving anything. Take away the ideological prisms and both strength and weakness look quite different. The institutions are neither the all-potent stuff of the Westminster sovereignty myth, nor the incompetent cretins suggested by post-war record (in terms of inability to obtain avowed goals). They are merely fairly good at pursuing the tacit, inevitable aims imposed by the historical pattern of British capitalism. It just so happens these aims are so unpalatable to so many as to be unsellable: there is no way of turning them into effective political interpellations.

The basis for such an odd polity is known to all economic historians, and indeed to most journalists specializing in 'the British crisis'. After its industrial interlude, from the mid eighteenth to the mid nineteenth centuries, the UK economy settled back into a more traditional, mercantile mode of exploitation. The 'Industrial Revolution' and its short-lived productive superiority gave added edge and impetus to Great Britain's colonial development-path; it did not produce a deeper alteration of course, or a political revolution. No second instalment of the 'bourgeois revolution' was to match and express the florescence of British manufacturing and engineering. Instead, the meridian of Victorian power witnessed a steady reabsorption of the new bourgeoisie by an older civil and state structure. The renewed overseas drive of imperialism brought life back into the latter, restoring its oligarchy and hardening a consciously archaic class order. Through the world dominance of sterling and London's financial institutions, capitalism was re-diverted into a more parasitic role – away from the river-valley industries of the early 1800s and towards external investment. It was this rebalancing of Britain's overall capitalist pattern that proved decisive for the following century. State strategy in peacetime has been determined by it.

Periods of war have of course brutally interrupted it, and produced – as social historians of both world conflicts remark – astonishingly successful socio-economic transformations. On each occasion the forced abandonment of liberalism led to dramatic state intervention and near-miracles of productivity within a 'siege economy'. These were manifested socially by the inhibition of class hierarchy: a kind of temporary radicalism amounting, during the Second World War, almost to apparent social revolution. And yet, in spite of such significant glimpses of an alternative path of development, the effect of spasmodic 'reindustrialization' was to restore the underlying state trajectory. Structure triumphed over the heady, widely held ideals of 1918 and 1945. Internationalization resumed its course under conditions somewhat different but – because of the victories and post-war alliances – hardly less tempting and propitious for the ruling class. *Dirigisme* and radicalism quickly and jointly subsided. The domestic industrial sector resumed its long-term decline, consistently sacrificed at every point of crisis to the outward-looking considerations of sterling and international prestige (shown for instance in spending on arms).

Imperialism turned into internationalization. But then, the former had always been predisposed towards the latter; that was its specific bent and form, culminating in the hegemony of sterling and City investment over the world market of 1900–1914. In spite of their superficial extension, British imperial interests were far less *intensively* dependent upon colonial and military rule than those of other systems. Many analyses of this 'investment empire' have demonstrated its relative autonomy from the areas actually governed or settled by the British. Free trade and movement of capital were far more crucial to it than colonies. Loss of the latter mattered little, provided that a viable, 'open' international capitalist order was retained – and of course, judged from a severely economic point of view, that was what the two world wars were fought to safeguard. After the second world conflict, particularly, the UK economy and state were able to enjoy an Indian-summer generation of relatively privileged access to the restored and American-guaranteed global market. The decay inherent in this situation was unmistakable from the early 1960s onwards – visible enough, at all events, to become the obsessive theme of British political argument. Yet it was not until the general economic recession of the later 1970s that 'decline' started to disband the British political 'consensus': that is, the underlying, tacit acceptance of post-imperial state strategy.

Regarded purely in economic terms, the latter represents the dominant interests of financial capital in alliance with a small number of UK-based multinationals – productive units too large for the domestic market and constantly in quest of both outlets and production facilities abroad. Since the City inherited its own overseas bias from empire, these two forces jointly constitute a permanent 'outward-looking' overbalance of UK capitalism. It is such irreparable disequilibrium that demotes British 'industry' in the sense dear to rhetoricians and Fleet Street's economic quacks. That is, the main body of (by world standards) middle- or small-scale industries founded on native capital, built up during the mid-Victorian era and then consistently deprived of adequate invest-ment and technological support since the later turning towards imperialism (New Imperialism, as it was labelled at the time).

But economic imbalance alone does not provide the thrust of the state's post-Victorian direction. Its external dependence is cor-related to internal asymmetries of class and region. The most celebrated account of this configuration was given by J.A. Hobson in his *Imperialism* (1901), depicting a nation increasingly polarized into an industrial North and a parasitic South living off the proceeds of empire. Nine years later, in a less familiar analysis, he perceived how the tendency had hardened into political form in the election of 1910.[1] A decade had settled the physiognomy of the Imperialist nation, far more emphatically than in the period before 1900. 'Two Englands' had emerged, '. . . a Producer's England and a Consumer's England, one England in which the well-to-do classes mould the external character of the civilization and determine the habits, feelings and opinions of the people, the other England in which the structure and activities of large organized industries, carried on by great associated masses of artisans, factory hands and miners, are the dominating facts and forces.' Most people do work in the South, but their labour is 'closely and even consciously directed by the will and the demands of the moneyed class, and the prestige of the latter imposes habits, ideas and feelings antagonistic alike to useful industry and to democracy'; while in the North both Liberalism and Labourism rested on an organized, skilled working class influenced by Nonconformity and relatively free from deference. Hobson thought this movement would soon develop to the point of challenging Southern hegemony: via the Labour Party, it would bring about a class *revanche*, where the intelligent, radical, egalitarian North would unseat the reactionaries and save civiliz-ation from Imperialism.

After the similarly crucial election of 1979 nobody can read Hobson's article without a shock of recognition. He was describing the politically formative moment of twentieth-century British society; 1979 saw the conclusion of the overall trend there made evident – the dissolution of its old nervous system. At the end as at

[1] 'The General Election: a Sociological Interpretation', *Sociological Review*, vol. III, 1910.

the beginning, Southern hegemony appears naked and unendurable: the regionally focused dominance of a uniquely extroverted exploiting class. But the recognition is tempered by hindsight. Accurate as Hobson's vision was, he could not understand how successfully Southern hegemony was to adapt itself, how easily it was to swallow those rising forces he was so confident about. The very same factors picked out so lucidly in the pages of *Imperialism* were to furnish the heartland area with unprecedentedly powerful means of social and ideal hegemony. And in the intervening period these have proved so effective that the North–South fissure, though never less real than in his description, was largely deprived of ideological salience. It was subsumed by the overall success of the metropolitan state's course. Labourism – far from redirecting that course – came rapidly to an organic accommodation with it. It settled for a corporate class compromise with internationalization, which was *also* a territorial balance. Wartime triumphs and postwar pickings, the adroit formulae of Keynes and Beveridge, and (in its own terms) the straightforward returns of City-governed capitalism all helped secure this.

Ideology shifted to make it possible. In Hobson's day the South had been won over to Tory 'Unionism', a hawkish creed wedded to the fantasy of imperial consolidation via tariffs and big guns. His own Liberalism, by contrast, still upheld a free-trade alliance between significant sectors of the bourgeoisie and the 'artisans' to whom he felt the future belonged. However, that alliance was foundering as he wrote. As a more directly working-class political formation emerged from the war years, the 'property-owning classes' simply appropriated the ideal gist of Liberalism. Much of the personnel and the electoral support of the Liberal Party gravitated over to Conservatism, as well as its doctrinal kernel. 'Freedom' then became its distinctive banner – a multi-functional gospel much better adapted to what were becoming the long-term interests of the ruling Southern elites.

Imperialism in the ideological sense was given too much importance by Hobson and others. It was a temporary aberration. The chronic outward thrust of United Kingdom capitalism was better served in the long run by cautious disengagement from direct political and military rule. Such pragmatism was less demanding and dangerous, both externally and internally. The New Imperialist dream of Chamberlain and Kipling aimed at armouring and systematizing Britain's overseas dependence – a course that would have carried it into even sharper conflict with other colonizing nations and demanded, ultimately, an authoritarian and interventionist state at home. Industry might have been saved and modernized by this counter-revolution. London's place as the central node of the capitalist money world would have been destroyed; so would the traditional mode of civil hegemony, or nonformal domination. A military and racist nationalism would have taken the strategic place of internationalization.

But of course, the notion of 'property-owning classes' had a deep ambivalence in the UK context. Preponderance within the plutocracy lay on the mercantile and financial side, well aware of the perils of ultra-imperialism. It was the middle and lower depths of Southern society that had been infected by Unionist hysteria, not the elite – as Hobson put it, 'Almost every old Cathedral city . . . nearly all the dockyard and service towns, the watering places and pleasure resorts, the county towns throughout the South, the old market towns', with their 'large classes of professional men, producers and purveyors of luxuries, tradesmen, servants and retainers who are more or less conscious of their dependence on the goodwill and patronage of persons "living on their means" . . .'.[2] Once war had demonstrated some of the consequences of an imperialist alternative, these masses were easily reherded into support for a more moderate, liberalized Conservatism. The permanent hegemonic bloc was constituted: an overseas-oriented, mercantile sector with decisive ascendancy over the industrialists at state level, this bourgeoisie as a whole then exerting sufficient authority – through the reformed Conservative Party – to maintain the order and direction of the system.

Rehearsals for an End

The Break-up of Britain originally failed to situate its nationalist problematic securely enough within this grander context: the general class and territorial disequilibrium of the UK state. The reader should remember, however, that it was written under polemical stresses, from inside an active national movement. In the Scotland of the seventies, socialists navigated uneasily between the

[2] Ibid., p. 109.

two primitive but vigorous opponents whose fusillades filled most of the political arena. On one side a bourgeois nationalism denied region and class altogether; on the other a lumpen socialism denied nationality any progressive significance whatever (unless its frontier ran through the middle of the English Channel). For the latter – inevitably a prime target for this and other tracts – the 'real problems' were 'exactly the same everywhere' in Liverpool as in Glasgow, in Cardiff as in Dundee (until, across the Channel, they suddenly became so different that withdrawal from the EEC was the self-evident answer).

Replying to this species of idiot bad faith diverted attention from the more important theme of the general articulation of class and territory within the United Kingdom state orbit. In fact, the national questions in Scotland, Wales and Ulster are lodged within the pernicious type of uneven development outlined above: a structural 'North-South' divide quite inseperable from the special historical form of the existing state. The underlying trajectory of that state is towards the eversion of the British political economy. The metropolitan heartland complex will become ever more of a service-zone to international capital – the conveniently offshore location for investment or reinvestment, insurance and speculation, guaranteed by both public and private institutions and underwritten by a famous social stability. Unnecessary to offshore success, the industries and populations of the Northern river valleys will eventually be shut down or sold off. There is no possibility of 'reviving' such an old, chronically deprived industrial sector on a scale capable of supporting UK capitalism's top-heavy metropolis; however, a significant manufacturing presence and significant employment prospects can be retained by turning over the North directly to foreign capital. To make the river valleys assembly-stages or branch-units of American, German, Japanese (and eventually Korean or Brazilian?) enterprises is the ideal complement to the main City-Southern strategy.

With the biggest of territorial empires and its insular emplacement, the UK state was once the epitome of independence; ironically, its historic parabola has carried it into an absolutely contrary fate – a chosen and inescapable dependence. 'De-industrialization' is in this sense no passing ailment, curable by budgetary medicine or programmes of crash investment. It is inscribed in the genetic programme of an abdicant bourgeoisie. The 'will-power' invariably solicited by Britain's revivalist pundits has no social substance. They are addressing an industrial sector utterly devoid of initiative, since the 1920s irrevocably inured to 'responsible' servitude. These traits are normally expressed in the doggy pathos of the CBI's spokesmen. When CBI President Sir Terence Beckett demanded a 'bare-knuckle fight' against Thatcher-Joseph monetarism in 1980 (medium-sized industry was then facing extinction on the cross of high exchange and interest rates) the result was national commotion and scandal. Beckett was forced to scramble his gloves on again the following day, doubtless regretting his acceptance of a post customarily reserved for pompous has-beens. No manufacturers' crusade was intended, he explained; merely a piece of highly coloured advice. Having attained its peak, the industrialists' rebellion subsided; in the ensuing two years the pace of de-industrialization quickened to breakneck level.

At the same time, Mrs Thatcher's sole genuine piece of 'radicalism' was bearing its fruits to the real oligarchs' table. Within a few months of taking office, her government completely abolished foreign exchange controls. Combined with the effects of North Sea oil revenues on the value of sterling, this offered unprecedented opportunities to the City. Outward investment soared, in inverse proportion to the growth of UK bankruptcies. Before long her deflationary high interest rates encouraged massive inflows of foreign capital to London's banks and brokerage houses: even within a context of world recession, the established pattern of Southern parasitism acquired boisterous new life. In this sense, 'Thatcherism' is merely the dramatic, relatively naked acceleration of the old state strategy. Labourism's putrefaction delivered over a significant body of Southern and Midland working-class support to her in 1979; her government was emboldened by this to plunge more directly along the path of internationalization than any before it, discarding some – though by no means all – of the usual vestments of consensus.

'Consensus' is one of the key amulets of the UK system. It is customarily invoked in an idealist perspective, to summon up a nation of nodding heads sagely in accord on fundamental matters. The material reality of consensus is, of course, a frequently semi-conscious (or even unconscious) acquiescence in the actual drift of the state and economy. It is, so to speak, what has consistently emerged from the supposed contest of wills and policies in Westminster and Whitehall – what is settled for in an often tacit practice, once all the ideological trumpets have sounded, all the taboos have reared their heads, all the 'impossible' difficulties been gravely registered and the representations of responsible opinion received. It is what is liable to happen, then. Consensus (or 'compromise') is the lowest common denominator of Great Britain's hunchback Establishment and economics. The record demonstrates the consistent hegemony of the City over the Treasury, and of the Treasury over the state (that is, over all governments). Anyone wanting to examine in detail just how this structure asserts itself through politics need turn only to the history of the Labour government from 1964 to 1967, a period now thoroughly turned over by memorialists and commentators.

Discarding 'consensus' in the talismanic sense means merely omitting a few of the means through which the real common denominator is realized. The patient was to be dropped bodily into the deeper waters of 'freedom' (the code for internationalization) rather than slid into them apologetically with the aid of comforters and balloons ('bailing out lame ducks'). This new rigour was accompanied by a steep rise in ideological decibels. Traditionally, 'Freedom' is a Conservative interpellation convoking *petty-bourgeois* resentment and ignorance into support for the patrician governing clique. Its real connotation is, of course, the freeing of the Southern non-industrial oligarchy on its eversive path (while 'state control' means braking the course via concessions and hand-outs to the river-valley interests, and the masses dependent on them). Benefiting from the rightist ideological climate of the 1970s as well as from Labour's backslide, Mrs Thatcher was in a position to inject unusual coherence into the Tory programme. The resurrection of monetarism provided perfect doctrinal disguise – the rhetorical 'hard line' ('No U-turns', and so on) counterpointing the actual thrust of her administration. This was, of course, only a magnification of traditional state strategy, relatively purged of consensual humbug.

Those who go on believing that her government was actually turning the theories of Friedman and Hayek into practice may safely be left to wrestle with their dilemma. A special niche of ideological Inferno must be reserved for them, next to the one kept for those who think Thatcher and Joseph were (phrases chosen from among thousands) 'picking industry up by the scruff of the neck to make it more competitive', or 'determined to slim down British industry at all costs'. There was never the slightest possibility of such a deformed economy responding in textbook fashion to the monetarist canons, least of all in the context of world slump. Mrs Thatcher's 'experiment' is no more than an attempt to utilize the recession to hasten and complete the dominance of finance capital.[3] The apotheosis of 'Freedom' *is* de-industrialization: Southern hegemony permanently liberated from the archaic burden of the Industrial Revolution's relics, the subsidies that prop them up, and the trade unions that agitate for them.

Not that anyone will ever preach this as policy, except on the journalistic fringe. No-one will ever need to. Everyone is in favour of modernization and restoring the healthy competitiveness of UK industry. It is simply that, *on the scale now demanded* by British decline and chronic imbalance, these are impossible programmes. Re-industrializing rhetoric is nothing but the coating on the pill of this reality. The 1979 Conservative regime's distinction was to promote the thinnest, most transparently absurd coating so far. The usual grubby pragmatics were replaced by a mighty Philosophical formula – a solution not merely to British woes, but to every error and economic ailment since the first coinage was minted. Britain's public is habituated to Ministerial shamblings which at least bear a homologous (if often dispiriting) relationship to reality. Thatcherism replaced these with a style of cut-throat theatrical *pronunciamientos* largely dislocated from actual British miseries. Precipitate aggravation of the latter was ideologized as the bitter medicine of a cure, in the stereotype 'recovery' sense; while each day brought the authentic final cure more clearly into focus – that is, the goal of successful de-industrialization. Having put its Industrial Revolution at last behind it, the globe-encircling empire will end as a colony. The most superior, advanced kind of colony, naturally: an enclave-state totally and comfortably occupied by capital.

Materially, it was North Sea oil that made the post-1979 fantasy

---

[3] The most acute analysis of this is given by John Foster, 'The Political Economy of Mrs Thatcher's Monetarism', *Quarterly Economic Commentary*, Fraser of Allander Institute, Glasgow, October 1981.

possible. In the earlier 1970s, nationalists were helped to power in Scotland by the Slogan 'It's Scotland's Oil!' The positive side to this mobilizing myth was obvious: oil revenues could make a lot of difference to a small country. Though censured as 'egotism' by our foes, there was also a negative aspect to the idea which these critics never, to my knowledge, answered or even came to terms with. That was the judgement, eminently safe to anyone versed in recent UK state lore, that otherwise the oil bounty would be wasted. Once in the grip of HM's Treasury it would infallibly disappear into the morass of 'general expenditure'. After Callaghan's Labour government refused to set up a separate oil-revenue fund in 1977, the game was over. Not only the Scots but the Britons had seen the end of their new wealth. It would go not into investment and 'modernization' but into propping up the old state – into another new interminable chapter of decline-management, lasting until the revenues themselves started to run out.

What not even the most cynical of us could imagine was how oil money would be employed to stage the mountebank production of Mrs Thatcher and her clique. The British state was not a doddering wastrel – an image whose contempt still harboured some benevolence – but an instrument of increasingly barefaced gangsters who expertly used the breathing space created by North Sea revenue to harden their grip. The monetarist redemption-drama originated in the City, spread to the Bank of England and the Treasury in the 1970s, and finally into politics. Though ideologized there into the general interest, these macro-economic policies remain (in words from the report referred to previously) 'based on the political interests of the City and are an attempt to strengthen the position of financial capital relative to other income and wealth categories in the economy.' The attempt was wildly successful. Oil, deflation, unemployment, high interest rates and industrial bankruptcy furnished dream conditions for London's financial apparatus in 1980 and 1981. Dollar weakness gave an added boost for most of that period, encouraging renewed confidence in sterling. 'Decline' had little impact here. A truth tactfully omitted from most parliamentary sermons and newspaper editorials.

It was the petroleum profits that allowed the reactionary offensive to take this special, rather unreal form. Only with them could City interests enjoy such a phenomenal consolidation *without* frontally attacking the working class. In their absence, the effects of the recession upon the system as a whole would have been far more crippling. Although an object of state stragegy, de-industrialization also constantly threatens the state: if it is allowed to assume too catastrophic a form the over-arching interests of financial circles are menaced by the repercussions. This is the authentic 'problem' of UK state politics – how to keep the process as painless as possible. 'Trouble' in this context is where river-valley mutinies shake confidence and risk a sterling crisis. But the oil inflow and recessionary doldrums together permitted an interlude of escape from the vice. This was, precisely, the interlude of Thatcherism: for a brief period it could be plausibly pretended that pure objective laws were being left to accomplish the labour of reaction. The scientific scrolls of monetarism were pulverizing the working class, not the ruling class or its state.

As Edward Heath discovered in 1973–74, *direct* attack can be destabilizing. When confronted by the likelihood of a miners' strike early in its course, Mrs Thatcher's regime simply surrendered. She refused to endanger her indirect tactic by frontal engagement in what recent history had unmistakably defined as the token, explosive example of 'class struggle'. The humiliation, it was rightly calculated, would rapidly be forgotten in conditions of worsening slump and trade union demoralization. With oil sustaining it, the City world would go on being insulated from this accelerated transformation. Its offensive would stay within the bounds of traditional civil hegemony – those limits that were temporarily breached in the confrontations of 1973–74.

It is such circumstances which explain the phoney side of the Conservative course, and make it more like a rehearsal for eventual conflict than the naked struggle so widely imagined after May 1979. In this respect it resembles many of the events and movements described in chapters of *The Break-up of Britain*. They were all – even the war in Northern Ireland – preparations for another, later round of more overt and decisive struggle. Like many other commentators and participants I thought this was the war itself – that the battle would escalate without interruption until a dénouement was reached. In reality they were episodes of phoney war, to be overtaken by a reflux of opinion and sentiment. The revolution is longer, more precarious and more circuitous in operation than we could understand.

The Movement to the Left

When the book appeared, hopeless stalemate at the centre of UK politics was being threatened by ambiguous or frankly right-wing peripheral movements. Since then, the central blockage has been shaken loose and Scottish and Welsh nationalism have moved markedly to the left. Although no comparable trend has emerged in Ulster, there are now some signs of change indicating that even there 1970s paralysis may be brought to an end. Most significant of all, a coherent general challenge to the grand strategy of the state has broken through for the first time since the death of imperial protectionism; and this new mainland nationalism has, as a consequence of the incorrigible abdication of the bourgeois strata, fallen into the hands of the socialist left. With the 'Alternative Economic Strategy', British socialists have acquired a new impetus and direction – but one that must sever them utterly from the old equivocations of Labourism, founded as that was upon a 'historic compromise' with the internationalizing state. The compromise got the working class what it could, at the cost of leaving long-term strategy alone (or, quite often, colluding actively in it). But what the new alternative proposes is not, *in British conditions*, just another variant of reformist tactics. It advertises a strategy the direct opposite of the underlying economic course of the last century – a path that the existing state structure could not conceivably pursue. The 'revolutionary' is not necessarily what appears so, or what thinks of itself as such. A programme of serious nationalist re-industrialization is neither revolutionary nor (of course) socialist, if viewed in the abstract. However, within the concrete context of the United Kingdom's deformed polity and economy, that is exactly what it cannot avoid being.

In all these ways the shift since 1977 seems extraordinary. The essays about England were focused on the peculiar vagueness and indecision of English nationality, as distinct from the over-stretched British racism handed down from the imperialists. They puzzled over Powell's failure to mobilize a rightist nationalism and the 'enigma' of Anglitude. The puzzlement was justified, but failed to perceive the connection between such uncertainty and the abdicant nature of the English bourgeoisie and its state-form: the latter's crucial thrust was against any genuine nationalism at the economic level, a fact that queered its assertion on all other levels as

well. The vacillating, muffled character of so much on the English
ideological register, its self-mocking archaism, the seesaw between
stereotyped 'patriotism' and the passionate wish to be for ever the
'good boys' of the West, between strangled pride and the
determination not to be just another small nationality like the rest –
these and other facets were apprehended, but improperly theorized.

From the same inadequacy proceeded a mistaken judgement
about English nationalism – the notion that, when things got bad
enough to drive the country into it, it would inevitably have a
blackly counter-revolutionary temper, 'bourgeois nationalism' at
its most beastly and irredeemable. There was nothing solitary about
this error. I doubt if any idea has been more widely held on the left,
especially the Marxist left. As well as the theoretical soporifics
mentioned here (Marxist apoliticism and 'internationalism', for
example) there were more solid excuses in the shape of Powell's
popularity and the antics of the National Front and other racist
groups. However, one determining factor that made so many fall for
the absurd 'nationalism equals racism' equation was, I can now see,
mere innocence. It was precisely in the absence of any seriously
articulated nationalist politics that paranoia had such a free rein. It
was the chronic impossibility of coherent bourgeois nationalism
that explained the strength and dislocation of Anglo-British
internationalism (and, probably, the relatively strong influence
there of the most rigidly internationalist Marxist creed, Trotskyism). In Britain – but above all, in England – internationalism
defines itself passionately and rather abstractly not against nationalism, but against a dreg-like *parochialism*, the stifling dross of
insularity and backwardness.

The same pessimistic notion lay behind a paper on Europe that
appears in the book, a critique of Johan Galtung that continued a
train of preceding assaults on British socialist opposition to the
Common Market.[4] On the whole, these still seem to me right in
what they asserted: 'left' opposition in the 1960s and early 1970s
was a nauseous combination of insularity and windbag wide-
worldism ('Europe is far too small for *us*', and so on), and a
European federal state was preferable to the persistence of the

---

[4] See for instance 'British Nationalism and the EEC', and 'The Left Against
Europe?', *New Left Review*, 69 (September–October 1971), pp. 3–28, and 75
(September–October 1972), respectively.

United Kingdom. However, what they did *not* grasp or state may have been more important (though none of the numerous critics saw the point either). Entry to the Common Market was a key replacement element in the long-term state strategy of Southern capital – 'Europe' being supposed to assume the same sort of role as territorial empire had done previously, the guarantor and support of its 'outward-looking' programme. There was also much steam and fulmination about industry, of course ('bracing winds of competition'), but that was as secondary as its subject. Were the EEC to wreak such a miracle, no doubt City men would have been pleased; if not, they could live as well, or better, with Euro-takeovers. 'Europe' was in that sense a humble predecessor of the monetarist runes of post-1979, a magic objective force bestowing cure from above. What it actually bestowed, in conditions of gathering recession, was modest opportunity for the financial sector and galloping de-industrialization up North.

These real coordinates of 'Europe' were obfuscated by abstract rantings about 'capitalism'. Those of short memory may need to be reminded that a decade ago the Common Market was a capitalist conspiracy designed to frustrate the advent (otherwise imminent) of British Socialism under Harold Wilson. Rightly indignant at such naivety, my stance of condemnation none the less went too far, and dismissed too much. It refused to credit the emergence of a left with a coherent national strategy, and in rupture with Labourism. The product of a world where *Tribune* and Denis Healey appeared destined to tandem forever on their wobbling course of political peonage, it despaired over-easily of English socialists, imagining 'British Socialism' as an interminable curse. Hence, 'left-wing chauvinism' was by definition warm-hearted idiocy which, if successful, could do nothing but push open the door to the real thing, inherently foul Great British nationalism. As for Europe, the implication of the position was an ultra-Europeanist outlook: United Kingdom socialists ought to forswear insularity (an ailment seen as encompassing nearly everything) and turn internationalism into authentic, day-to-day practice within the arena newly opened to them. This was wrong in another way, attributing too much to the genuine but limited possibilities opened up by entry to the EEC. And of course, in a quite tangential but (I can now see) disconcerting fashion, it was a stance that oddly echoed the outward drive of the ruling group itself.

Farther doses of retrospective wisdom make me feel I was unlucky in the timing of such efforts. A few years later I might have been more influenced by the women's movement, and capable of greater personal frankness in approaching the subject. The fact was that I felt intolerably and inwardly wounded by the anti-Europeanism of so much socialist opinion. This was the dilemma of an insecure national identity – common among Scottish intellectuals – that had reacted by over-identification with European cultures. I felt, no doubt with some exaggeration, that I owed everything that mattered to the latter; hence militant Great-English parochialism was a monster threatening everything, both native background and later achievement (or escape-route). No more need be said about it here. I would only add that the left's Alternative Economic Strategy, once it has freed itself from the delusion of being merely about economics, still has a very hard struggle on the political and ideological levels to eliminate the remains of such parochialism. Otherwise its new national-democratic identity will risk remaining befouled by the bilious scapegoatery of the anti-Common Market campaigns.

There were corresponding mistakes of perspective in other parts of the book. And again, the only solace I can now find is that my critics rarely identified these aberrations with any accuracy, or put forward more adequate ideas. On Scotland, for example, there was widespread alarm (not to say scorn) at the spectacle of a Marxist sympathising with the notoriously bourgeois nationalism of the SNP. Most of these reprimands still look like bilge, the product of reheated stereotypes and the sermonizing impulse so important to a frustrated left. The essential struggle promoted by the SNP – not to be confused with the crackpot ideology the party inherited from its past – was a progressive one all right. Had it borne some fruit in 1979, Scottish socialists and the Scottish working class would have benefited greatly from it. As far as the 'bourgeois' aspects of the 1970s national movement are concerned, I also remain convinced that in our specific conditions only the middle strata *could* have brought about such an awakening. But what very few people realized in the mid seventies was that this was a process cramped (and ultimately inhibited) by the underlying debility of the class that led it. In spite of the minority that had turned to nationalism, the majority remained sunk in a peculiarly Scottish torpor: a historical compound of respectable servility, Jekyllish conformism and fear of reversion to being 'natives'. The 1960s and 1970s were in truth an era when middle-class leadership and morale declined in Scotland; and in the later seventies, under the impact of recession, this basic decline became more like a rout. Thus what was wrong was not the bourgeois nature of Scottish nationalism, but the nature of the bourgeoisie itself: a class near the end of its spiritual tether, in quickening retreat from history. During the briefly optimistic years of the early seventies it had put out a nationalist offshoot, and toyed with the notion of independence; however, this was largely dalliance. Sterner pressures brought about a stealthy retreat whose dimensions were revealed in 1979 – as were the truer parameters of support for a national struggle.

This was all invaluable, if dispiriting, political experience. It bequeathed two vital legacies. The first was a far larger plateau of resistant support for nationalism. In spite of all the defection and post-1979 quietism, soundings reveal a body of hardened support much bigger than at any previous time. Secondly, the great trial-and-error experiment of the 1970s in Scotland has guided such support decisively towards the left. This is not the place to discuss the shape or the difficulties of that transformation. But the outline of its movement is clear enough: the failure of the older separatism and its anti-class ideology was a corner round which there is no returning, least of all in the conditions of economic and political crisis which will persist in the 1980s. In these conditions, the only 'tougher' nationalism that will stand a chance is a more socialist one able to deepen its popular appeal and work for some kind of tactical alliance with the Scottish labour movement (now seemingly more devoted to attaining self-government than it was during most of the 1970s).

Analogous (but perhaps less blameworthy) criticisms might be levelled at the essay on Wales. There also a much steeper defeat threw doubts on the political course of the previous decade, and a struggle developed to push the national movement leftwards – in this case, away from the cultural-linguistic nationalism focused on North and West Wales, and towards the socialism rooted in industrial South Wales.[5] As for Ulster, this appears to me now in a

[5] On this, and for other material on the leftward movement since 1979, see the symposium 'Looking Into the 1980s', and Dafydd Elis Thomas and Emyr Williams, 'Commissioning National Liberation', *The Bulletin of Scottish Politics*, nos. 1 (Autumn 1980) and 2 (Spring 1981) respectively.

rather paradoxical light. There was more wrong in historical and analytical detail with that contribution than with any of the rest; yet there was, I believe, less mistake about its predictive side than in the other forecasts that punctuated the first edition. My idea there was that, since the Protestant community is the real problem and cause of the 'troubles', no genuine political answer is possible until self-government is, somehow or other, forced down their throat and made to stay there (with whatever guarantees and supports are practicable for the Catholics). Nothing has invalidated this view since 1977; and there have been a number of shifts of opinion, both in Northern Ireland and on the broader stage of Irish and British debate, all giving it greater credibility. This is somewhat different from the movement to the left that has figured in the other instances of *The Break-up of Britain*. But then, Ulster is the only region of the British Isles where nationality conflict has been *so* acute that one may say a resolution of that issue (however summary and painful) is the precondition of any farther advance.

Permanent Emergency?

As I suggested above, 1979 opened an era of disintegration at the UK political level. Recession has shaken the ancient machine into partial break-down, even if the oil revenues have so far cushioned the drop and made a 'phoney emergency' lead us towards the real one. The party of the Southern oligarchy, with its 'radical' leadership and 'drastic' therapy, has been unable to avoid a caricatural and dangerously naked version of traditional strategy. This has proved at once fatally destructive of Toryism's old broad appeal, and another acid solvent of the consensus. With both wings of the old party system lurching into helpless self-liquidation, a period of political emergency has clearly been opened. How is this crisis likely to develop? And how will the national and regional strains described in *The Break-up of Britain* play a part in it?

As analysed above, the post-1979 collapse shows the following characteristics: a failure located at the state level, inherent in the entire structure that this state heads, has been forced into the open by the crude impact of slump. The political arena that had been formed by consensual suppression and mitigation of the underlying 'problem' has been ruined by the shift: both its partners have been delegitimated at once – a situation that plainly menaces the entire apparatus of civil hegemony, those elite hegemonic modes to which parliamentarism has been historically crucial. Hence, the state itself urgently requires a new political mechanism: a replacement sphere maintaining the relative autonomy of politics and with some hope of reviving mass confidence. It goes without saying that the real object of such a new alternative is the old cause – political hegemony must be restructured in order to keep the tacit mainstream strategy going, the 'outward' overbalance of UK capitalism's dominant stratum. This need defines certain cardinal poles of the new emergency formation's policies.

Its programme must be (1) restorative, promising the return of stability and 'harmony' after the disintegration of the former two-party formula into 'extremist' tendencies. A better yesterday is the key to its appeal. However, restoration also demands that the new model be (2) innovative, because the silent majority – Britain's comfortable-decline or muddle-through consensus – can now be rallied only by promise of some change perceptibly different from the 'new starts' of the previous generation. These changes must be political, constitutional or 'social' in appearance – that is (3) *not* economic in the shop-soiled sense of the reindustrializing growth fantasy. By the mid-1980s no-one will be able to take that seriously in any case: de-industrialization will have gone too far, and the last hope of remedy, oil revenue, will begin to dwindle. The underlying economic drive must be upheld by (4) staunchly European postures, since these have (as we saw) been made the token of internationalization. The spectre of UK economic nationalism can thus be held at bay, a task simplified (in the eyes of Establishment pundits) by the merger of nationalism and socialism in a rump Labour Party: this enables the former to be travestied as 'East European' Marxist nonsense. Any 'alternative' economic course can be discredited by the stigma of socialism, believed (not wholly without good reason) to be an incurably minority cause in Britain. Europeanism will of course in this perspective be one with (5) the continuation of Britain's 'good boy' function in NATO, tactful support of American leadership, and staunch opposition to follies like unilateral nuclear disarmament. Lastly, given the centrifugal trends of the 1970s and, above all, the menacing fissures opened up in 1979 between North and South, the revised recipe should incorporate some kind of countervailing therapy: the most plausible rhetoric here is (6) one of decentralization, understood as political disarticulation carefully metered and doled out from above. Devolution was a bit of ham-fisted partisan pragmatism, typical of the old style; the same aim, defusing potential separatism or river-valley mutiny, would be better realized as part of the other constitutional reforms indicated above (2).

Another way of defining the same priorities would be to say that what the *ancien régime* now seeks is a more permanent and flexible 'National Government' formula. That is, a reworking of its classical twentieth-century fall-back position, but rendered more elaborate and durable – a system, rather than a temporary coalition, designed for an emergency stretching as far as the eye can see. I have argued this case in a number of places recently, so will say little more about it here.[6] The aspect of the Social Democratic–Liberal Alliance ideology which calls for most stress in relation to *The Break-up of Britain* is, obviously, that of constitutional change and decentralization.

It is vital to the defensive elite operation represented by the astounding mushroom growth of the SDP that essential conservatism be concealed by a plausible progressive front. So far, this has been effortlessly accomplished. The reasons for such a triumph were unwittingly expounded in the earlier edition. The fact is that Labourism bequeathed such a mountain of unfinished (indeed, unapproached) business in the area of constitutional reform that it is child's play for intelligent reactionaries to pick it up and use it for their own ends. The simple, radical reforms that ought to have figured as automatic items in any self-respecting socialist pro-gramme – a written constitution, a new electoral system, principled devolution or federalism, and so on – were treated as irrelevant, or even as threats to the British way, and relegated to the limbo of the Liberal Party or the Electoral Reform Society. But at last this unspeakable misery has received its just punishment from events, more effectively than from the pages of any book. With contemptu-ous ease, the founders of the SDP have been able to distinguish themselves from a socialism still locked and hobbled in the rusting cage of the old Westminster model – demonstrating simultaneously

[6] For example, in 'The Future of Britain's Crisis', *New Left Review*, 113–114 (January–April 1979), pp. 43–69 (published also in Isaac Kramnick, ed., *What's Wrong With Britain? Perspectives on the British Crisis*, Ithaca 1979); 'Shirley's Party', *Quarto*, June 1981; 'The Crisis of the British State', *New Left Review*, 130 (November–December 1980).

the genuine appeal and novelty of 'irrelevant' radicalism. Meanwhile, the supposedly 'extreme' or Bennite left refuses even to contemplate electoral reform, and agonizingly wrestles its own democratic campaign over obstacles like the trade-union block vote. Of course, the political primitivism mentioned before goes on having some influence here; one thing the SDP–Liberal drive counts on is that socialists will be forced back on their own misery by resentment at the new foe – defending their traditional leg-irons as part of the 'Save Labour' crusade.

This excruciating dilemma of 'advanced capitalism versus backward socialism' is bound, on existing form, to be reproduced again over ethnic and regional issues. The new centre alliance has an appropriately suave programme ready to hand. Founded on the theft of Small-Is-Beautiful's clothes, it calculates that some form of harmless regionalism is the answer. UK local government is in parlous state anyhow, since the hapless reforms of the last decade. A more rational and popular rejigging of the system should appease the Scots and Welsh, without displeasing anybody too much; it might even be contrived to get rid of Ulster. Thus, alert action in the political sphere would achieve the real object: preservation and reinforcement of civil and economic unity, by the traditional metropolitan hegemony. For all its confusion and final failure, the devolution agony of the 1970s did come out of pressures from below; that was why it threatened break-up. In future, everything will come from above. The new Revolution-From-on-High will pre-empt by bestowal. The appalling technical hitches of the last round would be avoided by linking such regional government to general constitutional changes. And after the dispensation, strengthened central power would be in a far better posture to resist more annoyance from below.

On the other side, what strategy can be measured against this? The older British Socialism was overwhelmingly centralist in outlook; omniscient planning and uniformity of treatment were its trademarks, a subordinate and administrative statism indifferent to most of the ideas in a nationalist problematic. During the 1970s this strain stayed dominant within Labourism; it was responsible for much of the hostility to devolution, and managed eventually to cripple and contain the measures. It would be reassuring if the new socialism had emancipated itself from this legacy. There is, regrettably, small evidence that it has. It has evolved an alternative economic plan, but no equally impressive political strategy to accompany the latter, or to give a long-term structure to Benn's cadre rebellion. The big causes of recent years have made some impact: few New Labour Party militants would exclude nuclear disarmament or the women's movement from the new world, for example. It takes almost no effort to pledge new departures or scourge old shortcomings over race, rock music, the environment, Third World aid . . . and so on. However – returning to a main point stated earlier – these will not group themselves into a coherent programme automatically. Or at least, not upon the revolutionary level really demanded by and implicit in the AES. For that, the question of the state is central. No 'SPS' is conceivable or defensible without an intelligible reply to that question. 'Democratization' has become the new socialism's watchword; but if it denotes only party reform, community politics, policing the police and similar changes, the interpellation will be short-lived.

'Backward socialism' remains, in the United Kingdom context, an especially *political* description. And one element in that description is given by the national problem. It remains my conviction that it is crucial to the definition of any new democratic, socialist state. However, the urgency of the issue has been quickened since the book's first appearance. Perception of its importance has decreased among socialists; but this is cause for farther alarm and complaint, since the objective reasons for urgent concern have multiplied. The failure of 'Devolution' dampened interest; it ought to have engendered more anxiety than some other fashionable topics. This is true, above all, because of the very theme which has eclipsed the periphery from left-wing metropolitan attention: the affirmation of Labour's new left and its national economic programme.

The Alternative Economic Strategy is potentially far more centralizing than any of its predecessors. The state that tried to enact it would be different in structure and personnel, as well as in orientation. But, unfortunately, such a revolution could be 'democratic' in form while failing to acknowledge nationality. It could bring about a unitary state in a sense far more literal and defined than that of the old Kingdom, with its symbol-laden routines and unwritten idiosyncrasies. This could inflict upon us some of the vices of Jacobinism, as well as the benefits of equality: it could foster a new Great British identity and confidence under whose imperium regional or national trends would appear even more divisive and reactionary than at present. Participation in the new metropolitan ethos would be made a self-evident blessing, refusal a manifest sin (selfishness, narrowness, backwardness, and so on). Fuelled by the sort of foreign-hating paranoia prominent in the anti-EEC crusade – now aggravated to fever-point by defection from the Social Democrats, or 'Common Market Party' – this would amount to a style of nationalism corrosive of everything good about the current socialist breakthrough.

That nationalism in Scotland and Wales has become more socalist itself does not in any way mitigate the prospect. On the contrary, it may make it worse. The experiences of the 1970s have demonstrated conclusively that there is no preordained harmony among socialisms, and shown how sometimes socialism may exacerbate national antagonism. It was once widely believed that solutions to 'national questions' were a precondition of socialist or civil progress. There may still be some truth in this; but we also know now that the 'solution' will rarely be final, a relegation of mere nationhood to the historical files. These are facts more likely than not to recur, in new and more potent forms. Socialists in search of self-government are more, not less, likely to diagnose and resent great-nation chauvinism, overbearingness and egotism.

To those who have learned anything from recent history, then, the only possible safeguard must be to make an Alternative Strategy fully and freely federative in principle. That demands a different kind of state, with a vengeance. It points the way, perhaps the only way, to a 'Yugoslav' resolution of Britain's territorial issues rather than the 'Hapsburg' one I originally thought inevitable. There are great difficulties about any workable federalism in the conditions of the British Isles, which have been closely debated by political scientists. These would be amplified by any serious programme of British reindustrialization, conducted by more aggressive state and public-sector leadership. The chances of such enlightenment appear pretty small, when set against England's indurate metropolitanism – that hegemonic arrogance which such long experience has turned into daily bread. But there is the question: can a new English socialism shed its political backwardness in time? Having gone so far, is it really incapable of breaking with the shame and defeat of British Socialism?

October 1981

Postscript 2003:
21st-Century Hindsight

> 'This kind of political shame, which we feel only in
> the presence of the Good and the Innocent, lowers
> our eyes before those who will come after us …
> And do not most of us want, against the odds, to
> give our nations another chance?'
>
> Benedict Anderson, 'The Goodness of Nations',
> in *The Spectre of Comparisons: Nationalism,
> South-East Asia and the World* (1998).

When this book was first published in 1977, the publisher asked
whether a question mark after the title might not be more appropriate. After some argument, it was fortunately left out. Peremptory
statements can last better than nervous questions. New Left Books,
ancestor of Verso Books, held a reception for the book in London at
which the historian Eric Hobsbawm expressed in quite vehement
terms his doubts and misgivings about the book's prophecy. Later
he published his message as a critique in the *New Left Review*.[1] His
argument was that on no account should intellectuals try to 'paint
nationalism red' – that is, present it as an inherently progressive
or emancipatory phenomenon. The Soviet, Yugoslav and British
multinational states might be in mounting trouble. But troubles

[1] *New Left Review* (old series, no. 105, Sept–Oct. 1977): 'Some Reflections
on *The Break-up of Britain*', pp. 3–23. For a very different and much more
comprehensive critique of the ideas in *Break-up* I would urge readers to consult
Professor Joan Cocks's essay 'In Defense of Ethnicity, Locality, Nationality: The
Curious case of Tom Nairn', Chapter Five of her *Passion and Paradox: Intellectuals Confront the National Question* (Princeton University Press 2002). Although
Professor Cocks discerns a defence of 'ethnicity' where none exists, she nonetheless appraises the book in relation to the 1980s and the 1990s, rather than to
abstract notions of past history.

may be soluble, through the adoption of better policies (Communist, Civic-Liberal, Multicultural or other). To anticipate break-ups was therefore to risk hastening them – in effect, a wilful betrayal of enlightened principles.

Such misgivings seemed reasonable at the time. After all, Scottish and Welsh political nationalism were still uncertain and faltering growths, and the renewed 'Troubles' in Northern Ireland were in some ways reminiscent of earlier times rather than of new developments. English nationalism remained a curiosity, the fringe interest of academics and folklorists. Equivalent symptoms in Belgium, France, Italy, Spain and Eastern Europe could also be dismissed as marginal, or more frankly as 'reactionary' – nostalgia either for fascism, or for nations that never were. Karl Popper's *The Open Society* (1945) was still frequently invoked as philosophical justification. Its mixture of anti-Marxism, anti-Historicism and Liberal empiricism was still popular, and it would go on to enjoy a rebirth twelve years later, after 1979.[2] In general terms, progress was assumed to be a long-range and one-time transition: from the pre-historic condition of 'closed' or tribal cultures to one of 'open', liberal or social-democratic civilization. Nationalism was automatically suspected of seeking reversion from the latter to the former. It was putting the clock back, therefore, and reopening the door to the blood-politics of irrational communalism, and the atavistic voices of a former age.

The doubts voiced in *The Break-up of Britain* were of course instinctive rejections of this philosophical perspective, as well as discrete arguments about the political condition of the United Kingdom. On the other hand, they were never endorsements of ethnic nationalism either. With the benefit of one quarter-century's hindsight, I see no reason for disavowing that underlying position. At the same time, revising the philosophical foundations has proved damnably hard.[3] As for the condition of the UK, this has disappointed both parties to the old quarrel. It has been too tena-

[2] For the origins and fate of *The Open Society* see *Popper's Open Society After Fifty Years* (1999) edited by Ian Jarvie and Sandra Pralong.

[3] The author's latest stumbling venture in this direction was an inaugural talk at RMIT University in Melbourne, soon to be published as *Black Pluto's Door: Nations and Globalisation*. This suggests a general socio-historical explanation for the persistence and contemporary recrudescence of nationality politics, taking 'social nature' as starting point rather than modernity alone.

cious of life for nationalists, and yet done extremely little to satisfy protagonists of Union and greatness.

Internationalism and Politics

What passed for 'internationalism' in the 1970s was in truth an abstract and narrow creed, resting on pious and selective acceptance of certain Enlightenment ideas – those that could be made to look favourable to the state authorities of the era, and to some political parties of the moment.[4] Nor has this tendency to travesty lessened since the 1970s. Though from a different political angle, Neo-liberalism would in the 1990s carry it to new heights of absurdity. While proclaiming themselves revolutionary, the orthodox left movements of 1977 were even then turning into fossilised remnants.

However, ethnic nationality politics had its own narrow piety as well, derived from almost equally old counter-constructions of Romanticism, and from a misconstrued Social Darwinism. The species-differentiation which turned into 'nationality' is ancient; but the 'ethnic' label is very recent, deriving from colonialism and American dilemmas of the 1960s. The antagonism of these philosophies was to be artificially preserved until the 1990s, within the permafrost of Cold War fear and rigid confrontation.

As the latter has thawed out, so have the profounder received ideas that it for so long congealed. However, as this re-edition of *Break-up* appears, it should be emphasized how long the thawing process is likely to be. The Cold War lasted for longer than a conventional generation; recovery from it could occupy another. And the slowest region to thaw out is, unfortunately, the one where change is now most urgently and obviously needed: politics. Globalization will be tolerable only via re-constituted democratic polities, in an altered international order; yet politics and culture make up the zone upon which the dead generations weigh most heavily.

The causes of such uneven liberation are very deep-rooted.

---

[4] The most important study since then on Enlightenment is surely Emma Rothschild's *Economic Sentiments: Adam Smith, Condorcet and the Enlightenment* (2001), gentle in tone but abrasive in substance. She shows how misrepresentation of Adam Smith and David Hume began in the late 18th century itself, in a style recognizably similar to that of the Neo-liberal hysteria two centuries later.

They probably lie in the symbiosis of two factors, each tenaciously conservative in its own right. On one side is the modern or post-Westphalian state, the characteristic power-structure still evoked by the description, 'nation-state'. This extruded apparatus of authority is defined by separation from the society that it supposedly 'serves', but also controls. Abstraction is inseparable from the modern 'Leviathan', as is a resultant rigidity of both human organization and outlook: the typical traits of formal administration or 'bureaucracy'. State power looks first of all to precedent and establishment, backwards rather than forwards. This is 'How Institutions Think', the justly famous title of Mary Douglas's anthropological critique of modern bureaucracy; but it is also how they survive, above all when historically successful (as Western institutions were, in the 1980s).[5]

This tendency is automatically reinforced by the second conservative factor involved: the 'intellectuals'. As Antonio Gramsci observed from the bitter isolation of his prison notebooks in the 1930s, *gli intellettuali* are unavoidably conservative by formation, because they are nourished on a humus of accumulated and bygone culture. They may of course imagine drastic changes and departures from this inheritance (his own case, and that of the Italian Communist Party he helped found). Yet the sources of such imagination must lie in well-springs and traditions themselves inherited. Inherited, and often misunderstood or travestied, above all when a rising educated stratum attains office by revolution, or even via the representative process. Its self-justification then becomes allied to that of institutional existence, in the *staatlich* compound of 'our way' – a national course sanctified by re-written history, and turned into the apparently inevitable order of things.

Break-Up to Breakdown

Only two years after *Break-up* came out, a pseudo-revolutionary chain of events was launched in Great Britain that exemplified these characteristics. This was Mrs Thatcher's radical version of conservatism, founded on a 'liberation' of socio-economic forces and the roll-back of state responsibility for civil society. Though almost two centuries old, these Neo-liberal formulae were now

[5] *How Institutions Think* (1987).

pitilessly excavated to suit the conditions of the 1970s and 1980s.[6] Her New Toryism was accompanied by a reinforcement of the inherited United Kingdom framework of state. During the Thatcherite 1980s, an uncompromisingly British Union was stressed as never before. The aim was to extinguish all tendencies towards breakaway, as well as a discredited socialism. Like the rulers of the Communist East, Thatcherites were all for efficient and colourful local government – provided it stayed tame, and offered no political challenge to the imperium.

At the same time, intellectuals were recruited (or recruited themselves) into her altered hegemony, painting hereditary British nationalism in new colours as part of what was in truth a redemption of mildewed tradition. Once socially invisible, or frankly despised, Britannia's thinking reeds now found themselves regimented into bright-eyed Policy Units. The Unwritten Constitution was to be revivified by the new entrepreneurial culture, not challenged or replaced by it. A new intelligentsia was needed for this task, ostensibly 'radical' but essentially conformist – devoted, in effect, to redeeming British traditions by dazzling conjuring tricks.

Thatcher was deposed by her own party in 1990, when the contradictions of this stance had become electorally intolerable. But her counter-movement had some serious effects. Within a world still generally stultified by Cold War, the breaking-up process was held back in Britain for eighteen years. Her acceleration of economic change was accompanied by more than plain socio-political conservation: a distinct style of mummification now set in. In 1992 her successor John Major won an election giving farther respite to the old state. Five years of farther necrosis would be required, before a movement of sheer revulsion gathered strength, and forced a break at the general election of 1997.

When this moment of rupture did arrive, however, it failed to undo the state. New Toryism gave way to new Labourism. But New Labour was to succeed largely through failure: it refused to undo the Mummy's rags. Indeed it continued, and even intensified Mrs Thatcher's redemptive drive, striving more nimbly and visibly to keep Britain alive and 'great'. Instead of moving towards a new

[6] The most accurate retrospect on the great rehabilitation is *The Commanding Heights: The Battle between Government and the Marketplace That Is Remaking the Modern World* (2001) by D. Yergin and J. A. Stanislaw.

state and constitution, it plunged swiftly into a still more emphatic ideological campaign of resurrection.[7] But the political terrain was now unavoidable: mere vindication of century-old praxis was no longer enough. During the 1979–97 period, the movements for self-government described in the original text of this book had recovered strength again. They acquired new vitality, both from the absurdities of 'Thatcherism' and the obfuscations of Neo-liberalism. This recovery led them to an effective re-colonization of the Labour Party, and simultaneously towards positions clearly to the left of the New formulae of Tony Blair and Gordon Brown.

Thus what Thatcherites had perceived as 'backward' provinces were borne to centre stage in the post-1997 government. The latter had no choice but to satisfy the demands of Scottish and Welsh Party contingents, by this time firmly converted to 'home rule'. At the same time, the civil warfare in Northern Ireland persisted, and forced the British state towards a quite different version of self-government there as well. Neither the 'enterprise culture', the run-down of the welfare state, nor the chest-beating Britishness of the previous years had put a stop to disintegration. It merely slowed it down, forcing it to acquire deeper roots and a wider popular basis.

However, Blair's constitutional 'concessions' remained just that. 'Devolution' was intended to continue, or even to strengthen, the Union state and its Crown. Just as Thatcher's entrepreneurial Britain was meant to reanimate tradition, Blair's devolved kingdom was now seen as reinforcing its centralizing mainspring, the Unwritten Constitution of Westminster, and Britain's remaining world-power pretensions. The latter were destined for a renaissance under his rule. Indeed historians may well record this as the only genuine resurrection of the New Labour period.

In such a context, Devolution was little more than enhanced local government, and in no way a prelude to decomposition. Its purpose was restoration, and the safe renewal of British multi-national identity. Stability and continuity could not be put at risk by rash or unnecessary reform. A few compromises with political modernity may have become inescapable – for instance,

[7] In July 2002 I published an account of New Labour from 1997 to 2001 under the title *Pariah: Misfortunes of the British Kingdom* (Verso Books, London & New York). The last section tries to situate British misfortune within the broader context of political dearth and recession among the Atlantic seaboard states – the misfortunes of the later Enlightenment, as it were.

proportional representation in all three new assemblies. But within the prevalent sclerosis these were also sideways steps – Westminster's purpose was that they should weaken and moderate the new authorities. Like other *anciens régimes* before it, the British state was able to bend particular features of a newer political world to its own ends. As I suggested already, the 'think-tank' revolution of the 1980s and 1990s had been devoted mainly to clever emasculation in this sense.

In *After Britain* (1999) I analyzed the New Labour Millennium Dome project in the same light, as a political and ideological farce designed to supplant a vanished Socialism with a rejuvenated British nationalism. There is no need here to recapitulate details of this astonishing disaster. The vision was of a common roof housing examples of brilliant, forward-looking design – the credentials of a Cool Britannia in confident mastery of modernity, at ease with the dawning century. The reality was a costly parade of ineptitude and ambiguity, expressing all too accurately the dilemmas of a faltering realm. The wound to United Kingdom dignity and standing ought to have been fatal; but in fact most Britishers shrugged their shoulders at it – as if already too convinced of second-rateness and downfall to be farther affected. The former sense of invincible superiority had become a fatalism of decline, more inclined towards irony and self-mockery, and – again like the old Eastern Europe – towards an exaltation of the private over the public. Hence Blair's New Labour government could persist inertly in his constantly reiterated 'Project' – state-maintenance rather than state-renewal or reconstruction.

There is no need either to remind readers of the other disasters that followed upon The Dome. The two years leading up to Blair's second electoral victory in 2001 brought a whole series of them, ranging from the National Health Service, via a rail network breakdown, to the absurd mismanagement of a Foot-and-Mouth disease epidemic which overshadowed the election itself.[8] New Labourite

---

[8] At the time of writing, in late 2002, it has just been announced that Britain's most important rail link, the West Coast London–Glasgow line, will be shut down *for several months* to permit up-grading (i.e. making it safe for modern trains). This Ruritanian episode follows the earlier surrender of the network to market forces, in the shape of British Railtrack Ltd. After various fatal disasters, even Blair's government had to smuggle this company back into public control, to the profound consternation of share-holders and enterprise-zealots alike.

'triumph' in the subsequent vote now depended upon a novel phenomenon: massive abstention by the entire British electorate. Forty per cent did not participate (and the official figure was almost certainly an under-estimate). Far from being cured by New Labour, the revulsion of the later 1990s had sunk in and grown chronic. Blair's overwhelming Parliamentary mandate was based on less than a quarter of the suffrage. Nationalist campaigners in Scotland, Wales and Northern Ireland had always complained about the UK's 'democratic deficit' – the failure of central authority to permit them a voice. But by 2001, the Westminster system itself had become a standing deficit – a desertion of the English voters, as well as of the Celtic fringes. Maintaining Greatness now turned out to have its own peculiar cost: the formation of an abyss between state and society, and permanent political malaise.

Break-Up and Globalization

Were this the whole story, it would of course be tempting simply to extrapolate the 1977–2002 narrative forward. Surely 'break-up' is bound to pursue its course via farther stages, amid the debris and contradictions of a collapsing form of state? Over another twenty or thirty years? However, there is now a great deal more to the tale. Other factors have entered the scene, and a quite different global narrative now intersects with that of British decline and fragmentation. The break-up of Britain began in one age; but we can now be certain it will end in another, amid quite different rules, and disconcerting possibilities undreamt of twenty-five years ago.

To perceive the effects of this new conjuncture, one must return to the old one portrayed in *Break-Up*'s earlier editions. The main error there was a form of historical materialism that reflected both left- and right-wing preconceptions of the Cold War period. 'Uneven development' was the nub of that argument. The intensifying 'backwardness' of a post-imperial and post-industrial Britain was counterposed to the forward-looking impulses emerging out of its periphery. While nationalism naturally stressed ethnic or cultural motifs, the impulse of emancipation was also linked to a general idea of being 'held back'. And among the Marxists or Marxisant thinkers active at the theoretical level (including this author) it assumed a primarily economic form. Nationalism was in this period usually justified as a response to economic exploitation or imposed retardation – the political mobilization required to catch up with modernity.[9] It was only one more step to extend this justification to people and territories being unfairly tied down by 'backward' metropolitan centres. To the Baltic states, for example, escaping from Great-Russian inertia; Catalonia, always economically ahead of archaic Castilian centralism; Northern Italy, restrained by a central-southern Roman bureaucracy; or Quebec, the vehicle of a *revolution tranquille* aiming to leave hidebound British Canada behind.

Scotland remains the biggest factor in any political breakdown of the United Kingdom, and such convictions were strong there in the 1970s. This followed upon the discovery and exploitation of North Sea petroleum, mainly in Scottish territorial waters. 'It's Scotland's Oil!' was the resultant slogan. Even then, no prophetic insight was needed to see that, unless politically captured, the great windfall would disappear into futile attempts at propping up the Westminster *imperium*.[10] To both nationalists and home-rulers in Scotland and Wales, there seemed at least the possibility of using some of it for economic modernization – to re-industrialize, and rebuild out-of-date infrastructures, rather than wasting it upon state salvage operations, the 'special relationship' with America, and the purely commercial nexus of the City of London.

Such hopes were to be cruelly disappointed. A moribund polity talks new only to prop up the old. In 21st-century retrospect, it may appear obvious how things might have turned out differently. In theory, a state-led second-stage industrial revolution could have given new life to the island *imperium*. Could this not have been expressed in drastic constitutional changes, by the formation of a fully federal or confederal British state? Could democracy not have replaced Westminster – rather than the feeble parody of Blair's Devolution? In theory such plausible-seeming blueprints have multiplied from the 1970s up the present time and (it must be added) taken up far too much journalistic and academic space.

[9] The main culprit here was no Marxist. It was Ernest Gellner's immensely influential 1964 essay 'Nationalism', published in the volume *Thought and Change*. Gellner was a conservative historical materialist, much closer to Popper and (later) to George Soros and 1980s Neo-liberalism, than to forces of either the liberal or the socialist left.

[10] Christopher Harvie's *Fool's Gold: The Story of North Sea Oil* (1995) is a comprehensive indictment of the episode.

In practice, no such transformation was remotely possible. Mrs Thatcher's pseudo-revolution of 1979 onwards counted upon what she perceived as the natural bent of the British: an entrepreneurial leap forward, unleashing the potential of a civil society deemed still capable of miracles. Actually, the 'natural bent' of Anglo-British identity had long been a specific and historically-consecrated blend of commercialism and conservative hierarchy. 'Industrial revolution' had simply been one passing episode in this much longer national trajectory.[11] After 1997 the 'regressive modernization' of the Tories (in Stuart Hall's famous phrase) was taken up, and finally taken much farther by Blair's New Labour dispensation.[12] The political cast of Anglo-Britain had been quite favourable to post-World War II social-democracy; but under post-Cold War Neo-liberalism it was not so lucky – there proved to be in Mrs Thatcher's famed term 'no alternative' to craven surrender and precipitate apology for earlier sins.

So revivalism became the order of the day. The first action of Blair's Finance Minister, Gordon Brown, was to relinquish government control of economic interest rates to a City-controlled committee at the Bank of England. At the same time, approval of the special relationship with the United States mutated into subservience. Blair's government acted promptly to save the British Crown, and then prop it up, after its foundations were shaken by Princess Diana's strange death in 1997. Not for the first time in twentieth century history, the Westminster two-party order had become a de facto one-party system, devoted to safe modernisation. 'Safe' always means conservation of both state and national identity, in some earlier configuration – in this case, the palaeo-modernism of the British early 18th century. Hence the contradiction of Blair's rule: a paroxysm of phoney renewal was devoted to enhancing stability – always the most prized virtue of the British

[11] This point has been misunderstood in the most important recent reinterpretation of English nationalism, Liah Greenfeld's *Nationalism: Five Roads to Modernity* (1992). She sees England as the forge of modern national identities, rather than as an archaic template for certain aspects of nationalism. The misunderstanding has been reiterated in her new study *The Spirit of Capitalism: Nationalism and Economic Growth* (2001).

[12] Originally presented in various essays, Hall's thesis is most completely set out in *The Politics of Thatcherism* (1983) edited by Stuart Hall and Martin Jacques.

evolutionary order. British nationalism had come to rest upon a basic conviction of Providential grace and continuity – not a mentality of risk or societal adventure. Thatcher hatched a right-wing version of such redemptionism, between 1979 and 1997; now Blair and Brown followed with a left-wing one. Under conditions of unceasing fall, the labels of 'right' and 'left' became variations of a single inescapable process.

Really Existing Internationalism

But this fall is now *also* into the much greater abyss of globalization, and a one-world hegemony of capital. Even before leaving their anachronistic kingdom, the components of the archipelago are compelled to face and adapt to a wildly different *Heimat*. Cretinous variants of Neo-liberalism continue to dominate the media – in the Celtic fringe as well as in London – and of course perceive no problems of transition. All they see is undue slowness in the transition to a global nirvana.

The strain uppermost in Blairism derives largely from one particularly flatulent clamour of the 1990s: 'the end of the nation state'. The apotheosis of homo economicus after 1989 was at that time imagined as leaving ideological space only for individuals on the one hand, and a nebulous universal order – or 'borderless world' – on the other. Being both ill-defined and inchoately contested, this fog tended in practice to coalesce around either acceptance or refusal of United States domination. And for a retreating Britain, the parameters of profound acceptance had been established in advance by the mythology of its 'special relationship' between London and Washington. From the Suez crisis onwards, the relationship has fossilized into a form of self-colonization. Under the title of 'indirect rule', this abject posture was rather well known to British and other imperialists of the preceding age. Polyvalent dominance – Gramsci's egemonia – is most effective when the suborned have chosen their prostration. And normally, such elective subjection is founded on apparently sensible (if short-range) economic or career reasons: myopia re-attired as the national interest.

Over nearly half a century, such self-colonization has become a pillar of Britishness. It is close to being the heart of the surviving British identity. General de Gaulle thought that Britain would always choose the US and les anglo-saxons if put to the test. Today, this verdict of the 1960s appears sound (even if the General's own alternative French hegemony was to prove equally unacceptable). But here too globalization makes a profound difference. The UK's dismal prostration has persisted into a post-1989 world of near-universal subservience and collusion. Variants of self-colonization have become the political norm of Neo-liberalism. Most governments now strive to align themselves with what are presented as 'inevitable' global trends. However, this is not because they fear the eruption of American Marines or cruise missiles, or even the frown of the Washington court. Uncomfortable as the latter is, most of the world now dwells in a time of representative (or pretend-representative) governments. Pretend-choice is required for the action. Satrapy-leaderships must therefore persuade themselves (and their unfortunate electors) that there truly is 'no alternative'. Mrs Thatcher has lived to see her celebrated phrase become the formative slogan of an emergent world order: first-stage globalization. Politically speaking, Marx's great 'sorcerer' of modernity, capitalist free-market mania, has turned into a flock of carrion-crows living off the resultant symbiosis.

'Radical' ideologies of transnationalism are sometimes interpreted in the old historical-materialist terms, as an indirect reflection of single-market economics and multinational business practices. But one-worldism can also be read more straightforwardly: it is first of all the expression of an extensive suppression of political nationalism. National identities forged in an earlier modernization process, above all through revolution and warfare, now compete in an uncanny parody of their former hatreds and jealousies. Veiled abasement and stoutly denied complaisance have become the yardsticks of this transitional age.

The Social Darwinism of the early 20th century was a struggle for dominance; that of its end has become a competition for wilful curtailment and first-in-line status. Take for example, after September 11th, 2001, the swift, assertive and worldwide production of national credentials for President Bush's preposterous War Against Terrorism. From one week to the next, 'cracking down' on all symptoms of subversion became every nation's badge of renewed respectability. Establishment scoundrels the world over hastened to unite, with nothing to lose but their honour (in most cases discarded in advance) – and of course, the active political enthusiasm of their citizens. Like Blair's New Labour after its despicable 2001 general election, these knaves of globalism have been subsequently puzzled by mass apathy and indifference. How can it be that people prefer the honest emotions and colour of the Football World Cup, to playing their part in a world managed by mediocrities, and 'led' by a US President unable to fake himself a plausible election, even in Florida?

It seems reasonable to assume that the populations of the globe are approximately as resentful, inchoate, ingenious, ungrateful and potentially rebellious as they were before the End of History in 1989. But their experience since then has diverged sharply from what the zealotic blueprints demanded should occur. Rather than the 'inevitable decline' of the nation-state, what they have endured is more like its abnegation and abuse. Post-communism and the closure of Socialist short-cuts removed at once the justification and the morale of bourgeois governments. Obsequious mediocrity became the norm. Such are the politics of Neo-liberalism: the sanctified misrule of increasingly corrupt hirelings and tenth-rate windbags. In that sense, something of the original inspiration of *The Break-up of Britain* still remains justified. It misread 'uneven development' in over economic terms, when in fact it has always been a deeply human and social phenomenon. Frustrated rising standards is a goad like no other. But such frustrated anger was bound to be more salient in the post-Cold War than in any previous one.

Now, the Neo-liberal half-revolution dangled dream-like chances before the entire globe, thanks to the simultaneous bound forward in communication technology. But in the same moment, it condemned most populations to a limbo of non-attainment. Yet its 'politics' now consisted of servile patience plus ever more blatantly corrupt patronage, within a developmental queue extolled as 'nature' (human as well as economic). The only thing most living individuals could be sure of was that by the time modernity's American sorcerer got round to them they would be dead.

However, outside of economic textbooks, people have never wanted to live merely to reproduce themselves in less awful circumstances. Once change is imaginable, they want to mean something, or to 'stand for something' (other than being bottom of the resultant heap). Post-1989 globalization, unlike all its precursors, entered a world where change was universally imaginable, a daily summons to meaning and altered identity. Civilization derived from written words; now the 'Word' had become global, a drug reaching into the tiniest capillaries of collective awareness. Even before September 11th, 2001, how could it have been imagined that homo economicus would not dissolve in the resulting tidal force?

The Fate of Homelands

In other words, what the Neo-liberal universe has done is to generate an even more compelling recipe for democratic nationalism than its predecessor of 1750–1950. 'First-stage' globalization has been the brief era in which these possibilities have begun to hatch out and assert themselves – notably within the British-Irish archipelago, a primal theatre of both industrial and state development in the 18th century.

In the 1970s, when the lineaments of break-up first showed through, the smaller UK countries still imagined themselves as nation-states – that is, frustrated nationalities of the old order. By the year 2000 they were less frustrated, but the old order had largely disappeared. The dominant nation from which they sought political emancipation had become itself a new style of colony – the Sergeant-Major and cheer-leader of American-led globalization. Once conceived as a stepping-stone towards final independence, devolution now risks turning into a life-sentence as fleas upon the Washington organ-grinder's despicable monkey. As the subordinates of a subordinate state itself so cravenly supine, Scotland and Wales would then be contemplating genuine oblivion in all time coming.[13]

This prospect has proved less than overwhelmingly popular with the Scottish and Welsh electorates. If there is one thing that the

---

[13] The same is not true of Northern Ireland, naturally. The Ulster-Protestant population, still numerically and politically dominant, may end by refusing even devolved power, and demanding a return to full integration with the remains of the British Kingdom. This would mean voting for a quite unique destiny: to end up as invisible and impoverished fleas on a monkey that has in the meantime died. The Catholic population, presumably, would then become part of the conspicuously successful Republic of Ireland: booming, independent and independent-minded. Protestants would then have to choose between their present dead end, and becoming an influential regional minority in the Irish state.

Scots in particular do know all about, it is self-colonization. They lived with it for three hundred years after the Treaty of Union in 1707. Its pros and cons are second nature in a society that long ago reconfigured itself for mediocre self-management, in the absence of politics. The sententious moralism of the marginalized; disregard of democratic deficit for economic opportunity; cultural over-compensation and romantic chest-beating, to efface or embellish powerlessness; over-effusive loyalty to a distant cause and metropolis, welcomed and yet somehow never welcome enough – all these tropes of a supposedly post-national world are, alas, tired old family skeletons in Edinburgh and Glasgow. And after four years of devolved government, they look like being at least temporarily resurrected, rather than disposed of.

This is not a matter of policy. Within their limits, both the Edinburgh parliament and the Welsh assembly have argued for more social-democratic positions than those of Westminster, and in both countries some have been implemented. These achievements have been popular, and outside of Protestant Ulster there is practically no sign of any longing for return to the once all-powerful centre. In terms of social and economic policy there is no cause for either shame or back-tracking. But at the same time, there appears little appetite for farther advance or increased powers of the same sort. In 2001–02 every general survey or commentary revealed something more like fatigue, or general unconcern. A Scottish Council Foundation Report in May 2002 emphasized this sense of disappointment and dearth strongly, and the shrewd conservative columnist Allan Massie summed the matter up in the Scottish edition of the *Sunday Times*:

> 'The public is not convinced. They see politicians collecting full-time salaries and working part-time. And in the snatches of the parliament in session which TV presents us with, they see a pitifully low level of debate. Then, again, they hear politicians calling for a 'national debate' on this or that … (which) never materializes. No wonder so many – and not merely journalists – think things are going wrong, and find their hopes dashed.'

However, if a political system is accomplishing things voters approve of, like abolishing student tuition fees and public care for the elderly and handicapped, and yet still disappointing them, may this be because of things it is not doing? Massie does not miss the point, and concludes ironically –

> The parliament has been a resounding success ... (It) was devised by the Labour Party precisely to obstruct change, thwart reforms, and shield Scotland from radicalism. So far it has done so triumphantly ... Devolution was the change Scottish Labour needed to keep things as 'they've aye been here'. And it is working. (June 30th, 2002, 'Nothing Happens – Holyrood is Working')

In other words, it is preserving the United Kingdom for a time, as Thatcher did, but by more subtle means. It works by a modulation of self-colonization, rather than by suppression. And of course both the effect and the popular response are quite strongly conditioned by the altered general climate I have described. A particular powerlessness is being consolidated by the universal powerlessness. An emergent nationalism has found itself partly re-interred by the general paralysis and degradation of pre-2003 European politics.

Certainly, the stalemate derives in part from British constitutional sclerosis; but obeisance to the Neo-liberal dogmas of free trade and de-regulation also plays its part. The zeitgeist or faith of an age seeps into the fringes as well. It is quite logical for it to assume crass or caricatural forms there, as if potential reaction has to be repeatedly clubbed at birth. In Cardiff and Edinburgh, for example, daily overkill is guaranteed by the *Western Mail* and *The Scotsman* respectively. As for popular response, in a political world where self-castration has become the norm of independence, some despondency seems only natural among candidates lining up for the oath. Many nationalists in Scotland and Wales have tended to attribute such uncertainty to moral failings, or to treachery among leaders. But perhaps they should take a wider view.

If they do, then I think there is reassurance as well as warning-signals in this broader perspective. Underneath the present charades of apostasy and self-contempt, those deeper currents that have carried break-up so far are not slackening, but acquiring new force. Just as the tide in favour of home rule built up during the eighteen years of Conservative Unionism, so a new tide seeking real independence is forming itself beneath the façade of Blairism.

It will rise into the spaces left by New Labour's collapse, and by the increasing misfortunes of the old Union state. Manfred Steger concluded his recent overview of globalism by pointing out – well before the Iraqi war – how the 'Neo-liberal power base' is already losing its grip on the meaning of events, and alternative interpretations of the process are surfacing everywhere. Few wish to turn the clock back. But more and more are certain to seek a say in its ongoing machinery. As a result:

> 'More and more people realize that there is nothing 'inevitable' or 'irreversible' about the liberalization of markets and the deregulation of the economy... However, I fervently hope that new meanings will link 'globalisation', this central concept of our time, to a progressive political tradition that seeks to give institutional expression to a more democratic and egalitarian international order.'[14]

And the tradition he refers to is alive and well in Britain: in England, as well as in the periphery that most of this book is about. In 2002, as in 1977, it is far better represented by the disrupters than by the old British status quo. Through devolution, the deficit in democracy has been partly remedied. But this has in turn unavoidably created a deficit in leadership, largely responsible for the uncertainty of the present moment.

In the political readjustments of the break-up process so far, leadership problems have indeed figured prominently. Northern-Irish, Welsh and Scottish parties and governments have been constantly afflicted by these. However, is this surprising in new polities attempting autonomy (or possibly divorce) from such a profoundly conservative form of state? As I mentioned to begin with, 'ethnic' motives have had little relevance in this process – and sometimes been counter-productive. But where ethno-nationalism is lacking, civic nationalism is correspondingly more significant – and of

---

[14] *Globalism: the New Market Ideology* by Manfred B. Steger (2002), p. 150. Similar verdicts and attitudes are found in the work of Dani Rodrik, Charles Sabel and Roberto Unger: 'The creation of space to experiment with distinct national development strategies, suited to the circumstances, traditions, and aspirations of each country.' Creation of such spaces is exactly what the break-up of Britain has been (and still is) about.

course, this returns the argument to that political arena where the palsy of the Cold War and its Neo-liberal aftermath remains dominant. The prolonged absence of political revolution in the West has had its price – miseries of nervelessness and feeble cynicism, the decay of trust and social confidence, lapses into religiosity, and frantic searches for 'a lead' from somewhere or someone else.

I mentioned to begin with how the initial reception of *The Break-up of Britain* was conditioned by the environment of the 1970s – a world still enshrouded by both political and intellectual paralysis, and linked to dread of terminal conflict. The book came out at a moment when the social and national revolts of the 1960s were still being reduced to order. Democratic disorder was too dangerous to both sides in the Cold War. Always ambiguous in relation to progress, nationalism was now a more palpable nuisance and threat. It turned the clock back, from free-trade capitalism in the West, and from responsible State Socialism in the East – above all if associated with political dissidence, like anarchy or Trotskyism. Parties and nations (including would-be nations) were largely restricted to one single function in that world: to choose sides, and play a responsible part in the selected camp.

Nationalism has often been diagnosed as a substitute religion, or metaphorical faith – it invites transcendence in the name of a purer goal, for the sake of some visionary future condition. The individual is aware he or she may never know this; but the community (and offspring) could be luckier, and happier. As Benedict Anderson points out very movingly in *The Spectre of Comparisons*, it is difficult to think of an alternative secular vehicle for this somehow essential imagined goodness.[15] For the majority, perhaps; but to some extent activist or enlisted minorities did find a second emotional 'substitute' in parties, and especially parties of the political left.

These were characteristically communities in a much stronger than normal sense, which elicited some of the same feelings and

[15] From the same text quoted at the start of this postscript, in *The Spectre of Comparisons* (1998), Chapter 17. Anderson sums up the examples in his essay as follows: 'Each ... shows why, no matter what crimes a nation's government commits and its passing citizenry endorses, My Country is ultimately Good. In these straitened millennial times, can such Goodness be profitably discarded?' (p. 368).

attitudes as nationalism. This effect varied in relation to the social closeness and cultural spectrum of the organization in question. It was higher in Communist or sectarian movements than among social democrats – though the British Labour Party was (and maybe still is) capable of mobilizing very strong emotive adhesion. Everyone involved in British politics knows the man-and-boy Party member whose card is a kind of sacrament, and who regards defectors as little better than traitors to the movement's unrealised homeland. 'Class' in this perspective was quite easily made over into a virtual ethnicity – the disallowed but more authentic country of the oppressed. For proletarian internationalists the resultant homeland could also be (and regularly was) somewhere else: the Socialist mother- or fatherland, Soviet Russia, China, even Albania or Cuba. Religious surrogacy was therefore doubly displaced – sociologically into a political institution, and ideologically into an emblematic nationhood that stood in for the eventual native transformation. In *Communism and Nationalism*, Roman Szporluk showed how Marx and Engels themselves often manifested a deviant Germanness, and many followers were to discover their own variations on such spiritual displacement.[16]

It must also be recalled how in this mechanism passion is institutionalized, as well as re-routed. I referred earlier to the conservative features of both states and civil organizations (including parties), the social 'habitus' just as significant as their ideas and colourful rituals. Once routinely embodied, transvestism may assume the immutability of 'genuine' gender customs. Being taken for granted is far more contagious than logic – and will continue to be

---

[16] This is why left-wing anti-nationalism was so frequently and passionately 'nationalist' in voice: it expressed the same emotions, re-circuited through Party and an idealized (if distant) homeland – the body and the soul of a re-earthed transcendence. This always seemed to me true of E. J. Hobsbawm, for example, the first and sternest critic of *The Break-up of Britain* mentioned earlier. His forthcoming autobiography *Interesting Times* may make this clearer. Hobsbawm's great imagination and romantic concern for the oppressed and outsiders let him understand nationalism better than most liberals and socialists; but the same thing lent force and verve to a cosmopolitan stance sustained by his life-long Party membership. Critics have wondered why he was never capable of leaving such a manifestly discredited cause. But no one can leave a surrogate nation of the mind – a faith of brothers and sisters – as he might a mere political grouping.

so even while other social conditions undermine its very existence. The contemporary UK monarchy began life as a puerile imitation of 'authentic' dynasties like the Romanovs and Hapsburgs; by the time the latter fell, it was the embodiment of immemorial tradition and stability.

The Break-up of Britain had both the good and bad fortune to appear while such British habits were still strong, indeed stifling; many on the left were still possessed by them, and twenty-five years on such unconscious collusion remains widespread. Yet any more sustained comparison between then and the present also reveals a huge change. The contrast has become between a determined (if stricken) agent of history and a mere sleep-walker. In 1977 the Cold War political palsy still prevailed, a profound inertia favouring all the tropes of states, parties and intellectuals I have described. By 2000 most instinctive allegiance to 'establishments' had drained away, leaving hollow routines and vacant symbols behind. A combination of official servility with violent socio-economic changes led to universal 'apathy'; but such withdrawal is also a still voiceless wish for better political things – for democratic nations that peoples can more honourably call their own.

Steger's 'progressive political tradition' has still to be built up. The Cold War delusion (later underwritten by Neo-liberalism) was that existing Western forms of democracy are a sufficient, or even a half-adequate, foundation for the political life of the coming century. The new phase of British break-up will be part of that construction – a change for which no economic formula exists. Here more than anywhere else, it should now be plain that democratic advance is not possible within the confines of a three-hundred-year-old Constitution crafted for élite rule.

'Independence' in this new environment has become a matter-of-fact affair: simply the *sine qua non* of whatever fusion of democracy and nationality these particular societies can work out for themselves. But there will be little that is matter-of-fact about the actual process, as the end of Great Britain's life-line, the 'special relationship' to Washington, triggers the dissolution of the much more ancient and special relationships tying England and its Isles dependencies together. The 1707 Treaty of Union between the historic states of England and Scotland has always been the (largely unacknowledged) backbone of the British identity, as well as the emblem on its Union flag. Its maintenance always relied overwhelmingly upon an external reach and policy – imperialism, and its long-running aftermath. So it is less surprising than many think, to see it broken, in the end, by the external shock of an unpopular and shaming war.

In spite of the conservative purpose of Westminster legislators, Devolution has already been a tentative start along these roads for so long not taken. We can be sure it will develop, as the miasma of single-market globalism evaporates, and its British incarnation undergoes farther humiliations. With new leadership and under the different constitutions which they will create for themselves, Scottish, Welsh, English and Northern-Irish polities will go on to contribute to this new political order of things, instead of striving uselessly to conserve the old.

In provisional conclusion: *The Break-up of Britain* began its life in a still imposing, if narrowing river; by the time the 1981 paperback edition had appeared, the river had begun to feel the approaching rapids – which have accelerated for over twenty years, and attained a crazy pace even in the few weeks between beginning and finishing this new introduction. The thunder of a waterfall no one conceived of in 1977 is in everyone's ears, as Tony Blair sends off his ships and troops to assist America's assault on the Middle East, and millions demonstrate their passionate opposition in London, Glasgow and Cardiff, as well as in most other capitals of the world. In the altered world lying beyond these falls, it is surely unlikely the United Kingdom will survive in anything like its historical form.

Tom Nairn, October 2002,
Melbourne, Australia

Acknowledgements

Most of the contents of this book appeared previously in *New Left Review*, and it is to the *NLR* editors, and above all to Perry Anderson and Anthony Barnett, that my warmest thanks are due. Through them, the *Review* played a vital role in the inspiration, correction and final production of all the work here. This is of course not to suggest that they or other editors of *NLR* share all the views put forward here.

After *New Left Review*, the Transnational Institute played the greatest part in making the book possible. It came to the rescue at a difficult moment, and provided me with the means of working from 1973 to 1976. Among the many members of the Institute who helped, my special thanks are owing to Eqbal and Julie Ahmad, Helen Hopps, Dick Barnet, Marcus Raskin and – again – Anthony Barnett. Two of the later studies in the book were written in the Institute building at 20, Paulus Potterstraat, Amsterdam. May the TNI survive the murder of its Director, Orlando Letelier, and his colleague Ronni Karpen Moffit, and go on to pursue a still more radical programme in answer to the Chilean *Junta* and its allies.

I owe a special debt to Emma Tennant and *Bananas* for certain parts of the book. The last stage was written in London, thanks to the hospitality of James Cornford and Claire Lasko at their Outer Circle Policy Unit in Regent's Park.

There is a degree of repetition in the arguments which the reader should try to excuse. The different chapters were done at different times and for very varying occasions, over a period of seven years, and it was not possible to systematise them without some falsification. However, there is also some development visible in their progression, which I hope will compensate for the repetition. For the sake of chronological accuracy, the order is: Chapter 6, 1970; Chapter 2, 1974; Chapters 3, 5, 8 and 9, 1975; Chapters 1, 4 and 7, 1976.

Although no main part of the book was written in Scotland, that country's problems were never far from the inspiration of all of them. The final arrangements and alterations have been influenced by many discussions on the contemporary situation there, especially with Neal Ascherson, Owen Dudley Edwards, Lynda Myles, Gordon Brown, Hamish Henderson, Stephen Maxwell, Peter Chiene, and Isobel Hilton. At the same time, my thanks go to Michael Spens for providing a venue for such discussions, now and in the future.

2002 Update

For this twenty-fifth anniversary edition, a further range of acknowledgement is in order. Nothing of the original text has been changed, for straightforward historical reasons: *Break-Up* became itself a small part of the changes that ensued from 1977 onwards, and many are now interested in it primarily as a document of that era. There was a paperback edition of the book in 1981, edited by Neil Belton, and I have added the introduction to that here, as an additional tenth chapter at the end: 'Into Political Emergency'. But this is simply further documentation of the same era – including the author's persisting errors and delusions near the beginning of the Thatcher era in Britain.

More recently, encouragement for proceeding with the new edition came from Paul James and my other colleagues at the Globalism Research Institute of the Royal Melbourne Institute of Technology. This Institute deals with the politics and culture of globalisation – geopolitics rather than trade and economics. Working with Paul and our other colleagues has made me look back on the original text and its time in a different light. Of course others can judge better 'what is living and what is dead' of all that, no doubt more accurately than the author's own reassessment. At any rate, Australia has contributed much more to the latter than may be evident on the surface.

Mary Kalantzis and Bill Cope wrote a book called *A Place in the Sun* in 2000, and they have helped to provide a part of that for me at the RMIT University, offering much more than a job. It is from the time for research generously accorded by Mary's Faculty of Education and Community Studies, and Michael Singh's Department of Language and International Studies that the possibility of reconsidering *The Break-Up of Britain* arose. Then Bill offered to bring out the new edition at his Common Ground publishing house in Altona, Melbourne.

Simultaneously, I had the luck to meet Gerry Hassan and Denis Sullivan on a visit home to Scotland. They offered to publish a parallel edition from Glasgow, via their newly founded Big Thinking collective. Gerry in particular has been a constant source of support and stimulus. It is a special sort of joint venture which has reproduced such a half-historical text under two imprints, at opposite ends of the world.

In the new introduction I have attempted for this edition, the reader may be disappointed that each original chapter has not been updated separately. Again, the reason is simple. In the 1990s, history diverged more and more in the different parts of the United Kingdom, and more and more research was needed to follow these developments – far more than I could possibly attempt, from an Australian base. This is all the more true because of one gap in the original: the British micro-states. A residue of great-nation chauvinism in the 1997 author prevented him from understanding their significance. So I would have had to add new sections on the Isle of Man, the Channel Islands and Shetland as well.

A disconcerting amount of the work has been done in the interminable air between these opposites. Jet lag is the least of it: the deep, repeated shifts of culture lag and emotional disorientation, and the weird, indispensable simulacrum of universal culture furnished by today's internet have all played their part. But at least there have been two fixed points: Alan Roberts' garden of lemon trees, vines and passion fruits in North Fitzroy, and Millicent Petrie's home and family in Livingston, Scotland. Without them it wouldn't have happened, and I owe them special thanks beyond words.

2020 Update

This is the long-overdue republication of *Break-Up*. I'm especially grateful to Anthony Barnett for his support and encouragement, from the initial publication in 1977 down to the present. His new introduction is most welcome at this time, after so many changes and novelties. It helps us assess these changes and opens the way to new ones. So, thanks again Anthony, and to Verso for its continuing encouragement around the book.

Special thanks are due to Millicent.

Tom Nairn
Scotland, December 2020

Index

436